MANAGEMENT SYSTEMS

Second Edition

MANAGEMENT SYSTEMS

Second Edition

The Study and Design of Information Systems

Burton Grad
Burton Grad Associates, Inc.

Thomas B. Glans
International Business Machines Corporation

David Holstein
International Business Machines Corporation

William E. Meyers
Rich Products Corporation

Richard N. Schmidt
State University of New York at Buffalo

 The Dryden Press   Hinsdale, Illinois

To Pauline, Nancy, Anita, Betty, and Mildred

Copy edited by Wanda Giles

PREFACE

The life cycle of a management system consists of three stages: (1) the study and design of the system, (2) its implementation as a new system, and (3) its operation within the organization for which it was designed.

Most of the literature concerning management systems has heretofore concentrated on the second and third stages of the life cycle, leaving the first stage relatively untouched. There are two reasons for this concentration. First, computers promise substantial benefits and, once the decision is made to go ahead, there is typically great urgency to get them installed and into some kind of productive operation. Much of the available literature is a response to this pressing need.

Another reason for the concentration on the second and third stages is that there has been considerable difficulty in drawing together an appropriately tested body of knowledge encompassing the study and design of systems. While writers widely acknowledge the importance of the study and design stage, only limited recorded information concerning the procedural details of system development has existed. This situation appears to be changing, and there is a greater understanding of both the abstract and applied implications of information processing systems in a computer environment.

The purpose of our book is to present a thorough, detailed treatment of the first stage in the life cycle of a management system—its study and design. The material is given comprehensive treatment in order to provide a guide and workbook for beginning students in information systems design. Experienced practitioners will also find the book valuable if used selectively. Although the material we present implies that computer-based systems are to be developed, the concepts and procedures can also be applied to the manual and semiautomated processes that are used in many business systems.

Our book is therefore recommended for:

1. Systems courses for students of business, computer science, economics, engineering, and management.
2. Professional and technical training of systems analysts, system engineers, systems and procedures personnel, programmers, and others interested in system planning and development.
3. Use by management and systems design personnel in developing management information systems and information processing systems in commercial, educational, governmental, industrial, medical, and other organizations.

We want to emphasize why the book is constructed as it is. First, it is not concerned with teaching computers, programming languages, data base design, management information systems, teleprocessing, or any of the myriad of technical topics which are covered so well in the existing literature. Second, it is not intended to teach abstract concepts or to provide a survey of system planning and design techniques. Rather, it documents a particular rationale and procedure used by experienced practitioners to design useful management systems.

It is our sincere belief that in an education, training, or self-teaching situation it is vital to focus on methods, not just theory; on practices, not just concepts. Based on our own experience in teaching, we subscribe to an inductive approach to the subject of system study and design. Hence we use many examples (including one quite comprehensive case study) and illustrate each key point from different points of view and in different contexts.

While this approach makes the book somewhat long, it provides the teacher with an opportunity to select the sections of most interest to particular students, given their background, other courses taken, and their areas of specialization. We believe our book is unique in describing in such detail one successful plan of action for conducting a system study. It is procedure-oriented and in the nature of a cookbook. Since it deals with the practical aspects of analysis and design, it can be directly applied to both school and business problems.

We have divided the book into four parts. Part 1 outlines a general method for studying and designing a system from an organizational point of view. We explain the concept of three phases to cover the study and design of systems. These phases are discussed in detail in the subsequent parts. Part 2, the first phase in the study and design of a system, is *understanding the present system*. This part covers techniques for determining organization goals and for gathering and structuring data into a management report describing the present system. Part 3, the second phase in the study and design of a system, is the *determination of the requirements for the new system.* Here we show how goals, objectives, and activities can be translated into definitions of system inputs and system outputs, and how these determine the requirements of the system. An important aspect of this phase is the consideration of those present or planned resources of people and data processing equipment that will need to be part of the new system. The report containing the results of the findings in Phase II can be described as a system requirements specification. The third phase in the study and design of a system is the actual *design of the new system.* In Part 4 we describe the factors needed in designing a new system. Fundamentally, a set of alternative designs must be considered so that the final decision on a particular design will include proper handling of activity requirements, equipment configuration, costs, implementation, and conversion. Part 4 deals with the final report on a new system plan.

To make more systematic the work of designing systems, we present a number of documentation forms that serve useful purposes, both for the analysts who conduct the study and for managers who review the reports.

The examples, ideas, and illustrations provided are adapted from actual case studies in which the methodology presented in our book was employed. Names, identifying locations, and products have been changed; but the substance of the material quoted is taken from the actual reports produced in selected studies.

We make specific reference to nine studies by name: *Atlantic Distributors*, a Michigan-based warehouse chain; *Associated Retailers, Inc.*, a department store in Florida; *Butodale Electronics*, an 18-year-old Massachusetts corporation specializing in analog computers; *Collins, McCabe and Company*, a stock brokerage firm in Texas; *Custodian Life Insurance Company*, once a stock company, now a mutual company in Illinois; *National Bank of Commerce*, a moderate-sized bank in Kansas; *Supersonic Airlines, Inc.*, an international passenger and freight carrier with headquarters in New York; *Typical State*, a state well-known for its use of computers; and *Worthington Hardware*, a family-held wholesaling organization in California. The Butodale case study is used extensively to illustrate the three major reports mentioned above.

A glossary is provided to familiarize the student with technical terms in the area of computers, data processing, and systems.

An annotated bibliography has been included to give the student or professional additional sources to explore particular topics in greater depth.

For the classroom teacher a comprehensive instructor's guide is available to cover answers to the Questions and Problems and to suggest course outlines.

We wish to acknowledge the assistance of the International Business Machines Corporation in making available to us various published and unpublished materials, and we thank them for their kind permission to use them in this book. The concepts underlying our book were first published by IBM under the name "Study Organization Plan"; these were contained in IBM manuals and covered in certain courses.

Credit is also given to those companies, who must remain nameless, that participated in the evaluation of our approach to system studies and provided the basis for the various illustrations, examples, and case studies.

We also wish to thank the many individuals who contributed to the ideas expressed through planning, using, writing, teaching, and preparing the material. Two of our closest associates have died since the original material was formulated; Lee H. Baker of IBM and Robert R. Smith, a private consultant, were members of the team that created and tested these concepts. We have sorely missed their good counsel.

We particularly want to acknowledge the special efforts of Frank T. Dolen and Robert F. Walleck, both of IBM, who were instrumental in applying the concepts to smaller businesses and in preparing educational material. Sincere thanks are also due to Mrs. Eleanor S. Harris who typed many drafts of the original edition and to L. Kenneth Heath, Ray W. Oldham, William C. Tumelty, Harold W. Leffingwell, and Walt M. Whitmyre, all of IBM, who used and evaluated this approach with various firms. Richard G. Canning, a private consultant, helped initiate the work.

Tarrytown, New York	B.G.
Westport, Connecticut	T.B.G.
Cornwall-on-Hudson, New York	D.H.
Buffalo, New York	W.E.M.
Buffalo, New York	R.N.S.

January 1979

CONTENTS

CHAPTER 13

MEASURING THE PERFORMANCE OF SYSTEMS **276**

CHAPTER· 14

DOCUMENTATION FOR SYSTEM REQUIREMENTS **292**

CHAPTER 15

PREPARING THE REPORT OF REQUIREMENTS **314**

CHAPTER 19

DESCRIBING A NEW SYSTEM   403

CHAPTER 20

A NEW SYSTEM PLAN FOR BUTODALE   423

CHAPTER 21

STAGES 2 AND 3: IMPLEMENTATION AND OPERATION   449

PART ONE
OVERVIEW OF MANAGEMENT SYSTEMS

The three stages in the life cycle of a management system are (1) its study and design, (2) its implementation and installation, and (3) its operation, evaluation, and modification with the passage of time. Part 1 comprises an overview of the main concepts in the first of these stages. Chapter 1 introduces the main terms and concepts. Chapter 2 covers the three phases in the study and design stage: (1) understanding the present system, (2) determining the requirements of the new system, and (3) designing the new system. For each phase, the chapter explains the general form and content of a management report that contains findings presented by the team that studied the organization and designed the new system. Chapter 3 presents techniques and tools that analysts use in planning and carrying out a systems study.

Part 1 is a conceptual framework, designed to give the reader an overview of systems study and design. The subsequent three parts of the book develop these concepts more fully.

CHAPTER 1
INTRODUCTION

1.1 A CLARIFICATION OF TERMS

A *management system* is different things to different people:

1. It is the dynamic *structure* that holds an organization together and makes it function in a living sense.
2. It is the total set of governing *policies* and *procedures* that enables a business or institution to carry out its function and try to accomplish its objectives.
3. It encompasses rules for using the *resources* of an enterprise or an establishment within an enterprise and makes it an operating entity.

Notice that in each case we are talking about the dynamic use of physical and information processing, which applies the resources of people and machines, buildings and materials, money and information to accomplish a planned result for an organization. More formally, a management system is the method by which an organization plans, operates, and controls its activities and utilizes the resources of money, people, equipment, materials, and information in order to meet its goals and objectives.

The terms *organization*, *management*, and *system* call for clear definition. *Organization* generally means any business, enterprise, firm, establishment, or institution formed for a purpose. A part of an organization can also be considered an organization in itself. Organizations are inherently goal-seeking.

Management is used to mean those people responsible for directing the organization or its components toward achieving its goals, while a *system* is any dynamic entity that accepts or receives inputs, uses resources to perform physical and informational transformations, and produces outputs for further use.

Management systems are themselves hierarchical, to a point where there is a corresponding management system for each organizational entity. Thus, within a system there may be many subsystems directed toward specialized functions. One can talk about the business system, the accounting system, the personnel system, the production system or the information management system. While each of these is a system, its aim is to manage a specific resource or achieve only a part of the organization's goals. In contrast, the organization's management system focuses on the whole organization.

1.2 INFORMATION PROCESSING SYSTEMS

Since the emphasis of this text is on the information processing systems within the business management system, there are numerous discussions of computing and data processing. However, the concept of a management system did not result from the use of computers. Every functioning organization has always had its management system, even if not recorded or well understood. The introduction of data processing has forced clearer rules and procedures in order to gain the economic benefits from the computer's capabilities. Just as the introduction of industrial engineering brought formalism and order to physical processing, systems analysis and programming are bringing their type of formalism and order to information processing. The discipline needed to introduce and support computer-operated information systems has led management to think more precisely about its own structure and goals.

Another point should be kept in mind while reading this text: Information only represents reality; it is not reality. Yet much of the time management makes decisions based on recorded information. The value of the information depends almost entirely on its accuracy because accuracy or inaccuracy affects the quality of decisions. Therefore, information itself must be treated as a resource of the business.

The concept of information as a resource leads directly to focusing attention on the available information of an enterprise. This information, usually called the *data base* of a business, represents the sum of facts known about the firm's resources, history, and forecasts and plans for the future. This data base is fundamental to activities a business carries out to accomplish its objectives. The ability to relate multiple activities to a common data base and to provide improvements in accuracy, cost, and response has helped to make computers a cornerstone in the modern management system. Controlling the interplay between people and computers gives the information management system designer and the implementer great power to determine the effectiveness of a business.

This text often refers to management systems in general, although the requirements and design portions are aimed specifically at the information processing aspect of the management system. The reader will therefore recognize that the principles used apply to all management systems, not just to those concerned with information processing. The text also emphasizes that the information processing system exists within an overall management system that is designed to address the business or institutional goals and objectives. It is clearly not information processing for its own sake.

1.3 ADDITIONAL DEFINITIONS

Business vocabularies vary in explicitness. Each key word used in this book has a precise definition. As these terms recur, they will consistently carry the same meanings, subject to human interpretation.

We use the terms *management system* and *business system* interchangeably. The business system is made up of a number of individual systems. The words *enterprise*, *organization*, *firm*, or *business* in this text stand for the entire business system. A business is an assembly of people and resources organized into a complex whole for the purpose of fulfilling specific objectives or goals. Thus, a business may comprise all or only part of a company, an agency, a field office, or a government bureau, depending on how the business is defined by its management.

Goals are the contributions a business wishes to make to its environment, the ends to which an organization is directed. Goals can be translated into precise and quantitative *objectives*, which state what the business system must accomplish. Objectives can be measured.

The *environment* of a business is everything outside the scope of the study that influences the business. If a company is considered the business under study, then everything not in the company is in the environment. If one division of a company is selected as the business, then even the other divisions of the same company become part of the environment. The environment also includes external factors influencing the system, such as competitors and competitive products or services, geography, market status, customer goodwill, and so forth.

A business can be described in terms of its organization, goals, and activities. This text uses the word *activity* to mean a related set of operations having few ties with the surrounding environment. An activity is usually self-contained and directed toward satisfying one or more of the goals fundamental to the business. It generally starts with an input from the environment external to the business and ends with an output to that environment. However, some activities are concerned with the maintenance of resources and have no significant ties with the environment. Activities are the means by which an organization attempts to achieve its goals and objectives. A subsystem has many of the same properties as an activity but lacks the elements of goal direction and self-containment.

Activities are made up of operations. An *operation* is defined as something which, when initiated by a trigger, converts inputs to outputs, using resources to effect this transformation. The relationships of an operation are frequently internal; its inputs may come from another operation within the activity, and its outputs may be delivered to another such operation. A general model of the structure of an operation is shown in Figure 1–1.

A *trigger* starts an operation. It can be the first working day in the month, the eight o'clock whistle, or the arrival of a batch of invoices. Normally only one trigger is specified for each operation.

A *process*, or processing step, is an action that takes place within an operation. It can often be described by a transitive verb whose object is the input, output, or resource acted upon and whose modifiers can specify the conditions under which the process takes place. Examples of processes are:

1. Compute monthly withholding tax.
2. Locate information in personnel file.
3. Complete manufacturing report on scrap losses.

Each step in a business mechanism is a process. Related sets of these processes, started by some trigger, accepting some input, and ending with some definable output, form operations. Related groups of operations, preferably reaching to the external environment, comprise activities. Each activity or combination of activities is performed by a system.

Resources are the means of performing an operation. They may be imposed by the user or made necessary by the nature of the inputs or outputs. They include personnel, equipment, facilities, finances, materials, inventories, and information. Physical resources are stockpiled, or inventoried, to provide a time buffer between availability of and need for particular resources. In the same way information files provide a time buffer between operations; they keep historical information for later use and store operation rules for transforming inputs into outputs.

Figure 1–1 The general structure of an operation model

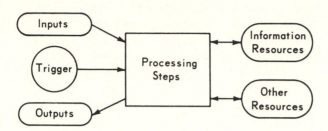

Customers, *management*, and *users* are the persons for whom a study is undertaken. When systems planners study some phase of the business that employs them, the customer is, for the purpose of the study, all or part of the company management. If the study is of another business, the customer is viewed as the management of that business. Even when working as advisors for other parts of their own business, systems planners should function in a customer-consultant relationship, since many times they will have to learn specific operations of the business as if they were outsiders.

The terms *systems planner*, *analyst*, *systems engineer*, and *study team* are used in their generally accepted meanings. Whether working alone or as part of a team, the responsibilities of a systems planner remain the same: searching out facts, organizing them into coherent descriptions, analyzing requirements, and synthesizing new systems.

Other terms, such as *activity requirements model*, *business model*, *overview*, and *synthesis* are explained when they are first mentioned or are illustrated by example. These and other terms are defined in the glossary of this book. Those not specifically defined will be understood in the context of their common usage.

1.4 GROWTH OF MANAGEMENT SYSTEMS

In their continuing effort to be competitive and yet conduct profitable, cost-effective businesses, managers explore many choices. A product or service can be redesigned to increase its attractiveness in the marketplace; advertising and sales promotion can be enlarged to reach a wider audience; internal cost reduction programs can reduce expenses; and the information system can be redesigned and updated for greater value. Of these examples, the search for new products or services and wider markets would usually draw the most attention, as areas without direct appeal are usually seen as less important. An existing system, for example, despite clear warning signs of inefficiency and obsolescence, often continues to be operated in the same old way, with only an occasional patchwork repair to keep it running. As a result, too many enterprises appear modern but operate internally with outdated tools.

With experience and growth, there is an increase in managerial maturity, sound judgment, and intelligent direction, whether the executives carry titles as owners, government bureau heads, agency directors, professional managers, or any others. This kind of management can detect and eliminate waste and duplication of services through a management system that is a sharp instrument of control and a generator of dynamic decision-making information. Many existing business systems have been designed around human capabilities and also around human limitations. Many have been built around outdated and poorly-structured organizations. Some systems still appear to use the classical bookkeeper perched on a high stool, pen (if not quill) in hand, carefully and laboriously making entries in a ledger. Other systems have been structured for a number of clerks, each busily performing manual calculations, punching keyboards of calculators, or performing other limited duties. Systems have been paced to human skills—and human fatigue, limited attention spans, and inaccuracy. Errors have been detected by one person auditing another's work through expensive cross-checking. Ironically, these systems have worked, because individuals have been able to compensate for many system deficiencies and errors. Even with the introduction of punched-card and batch computing equipment, systems often have remained tied to human capacities and machine specializations. Jobs have been divided into steps matched to machines. If volume grows, if something goes wrong, or if predictable bottlenecks occur, more machines are added, more people are hired, or the work is further subdivided.

In the 1960s equipment with vastly increased versatility and speed appeared on the market, but there was no immediate parallel improvement in systems control and methodology. Systems analysts and managers first thought the new machines could be superimposed directly on existing systems. And in fact this occurred, often with fairly good results. Work was processed faster and reports contained more detail. Thoughtful executives, however, began to realize that the increased speed was only a small part of the advantages of these machines. They saw that the new equipment and new concepts of organization could be applied to all of the information processing tasks of a business, including word processing, which is differentiated from data or number processing. They also saw how information processing tasks could be interwoven with such physical processes as numerical control of machine tools, automated order selection in warehouses, or responses to telephone inquiries in hotel reservation systems.

Out of this rethinking came a new approach: Redesign each system as a unified entity contributing directly to business goals and take full advantage of equipment capabilities as well as fast-developing management techniques. Here emerged the opportunity to tap the unrealized potential of a modern management system.

1.5 THE ORGANIZATION-WIDE APPROACH

The key to creating an improved management system is to approach it on an organization-wide basis. The business is examined initially in broad, general areas. Goals are identified in terms of what the business contributes to its environment. From this point, an approach can be defined and expanded into a management system which fulfills the goals of the enterprise. Functions not contributing directly to the satisfaction of a business goal will either be considered secondary in importance or eliminated. It is, of course, unlikely that many analysts will ever be put in the position of designing a total management system. Normally the decision will be to redesign one part at a time. This limitation does not invalidate the philosophy of this method; if anything, it increases its value. An analyst who sees a business or institution as a whole, relating individual parts to overall goals, can conceive interrelated, synergistic systems, rather than contradictory or inconsistent solutions.

The organization-wide systems approach is oriented toward goals and activities to attain them, rather than simply toward personnel, equipment, or organization structure. Consider an example. An aircraft flies passengers and mail between New York and London. This is a primary goal. To achieve it, certain takeoff and landing procedures are used. The aircraft is propelled, navigated, and controlled in flight, and it is prepared for the next trip. It is not necessary to mention in the statement of goals that a supersonic aircraft with an air-supported landing gear, piloted by a man named Eugene Irving, took off and landed on Runway 23. The goal is stated simply—fly passengers and freight between designated points—regardless of equipment or personnel. The purpose of a goal statement is to express the results the system must achieve. The statement ignores the processing details of the systems solution.

Under this systems approach, the organization is viewed as a single entity for which systematic solutions can be proposed. Past problem solving was based on a view of an organizational structure composed of individual elements. Because the systems approach offers more to modern business, this text advocates an integrated systems view. Part 1 of this book provides an overview of the methodology and documentation of such a system study.

1.6 ORGANIZATION GOALS

In an organization-wide view, information and physical systems are designed to support the primary goals of the business and are consequently closely identified with them. This is true whether the goals are formally written or present only in the minds of management. Profit making, while a common measure for nearly all enterprises (with the exceptions of government operations and other nonprofit situations), is too general for useful system consideration.

An organization tries to fulfill its goals to make its special contribution to the environment. For example, the primary goal of an appliance company is to manufacture and sell appliances. Profit making, though necessary for the company's survival, is only part of the governing framework within which the company must operate. Starting with the single goal of making appliances, the company may from time to time perform other activities for the purpose of adding to profit or increasing profit margins. By expanding into such activities as manufacturing component parts, fabricating metals, and financing purchases, the company adds new goals; and as it grows, the company may add departments, divisions, and subdivisions to meet the requirements imposed by more complex operations. The result of such growth and change is ordinarily a system of considerable complexity.

The many nonprofit institutions in society also extend their services and functions. Schools and colleges try to better educate their students and maintain effective cost control to limit taxes or tuition fees; they may add departments, expand facilities, and change their educational processes through such techniques as computer assisted instruction. Government agencies provide community management in villages, counties, states, and nations. Again, cost of functions is a key measure along with quality, timeliness, and effectiveness of services. Like businesses, these institutions are complex working systems.

These systems are total only in the sense that they are currently the sum of their parts. Over the years, primary organization goals may have been forgotten, new goals never formulated, and a number of secondary goals may have assumed unwarranted emphasis. Primary goals seldom include preparing reports (unless report production is the business) or sending bills (unless the business is a bill collection agency.) A goal-directed system calls for the reexamination and restatement of significant business goals.

1.7 ACTIVITIES

We have introduced two major concepts in the philosophy for designing systems: (1) the consideration of the management system as an entity and (2) the orientation of a systems study toward organization goals. A third concept, *activity formulation*, is another central idea of the study plan.

An activity, as defined, is a logically related group of operations. Performance of these operations results directly in the achievement of one or more business goals. Some typical statements of activities are:

1. Provide checking account service in a bank.
2. Estimate the cost of performing a construction project.
3. Provide demand for products.
4. Determine the distribution of power in a public utility.

As the principal element of an activity, operations transform inputs to outputs. Examples of operations are:

1. Prepare a market analysis for Product A from estimates and forecasts.
2. Compile a production schedule from orders and propositions.

As a logically related group of tasks or operations cutting across functional lines, an activity can often be made self-contained — made to stand alone, with few informational ties and little interaction with other activities in the business, and directed toward satisfying one or more business goals. There is no implied requirement that activities be formulated within organizational components or that future organization structure follow activity lines.

Approaches to Activity Formulation The study team can approach the formulation of goal-directed activities in several ways. One approach is deductive. From a statement of business goals supplied by management, activities are defined more or less intuitively. Detailed interviews are then conducted in the several departments or functions to verify the definition of the activity. Once there is verification, activities are fully documented.

A second way to define activities is the inductive approach. Initially, the team looks at the total resources of the business to secure an overview of costs and allocations. Then a detailed analysis of the operations is performed. Operations are sorted into logical groups of implied activities. Frequently, this requires a number of successive sorts to achieve useful arrangements among operations.

The composite approach begins with a goal statement from management. Then a major activity is identified and selected for documentation. Implied goals are formulated from the documents and are compared to management's stated goals to see if there is agreement.

Since the identification of activities and assignment of operations to activities presume a fresh look at a business, an acceptable procedure may require several iterations on the part of the analyst. This is expected if the business is to be properly divided into areas small enough to be grasped thoroughly by the study team. The analyst is the sole judge of the number and scope of the activities.

The activity formulation procedure can be explained effectively in the context of an actual case study of a company—Butodale Electronics—that has successfully applied the principles discussed here during a management systems study. Butodale is a fast-developing manufacturer of electronic equipment and has outgrown the model shop business system of its early days. Among the activities developed when Butodale's Phase I study reached the period of initial activity formulation was one called quotation and order acceptance. This activity consisted of receiving and processing inquiries and returning prices and delivery quotations to potential customers. However, the scope of this activity was confined mainly to the sales administration function and showed a cost of only $60,000 out of a total $16,000,000 in expenditures. The study team therefore modified the goal statements for the quotation and order acceptance activity and reshaped other activities in Phase II to reflect the situation more accurately. The outcome was quite different. Quotation and order acceptance was incorporated in an activity called "provide product demand." This activity not only responded to inquiries, but also covered the broader tasks of forecasting demand and processing proposals and orders for the entire company. The activity even included master scheduling. With its extended range, it cut across functional lines of accounting, sales, engineering, and management. In its revised definition "provide product demand" used $1,650,000 of the total resources figure and was a primary activity of the business.

After emerging from the formulation procedure, activities will generally have individual identities and defined boundaries. They will be of a certain size and will be describable in terms of the goals they satisfy. Obviously, the dynamics of a business enterprise will modify activities as time goes on, but for the purpose of putting the system into operation, this initial firmness is necessary.

1.8 FLEXIBILITY OF APPROACH

Anyone experienced in the design of management systems knows that there is an extremely wide variety of situations for which systems must be designed and that almost all situations differ from one another. The complexity of the problem is compounded by the fact that there can be a number of designs for each situation. To deal with these complexities this text presents a method that has a wide range of applicability to the formulation of systems and their designs.

Type of Business In the past, the framework of systems reference has been frequently overgeneralized or held within too rigid limits, centered on a single type of organization or application. The philosophy and methodology in this book are flexible enough to avoid the twin traps of rigidity and overgeneralization. This approach has been applied to such divergent business fields as wholesale distribution, banking, insurance, electronics manufacture, aircraft manufacture, and public utilities. After detailed analysis, study, and experience, it has been found that the approach can be used for organizations in the fields of credit, merchandising, transportation, communications, mining, construction, government, and education.

Size of Business Experience has demonstrated that the size of a business has no effect on the applicability of the plan of study. Both a small retailer and a giant multidivision manufacturing corporation have been studied within the framework. In the one case, a compressed version was used; in the other, the full plan was required. As the size of the enterprise varies, the design solution may call for large computers, mini-computers or intelligent terminals connected to time-sharing networks.

Resources and Time for Study While it is possible to use this method for a fast, comprehensive view of the business to aim at an improved business application, the method can also be used for probing a business in depth to portray its detailed structure and operating dynamics for redesign. Any level between these extremes may be chosen, depending on time, team size and quality, and study objectives.

Depth of Study The plan can be applied in varying degrees. Certain activities within a company can require more study than others, depending on the cost of data gathering and the potential and need for improvement. Forms developed to handle these aspects of studies—from overviews to fine details—are shown in Chapters 8, 14, and 19.

Level of Change The method is further useful over a range of levels in study refinement. Where an enterprise is interested in moderate systems improvement or direct computerization of an existing system, the plan provides a ready-made structure by which these objectives can be accomplished. In the other direction, it can be employed to support a study which will set in place a radically new system design.

SUMMARY

The objective of this book is the study of information processing systems from the management viewpoint. *Management*, *system*, and *organization* are the three most important words in the discussion. This book focuses particularly on those systems involving computers and information processing functions.

As a business grows, so does its need for refined, sophisticated systems. The design of these systems requires a definition of business goals within an organization-wide approach. A flexible approach to systems study and design permits a basic methodology to be used regardless of type and size of organization, size and length of study, depth of study, and level of change desired.

QUESTIONS AND PROBLEMS

1–1 Obtain the dictionary definitions of *organization*, *management*, and *system*. (Use Webster's *New Collegiate Dictionary* if possible.) Discuss the similarities and differences in the definitions.

1–2 Obtain definitions of the word *environment* from a dictionary. How can these definitions be applied to the environment of a management system?

1–3 Discuss the similarities and differences of *activity*, *function*, *operation*, *system*, and *process*.

1–4 Figure 1–1 depicts the general structure of an operation model. Let us assume that eating dinner is an operation. How can such an operation be described by the model in Figure 1–1?

1–5 Name and define five different types of resources that an organization possesses.

1–6 Name at least five different types of organizations. What criteria can be used to separate one organization from another for the purpose of examining goals and activities?

1–7 The text states that business systems have matured considerably over the years. However, many organizations are successfully operating today without modern systems. How can these organizations exist?

1–8 If every organization has a management system, why are so many organizations unable to achieve their desired goals?

1–9 Discuss the concept of activity formulation.

1–10 Name and describe five variables which help determine the range and scope for a business study.

CHAPTER 2
THE STUDY AND DESIGN OF A MANAGEMENT SYSTEM

2.1 THE LIFE CYCLE OF A MANAGEMENT SYSTEM

We envision three stages in the life cycle of a management system:

1. Study and design the system.
2. Implement and install the new system.
3. Operate, evaluate, and modify the system.

The key words associated with each of the stages are shown in Figure 2–1. In this section we shall cover each of the stages by expanding briefly on the key words in the figure.

The purpose of Stage 1 is to design a new system for the organization or for a defined part of it. To accomplish this, one must recognize and define the specific problems to be solved. Generally, one defines the problems of the organization by determining the objectives of both the organization and the system through a study of the present system. If there is no present system, as in the case of a new organization, the study typically views similar operations in at least one other organization.

From the study emerge both broad and detailed understandings of what the system is required to do. These understandings, coupled with information concerning the future direction of the enterprise, lead to the specification of the system requirements: "What must the system do?" and "How well must the system perform?" Answers to these two questions will provide the design objectives of the new system. Then the new system can be designed. Although it seems self-evident, it is almost universally ignored that analysts designing a system and the management for whom the system is being designed must work together in order to insure a proper outcome.

Once the new system is designed, it is necessary to consider the assembly of people and equipment that can carry out the information processing work imposed by the design. In a typical situation the analysts usually consider several configurations of personnel and

Figure 2–1 The three stages in the life cycle of a system.

Stage 1	Stage 2	Stage 3
Study and Design	**Implement and Install**	**Operate, Evaluate, and Modify**
Recognize problems Determine objectives Study present system Determine system requirements Design new system Propose solution	Design detail system Design data bases Develop programs and documentation Validate and test system Convert to new system	Operate system Analyze performance Modify system Maintain system Enhance performance

equipment, some of them quite different, but all of them able to carry out the work of the design, though with varying degrees of effectiveness and cost. It is the responsibility of the study team to search out the best people and equipment in terms of total cost and efficiency.

The analysts' final work is to report on the main features of the system they have designed. The report should include recommendations for any new equipment needed to handle the tasks.

The overall purpose of Stage 2 in Figure 2–1 is to implement the newly designed system by converting the plan into reality. The first step involves analysts' explanations of the details of the system design. Input and output files must be designed, flowcharts and system diagrams prepared, programs written for the computer, and test criteria and test data organized. The data flow through the system must be tested. The real data of the system must be processed, and the outputs of the system must be checked to insure that they conform to the set specifications. This verification often takes place in parallel operations in which computer operation results are compared with the existing system. Finally, there is full conversion to the new system; and after a suitable monitoring time to assure accuracy, the new system becomes part of the normal operation.

Imp Stage 2 info.

The third stage in the life cycle of a management system involves operation, evaluation, and modification. When the new system is placed in day-to-day operation, all problems, errors, and other difficulties must be solved realistically. The efficiency of the new system must be checked closely to make sure it continues to meet the set specifications. It is not unusual for unforeseen difficulties to force modifications to the new system. Managerial personnel, who usually receive the outputs, are able to spot deficiencies; if they do, the system must be modified.

Elements in the external environment can exert great influence. For example, a change in government regulations might have an impact on the system; stockholders, unions, customers, vendors, and even policies of other countries could affect it. Through all events, the system must be maintained, serviced, and kept operational. To this end, personnel must be trained, equipment must be maintained, and everything that can affect the operation must be monitored to make sure it is able to meet management objectives. The three stages in the life cycle of a system are not mutually exclusive; they overlap in various ways and at various points.

2.2 THREE PHASES OF STUDY AND DESIGN

The implementation and operation stages are covered in numerous articles, manuals, and books. However, there is limited material describing the vital first stage of study and design.

Figure 2–2 shows that the study and design stage is separated into three phases:

Phase I   The existing system is studied to gain insight into the organization and its key relationships.

Phase II   Results of the Phase I study are blended with forecasts of foreseeable needs to develop accurate specifications of system requirements.

Phase III The new system is designed from specifications of its basic requirements and then communicated to management in the form of a new system plan.

One theme of this book is that application study and design should itself be treated as a system to be planned, organized, managed, and controlled just as any application system. This means one must understand the goals and measurable objectives, the limitations and constraints, the tools, equipment, and personnel of the project. The book suggests specific procedures, techniques, and forms to carry out the complex work involved in planning and proposing an improved or new application system. They have been tested and found useful but have realistic limits. They simply provide structures to assist competent people in doing a job better, faster, and with greater benefits to the user of the system.

Figure 2–2 The three phases of Stage 1 in the life cycle of a system.

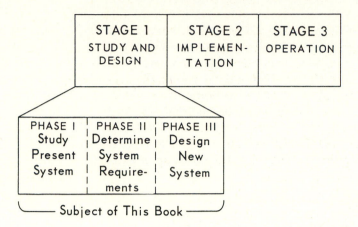

The area of automating information systems is subject to frequent change, and what seem to be radical new concepts appear from time to time. But sound study and design techniques still have the same significant value that they have had in the past:

1. While systems have grown from batch applications where inputs are collected and run at daily, weekly, or monthly intervals to online applications where each input is processed on receipt, analysts still need to study each type of transaction (or message) to understand its implications for data entry, verification, and control.
2. While data storage has expanded by many orders of magnitude, and individual application files have become common system data bases, the importance of file and record analysis has not diminished.
3. While computer equipment configurations have changed from a single Central Processing Unit (CPU) with local input/output devices to distributed systems including terminals (programmable and preprogrammed), communication lines, micro- and mini-computers, multiple levels of data storage and interconnected CPUs, the emphasis on system performance and flexibility remains strong.
4. While applications themselves become farther-reaching— dealing not just with routine fixed format records, computing arithmetic values, and printing formal reports, but now

including text entry and edit, graphic presentation of information, process control signals, and even picture and voice manipulation—the need for thorough application understanding is even more valuable in designing good, profitable systems.

5. While large leading edge users are concerned with complex networks of computers and peripheral equipment, there are still vast numbers of smaller businesses or individual units within larger organizations that are just starting to use computers. They need good study and design tools to insure that their first system installations will be productive and economically worthwhile.

As we explain the three phases of study, requirements, and design, the student should view them from a systems-oriented standpoint. These approaches and techniques evolved after study of existing application development methodology, establishment of requirements for new study concepts, and design and testing of the proposed solutions. This methodology is a system solution to a management system problem—how to plan and direct the design of application systems in a predictable, credible way.

2.3 UNDERSTANDING THE PRESENT SYSTEM

In order to understand the present system, analysts try to determine what is done in the organization: What inputs are used, with what resources, to achieve what results? This will hold true in a conversion study where a manual system is being transferred directly to a computer, in a study aimed at improving or modifying an existing system, or in a major advanced system study leading to a new concept and design. In all cases information is collected and organized into a pattern that permits an understanding of the organization as it presently operates and reacts to its environment.

A document entitled "Present Business Description" is the formal output from Phase I. It contains three major sections—general, structural, and operational.

The general section includes a history of the enterprise, its goals and objectives and major policies and practices, industry background, and government regulations.

The structural section contains a model of the business, describing it in terms of products and customers, materials and suppliers, fi-

Figure 2–3 A model of a business system.

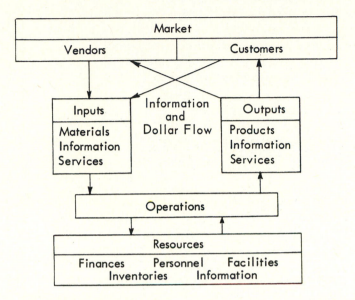

nances, personnel, facilities, material inventories, and information files. A simple example of a business model is shown in Figure 2–3.

The operational section employs flow diagrams and statistics to present the operating dynamics of the business. These diagrams and charts reflect how the resources of a business respond to inputs, perform operations, and produce outputs. An appendix can be added to cover the detailed working documents needed to explain operations, identify documents, and define the files in which the organization's information is stored.

The management systems approach can be applied to all system studies. Conversion studies are directed to changing only the physical method of performing a job. Here the intent is to insure that all key functions are properly performed on a suitable computer. However, improvement studies often lead to functional changes in the system being investigated. More emphasis is placed on combining or eliminating functions, changing the timing of operations, and improving information availability and accuracy. In both conversion and improvement studies, the general and structural sections can be completed quite rapidly, with more time allocated to the compilation of data for the operational section. The application of the philosophy and methodology in this text often leads to extending the scope and the potential benefit of conversion and improvement studies beyond management's initial objectives. In the advanced study, where the objective is to be consciously and deliberately free from past limitations, understanding of the present system is still necessary before present and future system requirements can be defined and established; but emphasis shifts toward the general and structural and away from the operational details.

2.4 DETERMINING SYSTEM REQUIREMENTS

In determining the requirements of a system, two main questions arise: (1) What is the system required to do, now and in the future? (2) How well must it perform to fulfill these requirements? To find out, facts about the existing system are blended with information and projections about the future. Additional information is generated through forecasts and predictions of future markets, new services, product volumes, design changes, business trends, advanced processes, regulatory law, and revisions in product mix. If management intends any changes in policy or objectives along the lines of increased specialization or diversification, such plans must be considered in requirements for the future. A proposed system will have to take into account seasonal patterns in labor and costs, as well as market penetration by competitors. Phase II, then, is a mixture of analysis, synthesis, forecasting, construction of models, and trade-off evaluation.

One critical requirement that is often overlooked is the system's ability to adapt to unpredictable future changes. Clearly, analysts cannot know what specific changes will occur, but history and common sense tell them that significant modifications will be needed if the firm is to remain productive and profitable. Therefore, a system must be built which can be readily modified to accommodate change. In this process, analysts may trade off short-term efficiency to provide longer-term value.

Collection and review of information are the first steps in determining the requirements of the system. Next, the study team must combine creative ideas with precise scientific techniques to generate realistic requirements. Systems analysts are increasing their use of the techniques and methodology of management science and quantitative analysis. Operations research, for instance, which started when statistical and mathemathical techniques were applied to military problems during World War II, has produced many worthwhile solutions to complex business problems.

The approach used in Phase II is much like that of an architect designing a new house. First, the architect has the future owners describe their plans and ideas and learns the income, sizes, and ages of the people who will live in the house. The architect then observes their present dwelling in terms of taste and preference and notes the arrangement and sizes of recreation, relaxation, and work areas. The next job is to bring the clients' desires in line with their budgets. Will they give up a screened porch and an extra bathroom to have a third bedroom? Will they postpone some landscaping and keep the air-conditioning system? With this background information, the architect can formulate requirements within the boundaries of available funds and draw up definite specifications which will lead to a satisfactory design.

Specifications are of prime importance; their precision and accuracy control the eventual effectiveness of solution design. Analysts who study a system to determine its requirements must report their conclusions to the management of the organization in a report called the "System Requirements Specification" (SRS). This document contains a series of information packets, each giving the requirements for a separate activity within the organization. (An activity is a combination of operations leading to the achievement of one or more business goals.) The content of the report for an organization with three principal activities is shown in Figure 2–4.

The activity specification packets are introduced by a summary section stating the overall goals and objectives of the business, defining the scope of the study, and summing up the reports to follow. Each SRS packet has three main sections: general, operations, and measurement.

The general section describes the goals and objectives of the activity and its scope and boundaries and lists such considerations as policies and costs not mentioned in more specialized sections. An activity requirements model shows the relationships among logically-required and imposed inputs, operations, resources, and outputs. Figure 2–5 shows an activity requirements model for one activity of an organization.

The section on operations specifies what the system designed for the activity must do, what operations it must perform, what inputs it must accept, what outputs it must produce, and what resources— personnel, equipment, facilities, materials inventories, and information files—will be required. This specification is of the minimum

Figure 2–4 Structure of the document containing specifications for the requirements of the system.

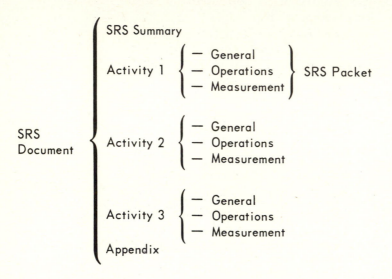

requirements for input, output, and resources imposed by management or logically required to achieve a goal. The more resources imposed, the less freedom the study team has in designing the new system. Thus, the analysts must do everything possible to see that Phase II includes only those specific inputs, outputs, and resources logically required or mandated by management.

The section on measurement states how the system design is to be evaluated as it performs the stated tasks of the activity. Measurements are identified and acceptable limits and present performance levels determined in terms of time, cost, accuracy, and volume. Cost/benefit analysis integrates the various value elements.

If there is an appendix, it contains material which supports and amplifies statements of essential operations. This material is composed of the various documents that the analysts have prepared during the course of the study. Message and file sheets, resource lists, flowcharts or decision tables for operations logic, and definitions of measurement factors are included.

Conversion and improvement studies have often been undertaken without extensive investigation into present and future requirements. One danger in this course of action is that existing operations can be made more automatic, even though they are no longer essen-

Figure 2–5 An activity requirements model showing the required relationships within an activity.

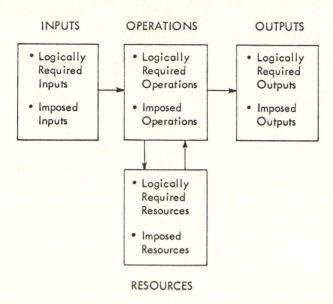

tial or even useful. Another danger is that future changes may show that the newly-designed system is not adaptable and is therefore inefficient.

2.5 DESIGNING THE NEW SYSTEM

Once the requirements for the new system have been specified, it is designed and described. A high level of creative contribution is desirable from the design team if the system is to successfully support the enterprise over a span of years.

The requirements specifications from the Phase II report actually become the design objectives. Then, design alternatives are formulated and described to see how effectively they meet requirements. If more than one activity is to be designed, the analysts must examine and integrate input, output, file, operation, and equipment characteristics for all of the activities.

The activity-oriented solution is then expanded, with specific equipment being selected for each alternative solution. The best system is chosen through careful evaluation. An implementation plan is then devised to show the cost and schedule for detailed systems design, programming, installation, conversion, testing, and personnel training.

The main effort of the analysts toward the latter part of the study is the preparation of a report containing the design, or alternative designs, for the new system. This document is the "New System Plan." It should carefully spell out the justification for installing the new system in business terms—its impact on revenue, investment, and expense. These benefits should be compared to the costs for developing and operating the new system.

It is useful to management personnel reviewing the recommendations to have the report cover five main subjects: (1) a managerial summary, (2) a description of the new system in operation, (3) a plan for implementing it, (4) an appraisal of the economic value of the proposed design, and (5) an appendix containing the key supporting data and information on which the report was based. These divisions are customarily preceded by a preface containing a letter of transmittal, an introduction, and a table of contents. Each of the five main parts is named and described below.

The *management abstract* section reviews the work of the first two phases, outlines the proposed system as it will operate, surveys the implementation plan, and emphasizes the system's potential for profit improvement, reduction of costs, and associated benefits. Since it is a synopsis of the entire study for management evaluation, it concisely describes the main points of the system.

The *new system in operation* section relates the way the system will work, needed equipment, operating personnel responsibilities, and expected operating costs.

The *implementation plan* section describes the various steps of installing the new system, showing costs and time schedules.

The *appraisal of system value* section describes the benefits to be derived from the new system, tells why other designs were rejected, and projects the advantages over the lifespan of the system.

The *appendix* includes a selection of important supporting data not shown in other sections. It supplies the technical reinforcement of the system, making it more comprehensible.

The "New System Plan" is the culmination of the entire systems study and should provide a well-documented, thoroughly analyzed framework from which the implementation and operation of the system may be inaugurated.

SUMMARY

A management system may be considered as passing through a three-stage life cycle: study and design, implementation, and operation. The study and design of a system can be performed in three phases: understanding the present business system, determining systems requirements, and designing the new system. The objective of the first phase is to determine what is now done, using what inputs, with what resources, achieving what results. This phase includes the preparation of a model of the business system. In Phase II, facts about the existing system are blended with estimates and plans concerning the future. Phase II is a mixture of analysis, synthesis, forecasting, construction of models, and quantitative assessments. Phase III can require an even higher level of creative effort. In this third phase the reports of the first two phases are used as the basis for design objectives. Design alternatives are then formulated, described, and evaluated.

QUESTIONS AND PROBLEMS

2–1 Figure 2–1 shows the three stages in the life of a system. On the basis of the steps listed for each stage, which is the most difficult stage, and which is the easiest stage?

2–2 What are the objectives of each of the stages in the life of a business system?

2–3 What would be the dangers of going directly into the Stage 2 implementation of a system instead of carrying out a Stage 1 system study and design? Are there cases where you would skip Stage 1?

2–4 Would there be any reason to conduct a Stage 1 systems study and design without going through with implementation? Why?

2–5 The text describes three phases for conducting a systems study. Rank the phases in order of importance in developing a successful system. Explain your reasons for the ranking.

2–6 What is the purpose of each of the three phases in Stage 1?

2–7 Discuss the contents of the report which is prepared after Phase I is completed.

2–8 Figure 2–3 depicts a simplified model of a business system.

Does this model really depict the system for any organization?

2-9 If Phase I defines the present system as it now exists, why is it necessary to determine systems requirements in Phase II? Are not the systems requirements already defined in the Phase I study?

2-10 What two main questions arise in determining the requirements of a system? How does one find out the answers to them?

2-11 Let us assume that your reading and studying of this book can be defined as an activity. Can such an activity be expressed in the structural form shown in Figure 2-5?

2-12 Discuss the contents of the New System Plan.

CHAPTER 3
PLANNING AND CARRYING OUT
A SYSTEM STUDY

3.1 PLAN FOR THE STUDY

A careful plan of action must be prepared before a system study can be carried out. The plan should state the purpose and scope of the work to be performed, show how the study team will be selected, and indicate how the time and resources of the team are to be employed. It should reflect the desires of management as well as the technical considerations of the study team.

This chapter focuses on four subjects: planning for the study, gathering information about the business, techniques to use in the requirements and design phases, and methods of documentation and report preparation.

The plan for the study can be amplified as extensively as management requires. In a small business where one or two people can handle all the study tasks the plan might evolve from conversations between the manager and the analysts. In large companies where the study could continue over many months, this informal planning would be unsatisfactory. In the latter case, the study purpose would have to be precisely agreed to, as would areas for inclusion or exclusion, depth of study, and a cost budget. From a general agreement on the scope of the project, detailed schedules would be prepared to include personnel assignments and the sequence in which work will affect each selected area of the business. In any case, the study plan should be recorded for review, approval, and later measurement.

Managing a system study is itself a system problem. Much thought has gone into the ways in which the team leader can plan and organize the various data collection, analysis, and design tasks. First, the tasks must be identified, sized, and put in sequence. Next, the available people should be assigned to the various tasks with a clear understanding of what is to be done, why it is needed, when it is due to be completed, and how the information, requirements, or solutions are to be recorded. Finally, careful follow-up and feedback are essential to maintaining effective control of the work.

Even if the scope of the study, team composition, time schedules, and task assignments are planned in some detail, no plan can envisage many of the problems which will be encountered or the precise length of time each task will take. For example, in one study several product lines were to be examined as separate units. Although this seemed to be a relatively straightforward assignment, examination of the files revealed that the records were maintained by functional responsibility (engineering, manufacturing, and accounting) and that there was no continuity or common classification for the different product lines as they were processed through the business. Much additional time had to be spent analyzing the files in each function to produce a complete product line analysis. Therefore, even though a valid plan has been prepared prior to starting the study, experience shows that it must be reviewed frequently and modified to include recent events and changes in thinking.

Initiating a system study involves four principal functions: selection of the team leader and setting up effective relations with the management of the organization to be studied, establishing the scope and boundaries of the study, selecting the team to carry out the study, and setting in place the scheduling and progress control mechanisms to manage the study. The four topics of leadership, scope, team, and schedule will be covered in the following sections.

Leadership and Management Relations   The individual assigned to lead the team should have demonstrated abilities in planning, organization, and administration. The team leader has the problem of coordinating the entire project, laying out time, cost, and personnel schedules; reporting progress to management; selecting members for the team. The leader must also understand the scope and purpose of the study to the degree that work can be reduced in some areas, while coverage in others is expanded. The team leader is the one person who can never lose sight of end objectives, total costs, and management expectations.

The leader's attitude influences the team's approach to its work. As a technical manager or as an administrator, he or she must be able to motivate people to work effectively and develop a climate in which competitive drive is directed toward the best ways to accomplish a task, rather than on the interplay of personalities.

Among the personal relationships the leader and the team will work on in the course of a study, none will be more critical than building mutual understanding with management. Once a good working relationship has been established through the resolution of study goals and scope, the team must keep management periodically informed of progress. During these review sessions, progress is summarized and measured against scheduled completion dates; current problems are discussed and resolved; and projected schedules are reviewed for the period ahead.

Progress meetings usually are brief and informal. However, when a major checkpoint such as the end of a phase is reached, longer and more formal presentations will be necessary. Other members of the business are invited for evaluation of critical areas. Some aspects of these reports (for example, activity formulation) will require considerable sales ability, especially if recommendations depart substantially from past practice. In all these contacts among the team, management, and operating personnel, the team must cultivate the consultant-client relationship, even if the team is part of the organization under study.

Scope and Boundaries The scope of a system study defines the range of what is to be considered inside the study and what is to be excluded. Organizational components, products or services, and locations to be analyzed are usually specified precisely. The word *scope* is used to relate to what is to be covered, while *boundaries* refers to what is not to be in the study.

From this clear-cut beginning many complexities can arise as the team comes to a good understanding with management or even within itself. Often, managers will initially state a systems problem as they see it and wish it to be corrected—for example, long delivery cycles, poor credit-risk selection, slow response to customer inquiries, or high employee turnover. But these are often symptoms, not causes. The team must turn these statements into purposes and then logically establish scope and boundaries to match the purposes.

The basic approach is direct and straightforward enough. But throughout their work, study teams will be called on to make decisions concerning the quality and depth of their own efforts, and these decisions require mature, objective judgment. If there are differences of opinion with management over the scope and objectives of the study, how far does the team press its views on issues of substance? When the work for each phase is completed and the report is written, how can the effort be measured as to completeness and competence? What pitfalls must be avoided in conducting a study? What level of accomplishment should be set for a team? These questions and others will be asked time and again, often without satisfactory answers.

Although team leaders should try to adopt managerial viewpoints, it may be difficult at times to reconcile desires of the team and practical judgments of management. A team that has developed enthusiasm for its work may suddenly be confronted with constraints such as restrictions on the project scope, or by limitations on modifying inputs, outputs, and resources.

Usually, these constraints result from managerial judgment of what is necessary and proper for the well-being of the organization. For example, study objectives in the beginning may have been stated as the nominal improvement of an existing system or as the direct conversion of an existing system without any change at all in the present procedures. The study team may accept such an objective at first; but after delving into the business, it may find opportunities for making considerable improvement, if given more time and people. Management may wish to stay with the initial scope and objectives. Similarly, management may request the continuation of a certain document within the system because it is well recognized in the trade, or it may decide that the present equipment is satisfactory and should be incorporated into the new system design.

When these constraints materially interfere with or severely hamper system design, the team leader must make a strong case for their relaxation. The position, however, must be supported with a well-considered and documented analysis of expected costs and potential results. Should management persist in its position, the team has no alternative but to accept the restrictions. Most of the time this will not be a difficult problem, and compromises can usually be worked out. It is safe to say that all system studies are done within a set of various constraints. Such constraints normally are not sufficient as excuses for not designing a profitable, workable system.

Team Size and Composition Purpose, scope, time, and depth of study will determine in large measure the size and composition of the team of analysts making the study. Under normal conditions, there should be at least two members on the team, even if the business is very small and the study quite limited. Two people working together can furnish enough stimulus to each other to make their efforts far more productive than one person working alone. Whatever size the team, individual talents should complement one another. For example, if one member has a knowledge of methods and procedures, then his or her counterpart should be knowledgeable about the business system as it presently functions. Large-scale studies might require the skills of a mathematician, an operations researcher, or an economist if a quantitative investigation using management science techniques is contemplated.

Requirements for specialized knowledge and skills vary considerably. Knowledge of functional subjects such as accounting, manufacturing, engineering, and production control will be needed; knowledge of special techniques such as simulation may also be necessary. A requirement in many studies is the skill of computer systems synthesis—for example, familiarity with computer characteristics and with communications networks.

When the study team is selected, management may consider this a good time to announce the study to those individuals within the business who will either be affected by it or who will be contributing time and effort to it. This announcement is particularly important for individuals who will come in direct contact with the study team or be interviewed during the course of the study. The communication of study plans to employees is a management responsibility, but one which is often not given sufficient attention. Experienced systems analysts know that an effective study requires employee cooperation, particularly at the supervisory level. As far as practical, all employees should be included among those who should be told of the plans for the study. The manager responsible for authorizing the study should personally announce it and demonstrate support for the effort.

Schedules and Progress Control Business size, study purpose, allotted time, and team size are variables affecting study schedules and costs. A detailed study of a small business by a two-person team might be conducted in one week to one month if all goes well. For a multimillion-dollar concern, the same two-person team could probably not undertake more than an overview study in a like time period. Examining the operations of a single department of a large company, however, could be a reasonable goal to accomplish in one month.

The level of study refinement has a major influence on time schedules. Improvement and conversion studies require less background information than do more comprehensive system studies. For example, operational data, rather than general or structural data, is of more consequence in Phase I for improvement and conversion studies. Similarly, if time does not permit close analysis of system requirements in Phase II, then the present system description might have to serve as the initial statement of requirements. During Phase III, a conversion study will emphasize new equipment and procedural changes necessary, while Phase III for improvement studies means modification of existing systems rather than bringing in new equipment. Time schedules will be considerably shorter for these kinds of studies than for a more extensive study. Note that if a business is planning to use a computer for the first time, the nature of the study will tend to be more time-consuming.

Even when the plan is applied in its complete version for large-scale studies, certain compressions of time are possible. For example, although the phases of understanding the present system, specifying system requirements, and designing the new system are generally performed in series, there are many opportunities for conducting parts of the study simultaneously if team size permits. Thus, in Phase I several persons can collect data for the general and structural sections at the same time. Similarly, in Phase II the activities are fairly autonomous after reformulation so that the requirements for each one can be analyzed separately and simultaneously.

Activity formulation is an example of a sequenced task which does not lend itself to telescoped scheduling; it requires time to define and also time for review through successive evaluations. In contrast, parallel interviews can often be carried out, or interviews can be scheduled to fill in open periods in the work plan. But one caution in assuming too much overlapping and compression is that interviews take time, and management may be too busy to review results when the team is ready. Time is not easily compressed in this work if results are to be worthwhile. A logical planning process starts with identifying the tasks to be done, estimating how long each will take, and indicating potential areas for overlap, thus providing some buffer time.

In determining the time requirement, analysts will want to use techniques such as Gantt charts, program evaluation and review techniques (commonly called PERT), or the critical path method (known as CPM). There are computing programs to assist in project control by simplifying the tasks of function planning, schedule entry, progress reporting, and completion projection. These charting and control techniques which are noted in the text should be learned through one of the texts referred to in the bibliography.

There are two major ways in which the time required for a system study is determined. The first can be called the addition method and the second, the subtraction method. In the addition method, the time for each part of each phase is determined. Where possible, operations that can be overlapped are scheduled to run simultaneously.

Then the separate times are added together to arrive at the target date for the completion of the design of the new system.

In the subtraction method, management usually sets the target date by when the new system must be in operation. Then the analysts must predict the time necessary for Stage 2. This time is subtracted from the target date, thus determining the time remaining for the completion of Stage 1 work.

The addition method is normally used, but circumstances sometimes require the subtraction method. Management's attitude in such situations is that it needs a system in operation in twelve months, even though it may not be as efficient as one which would not be ready for two years.

One tool which can be used throughout the study for management and control purposes is the computer itself. There are many programs available today to assist in the administrative tasks of running a study. There are programs for project scheduling and rescheduling, project budgeting, documentation of results, analysis of data collected, and preparation of reports. A well-run study will make sure that these techniques and programs are known and effectively used by the team members.

3.2 STUDY TECHNIQUES

An analyst employs many different techniques for understanding an existing management system and for designing a new one. Techniques of information collection, analysis, and synthesis are used with varying degrees of emphasis throughout the three phases in the study and design of a new system. Figure 3–1 presents a rough guide to the amount of effort devoted to these three techniques. The shaded areas represent the amount of effort. Thus, in the first phase the main emphasis is on collection, with little analysis and minor synthesis. In the second phase, analysis dominates, with little collection and synthesis. In the final phase, the effort is mainly that of synthesis, with less analysis and minor collection. The outputs from each phase are also shown in Figure 3–1.

Collection is the accumulation and recording of information with a clear objective in mind. Only significant data are selected, and just enough is collected to be useful in the study. The questions of what is significant and how much is enough are discussed in subsequent chapters.

Figure 3–1 Degrees of emphasis on techniques of documentation, analysis, and synthesis during the study and design stage of a system.

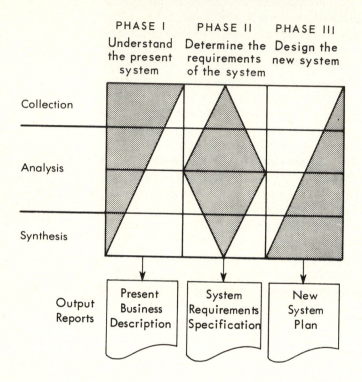

Analysis is the breaking up of study subjects into manageable elements for individual evaluation.

Synthesis, as opposed to analysis, is the combining of parts or elements into a complex whole; it is the reasoning involved in advancing from principles and propositions to conclusions. An example of synthesis in Phase II is the formulation of future business goals. From sources such as the present system description, statement of present system goals, analysis of demand for current and future products and services, and interviews with management, information is organized and integrated by weighing values, dropping extraneous considerations, and extracting meaningful facts to produce a set of goals and objectives that are representative of the business.

Among the range of management science techniques, simulation is particularly useful in a system study. A simulation is an experiment in which real-world conditions are imitated in a model to replicate, as closely as possible, the manner in which a particular system design would perform, if implemented. Decision rules can be tested for validity over a range of situations, or an entire business system can be evaluated for effectiveness of operation. For example, one simulation performed on a computer examined in a matter of minutes the operations of a small factory over a whole year.

Other kinds of models are also useful in systems work. *Queuing models* investigate problems surrounding waiting lines; *Monte Carlo models* introduce variable values into simulations for problems such as production scheduling. Some models are simply descriptive; others must be manipulated to arrive at an acceptable solution. Some models accept relatively fixed information only; others permit substantial data variation. *Optimizing models* employ the techniques of calculus, game theory, and linear programming. Almost any operational system can be described by one or more models, although design and construction of the complex models generally require considerable mathematical skills and may take months to complete.

Unfortunately, much of the information needed both at the descriptive level and at the detailed, quantitative level is not readily available and certainly not in the form desired. This book is concerned with content, structure, and form; it also gives examples to show first how to obtain or develop the information needed and then how to organize this information for use by the team and display it to management.

3.3 INFORMATION SOURCES

When one considers the problem of gathering data and information, it is possible to identify three main sources:

1. Examining internal and external records.
2. Interviewing supervisory and operating personnel.
3. Observing and recording the actual dynamic processes.

All three sources will be used at various points in the study. Record searches predominate in enterprises with well-organized record and file systems. Interviews and observation are used most where the record system is not so satisfactory, or to verify and refine historical data and reports.

To develop data-gathering plans, analysts must first organize their own file systems. A binder, with dividers for each major subject, is one way of collecting general and structural information in an orderly fashion. The binder has the advantage of visually demonstrating the degree of documentation for each topic as data are collected. When the report is written later, the analyst reorganizes the compiled data from the binder (and from others, if the study is a large, decentralized one), and prepares a coherent narrative or series of exhibits to summarize findings. While this is described in manual terms, it is often advantageous to use computer files as a means of recording information and displaying it for review and analysis.

Business information exists in many places, some external to the enterprise, others internal. In most cases, the analyst seeks out data from a wide variety of sources, then verifies the results with personnel who are closely acquainted with the subject matter.

Examining Records and Reports During early planning sessions with management, a study team should develop a list of sources for material relating to the general and structural sections of the report it is to prepare. If a large number of references are available, the problem is usually one of condensing pertinent facts.

Unless the data has been published or well organized, a number of problems arise. To reconstruct information from manual or even computer files is time-consuming; such files may be in use, inaccurate, or perhaps maintained in classifications not useful to the study. Operating personnel in the marketing department may file their records according to the customer order number; the engineering department may use drawing numbers; and the manufacturing department may keep its records according to shop order numbers. Files may be dispersed and decentralized in large companies with some historic information stored at remote locations and thus not easily accessible. When this happens, the analyst should make a preliminary list of requirements and should request clarification on how the data can best be obtained. A complete knowledge of files and records will be necessary in an extensive study; the sooner an analyst becomes acquainted with them, the easier the entire task will be. To the extent that computerized data bases and search and statistical tools can be used, the study time can be shortened and the quality of the information improved.

External data can be formal or informal. Trade publications, government bureaus, and credit associations are formal sources; and their information is fairly standardized and objective. Brokerage reports are often quite revealing in their appraisals of a company. Informal sources, such as customers of a bank, policyholders of an insurance company, or the audience of a TV network, are somewhat less objective, but still offer critical and useful evaluations. Vendors and suppliers to manufacturing concerns may also be considered in this category.

Frequently, information for understanding an organization can only be obtained by asking the personnel involved. This goal should be kept in mind during interviewing.

Interviewing The interview is perhaps the most fruitful, but the most unpredictable, means of securing information. It is valuable when the analyst has the person's trust and confidence; it is unproductive when there is anything less. Still, more significant data are gathered by interview than by any other single method.

Interviews customarily start with the top levels of management. Middle- and first-line management then become the main sources of information during the study, along with professional specialists. Later, individual office and plant employees may have to be interviewed concerning their particular job assignments.

The confidence of persons being interviewed must be earned, not presumed. People become suspicious and distrustful if there is even a vague threat, imagined or otherwise, to their job security. With this in mind, the analyst should make the interviews informal and concentrate on establishing a working relationship. In the process of gathering data, analysts conscientiously avoid any connotation of making stop-watch studies or of appearing to be efficiency experts. They must encourage the feeling that they have become a part of the business, but they must not get involved in day-to-day problems. This advice would apply whether the analysts are making the study for their own company or for an outside firm.

In the first interview (more than one is sometimes needed), the analyst is interested in establishing an atmosphere of trust and confidence; consequently, he or she will take few notes and will attempt mainly to understand the individual and the working background. Deep resentments develop against outsiders who imply they are exceptionally knowledgeable or who convey an attitude of being out to clean up a mess. In one case, a team was working in an organization where the employees felt they were already overburdened with work. The team members made a basic mistake: They tried to show management their capability by eliminating two positions in a certain department after one week's study. When news of this got around, everyone perceived job security as highly threatened, and the team was never able to establish confidence with the people. This resulted in a failure to secure accurate answers during subsequent interviews.

A good interviewer, without seeming to, takes command of the situation and encourages conversation without asking many direct questions. Among other considerations, the interviewer must be prompt for the interview, adhere to the time schedule and subject matter, and make further appointments when they are convenient to the person being interviewed. Where possible, interviews are conducted in surroundings free from distractions; a subject's own office — or that of a superior — almost always creates problems.

A thoroughly planned schedule will reduce the need to repeat interviews, although analysts often find a few individuals who are so knowledgeable about the organization that they will tend to return to them for additional information. However, a balance among the personnel contacted prevents bias from creeping into the information and spreads the interview load more evenly. As interviews are carried out, careful consideration is given to the length of time for each session, frequency of repeats, and individual productivity of each interview. There is no fixed rule for this, as the person being interviewed is often the best lead to what is appropriate for length and frequency of interview.

While interviews may be used at any point in a system study, data gathering for the general and structural sections of the report is mainly a problem of collecting recorded information. Some interviews are injected to identify specific goals of the business, potential problem areas, and areas of operations where there are particularly good prospects for reducing costs and improving efficiency.

When operational data are being gathered, the analysts have to be thoughtful and interpretive, since they will be formulating activities to agree with what they have learned about the business. Much of the time there is no precedent to rely on, and replies to questions reflect assumptions, estimates, and judgments. It requires resourcefulness on the part of the analyst to ensure that activity costs, time cycles, and the flow of events are reasonable. One of the most important tasks is therefore to separate fact from opinion early in the study.

A serious problem that arises frequently during the accumulation of data, both from records and from interviews, is that answers to many questions are not known, and there is no time to conduct a thorough historical search. The analyst then relies on direct observations or uses estimating and sampling methods to get the needed facts.

Observations and Projection Sometimes, file searches and interviews are less than adequate data-gathering methods. This is particularly true in a business which is new and growing, where little management time or effort has yet been spent on such things as time standards, long-range budgets, planning records, or material costs. This also holds for the established business where more attention is paid to gross dollar budgets than to cost breakdowns of individual operations. In one case, a communications system was considered by a company having no records of volume and frequency data on which to base analysis of requirements. In cases such as this some kind of estimate must be made based on observations.

Estimating is an accepted method of developing data; but where possible, estimates must be checked with control totals or verified by interview. If, for example, three activities—and no others—cut across a single department, activity costs in that department should roughly equal the overall department budget. However, if only one activity is to be studied, a realistic checkpoint to verify the analyst's and the supervisor's estimate should be developed.

Since estimating data is a valid and acceptable procedure in systems work, it will save time as long as recognized checks and balances are applied to verify the accuracy of the assumptions. In some situations, estimates made in this manner are accompanied by data obtained from samples.

Sampling is a measuring technique which can be applied formally or informally. One form of sampling, known as work sampling, can be employed to analyze the actions of people, machines, or events in terms of time. Sampling is particularly useful on nonrecurring or irregularly occurring events where procedures have not been issued or data are not available.

A major advantage of sampling lies in the relatively low cost of obtaining data without disrupting or intruding on normal work routines. A second advantage is that there may be a substantial reduction in the time needed to obtain the necessary information. From relatively few observations, inferences can be drawn concerning the total work under study. The analyst actually uses some form of sampling, however informal, throughout a study. Analysis of last month's incoming orders, random selection of one file drawer for review, and observations of clerks working in a tool crib at a particular time are all examples of informal sampling.

When tracing a single activity through a business or working in an area where data are not available or well classified, sampling becomes a necessity. In a data entry area, for example, the analyst may want to find the amount of machine and operator time consumed by customer billing in relation to the amount of time spent performing all operations.

If the actual sampling is done by someone else, the analyst should determine the sample size and the specific times that observations are to be made. For example, a customer billing sample on the 30th of the month probably would not represent the effect this job has on the facility over a month. Rigorous sampling plans are very complex. When the inferences based on samples are of critical importance, it is sensible to employ the services of a qualified statistician.

3.4 TECHNIQUES FOR ANALYSIS AND DESIGN

In approaching its work, the study team may perform in a routine manner and produce acceptable solutions. Or it may find itself in a situation that provides opportunity for the creation of quite original systems. In fact, an unusual design may be required if the new system is to contribute significantly to the profitability and efficiency of future operations. Other times, straightforward and simple improvements may be very effective. A combination of methods frequently is needed to design a truly improved system. It must be remembered that design problems and opportunities are shaped by the two factors that affect all other aspects of organizational life—time and money. These are in limited supply in all organizations. When it comes to design, practical executives usually prefer an ordinary system that is sure to work to a highly creative system that may not or to one that requires too much time to develop and validate.

There are various techniques for resolving the problems encountered by the study team. Two of these are trial and error and application of scientific analysis and synthesis. Each is helpful, but techniques merely set up the problem for the analyst to solve. Once these techniques have been applied, then logic, hard work, and insight are necessary to achieve results. But success does not come only by inching forward or by making changes in small increments. It can also be achieved suddenly after extended periods of hard work and application. Consider the following illustrations.

For many years, the accepted way for an engineer to describe a product's structure has been through a bill of materials. This document is a critical input for manufacturing, and much effort is expended on its form and arrangement. The use of collation charts and single- and multiple-level parts explosions are two examples of improvements in form and arrangement. With the advent of the computer, the manual bills were simply converted to magnetic tape or punched cards or stored in memory. Then somebody had a new thought: bills of materials need not be stored at all if the design logic stored in the mind of the engineer can be reconstructed and stored in a computer program. If the design logic is stated in such a way as to make the transformation possible, product characteristics can then be generated directly from customer specifications.

As another example, consider a company that maintained a 50,000-card standard cost file. The average record for a part contained ten to twelve lines. Because of its size and complexity, the file was updated just once every two years; consequently, material and labor variances ran as high as 50 percent. A major cause of these high variances was that the price of a key raw material sometimes changed every few weeks. Since this raw material was used for a large number of parts, making the changes posed such a massive clerical problem that master records were not modified. The company decided to keep the equipment and system it had and to wait until it could afford a computer with a large enough memory to store the entire file on a random-access basis. However, the systems team understood that the amount of each raw material used on each part was fixed and known. If this amount were stored on the cost card for each part, then the correct current standard cost could be determined by calculation, and the entire standard cost system could easily be processed on existing equipment.

The analyst who can find the essential nature of business problems and detect the fine interrelationships which exist among operations is usually able to considerably extend the profitability of the system. To a systems engineer operating from a systems approach, the general statement of business goals is more important than the particular; it incorporates functions, rather than the means by which functions are performed. From this viewpoint, a railroad does not run trains from one terminal to another; it provides a transportation service for passengers and freight between designated points. A door is not a rectangular construction of wood and metal with hinges; it is a means to control entry and exit. Through generalized concepts analysts lift their thinking out of conventional molds. Each design study can then be viewed as an opportunity, not a problem.

In some studies there are a number of chances for analysts to depart from good practices. Even the best-intentioned and most farsighted team leader may fall prey to certain common pitfalls.

A common error, and a most serious one, is improper problem formulation. Problem areas are often specified or pointed out by management. The study team should take time to evaluate whether the problem has been correctly stated and is actually the one to be resolved. For example, the problem of devising a better method for handling customer complaints could actually be a problem of product quality. The basic problem is not always obvious, and much time can be wasted tracking down a problem that does not exist or one which has been improperly formulated.

Another danger lies in a team's tendency to concentrate on the techniques of problem solution and thus lose sight of the problem itself. In mathematical modeling techniques, for example, it is fascinating to investigate all the possible combinations of solutions generated when resources and inputs are altered slightly. A team can become so engrossed in operating the model that it loses sight of the original problem.

There is also the problem of deciding how much documentation is needed to support recommendations and future phases of study. It is easy to say that the main rule of documentation is not to collect too much or too little, but this does not resolve the dilemma. This problem is closely related to two others: (1) What are the significant areas to investigate? (2) How deeply should they be probed? Analysts working from the overview level in Phase I, for example, will occasionally have to work at deeper levels when the situation demands, then return to the overview level as soon as possible. The key to knowing when to probe deeply and amass a greater quantity of data is closely tied to understandings reached at the beginning of the study.

Experienced study teams typically view an organization objectively to maintain proper balance among events. Whenever a period of deep observation occurs, the analysts should stop for a while to consider what they have accomplished and where they now want to go. In addition, there should be a clear indication of which areas are important, or not so important, soon after the study begins. Priority should be assigned to the significant areas of opportunity on which major effort will be expended. If the parts of a study are always related to the whole, and major opportunities identified, this knowledge usually leads to a correct decision on how much and how deeply to study.

A common shortcoming in study teams is the consideration of too few alternatives. There is seldom only one way to define, attack, and solve a particular problem. Successful teams consider commonly-known, standard options and supplement these with others they have developed to satisfy the special requirements of the situation. This is most important when standard alternatives are only somewhat satisfactory. The invention of a wholly new approach to address special conditions can contribute greatly to effective system design; but of course the team normally should not try to develop new techniques if standard ones work satisfactorily.

The last common failing is excessive ambition, the attempt to cure all ailments with one potion. Only so much can be accomplished in a study, once the constraints of time, cost, and personnel have been defined. If problems have been formulated correctly, a careful study plan worked out and followed, and a reasonable number of choices evaluated, this is all that can really be expected of a team.

3.5 STUDY DOCUMENTATION AND REPORTS

Although the study team keeps management periodically informed of progress and plans, the reports at the end of the three phases, whether presented orally, in written form, or both, have special importance and therefore require extra effort. These reports are the basis for management's decision on whether and to what degree the system implementation and operation stages are to be undertaken.

A written report is desirable; an oral presentation is also advisable. The team must examine the written report for adequacy, consistency, unity, conformity to assignment, proportion, clarity, completeness, simplicity, and accuracy. There should be a logical structure of information from introduction to conclusion; form should be the same from one section to another, with events logically leading from one to another. The language should be understandable, events explained with commonly-used terms, and sentence structure free of awkwardness. Further, the report content should be complete and concise. There should be adequate supporting material included for each topic. Lengthy narrative can be avoided with visual displays, such as graphs, diagrams, and tables.

Oral reports are often most effective when visual aids and an informal presentation are used. Instead of covering the same ground as the written report, the oral presentation concentrates on selected important features. Where practical, the written report should be distributed to the management personnel prior to the oral presentation. Management personnel can review the material in detail and thus be in a far better position to benefit from the team's discussion with them.

3.6 QUALITY OF DOCUMENTATION

Data quality is important during all phases of study, but especially so in Phase II. The validity of the specifications of the new system are being tested here before system design. As data are collected, manipulated, organized, and presented in report form, they must be checked and rechecked for objectivity, reliability, accuracy, validity, relevance, completeness, and usefulness.

Objectivity is the absence of bias in information. For example, the statement "Henry Anderson is one of our sharpest, most productive salesmen" is one of personal bias, while "Last month Fred Miller sold thirteen whole life policies worth a total of $175,000" is objective. Emphasis on factual statements, with few adjectives, creates objectivity.

Reliability means that the same measurement repeated several times on the same object will not produce markedly different results. Should the results differ substantially, the process would be considered unreliable to the extent of the spread in measurement.

Accuracy is the absence of constant error. Measurements are subject to constant and variable error: a speedometer may be 5 percent high on all readings (constant); a cutting tool may register -0.005 in one cut and $+0.005$ on the next (variable).

Validity means that a measurement really measures what it is supposed to measure and nothing else. For example, the number of hours an experienced instructor spends attaining proficiency to teach a subject is not a valid measure of the number of hours a beginner will require to effectively learn the same subject.

Relevance is the applicability of information to the subject under consideration. An individual's grades in a logic course may be related to his or her potential success as a computer programmer; the number of training sessions required to teach repair of engines may be related to the number of sessions required to teach repair of transmissions.

Completeness is the presence of all relevant factors of information. A decision on reordering stock, for example, could probably not be made if information on previous stock usage were not available.

Usefulness is the relationship between the significance of a result and the cost of obtaining that result. This is a rough and relative measure, which says that if the value of a result is considerable, and its cost is low, then it probably is a good buy. Conversely, if the value is not substantial, but the cost is high, it may not be a good buy. For instance, if the cost of a real-time feedback system to record parts completions as they occur is high, and the significance of this online timeliness is not important, the usefulness of the feedback system is low. At times, a particular result may be absolutely necessary, and therefore the cost has to be accepted, whatever the usefulness.

Many study teams today set up the data collected about a business in a computer data base so that it can be easily analyzed, retrieved, and displayed. Here again, we find a computer system invaluable in assisting with the management system study. The information may be used in a batch, or offline, mode, printing reports by various organizing criteria; or it can be available online so that the analyst can probe the facts and display significant summaries as required.

The team organizing study material must present the information to more than one kind of audience. The management group must read, understand, and approve the output reports from each of the three phases, while specialists must check and use the data to write detailed systems procedures and computer programs in the implementation stage. Therefore, the display of the results has to be carefully planned to use effective reporting techniques. Visual devices such as graphs, charts, and schematics, and a good narrative form are effective in meeting management's requirements for clear but brief summaries. Flowcharts, decision tables, and procedure statements are effective in meeting the more detailed requirements of analysts and programming specialists. These various documentation techniques are described in later chapters.

SUMMARY

A system study requires a plan of action. A time schedule is necessary, and the estimated time will vary depending upon the purposes of the study. Before the study begins, meetings are held to define the scope of the study and to determine the size of the study team. In order to obtain maximum cooperation, announcement of the study should be made to the personnel whose functions will be reviewed.

Much of the information sought during the study can be secured through interviews with personnel in the areas being studied. These interviews are critical to the success of the study, and care must be exercised in scheduling and performing them. Collection, analysis, and synthesis are used in different degrees in each of the three phases of the study. Collection of information is important, particularly in Phase I.

More than one method of reporting may be necessary, because the information gathered by the team will be presented to more than one audience. Flowcharts, narratives, decision tables, and procedure statements are some reporting techniques which can be used. The design of the new system provides an opportunity for creative solutions to the problem. New approaches should be considered. Although the scope and objectives of the study may be well defined and agreed to, management may exert certain constraints and the team must use caution to perform within those constraints and still achieve desirable results.

QUESTIONS AND PROBLEMS

3–1 Why is it that the top executive of the company is so important to the success of a system?

3–2 Which type of reporting technique would be most applicable in presenting the results of a systems study to:
a) the president and executive officers of an organization,
b) the manager of a department whose functions were studied, or
c) an equipment manufacturer who is evaluating the type of equipment required?

3–3 Give two examples of pitfalls which can be encountered in conducting a system study.

3–4 What are management constraints? Why are they so important in the design of a system?

3–5 What subjects should one or more members of a study team know if the team is to study and design an information system for a telephone company?

3–6 What subjects should one or more members of a team know if the team is to perform a major customer information systems study for a commercial bank?

3–7 List ten steps which should be estimated in determining the time schedule for a system study.

3–8 State three ways in which the time schedule required for a study can be reduced.

3–9 In Figure 3–1 the amount of emphasis on collection decreases from Phase I to Phase II to Phase III. Does this decrease seem reasonable?

3–10 Although direct interviews are a valuable source of data, what are some of the pitfalls of interviewing?

3–11 Describe two data collection methods designed to reduce the time requirements of a study.

3–12 Why might the analyst have difficulty in obtaining complete information about the existing system through interviews with supervisory personnel?

3–13 Even though many systems are automated today, the text stresses the importance of proper announcement of the study and correct interviewing techniques. Since these are people-oriented problems, why be concerned about them in this automated world?

3–14 Why is it necessary to sell the results of the study to management if the study team is already a part of the company?

PART TWO
UNDERSTANDING THE
PRESENT SYSTEM

Part 2 presents some detailed aspects of the philosophy and methodology used to understand the present business and its management system. If a study is being made for one part of an enterprise, the same words—business, organization, and system—refer to that part of the enterprise being studied. The environment will then be all elements outside the area under investigation.

Part 2 covers the methodology of gathering data and organizing it into a report used by management to direct the further efforts of the study team. This section explains how the existing business applications are reclassified into goal-directed activities for study and analysis. To clarify the meaning and usefulness of the new concepts and terms, examples taken from actual system studies are used.

CHAPTER 4
UNDERSTANDING THE PRESENT SYSTEM

4.1 OBJECTIVES IN UNDERSTANDING THE BUSINESS

Designing and selling a new system solution requires the ability to grasp current business practices. Management will expect careful financial comparisons between proposed solutions and present methods. But an equally important reason for understanding the present system is to provide the analysts with an understanding of the business, its goals, successes, and problems. How can one be confident in the requirements statement for a new system unless one has been thoroughly immersed in the current procedures? This question introduces a serious danger; the analysts' purpose is to understand, not necessarily to accept. It is vital during Phase I to question and evaluate effectiveness and reasonableness.

The Nature of Phase I We can speak of Phase I as a plan for characterizing the present business system with particular focus on its information processing activities. The analysts collect data on the functioning of the current system and its general, structural, operational, and financial characteristics. All of these data must be displayed in an organized format for presentation to management to validate the team's understanding of the business. The data must also be documented and filed in such a way as to support the team's efforts to establish requirements and formulate a system solution.

It is convenient to examine the information to be collected in terms of how it will later be displayed for management and documented for further use by the team. The balance of this chapter will therefore examine the "Present Business Description" report which communicates to management the team's understanding of the present system. It will then focus on techniques for preparing the needed information and finally will provide an overview of helpful documentation forms that record the details of the present operations.

This chapter is an introduction to Chapters 5, 6, and 7, which discuss the principal elements in a present business system study: gathering, analyzing, and displaying general, structural, and operational information.

4.2 THE PRESENT BUSINESS DESCRIPTION REPORT

A recommended overall form of the "Present Business Description" report is shown graphically in Figure 4–1. In real situations the layout and content of individual sections will vary considerably from business to business. However, the report is usually divided into three major sections: general, structural, and operational. The body of the report is preceded by an introduction; an appendix customarily is added for important support documents.

The Report Sections The general section should contain a history of the enterprise, a statement of goals and policies, and an assessment of its position in relation to competition. The structural section normally describes the inputs, outputs, and resources of the business. The operational section contains details of the operating dynamics of an enterprise with emphasis on the flow of events, time cycles, and costs.

This report is more than a static model or description of an enterprise. As a study team becomes acquainted with the customs, practices, personnel, and operations of a business, it will discover areas of strength and weakness and will develop an awareness of trouble spots and problems. Among other tasks, specific business goals are defined, and a suitable group of activities is formulated; operations and functions are recorded; and evidence is acquired on high-cost areas that are sensitive to reduction by introducing system changes.

Initially, the business is described in broad, general terms; then it is described by activity classifications assigned by the study team. Under this latter approach, a business is viewed according to the activities or groups of operations necessary to achieve one or more of its specific goals. Looking at a business from more than one angle is much like an engineer preparing a drawing for a complex casting. Side and end views are not sufficient; cross sections are also required.

All these viewpoints affect the design of the new system, and the objective of the analysts is to obtain the understanding necessary for such design. The output report formally documents their findings so that the information is recorded and available for further use. In effect, this becomes a data base of information on the current system.

Figure 4–1 Structure of the report describing the present business.

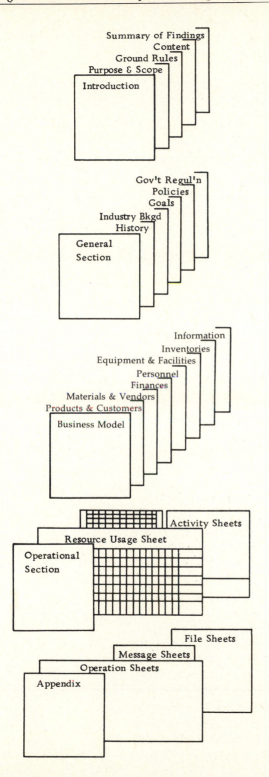

4.3 TECHNIQUES FOR PREPARING THE PRESENT BUSINESS DESCRIPTION REPORT

The document which we call the "Present Business Description" report can be prepared in a variety of sizes, arrangements, and styles. Within its overall framework, it is possible to look briefly at a business, determine general goals and operating methods, sketch structure, and arrive at a picture of operations. On the other hand, it is possible to probe in depth to produce an extremely detailed report of the structure and its operating dynamics. Which of these views, or which of the various intermediate levels a study requires, can be determined only in terms of the study purpose, team size, time allowed, and size and complexity of the business.

In performing a system study, time is usually critical. Most studies are intended to proceed through the full three-phase cycle. The latter two phases are particularly difficult to compress in time, so the study of the present system must usually be completed quickly, but adequately.

Many system studies are done without a formal report of findings by the analysts. It takes time, effort, and ability to reduce such information to written form. Often there is great pressure to get the new system into operation. Shortcuts to save time usually involve the elimination of formal documentation. Nonetheless, understanding is essential to design and must be obtained, whether or not it is formally recorded.

Purposes and Variations Approach and methodology can vary for each of the many purposes for doing a study and report. For example, detailed operational data are important for a conversion study, since they are the information which will be used directly in writing the new computer procedures. In a major system design, however, general and structural data are of equal significance because of the deep insight into the business required to perform the subsequent analysis and design steps.

An overview provides a broad understanding for the complete reconstruction of an information system. This broad view of a large business discloses the critical areas where the most dollars are being spent or where the most profit is being made. In an advertising agency, for example, a preliminary overview might disclose that of four activities—films, technical literature, space advertising, industrial promotions—space advertising alone is responsible for 80 percent of agency income. If profit figures for the other three are not out of line with capital investment and costs, space advertising becomes the important area for further study.

A preliminary overview may disclose parallel operations which have much in common, in which case a study of one operation would be representative of the whole. In one distribution business, for example, there were thirty-one warehousing sites; three of these had limited assembly functions, while the other twenty-eight simply stocked products. Twenty of the twenty-eight carried a single product line; the other eight were multiple-line warehouses supplying major population centers. The system analysts studied two single-line warehouses, one multiple-line warehouse, and one warehouse with limited assembly functions. From these they produced a satisfactorily representative picture of the entire business. Successively more depth is represented by intermediate and detail views. Most studies require some investigation at these detailed levels for operations.

There is yet a further level of data collection usually needed to successfully carry out a system study. This detailed documentation is the factual foundation on which the activity formulation will be built. Therefore, in addition to the general and structural information collected during Phase I and displayed in the "Present Business Description" report, a set of forms is recommended to obtain the technical details of an on-going business. The basic documentation forms are covered next.

4.4 DETAILED DOCUMENTATION OF THE PRESENT SYSTEM

At this time only an overview of the forms used in a system survey is needed. An understanding of their purpose and relationship will aid in grasping the nature and flavor of the present business study.

The basic purpose of a survey is to determine quickly what is done, from what source, with what resources, to achieve what results. More specific purposes include the need to understand how a system or activity fits into a larger organization, that is, into its environment. A coherent description of present operations is needed as a basis for further analysis of how well an existing system meets present or projected demands. Quick surveys can also determine costs of personnel, machines and equipment, material, and facilities; they can provide a picture of overall efficiency in terms of elapsed times in a sequence of operations, unit operations times, and operating volumes.

A system survey seeks only the information needed to provide understanding of the system or activity for its particular purpose. Its aim is to show how people and equipment, using such resources as material inventories and information files, respond to inputs to produce outputs and results.

Documentation forms for describing a system must be easy to use if they are to be valuable for surveys. They must also be logically organized to clearly segregate and identify the key information needed for understanding a system in operation.

The Purpose and Interrelationships of Forms The five main purposes that the documentation of an existing organization must serve are: (1) to find the cost of using resources for activities, (2) the description of activities, (3) the description of operations, (4) the description of input and output documents, and (5) the description of records and files. The five documents described in this chapter were developed to satisfy these purposes. For convenient reference they are titled to correspond to the above purposes: (1) resource usage sheet, (2) activity sheet, (3) operation sheet, (4) message sheet, and (5) file sheet.

The relationships among these forms are illustrated in Figure 4–2. The organizational structure and a cost analysis of the activities appear on the resource usage sheet. The flow of the activity itself is displayed on the activity sheet.

The arrow in Figure 4–2 connecting the activity sheet and the resource usage sheet represents two kinds of relationships, one direct and one indirect. The direct relationship is that the activity sheet shows the pattern of operations for a given activity, and the arrow points to the major row of the resource usage sheet showing the cost structure for the activity as a whole. The indirect relationship is that the analysts may have used some of the volume and time data from the activity sheet to assist in estimating costs shown on the resource usage sheet.

Operations within each activity are further described on the operation sheets, with details on information inputs and outputs (from or toward which the operation works) and information resources (with what the operation works) provided on message and file sheets. These forms permit the analyst to describe the activity in motion; they reveal the flow of incoming materials or information through the internal workings of the system to output.

The resource usage sheet fits each system under study into its larger context. It shows the organization and structure of the business

Figure 4–2 Relationships among the five basic documents used in studying an existing organization.

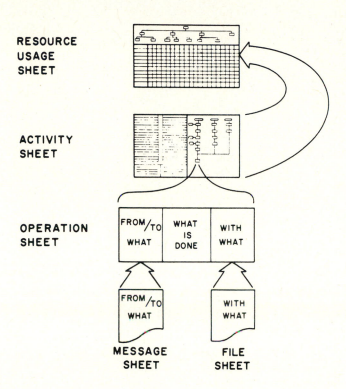

environment. It also provides a rapid analysis of costs for the organizational components and shows the cost impact for each activity or system.

The activity sheet traces the flow of a single activity, breaking it down into its major operations. Each activity sheet presents as large a group of related operations as can be handled conveniently. It includes a flow diagram of the activity with individual blocks representing various operations (each of which can be more minutely described on operation sheets). Key characteristics such as volume and time can be recorded in tabular form.

The resource usage sheet and the activity sheet together provide a quick look at a business system. The operation sheet and the message and file sheets provide yet closer views.

There can be an operation sheet for each block on the activity sheet. It is used for recording the related processing steps that form a logical operation. It describes what is done, with what resources, under what conditions, and how often to produce what specific results. Its primary purpose is to show the relationships between inputs, processes, resources, and outputs.

The message sheet is one of two forms that support the operation sheet. It describes the inputs and outputs — in effect, to whatever level of detail the management and the analysts desire, from what source or toward what result an operation is working.

The file sheet describes a collection of records, an information file; it is the second of the two forms supporting the operation sheet, and shows with what information the operation works.

These five forms are useful for providing a coherent description of a system. Moreover, they can be used at several levels of detail. The resource usage and activity sheets together display the dynamic mechanism of an activity; together with the operation sheet they provide a fairly detailed operational view. The operation sheet by itself permits a look at critical operations and, when it is supported by the message and file sheets, provides a closeup of information used in or produced by such operations. Message and file sheets by themselves permit observation and analysis of information inputs, outputs, and resources, with again a variable level of detail as desired by the analysts.

When describing what is done (on the operation sheet, in the field reserved for process description and qualifications), the observer can choose from several levels of detail by exercising a choice of verbs. Such verbs as *prepare*, *reproduce*, *update* are descriptive of processes at one level of detail. Computer languages, such as Cobol, PL/I, or Fortran are examples of more detailed descriptions.

The techniques and forms discussed in this text have been tested by use in system studies of a number of diverse businesses. While they are not the only answer to the problem of describing the characteristics of a business system, they have proved workable; and they do guide the analyst in a logical study of system characteristics. They are broad gauge in approach, so in specific instances there may be tailored-to-order techniques that are more powerful or more descriptive for a particular problem or design solution. For example, certain computer-room procedures may be more efficiently described by a symbolic flowchart (with narrative description giving volumes and flow rates), and supported by record and report layouts. In the event that a specific technique has proved successful in a particular area, it should be used. The analysts may also design any forms desired. It is simply the content that is relevant; and with the amount of data collected during a study, analysts must use some kind of systematic collection and recording mechanism. Forms are like road maps for analysts.

SUMMARY

The first stage in constructing a business system is study and design. There are three phases in the study and design stage, the first of which is understanding the present business. This awareness must precede the determination of the requirements of the system; it functions like a data base. This phase produces the "Present Business Description" report, which can be written in a variety of ways, but usually consists of an introduction, a general section, a structural section, an operational section, and an appendix.

Detailed documentation can include a resource usage sheet, one or more activity sheets, and the necessary operation, message, and file sheets. While these are of substantial value to analysts, they are only included in the "Present Business Description" report when they are critical to the conclusions.

QUESTIONS AND PROBLEMS

4–1 What is the primary reason for studying the present business?

4–2 Describe some of the sources for general and structural data for a Phase I report.

4–3 Why would a company dictionary be important to systems study and implementation?

4–4 Define the following terms as they might appear in a company dictionary:
a) hourly rated worker,
b) discount,
c) gross pay,
d) federal withholding tax,
e) employee,
f) charge account number,
g) net pay.

4–5 Would the report presenting the study team's findings during their study of the present business have any value for management of the organization concerned even if the study stopped there? Explain.

4–6 In Figure 4–2 the arrow between the activity sheet and the resource usage sheet suggests that the data from the activity sheet flows into the resource usage sheet. Is this true?

4–7 How do the five documents described in this chapter together form a coherent description of the system?

CHAPTER 5
GENERAL BUSINESS DESCRIPTION

5.1 PARTS IN THE GENERAL SECTION

The general section of the report describing the present business system should clearly and concisely convey the major features of a business in narrative form. It is usually composed of five parts: (1) history and framework, (2) industry background, (3) goals and objectives, (4) policies and practices, and (5) government regulations.

This chapter discusses the following topics for each part of the general section:

1. Content and type of data required.
2. Methods for data collection, including sources of information.
3. Examples of how the information might appear.

5.2 HISTORY AND FRAMEWORK

The present goals and practices of an organization are often shaped by the important events in its history. The report section dealing with the organization's history and framework identifies major milestones which have influenced the present direction of a business.

The Nature of History Reporting Important historical information includes ideas, attitudes, and opinions of key management and operations personnel; excerpts from the original charter; stated reasons for starting the company; mergers and spinoffs; expansion or curtailment of product lines and services; and reasons for changes in name or products. In addition, the growth of the physical plant and numbers of employees over the years are mentioned, along with a general identification of current products and services.

The following statement of the history and framework of Butodale

Electronics is an example of how this kind of information can be displayed:

The Butodale Electronics Company was established in 1961, incorporated in the State of Massachusetts. It was founded by four engineers and scientists who had worked together for a number of years in a large corporation on advanced government project work. Their main objective was to aid research laboratories and manufacturers in design and production of the latest radar, radio, and other electronic equipment through use of analog computers and other specialized technical facilities.

It is significant that the corporation sales have increased from $170 thousand to $15.9 million since its founding. Some of the major milestones in the last five years were:

1. Establishment of the Worcester Computation Center to develop new fields of application for the analog computer (for example, heat transfer, nuclear engineering, process control engineering).
2. Establishment of the Long Beach and Rio de Janeiro Computation Centers to extend what was started at Worcester and to educate prospective customers in the use of analog computer techniques.
3. Opening of additional sales offices in Chicago and Fort Worth.
4. Expansion and modernization of the original plant in Danvers.
5. Starting a major drive to secure overseas business, particularly in South America.

Butodale's major product lines have expanded during this period to include small general-purpose analog computers, instruments and data plotters. (None of these new lines have developed to more than 10 percent of the total annual sales volume.)

The above material implies certain objectives (for example, expansion of overseas operation) and even provides reasons for starting the company. The remainder of the statement goes on to describe recently-added product lines.

Data Sources The Butodale history is one and a half pages in the report, while the history of the National Bank of Commerce requires three and a half pages. Length can vary; it is important only that the narrative reveal useful facts. In their initial meetings with management, analysts customarily request certain general information: annual reports, current and back issues; a prospectus or other SEC (Securities and Exchange Commission) reports; copies of speeches by management personnel concerning the business; employee orientation handbooks; and published texts on company history. A history of key events about a company is put together from such material.

In addition, large commercial banks such as New York's Chase Manhattan, Citibank, Manufacturers Hanover, and Marine Midland, California's Bank of America, and Philadelphia's First Pennsylvania often publish reviews of important industries, and these can be used as source data. These summaries are oriented chiefly toward the investing public, but are handy references for history.

Sources of financial and operating data such as *Standard & Poor's*, *Dun & Bradstreet*, and other industrial and commercial registers can be scanned for general information. Biographical registers such as *Who's Who in Commerce and Industry* are valuable when the personality of one man has strongly influenced the enterprise.

Where a study is directed toward one element of an enterprise, the company's historical data will be of less importance and can be substantially reduced. Instead, it may be on target to discuss the history of the particular location or department. Why was the organizational component created? What particular problem or opportunity was it designed to address?

This history and framework section naturally leads to the industry background section.

5.3 INDUSTRY BACKGROUND

The industry background part of the report on the present business places it in perspective within its industry. Comparative data that indicate why one company is successful and another is not, along with facts on the entire industry, should be included if available. Areas of concentration, strengths and weaknesses, and market potential of the major companies should be assessed. Here, the word *industry* is being used generically; it is meant to include organizations and institutions of all kinds.

Form of Industry Background Reporting The nature of the industry should be summarized briefly, showing demand for its products and services, technological developments leading to progress, growth characteristics and trends. Among individual companies, comparable statistics can be prepared on sales volume, product and service likenesses and differences, territories served, profit margins, and other factors. This is sometimes difficult to do, since many multi-product-line companies do not release statistics by divisions. However, there often are historical or trade association data available that will permit some kind of comparison, and changes in U.S. federal laws require more detailed breakdowns for publicly held corporations.

The following example is taken from a study. It illustrates the kind of material found in industry background sections:

Butodale is in the electronics industry and specifically in the analog computer area. Analog computers are widely used industrial tools which fall into two categories, general-purpose and special-purpose computers. There is considerable competition in this industry; some of the biggest competitors are ABC Instrument, Jones Instrument, and National Systems, Inc. Many investment analysts feel there will be continued growth for the general-purpose computer but this growth may not be at the same rate as in the past. The company agrees with these conclusions and, therefore, there is considerable stress put on finding new markets and new products. In order to uncover these areas and products the company has set up a New Products Committee and a Market Analysis Section. It is the specific purpose of these groups to plan future growth and to direct engineering effort towards this growth in order that the company may maintain a planned growth pattern of 20 percent per annum, or greater.

Some of the product areas under scrutiny are instruments, special-purpose computers, and process control equipment. Likewise, industry statistical analyses by marketing areas are developed in order to concentrate effort in the proper industries. There has been no designed plan to integrate this company through component manufacture; however, it is not opposed to this type of growth if necessary to insure a reliable source of supply, and if excess capacity can be sold profitably. Recently the company absorbed the Premium Capacitors Company and is now building high-quality capacitors.

Sources for Industry Background Reports A useful source of background information is the industry's technical paper or magazine. Almost every industry is served by at least one such publication; some are quite objective and informative. Editorial and research staffs of these publications frequently have files of industry statistics; a few publications issue an annual statistical review which summarizes the state of the industry or field of operations. For example, *Aviation Week and Space Technology* publishes, in the first issue of the year, a special report on the state of the worldwide electronics business, with projections for the year to come.

The Department of Commerce publishes a wealth of material on U.S. industry and trade. Government data are as a rule more objective, but less current than information found in business publications. The Census of Manufacturers, for example, maintains diversified industry statistics which can be used to verify other data. The

Department of Agriculture publishes data on the food processing industry; information on the alcoholic beverage trade can be secured from the Treasury Department; data on the prescription and proprietary drug business may be requested from the Department of Health, Education, and Welfare.

Data bases being developed by the government are invaluable sources of information which should be used whenever the material is suitable. In addition, there are now statistical information organizations from which data can be purchased, often in computer readable form if desired.

5.4 BUSINESS GOALS AND OBJECTIVES

Goals and objectives, as used in this text, have to do with the same general concept. However, this book defines goals to be statements of purpose, while *objectives* are the measurable and quantifiable means of achieving them. A clear understanding of business goals is necessary before activities can be properly formulated. In this section of the report the requirement is for specific rather than general statements. Goal definition, good or bad, may strongly influence the final system design since activities are keyed to it.

The Definition of Goals The definition of these goals is normally a relatively brief list of a half-dozen or more specific statements. As an example, in the report prepared for the Butodale Company, the preliminary goal statement reads:

A major objective of this corporation is to expand sales and profits which will guarantee a proper return to stockholders and offer continued opportunity to employees. The present sales goal is to increase gross by at least 20 percent; a net profit goal of 7 percent of sales and 15 percent of net worth has been established.

However, phrases like *expand sales* and *guarantee a proper return to stockholders* were considered too general. In subsequent discussions the goal statement was revised to read:

1. Manufacture and sell standard computer equipment and accessories.
2. Design and manufacture special computer models and accessories to satisfy individual specifications and requirements.
3. Offer computation services and engineering consultation on a fee basis to industry, commerce, and schools, among others.

4. Manufacture spare parts and components for sale to the trade.
5. Repair and maintain installed equipment.
6. Conduct research on new products and services to support present lines and initiate new ones within Butodale's area of knowledge and proficiency.
7. Compensate employees and suppliers for services, and provide a satisfactory return for investors.
8. Demonstrate competence and quality in every product to clearly show advantages over competitive equipment.

This second statement was far more definitive and revealing of the goal structure of the business. These eight points were subsequently incorporated into the report of the second phase of the study. For comparison, let us examine goal statements for another type of industry.

In the present business report for Custodian Life, the analysts found it appropriate to identify most of the organization's goals with a standard of attainment. Following is the statement from the section containing the goals and objectives for Custodian:

Competition is the dominant factor in the insurance industry and reaches into many different areas of a life insurance company. In the past decade, ordinary life insurance in force in the U.S. has doubled, while group insurance has shown an even greater increase. Custodian Life confronts this highly competitive, rapidly expanding market place with these goals and objectives:

— New business production each year to equal 16% of the insurance in force at the beginning of the year.
— A net gain in insurance in force of 10% each year.
— A termination rate not greater than 6% per year of the insurance in force at the beginning of the year.
— Development of the accident and health insurance business by an increase in the annualized premium of 49% over the previous year.
— Expansion of operations into seven additional states during the next twelve months.
— A well-balanced operation with proper consideration given to all groups within the company.

This statement could have been more specifically directed toward the individual services the company offers and the markets it serves. However, management felt the goals so expressed were adequate as they stand.

These two sets of statements reveal several things about the philosophy and methodology of stating the goals of organizations. It should be clear that a wide variation of statements is possible, depending on the analysts, the industry, management personnel, and the sources available. While directives, management statements, and other internal publications offer clues to business goals and objectives, the ultimate sources of information are the personal interviews with owners or top-level management. As the Butodale example pointed out, managers often express goals quite generally. A rather searching self-examination may therefore be necessary to produce adequate goal statements.

Goal formulation is a worthwhile endeavor. Organized thinking differentiates the goal from the problem. For instance, management may be concerned about a drop in revenue from a particular product line. The immediate reaction may be to blame the relatively long delivery cycle required to fill orders. The goal seems to be to reduce the delivery cycle. However, the real goal is to improve the sales rate, which may or may not be affected by cutting the response cycle by 50 percent. Even if a problem is resolved, the customer will not be satisfied unless the goal is realized. Thus, goal specification is exacting, but necessary.

5.5 POLICIES AND PRACTICES

The goals and objectives of a business should be reflected in its policies and practices. Some will be common to the industry or field of concentration; others will depart from industry practice as suits the requirements of a specific enterprise.

The Nature of Policies   Policies, which are simply stated courses of corporate action, would include codes of ethics, plans for expanding into new territories, approaches to advertising and publicity, attitudes toward employees, viewpoints on promotion, and the like. Policies are ideas, attitudes, and philosophies, as distinguished from procedures or methods; and the analyst must keep these differences in mind as he compiles the policy statement.

Butodale's policies are oriented to the employee, as can be determined from the following excerpt from the report for that organization:

Some of the major policies instituted by Butodale have unquestionably helped the company attain its position of eminence in the analog computer industry. One of these policies is the corporation's attitude toward its employees. Butodale has developed a labor philosophy in which it endeavors not to infringe on the private lives of its people, while offering liberal employee fringe benefits, including educational opportunities. The company makes a strenuous effort to keep layoffs to an absolute minimum. This policy has resulted in a fine labor-management atmosphere. It has made itself felt in pride of workmanship and company loyalty hard to equal in modern industry.

In contrast, the policies and practices for the National Bank of Commerce are much more detailed, as shown by the following statements in the report for that organization:

For individual and commercial customers and prospects

1. Accessible, flexible facilities for deposit and receipt of cash, checks, bonds, drafts, and other negotiable instruments.
2. Interest-paying system to encourage time deposits.
3. Safekeeping facilities for valuable records.
4. Personal, confidential, knowledgeable consultation on all financial matters.

For correspondent banks

1. Direct sending service and fast collection of cash items.
2. Full draft collection service.
3. Fast currency and coin shipment service.
4. Valuable document safekeeping facilities.
5. Assistance on large loans and advice on trust matters.

For loan customers and prospects

1. Facilities and experienced personnel available for consultation and financial advice on all loan matters.
2. Readily accessible facilities for the closing of (and payment on) personal, commercial, or mortgage loans.
3. Extensive advertising program to attract loan prospects to the bank for consultation.
4. Specialists available with a broad knowledge of income-producing investments.
5. Specialists available having detailed financial status information on local individuals and businesses.
6. Analysts available who are well informed on relative valuations on all types of property.
7. Flexible interest-charging structure to encourage large loans and rewards for those who pay when due.

Planned practices to meet goals

1. Expand advertising program to reach more potential customers.
2. Enlarge drive-up banking facilities.
3. Increase emphasis on "Installment" type loans.
4. Modernize and reorganize physical and manpower facilities as necessary for most efficient operation.
5. Maintain an electronic data processing center using the latest computer equipment for processing paperwork; offer such services to local industry at an attractive cost.

There are a number of other dimensions to the policies and practices statements. If relevant to the business, the analyst should cover special contracts and agreements such as royalty arrangements, licenses for patents, long-term leases of facilities and equipment, and special marketing relationships. Union contracts may also reflect key business directions or constraints which will have to be considered in any proposed changes to operational practice. These are the kinds of considerations that help the analyst understand the history and future of an organization.

Sources of Policy Information Most companies prepare and publish standard operating procedures, operating and policy instructions, directives, and other internal declarations stating corporate policies, standards, and attitudes. Published information of this type should, where practical, be supplemented with statements from top management verifying or correcting items listed and the analysts' interpretations. Company advertisements and publicity releases also reflect the corporate personality, indicating areas in which the company currently operates or seeks to become established. House publications, too, frequently discuss policies, practices, and attitudes; but they may not be totally objective in viewpoint.

5.6 GOVERNMENT REGULATIONS

In virtually any enterprise in today's world, government regulations have some impact on the policies of the organization. For this reason, analysts of management systems must consider them routinely.

For consistency, all explanations and examples are given for United States–based operations and relate to U.S. laws and institutions. Obviously, this must be modified for any company that is doing business in other countries or is based outside the U.S. Depending on the application area, it may be necessary to take a worldwide view to gain a proper understanding of the present system and future needs, but government regulations at all levels — federal, state, and local — often influence the way a business is conducted.

A discussion of regulations in the present business report should answer three basic questions:

1. Which government regulations help the company do business (for example, charters, tariffs, franchise enabling acts, subsidies)?
2. Which restrict its business activities (for example, utility regulations and regulations on financial enterprises)?
3. Which affect its record-keeping or operating practices?

Rulings of the Federal Aviation Administration determine form and content of some airline reports; rules of the Federal Communications Commission require certain reports from communications facilities in specific form; rulings of the Securities and Exchange Commission affect the record-keeping of brokerage houses. However, the general SEC requirements affecting stock issue for publicly-held corporations would normally not be spelled out in the report, nor would laws regarding monopolistic practices and restraint of trade. These and income tax rules would only be spelled out if they were of unusual immediate significance to this business.

Other government regulations besides federal laws will affect policy and practice. For example, the attitude of the local government regarding industrial waste or pollution must be heeded. Often such rules will be geographically selective or refer to particular lines of business. However, they may sharply influence management decisions. This kind of informal regulation is noted in the report.

Having established the philosophical setting for the section on government regulations, a specific statement taken from an actual report can now be examined. In the following quotation from the National Bank of Commerce report, it is noteworthy that both permissive and restrictive regulations are mentioned.

National Bank of Commerce, organized in 1891, was chartered for business under the National Bank Act of 1864. The National Bank Act created a Bureau of Controller of Currency in the Treasury Department. The Controller, who is Director of the Bureau, has the power to charter national banks and is responsible for the examination, supervision, and rules relating to the operation and powers of such banks. Where state banking regulations are in conflict with national regulations, the national bank is normally required to comply with the state regulation.

National Bank of Commerce, like all member banks, must operate within the limits of the regulations of the Federal Reserve System. Responsibility for Federal Reserve policy and decisions rests on the Board of Governors, who are appointed by the President and approved by the Senate for a term of 14 years; the twelve Federal Reserve banks; and the Federal Reserve Open Market Committee. All national banks must be members of the Federal Reserve System, hold Federal Reserve stock, and must maintain legal reserves on deposit in their district Federal Reserve Bank. National banks must furnish a financial report when requested by Federal Reserve, and are members of the Federal Deposit Insurance Corporation, which guarantees each depositor against loss up to a maximum set by FDIC.

National Bank of Commerce must constantly adjust policies and operational procedures to meet the requirements of new Federal Reserve regulation interpretations.

The statement then lists the areas covered by the regulations of the Federal Reserve System.

Regulations may not always have a direct effect on an enterprise, but still may influence business policies. A statement in the Butodale report illustrates this point:

Government regulations do not play a major role in company plans. However, a significant percentage of sales is subject to renegotiation. Since the government sets profit objectives as a percent of sales, this has an effect on company plans and strategy.

One might expect management to know all about such regulatory information as noted in the above statements. However, management personnel may change, regulations may vary both in content and interpretation, and the organization itself may have changed since the last time management took a serious look at such information. For these reasons, the section on government regulations can serve a useful purpose to management as well as to the study team itself.

Analysts usually look in books and journals related to the industry for general information on government regulations. Annual reports and other company publications sometimes disclose the effect of government regulations on a business.

Commerce and financial laws enacted by the various states, for example, are specifically restrictive on banking and insurance operations; and utilities are closely regulated by state utility commissions. Franchises are examples of permissive regulations, as are federal laws which grant subsidies to industries. Summaries of the legislation, and perhaps the laws themselves, should be read for an accurate appraisal of their impact on the business. The company's legal department should be consulted in making this appraisal.

The discussion of government regulations normally terminates the general section of the analysts' report on the present business system. This general section is then followed by the structural section, which describes the inputs of the business, its resources, and the outputs it produces. The philosophy is that the general section presents the setting for the goals and environment of the organization, whereas the structural section presents other realities—what it receives from the environment, what resources it has to operate upon the inputs it receives, and what it provides back to the environment. The structural part of the report is the subject of Chapter 6.

SUMMARY

The general section of the report of the present business system is composed of history and framework, industry background, goals and objectives, policies and practices, and government regulations. Historical information includes opinions of key management personnel, original charter, reasons for starting the company, mergers and spin-offs, expansion or curtailment of product lines, and reasons for changes in name. The industry background part of the report places the business in perspective within its industry; useful sources of information are the industry's technical papers and magazines. Information on the goals and objectives is of prime importance in the formulation of activities. Directives, management statements, and other internal publications offer clues to business goals and objectives; but the ultimate sources of information are the personal views of owners or top-level management. The goals and objectives of a business are implemented by its policies and practices. Published procedures, policies, and directives supplemented with statements from top management supply the information for the policies and practices part of the report. Government regulations can often influence the way a business is conducted. The report should include information about which government regulations help the company, which restrict the company, and which affect its record-keeping practices.

QUESTIONS AND PROBLEMS

5-1 What is the main purpose of the general section of the present business description?

5-2 What is the major purpose of the history and framework section of the general section of the present business description?

5-3 Summarize some potential sources of information for the industry background section of the present business description.

5-4 When studying a manufacturing process of a company, it may be desirable to classify the production facilities used in the plant. What sources of data could be used for such classification?

5-5 Chapter 5 contains the policies and practices of the National Bank of Commerce. What information might these policies and practices envision for the bank's customers?

5-6 Chapter 5 contains a selected statement of the history and framework of Butodale Electronics. The third item in the example reads, "Opening of additional sales offices in Chicago and Fort Worth." Could the statement be changed to "Opening two additional sales offices?"

5-7 Government regulations vary from one industry to another. Classify the following industries as to the degree of government regulations a study team might encounter during a systems study. Use a classification system of very much, some, and little or none.
a) dairy,
b) brewery,
c) advertising agency,
d) computer manufacturer,
e) trucking company,
f) stock broker.

CHAPTER 6
STRUCTURAL ASPECTS OF A BUSINESS SYSTEM

6.1 STRUCTURAL ELEMENTS

The three major structural elements of a presently operating business management system are *inputs*, *outputs*, and *resources*.

Inputs Inputs for a product-oriented organization or system are normally the materials that are received or bought from its suppliers. For example, a company manufacturing a whipped topping would have coconut oil, corn syrup, and water as three major inputs. These inputs might be supplied from three separate sources—an oil company, a corn products company, and the city water authority. A milk company would receive milk from dairy farms and cartons from a paper-container manufacturer as two major inputs. Each company would probably receive many other inputs.

Outputs Outputs are normally the products that an organization sends or sells to its customers. Customers, like vendors, are part of the environment. The above two companies can provide examples of outputs. The whipped topping company transforms the oil, syrup, and water into a whipped topping to sell to bakeries, hospitals, and individuals. The milk company, having pasteurized the milk and filled bottles or cartons, sells it to retail stores, restaurants, hospitals, and individuals.

Resources The two companies transform, package, and sell; but they must have some means of carrying out these operations. These means we call resources. Resources are made up of financial support, people, inventories of material, files of data, and production and information processing facilities. Thus, the whipped topping company has to have money, managers, chemists, salespeople, and machine operators; storage space for input materials and the finished product; and physical facilities such as a plant, blending equipment, freezer, and sales office.

Now we can draw an accurate analogy between an information management system and a manufacturing process. The processing of information is usually a service to the rest of the business. The information management system must receive inputs from the environment (that is, customers and suppliers) or from other elements of the business. Its own outputs then become financial reports, factory instructions, and purchase orders to give to other business components, vendors or customers. To carry out these information processing tasks, there must be physical resources to store previously recorded information as well as processing instructions to collect, calculate and display information.

These three elements—inputs, outputs, and resources—constitute the structure the study team must understand in order to design a new system. Also of fundamental importance is the understanding of the operations by which inputs are transformed into outputs. These operations will be discussed in Chapter 7.

Sources of Structural Information As in the general section, analysts must search for data. The sources used as a foundation for the general data can again be used for the structural aspects of the system. It is necessary to discuss the sources in detail only where they are new.

It would be of little value for analysts to collect a large quantity of data if they had no idea what they were looking for or what they were going to do with the information once it was obtained. For this reason, a business model is used to identify the structural elements and the relations among them. We showed the general outline of such a model in Figure 2–3. Now we present one in more detail.

6.2 BUSINESS MODEL OF THE STRUCTURE

A model of the business sets up the framework for exhibiting the relationships among the inputs, outputs, resources, and operations. The model serves a useful purpose by establishing a classification system for displaying data.

Elements of the Business Model Elements of the business model will vary in emphasis for different industries and enterprises. Physical inputs and outputs are stressed in most models for a manufacturing enterprise, while resources predominate in analyzing an employment agency. Deposits and loans are input and output classifications for a financial institution, but money in general is a resource for other enterprises.

Note also that one can deal with the enterprise as any logical grouping of functions of people or facilities. It can be at any level of the organization from the whole company to a relatively small department or section. It can be separated by product line or type of service. It can be distinguished by geographic location or class of customers. In all of these cases the same principles apply, but they must be sensibly adapted to the particular situation.

Figure 6–1 is an actual model prepared for the Butodale company. Note that the environment contains both vendors and customers. We see that Butodale deals with 850 vendors. The analysts classified the vendors according to the dollar volume of their purchases. This classification revealed, for example, that fifteen vendors supplied over $100,000 worth of materials each per year.

The model shows that the combined 850 vendors supply Butodale with fifteen classes of items ranging from transistors to converters, and that the total cost of these materials amounts to 45 percent of sales. Probably, the analysts based their summaries on individual dollar figures obtained for each of the materials. This additional information is of interest to management and to the analysts later when they design the new system.

The inputs become involved in company operations, which in the present system study for Butodale were organized as marketing, engineering, production, accounting, and purchasing. The new design may change it considerably, but before there *is* a new design, the present situation always must be defined.

The operations of an organization are carried out using resources. In Figure 6–1 we see that the analysts classified the resources into four main categories: finances, personnel, inventory, and facilities. For each category, they have set up subclassifications which they list in the model, accompanied by figures to indicate dollar or physical amounts.

The model then shows that the inputs are converted into outputs, which for Butodale are called products. The major product is the general-purpose analog computer which makes up 72 percent of sales. The other products sold to customers are listed, together with their relative importance as reflected by the percent of sales figures. The analysts also note here that 9 percent of all output is sold in South America.

Outputs are delivered to the environment which, for the Butodale

Figure 6–1 A business model for Butodale.

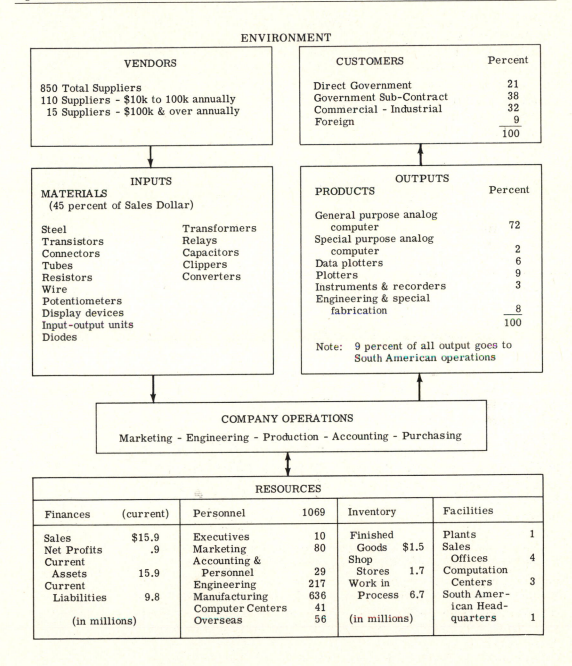

ENVIRONMENT

VENDORS

850 Total Suppliers
110 Suppliers - $10k to 100k annually
 15 Suppliers - $100k & over annually

CUSTOMERS	Percent
Direct Government	21
Government Sub-Contract	38
Commercial - Industrial	32
Foreign	9
	100

INPUTS

MATERIALS
 (45 percent of Sales Dollar)

Steel	Transformers
Transistors	Relays
Connectors	Capacitors
Tubes	Clippers
Resistors	Converters
Wire	
Potentiometers	
Display devices	
Input-output units	
Diodes	

OUTPUTS

PRODUCTS	Percent
General purpose analog computer	72
Special purpose analog computer	2
Data plotters	6
Plotters	9
Instruments & recorders	3
Engineering & special fabrication	8
	100

Note: 9 percent of all output goes to South American operations

COMPANY OPERATIONS

Marketing - Engineering - Production - Accounting - Purchasing

RESOURCES

Finances	(current)	Personnel	1069	Inventory		Facilities	
Sales	$15.9	Executives	10	Finished		Plants	1
Net Profits	.9	Marketing	80	Goods	$1.5	Sales	
Current		Accounting &		Shop		Offices	4
Assets	15.9	Personnel	29	Stores	1.7	Computation	
Current		Engineering	217	Work in		Centers	3
Liabilities	9.8	Manufacturing	636	Process	6.7	South Amer-	
		Computer Centers	41			ican Head-	
(in millions)		Overseas	56	(in millions)		quarters	1

model, is composed of customers. The customers are divided into four groups. We can see immediately that Butodale depends heavily on government contracts, with direct and indirect government sales being 59 percent of total sales. Only about one-third of sales go to domestic business organizations. Another point revealed is that Butodale does not have a significant retail business.

The business model in Figure 6–1 was not simple to prepare, even for experienced analysts examining a well-run organization with good records. The model is always of great interest to management, for it puts the elements and relations among them together as an integrated whole so that the system can be seen as an entity.

Relationships between Total System and Information System The reason for initially examining the whole enterprise rather than just its information management system is that the information system exists to serve the overall business needs. It is therefore critical to understand this business structure before trying to understand and evaluate the information processing activities. Furthermore, if one is to justify the value of a new information system, it will often be necessary to show how this change will affect the business costs or revenues and hence the bottom-line profits. These benefits might be derived from replacing existing information processing functions, from improved control of production costs, or even from better management of materials and parts inventories.

In many businesses and institutions, the real product is an information service. Many government organizations prepare reports and statistics. Banks and insurance companies process information to provide a financial or security service. In these cases an even greater proportion of the total costs and total revenues are explicitly dependent on the quality and effectiveness of the information management system. The business model should reflect this structure; it should highlight the essential ingredients in the business.

The model can be fashioned into many different patterns to conform to the type of company, industry, product, or similar variation. Yet in its overall pattern the model remains much as is shown in the example. One can include greater detail if needed, but too much detail in the figure itself can make it unwieldy, and what should be emphasized might be obscured. The general model of the overall structure is probably best portrayed in general terms. Nonetheless, details are of prime importance in getting the information needed for building the new system; for this reason, the remaining sections of the report are devoted to these details. The first area is the firm's products and the markets in which it sells them.

6.3 PRODUCTS AND CUSTOMERS

The marketing aspects of an organization are of critical importance for practically all organizations, regardless of other considerations. This area is fundamental in the study of an existing system. Of the many possible ways of viewing the marketing function, we emphasize the products of the business, since they are the outputs, and analyze them in conjunction with the customers who purchase them. Even ultimate consumers who use them, who may or may not be customers of the company itself, may be included in the study. However, the time and cost of going to this level of effort usually prohibit much exploration of ultimate customers for manufacturing or wholesale organizations.

The analysts should begin their study of the existing products and customers by describing the market for the enterprise's products and services, with emphasis on sales and distribution characteristics of existing and planned products as well as information on past and future trends of product demand. Where possible, marketing methods are analyzed. Some of the questions the analysts might try to answer are: Does the enterprise sell directly to the public, or through agents, wholesalers, retailers, and franchised dealers? What specific promotion or advertising strategies are used? What part of the sales dollar does advertising represent? How do products compare with those of the competition?

Discussions of sales or distribution methods also provide insight into the marketing aggressiveness of an enterprise. A map can be plotted to show locations of sales offices and warehouses, sales representatives, and sales wholesalers or retailers. If products or services are sold on long-term contracts, this fact should be included in the report.

Information on trends in product mix, shifts in the composition of income, and breakdown of income by major product lines customarily is noted where these factors contribute to a total picture of the market.

Some examples are relevant here. In a report for the Worthington Hardware Company, the description of products starts by breaking Worthington's sales into nine departments.

The Worthington Hardware Company maintains an inventory of approximately 35,000 items. These items are shown in a general catalog (the index to this catalog is attached in order to identify the products).

The 35,000 items are classified into departments as follows:

Department	Estimated Percentage of Total Items
Athletics	8
Guns & Ammunition	4
Fishing Tackle	7
Electrical	7
Housewares	22
Stoves	2
General	17
Tools	24
Builders' Hardware	9

The list discloses the range of products, and to some extent defines the market area. Builders' hardware, for instance, is purchased mainly by the building trade. The Worthington organization is predominantly sales-oriented, as could be expected of a wholesale distributor, and the analysis in Figure 6−2 compares income, profits, and expenses for the nine departments. The following note was part of the report and explains the way some of the data in Figure 6−2 were adjusted by the analysts:

Overall, hardware departments contribute approximately 70 percent of sales and sporting goods departments 30 percent. Promotion department's sales were included in all department sales prior to the current year. The promotion department plans to publish a promotion booklet four times a year for hardware (spring, summer, fall, and Christmas), and once a year for sporting goods (Christmas).

It is important that analysts support their tables and graphs with solid statements that point out the highlights of the evidence.

For Worthington, the market can be explained satisfactorily in terms of departmental output and profit margins. However, the same type of display would not be suitable for the National Bank of Commerce. Instead (and just as effectively), the market for services was described in its report by showing how the level of available loan funds is determined, and by itemizing the types of output services which use these funds. The following statements from the report illustrate this point.

Figure 6–2 Two types of product analysis taken from the structural section of the report of present business for the Worthington Hardware Company.

Department	Thousand $ Gross Margin	% Gross Margin	% Expenses	Net P/L %	P/L % to Total Sales
Athletics	121	18.9	19.5	- .6	- .04
Guns and Ammunition	188	18.1	16.6	1.5	.25
Fishing Tackle	67	10.8	18.9	-8.1	- .73
Electrical	83	16.2	14.8	1.4	.12
Housewares	176	16.3	19.4	-3.1	- .58
Stoves	13	24.9	24.1	.8	.08
General	160	22.7	22.9	- .2	- .19
Tools	155	20.6	19.6	1.0	.20
Builders' Hardware	167	21.9	21.8	.1	.03
Total	1130	Avg. 18.3	Avg. 19.2	Avg. - .9	Avg. - .86

Departmental Profit Picture — Previous Year

Comparison of Departmental Sales

	Previous Year % (9 mos.)	Current Year % (9 mos.)	% + or −
Athletics	9.4	9.1	- .3
Guns and Ammunition	14.6	14.9	+ .3
Fishing Tackle	11.6	7.9	- 3.7
Electrical	6.3	7.1	+ .8
Housewares	18.2	16.3	- 1.9
Stoves	.3	.4	+ .1
General	12.5	10.8	- 1.7
Tools	12.5	12.8	+ .3
Builders' Hardware	14.6	14.4	- .2
Promotions	--	6.3	+6.3

Output Products

The National Bank of Commerce furnishes loan money and banking services primarily in Shawnee and Wabaunsee Counties.

The amount of loan money available for output to customers is determined as follows:

Total deposit money
Less outstanding regular loan money
Less long-term outstanding investment loan money
Less cash and reserve
Equals available loanable funds.

Output Services

1. *Demand Deposit* Check collection and payment service is offered in order to increase the percentage of demand deposits that can be loaned (or

invested) to create interest and fee income. A small fee is charged to cover a portion of the handling costs.

2. *Time Deposit* Interest dividends are paid to savings depositors to encourage larger deposits and therefore increase loanable funds.

3. *Loan* Secured or unsecured loans for long or short terms are offered. People experienced in all types of loan financing are available to the bank's customers and prospects.

4. *Trust* Trust service is offered to encourage new and retain existing trust deposit funds. A fee charged for administration of estate and pension trusts creates income for the bank.

5. *Correspondent Check Clearing and Collection* This service primarily benefits local industry and surrounding banks. Rapid clearing and collection service encourages large deposits, which creates more loanable funds.

6. *Safe Deposit* Document safekeeping service is offered to provide a maximum security area for a customer's valuable documents. Fees for use of the Safe Deposit area create income for the bank.

Borrowing Customers (Receiving output money)

Individuals
Commercial businesses
Government
    Local, state, national (includes bonds and securities)

Types of Loans	Percent of Outstanding Total
Real estate	20
Financial institution	4
Purchase or carrying securities	3
Farm loans	5
Commercial and industrial	48
Automobile installment	6
Retail consumer installment	5
Single-payment household and personal expenditures	9

A general policy of the bank is to have outstanding loans equal about 40 percent of total deposits.

Depositing Customers (Receiving output services)

Individuals At the present time the bank has 24,000 individual deposit customers. Records show a total of 36,500 accounts. However, studies show a 50% account duplication between savings and checking.

Commercial 2,200 community business establishments are customers of the National Bank of Commerce. The records actually show 2,500 accounts, but some customers have multiple accounts. Both large and small businesses use the service offered.

Banks   Out of 609 banks in the state, 277 have active correspondent agreements with the National Bank of Commerce. The records show 365 accounts; however, 88 are considered inactive. The primary market appears to be the area within an 80-mile radius of the bank due to one-day check clearing desired by most banks. About eight banks in the primary market area offer correspondent bank service and are considered competitors.

Government   Local, state, and federal government units are customers. The federal government is the largest single depositor.

The dollar volumes of business can be broken out geographically or regionally, by distribution channel, and by customer or customer type if this method of analysis contributes to a balanced explanation.

In Figure 6–3, which shows four graphs from the report of products and customers for the Custodian Life Insurance Company, the information does not fall under exact product classifications but does illustrate sources, trends, and premium/expense relationships, many of which are important output factors. These graphs again illustrate the point that the contents of the report vary with the circumstances.

For sources of information, the analyst will find it fruitful to consult sales catalogs and other promotional literature. These contain data on products and services. Furthermore, the company's marketing executives will be able to provide extensive analyses of the markets. More often than not they will have available a number of reports showing sales figures by various categories. Following are some examples of data they may be able to furnish:

1. Sales tabulations by customer order, store, warehouse, industry, region, territory, and salesperson
2. Industry and company sales forecasts
3. Shipments reports
4. Advertising outlays
5. Product line profit margins
6. Budget sales output
7. Financial operations statements
8. Sales quota reports
9. Warehouse turnover
10. Sales expense reports

Thus far the environment has been viewed as the destination for sending the outputs of the organization. The environment also furnishes inputs for the organization.

Figure 6–3 Example of the type of information that may be presented in the products and customers section of a report on the present condition of a business taken from the Custodian Life Insurance Company report.

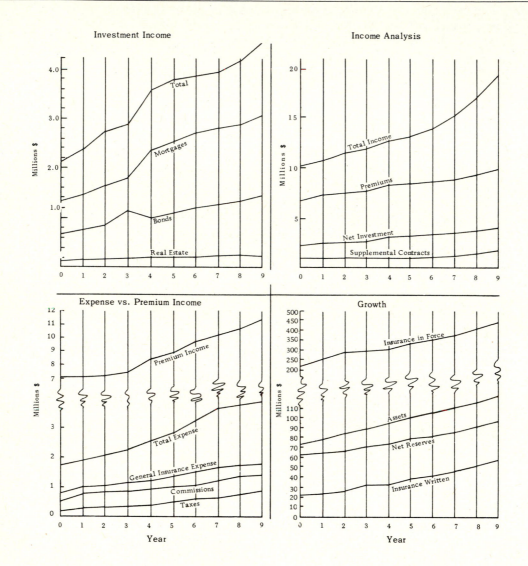

6.4 MATERIALS AND VENDORS

To produce outputs, the organization must have access to its environment to acquire materials from vendors. As with products and customers, analysts usually gather information on materials from various sources. Some of the sources of data and some of the methods of presentation follow. Input materials and services can be classified by source, type, total and unit cost, availability, cyclic need, or other features. Major suppliers (sources) are customarily ranked according to annual dollar volume. Procurement practices and competitive conditions in the market should also be appraised as they affect many segments of the business.

In the structural section of the report, an analyst is concerned primarily with the input materials, services, and inventory resources essential to fulfilling goals of the business. Therefore, office supplies of a manufacturing enterprise or water used to cool grinding equipment in a job shop usually are excluded, while raw materials used in the manufacturing enterprise to produce goods ultimately sold on the market are included.

In some types of vertically-integrated enterprises and some service organizations, relatively few products are procured from outside companies. Several large U.S. manufacturing enterprises, for instance, are so organized that subsidiaries supply everything from raw materials to subsystems of the finished product. Under these conditions, if only one division of the company is being analyzed, the others are treated as part of the outside environment and therefore become potential customers or vendors (outputs or inputs) for the business.

These three examples from manufacturing, wholesaling, and life insurance businesses clarify the above general concepts. In the first illustration note the coverage of the procurement and inventory practices in the statement on the problems of delivery and quality control:

Approximately 45 percent of the sales dollar at Butodale is the cost of material. Some of the major purchased materials include steel, transistors, tubes, potentiometers, display devices, transformers, capacitors, connectors, relays, wire, and resistors. At present Butodale controls this material by a procedure based on relative annual parts cost. It is important to note that the time lag for material purchased varies from two weeks to four months. An order record card is sent to the buyer, who originates the purchase authorization. Different buyers handle different classes of items. Fifty percent of the time the buyer inspects the order record card; selection is automatic the rest of the time. Ninety percent of the items handled through the inventory control section have Butodale part numbers, which makes processing very fast. When part numbers are missing or not assigned, it is difficult to determine if there is such an item, or if it is ordered directly by name and charged to a project. The company has about 850 suppliers, 125 of whom could be considered major

Figure 6—4 Example of a table of data concerning the materials and suppliers of the Worthington Hardware Company.

	Purchases	Percent of Total	Average Inventory	Percent of Total	Turnover
Athletics	$ 331,850	10	$ 157,905	11	2.4
Guns & Ammunition	561,362	17	256,297	18	2.6
Fishing Tackle	287,549	8	172,309	12	1.9
Electrical	242,294	7	110,865	8	2.9
Housewares	512,356	16	137,474	10	4.3
Stoves	26,091	1	36,969	3	1.0
General	302,370	9	115,530	8	3.3
Tools	395,163	12	118,287	9	4.6
Builders' Hardware	401,165	12	213,704	15	2.5
Promotions	261,125	8	88,337	6	3.8
Total	$3,321,325	100	$1,407,677	100	3.0

suppliers; of these major suppliers, 110 receive $10,000 to $100,000 of business annually, and the remaining 15 receive $100,000 and over annually. The company endeavors to have multiple sources, but because of the high quality of Butodale equipment, this is not always possible. A limited number of very expensive attachments for systems input and output are required, the purchase of these units is forecasted and an agreement negotiated with the supplier, giving an annual requirement with quantities to be delivered at specified dates. This arrangement seems to work satisfactorily. In view of the high quality standards set by Butodale, all incoming material must go through a stringent quality-control check. This, on occasion, causes material shortage if inferior material is received. Records are maintained to reflect these conditions, and to eliminate recurrence of such conditions.

A second example is a table of data concerning the materials and suppliers of a wholesale company—Worthington Hardware. One can well imagine that a wholesaler is not likely to have much raw material or many problems with inventory in the process of being manufactured. Thus, the materials and suppliers will differ from those of a manufacturing concern. Consequently, in the report for Worthington the analysts prepared the information shown in Figure 6–4. There is a straightforward listing of purchases and turnovers for each product line ranging from athletics to promotions. These types of data give a ready reference to the two major variables that interest management—the status of shelf goods and the movement of shelf goods. Not only are the primary figures given in dollar amounts, but also as ratios, for greater understanding.

An organization that has no products or materials in the usual physical sense, but only customer service and financial credit, presents a different picture. In those types of businesses, for example public utilities, the availability of supplies must be projected over long periods. For such cases, reserve and emergency sources can be described. In lending institutions, the nature of input fundings, types of investors providing funds, and data on the amount of funds secured in the various categories is normally included. The following material and suppliers narrative taken from the report for Custodian Life is a case in point:

Insurance companies must look to the field of investments to put their premium dollars to effective use. These investments provide a return which is an important factor in the successful operation of the business. Custodian Life looks to three major classes of suppliers to provide these materials (better referred to as investments) which bring a steady income to the company.

The first class, and most important, is the mortgage market, in which $69 million, or 54 percent of the ledger assets, were invested as of July 31. The mortgage investment policy is directed towards single residential loans and two-family residential buildings. However, multifamily and commercial buildings are approved, with the maximum loan on such properties being $1,000,000. The general terms and limitations applicable to each class of mortgage are determined by the investment committee based upon recommendations made by the mortgage loan department. During the past fiscal year, the net income from mortgages was $2,973,000.

The second class of supplier is the bond market, in which $48 million, or 38 percent of the ledger assets, were invested as of July 31. U.S. Treasury issues are by far the greatest single market, followed by public utility securities in strong second place. The remainder of the market is diversified with balanced holdings in industrials, municipals, Canadian governments, and railroads. The net interest earned from bonds amounted to $1,457,000 during the past fiscal year.

The third class is real estate. This is a very minor item, representing less than 1 percent of the ledger assets. The real estate holdings consist primarily of the home office buildings and several properties adjoining the home office. Operating in the three markets listed above, Custodian Life has a net investment income of $4,602,000 for the past fiscal year. This amount was second only to the premium income, and provided resources with which to operate the company successfully.

Figure 6–3 revealed trends and relationships for several of these input factors.

When seeking information on materials and suppliers, the analyst should first consult the purchasing department or accounts payable unit in the accounting organization. These departments often compile summaries of dollar expenditures by individual suppliers for a number of different reasons; for example, the Small Business Administration requires periodic reports from government contractors on purchases placed with small business concerns. For internal control reasons, accounts payable units usually maintain records by vendor to prevent duplicate invoicing, cost accounting may keep records on unit costs, and quality control and inspection sections may have data on vendor performance. Any or all of these functions should be checked for vendor information.

In addition, current operating reports possibly contain information on such variables as commodity lead time, material cost variance, vendor evaluation, and analysis of cash payments reports.

After an examination of the organization's inputs and outputs, one next views the resources used for the transformation of inputs into outputs.

6.5 RESOURCES

Resources are those means used by an organization to change inputs into outputs. A convenient classification of resources is: finances, personnel, facilities, inventories, and information.

The roles that money, people, and machines play in processing inputs into outputs are clear enough, but inventories and information are somewhat special.

Inventories and Information Inventories provide a time buffer between receipt of inputs and their use or, conversely, the preparation of outputs and their distribution. Inventories usually refer to physical materials.

Information can be viewed as an inventory-like resource. For instance, patents, trade secrets, people's knowledge or experience, previously documented procedures, and historical records all provide an information inventory or data base which serves as a time buffer between initial availability and final usage.

Because it is so difficult to document what is in a person's mind, it is most convenient to include only the records and files portion of this resource. In the next sections are the five classes of resources: finances, personnel, facilities, inventories, and information.

Nature of Resources It is of interest to consider the nature of each type of resource in order to understand the key role it plays in the operation of a business. For instance, people and equipment are not consumed in a production process, but their time usage must be scheduled and controlled. Equipment wears out, it requires maintenance and represents a significant medium-term investment of financial resources. People require training, may leave without warning, and are subject to relatively unpredictable variations in productivity and quality of performance.

In contrast, materials and money are consumed in the production process and must be replenished through allocation of revenues and borrowing. Each of these resources can be stockpiled, or carried in inventory for later use. This separates supply from consumption, but also represents an increased investment of financial resources, which in turn requires greater profit on sales to provide a satisfactory return on the total investment.

Information is a different kind of resource. It can be stockpiled like material and is subject to time obsolescence and quality assurance. However, it is not consumed by usage and can be reused many times. It requires an investment to obtain and maintain accurate, timely data; and it costs money to store and retrieve it easily and rapidly.

Timeliness, accuracy, and availability of information are important factors in designing and evaluating a new system. They must be translated into cost equivalents in order to determine the increased value of a new solution over the present business system. Two other general concepts may be worth considering as one looks at the resources of a business—acquisition/storage costs and quality assessment.

Inventories are normally analyzed in terms of their cost of acquisition and cost of retention versus the potential risks of delaying the manufacture of needed products or having to buy to order. In the same way, information value can be measured in terms of its costs for acquisition and retention (recording, transmitting, storing, and retrieving) and the implicit revenue loss or cost increase because of inaccurate, out-of-date, or inadequately detailed data.

Quality of physical inventory is normally determined by incoming quality control procedures; this prevents problems when the user needs the materials. Similarly, information accuracy can be assessed by quality checks when the information is acquired; this tells the user how much to depend on the data when they are used.

6.6 FINANCES

Financial resources are relatively easy to document if the company is publicly held or if government regulations require disclosure, though divisional or departmental data may be limited. Where a company is a proprietorship, partnership, or a closely held corporation, financial data are usually confidential; in such situations analysts must particularly guard against disclosure of financial information to unauthorized persons.

For the typical organization, the main exhibits in the financial resources section are a balance sheet of financial operations; a statement of income and retained earnings; and an overhead, or expense, statement. The balance sheet and earnings report forms prepared for an annual report are usually satisfactory for displaying these data. The emphasis on detail varies with the type of enterprise; for example, the statement of a bank's status usually lists the outstanding loans separately under assets, and lists deposits, capital, and reserves under liabilities. Reserves held by an insurance company or receivables and debt-retirement items of a finance company may be similarly featured. A consolidated overhead or expense report should be prepared as the principal means for exhibiting the cost and expense allocations for the organization.

Financial statements are generally appended with notes that explain or amplify important transactions. In this area, the analyst deals with all financial aspects, even those that can be thought of as inventories of money.

Company balance sheets and statements of earnings are not illustrated here, since they are published widely. In presenting this information for management purposes, it is a good technique to show relations by plotting the data on graphs; for example, financial progress of the enterprise can be compared to its industry, or to major competitors, or to industry leaders. Exhibits taken from the report prepared for the National Bank of Commerce illustrate this type of display as shown in Figure 6–5.

Other financial documents will be summaries of budget reports for particular business units (where these are only a part of the enterprise); this may show revenue, expense, and profit and loss information for the organizational component. It will certainly break down the costs and income by type of expense item and class of product or service provided. These may be displayed in the same form as an income statement and, where appropriate, as a balance sheet.

Figure 6–5 Three exhibits taken from the financial resources section of the structural part of the report on present business conditions for the National Bank of Commerce. All figures in millions of dollars.

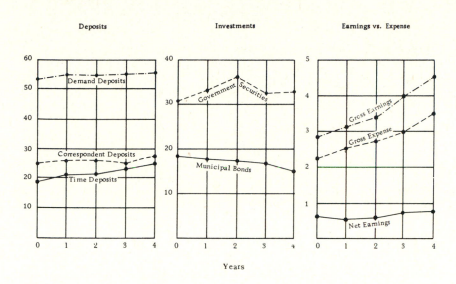

Before preparing the finances section of the report describing the present business, the analysts should arrange interviews with the financial officers to find out what information is considered available and what is classified as confidential. Such records are normally acquired from the controller; if a division or department of a large company is under study, budgets and cost-distribution records are usually easy to obtain from the financial manager. Outside analysts may have to study the profit statements privately. Occasionally, the officers of an organization will not give the analysts access to certain financial data. This situation occurred, for example, in a study of a major manufacturing concern. The study team compensated for the tight security on financial data by using ratios that were customary in the industry for companies of this size and by searching for support-ing information in published articles and other appropriate external sources including *Moody's Manuals of Investment* and *Dun & Brad-street Ratings*. From these sources they were able to prepare an ac-curate finance section.

Where data are related to business units, analysts will need month-ly financial reports usually provided by the unit managers. Where more detail is required, product cost reports and general ledger rec-ords may have to be searched. Money is the common denominator by which businesses measure themselves. Financial reports provide a special model of the business, fundamental to understanding what is now going on and, most significantly, to assist in making trade-off decisions for any future information management system.

Based on primary data in money terms, analysts can prepare a large number of derived relationships in the form of ratios, correlations, and trends. There is a limit, however, because it takes time and effort to prepare this information and to present the results graphically. Consequently, a study team must settle for the techniques that are most informative in the circumstances under which they are working. Their attention must then be redirected from financial resources to human resources. These we consider in the following section.

6.7 PERSONNEL

Human resources are of major importance in a study of any organization. Information on personnel is needed in both the structural and the operational sections of the study.

Even where there is a large investment in buildings, equipment, and materials, people are the cornerstone of a business. They are the system drivers. They control the use of the other resources. Clearly one has to think about the different functions people play in the organization from top-level decision makers through intermediate-level planners and managers and operational personnel who carry out the working functions.

Sources of Personnel Information An organization chart is customarily the first exhibit in the personnel resources section of the report. If such a chart does not exist, the analysts should draft one from data provided by the personnel department of the company.

Reports which classify employees by organizational component, skill, location, salary, and other categories often indicate important facts about the business not readily apparent from an inspection of its organization chart.

Other valuable facts concerning personnel are union membership and union relations, local labor markets, turnover statistics, fringe benefits, stock options, and profit-sharing plans. Management attitudes on personnel subjects and comparisons with other businesses drawing on the same labor pools are often pertinent and should be included.

In searching for information permitting the analysis of personnel costs by organization component, product or project, and other cost-distribution categories, analysts should first turn to the accounting departments. The information gained there can be supplemented by interviews with personnel administration and accounting supervisors. From these sources one can obtain such additional factors as the classifications of the employees.

The Personnel Report The human resources may be summarized in displays similar to those used for financial resources. The number of people assigned to various business functions, their skill mix, and average cost per employee (including training and benefits) can be shown through tables and graphs as current pictures or trends over time. Ratios of people to product or people to service units may also provide valuable insights.

Some companies have organized excellent records on employees and include personal statistics such as formal education, degrees, special courses and training taken, and skills other than those used on their current job. The trend toward more complete records has been accelerated with the wider use of computers and additional government regulations which attempt to assure fair and equal treatment for all employees. A careful search in several sources, supplemented by interviews, is still the general method for obtaining data on the organization's personnel resources.

6.8 EQUIPMENT AND FACILITIES

The facilities of an organization generally include items such as the land the company occupies and the size, value, and arrangement of buildings, equipment, communications networks, and computers.

The Facilities Report The data presented in the section of the report covering an organization's facilities are usually itemized according to manufacturing plants, sales offices, research facilities, warehouses, and distribution facilities. Information concerning the area of buildings, whether the facilities are leased or owned, and plans for new construction are useful types of data in support of this list. Major items of machinery or other equipment involved in the activities under study should also be classified and listed, with capacity figures added if meaningful. Equipment listings are often supplemented by layout diagrams of plants and offices.

In certain types of business, the communications network (for example, the communications terminals for a brokerage house with multiple locations) is a most essential facility, and its performance should be covered in some depth. A map with connecting lines to point out inter-office connections and switching centers is a good visual aid to show the different locations and to show the dispersion of sales offices and manufacturing plants. Operating and original costs, current and projected volumes and capacities, and response speeds are important. The time and length of queues, periodic fluctuations, and volume trends can be recorded here since they will be useful to management later when the operations information is presented. Data are usually shown in visual form, such as graphs. When obtaining data, analysts usually find that equipment and facilities are generally well documented. Information may be extracted from plant accounting records or from details maintained in the manufacturing or engineering departments. Communications network data is obtained from equipment vendors or from user personnel. Computer information can be obtained from the data processing organization and from users of stand-alone systems.

6.9 INVENTORIES

Physical inventories include raw materials, parts, assemblies, and finished products. These physical items, kept in larger supply than needed for current operations, serve as buffers between the peaks of usage or demand and the capacity to produce or obtain supplies.

The Inventory Report In the inventory resources part of the report, the physical inventories should be classified by type (raw materials, components or parts, in-process or semi-finished assemblies, and completed products), inventory level, location, value of stock, and cost of maintenance. In some cases, it is difficult to separate facilities from physical inventories. A distinction must be made, however, between stocks consumed in the operation of the business, and permanent facilities. Thus, in the case of a water distillation plant, the tank is a facility, while stored water is an inventory.

Characteristics of inventories found useful for management include: level, flow (both inputs and outputs), turnover, age, cycle, demand, access, and reaction capability to changes in demand. Obsolescence factors are also important since stock usually becomes less valuable with the passage of time. In the case of physical stocks, the value of raw materials is more accurately predictable than the value of some kinds of finished products which are subject to technical obsolescence.

Note that the inventories in a bank or insurance company are really investments and cash equivalents. These can most easily be handled as part of the financial section. It is a strain to treat them like physical inventories.

Sources of Inventory Information Analysts should consult several sources in their search for inventory resources. Generally, physical inventory records are located in the accounting and manufacturing departments. Accounting records typically show inventory changes through shipments to customers and receipts from vendors. There may also be classifications by type of material (raw or in-process), consignment and warehouse balances, and material budgets. The manufacturing department customarily maintains files in stockrooms, accumulation areas, and inventory control sections; it reports inventory status by units, age, manufacturing losses, amount of surplus and obsolete, and special budgets. For inventory policies and practices, the study team should consult the inventory control supervisor or cost accountant.

6.10 INFORMATION

Information files include operational experience, decision rules and logic, and historical data concerning operations. A file of account records, a sales catalog, and a library of programs for a computer are examples of information resources.

Besides files of records, there are other kinds of information inventories which cannot be overlooked: standard procedures and instructions and that information retained in people's memory. This is edited information, refined by years of application and practice. This latter resource may be less accessible than files, but it is often more valuable.

One of the benefits of computers has been the ability of system designers to convert the store of information from the human mind into computer programs. Management personnel have often not recognized this potential of computers, but the situation is changing and greater consideration is being given to this aspect of system development and application.

Covering information resources in structural terms is the purpose of this section of the "Present Business Description" report. However, the operations section really focuses on the information processes of the business, including detailed data on files, records, messages, and other information elements needed to run a business successfully. In the structural section, then, the analyst should concentrate on the physical characteristics of the information resources: what they are, where stored, in what physical form, the means of access, and other relevant subjects.

With all this information collected over a period of days or weeks, the study team is ready to develop the structural section of the report of the present business. At the same time the team must be planning the collection of data relating to operations carried on within the organization.

SUMMARY

Inputs, outputs, and resources are the three major elements in the structural view of a management system. Operations transform inputs into outputs. Resources are needed to implement operations. A business model exhibits the relationships among the inputs, outputs, resources, and operations. The pattern of all business models is much the same; but variations of content are required to conform to the particular company, industry, and products.

The marketing area of an organization sells outputs to customers, and this component should be included in the study of an existing business system. Materials from vendors are the inputs to the organization from the environment. Resources, which are the means for changing inputs into outputs, can be classified as finances, personnel, facilities, inventory, and information. Analysts should review files and reports and interview personnel to obtain information about the resources of the organization.

QUESTIONS AND PROBLEMS

6-1 What are the three major elements of the structural aspects of a system?

6-2 What interest would management people have in the inputs of the organization?

6-3 What does the structural section of the present business description represent?

6–4   The text lists five categories of resources: finances, personnel, inventory, facilities, and information. Which category is the most valuable to an organization? Why?

6–5   If the information presented in the report of the existing system is so valuable, why is it necessary to conduct a study to gather the data? Why does the company not maintain structural data on a current and continuing basis?

6–6   What might be the input pattern of the structure of the business office of a telephone company which is open from 8:30 A.M. to 5:30 P.M.?

6–7   In the structural part of a manufacturing system, the term *family* may be applied to a group of parts with common geometrical or electrical characteristics such as shafts, printed circuits, motor laminations, brackets, and so on. If a team is studying the manufacturing process in a given company, what might be the team's source of data for establishing family groupings?

6–8   Many data processing departments assign an identification number to each report produced by the department and maintain a description of the contents of each report and a list of recipients. Of what value would such information be during a systems study, especially where the structural aspects are concerned?

6–9   Structural data can be viewed from five levels:
a) Routine data,
b) Control totals,
c) Control ratios,
d) Mathematical models,
e) Mathematical models integrated with routine data.
Of what value is it to consider these five levels of data when studying the structural aspects of a system?

6–10 What are the main elements of the business model, and for what purpose is the model used?

CHAPTER 7
INFORMATION PROCESSING OPERATIONS

7.1 THE SETTING

While Chapter 6 discussed the way a business is structured to provide services and products, this chapter concentrates on the information processing system which, of course, is the main subject of the information management system study. Information processing operations refer to the dynamic (that is, time dependent) functions involved in carrying out the data processing aspects of the business. Examples are the reservations systems of airlines, hotels, and car rental agencies where the time response characteristics are critical to the company's success.

This chapter does not simply record how information processing is now performed. Rather the chapter analyzes what is done, as the functions are grouped by activities; displaying supporting volume, cost, and time statistics.

Five forms are used to capture this integrated picture of information processing in a business. They were shown in Figure 4–2: resource usage, activity, operation, message, and file sheets. This chapter focuses particularly on the resource usage sheet and the activity sheet.

7.2 THE INFORMATION SYSTEM

The information system consists of activities, operations and processes which produce outputs needed to record events and provide analyses for human decision making. One must keep in mind that the information system serves the needs of the people who direct the business, not vice versa. In documenting a present system, an analyst must make sure that information functions are a means for serving business goals and that they are a way of extending people's capacity to make better decisions in more timely, cost-effective ways.

One approach to understanding the present information system is to assume that the current organizational structure accurately reflects the business goals. On this basis, an analyst can document the information flow and processing costs on a department by department basis. This is certainly an acceptable procedure and in many cases is the only practical course available. However, deeper insights can be obtained when the analyst takes a more fundamental view and identifies business goals and associates with them the information processing activities used to realize these goals. This overall view is that an existing information system is typically composed of people and computing equipment processing input and file data to produce output reports and update the file records.

This text examines the second approach. Certainly, the analyst can always take the alternate route of using present applications as identified activities. This will even be quite appropriate for improvement or conversion studies, but it will not often lead to the significant results obtained with full activity formulation.

Since activities are central to representing the present business information processing operations, activity formulation and the collection of operations data are the next subjects to consider.

7.3 ACTIVITY FORMULATION

The determination of business goals and the formulation of activities are probably the most important tasks that analysts must perform during a present organization study. In the method under study, analysis and new system design are based primarily on activities. Activity formulation goes far beyond conventional data organization. It requires considerable thought concerning the business in terms of goals, objectives, and purposes, as these may contrast with the existing organizational structure. This analysis calls for judgment and insight on the part of the analyst who must listen to and interpret the established views to analyze and reformulate them as basic activities.

The initial definition of activities may be modified as the analyst becomes more familiar with the business, but early definitions and boundaries usually do not change significantly. Therefore, activities evolve from intensive examination of the nature and practical requirements of the business; they are not formulated quickly or casually. It is necessary to discuss ways to arrive at activity definitions through a series of approximations and successive refinements as no

Figure 7–1 Butodale's organization and cost of activities displayed on a resource usage sheet.

NOTES

1. ORGANIZATION CHART DOES NOT INCLUDE COMPUTER CENTERS OR FOREIGN OPERATIONS, A TOTAL OF 97 PERSONS.

ORGANIZATION CHART

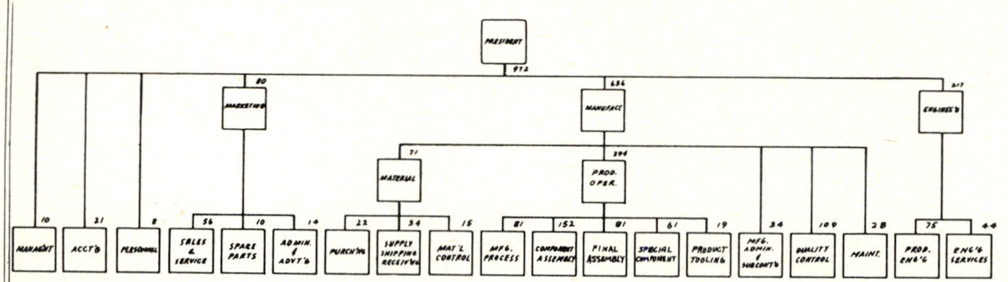

Resource Usage Sheet

Study BUTODALE ELECTRONICS
Analyst R. L. CASEY
Date

NOTES:

(BALANCE SHEET)

		MANAG'NT	ACCT'G	PERSONNEL	SALES & SERVICE	SPARE PARTS	ADMIN. & ADVT'G	PURCH'NG	SUPPLY SHIPPING RECEIV'NG	MAT'L CONTROL	MFG. PROCESS	COMPONENT ASSEMBLY	FINAL ASSEMBLY	SPECIAL COMPONENT	PRODUCT TOOLING	MFG. ADMIN. & SUBCONT'G	QUALITY CONTROL	MAINT.	PROD. ENG'G	ENG'G SERVICES	TOTALS	ASSETS	LIABILITIES
PERSONNEL		230,000	115,500	48,800	448,000	41,000	84,000	149,600	183,600	61,500	421,200	638,400	356,400	268,400	134,900	326,400	632,200	142,800	642,400	964,800	5,889,900	CASH & RECEIV. 6,604,560	CURRENT NOTES 7,710,000
MACHINE & EQUIPMENT			22,000	1,000	10,100	2,000	3,000	3,000	10,100	24,300						5,000					80,500	INVENTORIES	OTHER
MATERIAL			14,000	6,000	342,00	7,000	11,000	12,000	21,000		46,000	75,000	46,000	32,000	10,000	20,000	58,400	162,900	116,600	72,600	1,052,600	9,338,012	2,051,506
MISCELLANEOUS		515,400			251,600		167,300	872,200			18,000	6,000					31,000	15,000		6,000	1,882,500	FIXED ASSETS 2,265,208	LONG TERM 567,249
		303,700						6,384,000													6,384,000		OWNERSHIP 7,813,246
TOTAL		1,049,100	151,500	55,800	1,051,700	50,000	265,300	7,420,800	214,700	85,800	485,200	719,400	402,400	300,400	144,900	351,400	721,600	320,700	759,000	1,043,400	15,593,200	18,207,780	18,142,001
ACTIVITY NAME	PERS.	24,000	25,260		448,000		84,000												126,400	148,300	855,960		
PROVIDE	EQUIP.		2,800		10,000		3,000														15,900		
PRODUCT	MAT'L.		4,100		342,000		11,000													2,200	359,300		
DEMAND	MISC.				251,600		167,300													700	419,600		
(001)	TOT.	24,000	32,160		1,051,700		265,300												126,400	151,200	1,650,760		
ACTIVITY NAME	PERS.		21,760					36,000	70,400	32,600	421,200				34,900	84,600	108,100			44,500	854,060		
PROVIDE	EQUIP.		4,800					1,000	3,300	8,400						1,700					19,200		
MATERIAL	MAT'L.		1,600					5,000	9,300		46,000				1,500	5,000	18,000			2,800	89,200		
	MISC.							2,940,400			18,000						4,500			500	2,963,400		
(002)	TOT.		28,160					2,982,400	83,000	41,000	485,200				36,400	91,300	130,600			47,800	3,925,860		
ACTIVITY NAME	PERS.		8,500					37,600	12,800	3,000		638,400		268,400	66,500	112,800	294,800			43,500	1,486,300		
PROVIDE	EQUIP.		510					1,000	2,000	4,100						2,700					10,310		
COMPONENTS	MAT'L.							4,000	6,000			75,000		32,000	5,500	8,000	6,700			3,800	141,000		
	MISC.							1,003,900				6,000					13,000			500	1,023,400		
(003)	TOT.		9,010					1,046,500	20,800	7,100	719,400	719,400		300,400	72,000	123,500	314,500			47,800	2,661,010		
ACTIVITY NAME	PERS.		7,500					42,000	51,500	3,900			356,400		33,500	129,000	229,300			91,300	944,400		
PROVIDE	EQUIP.		1,000						3,300	1,100						600					6,000		
END	MAT'L.		510						3,200				46,000		3,000	7,000	33,700			13,900	107,310		
PRODUCT	MISC.							984,000									13,500			2,800	1,000,300		
(004)	TOT.		9,010					1,026,000	58,000	5,000			402,400		36,500	136,600	276,500			108,000	2,058,010		
ACTIVITY NAME	PERS.		8,700			41,000		34,000	48,900	22,000									516,000	637,200	1,307,800		
PROVIDE	EQUIP.		310			2,000		1,000	1,500	10,700											15,510		
ENGINEERED PRODUCTS	MAT'L.					7,000		3,000	2,500										116,700	49,900	179,100		
AND SPARE PARTS	MISC.							2,327,900												1,500	2,329,400		
(005)	TOT.		9,010			50,000		2,365,900	52,900	32,700									632,700	688,600	3,831,810		
ACTIVITY NAME	PERS.	206,000	43,780	48,800														192,800			441,380		
PROVIDE	EQUIP.		12,580	1,000																	13,580		
MANAGEMENT,	MAT'L.		7,790	6,000														162,900			176,690		
PERSONNEL, AND	MISC.	819,100																15,000			834,100		
FACILITIES (006)	TOT.	1,025,100	64,150	55,800														320,700			1,465,750		

one best method exists for defining business goals and for formulating activities to carry out these goals. However, the study team may select from three general approaches to arrive at a definition: deductive, inductive, and composite. All three presume that the team has completed investigations for the general and structural information, prepared a functional organization chart, and broken down the total business costs to show the cost of carrying out departmentalized functions for one year. Within each department the costs are further subdivided into the costs for personnel, facilities, equipment, materials, and miscellaneous items. The resource usage sheet in Figure 7−1 shows Butodale's main departments (management, accounting, personnel, and so on). The cost figures in the summary row under the departments are the subdivided costs of carrying out the departmentalized functions. For example, it cost Butodale $1,000 during the year for machinery and equipment in the personnel department. At this point the activity names and detailed cost data would not yet be available.

The analysts' method of choice is determined largely by how well the management goals are understood and can be stated early in the study, how much freedom the team has, and how far activity definition and scope may depart from existing organization patterns. The deductive method is normally followed when restraints have been placed on the study team by management or when goals and activities are well defined in the beginning; the inductive method is used where relatively few constraints are placed on the team, there is considerable freedom of action, and substantial data gathering is permitted before arriving at an activity definition. As a result, the deductive method is closely associated with studies leading to the improvement and conversion of an existing system, while the inductive method is more appropriate when an innovative solution is required. The composite method is best applied when only one or two activities determine the business results.

7.4 ACTIVITY BOUNDARIES

An activity is a set of related operations, usually self-contained with few ties to the surrounding environment, directed toward the fulfillment of one or more goals of a business. It can be viewed as a logical business unit. Most companies lack complete operational integration, and overlapping of activities occurs. In addition, organizations are frequently structured along the lines of primary business functions, not lined up with respect to information processing activities. A principal reason for defining activities is to be able to separate a business information system into relatively independent elements that can be easily understood, analyzed, and evaluated. A small business may be treated as an entity, but in larger concerns size works against the analyst. In a very large company, one can quickly lose sight of the objectives set up for the study; analysts must constantly guard against this possibility. The organization focus on functional patterns (for example, marketing, engineering, manufacturing, administration) usually does not resolve the problem because this organizational structuring conceals the information processing flow of a business.

The activity-oriented systems approach, based on goal-directed activities, focuses the attention of management and the study team on the information processes of a business. This certainly does not mean that the business organization is realigned into new patterns. However, one can best conduct an activity-oriented business study through these activities. The activity structure must be made clear and logical to management, who ultimately will have to make judgments and decisions in terms of activity alignments. Also, activities should not depart so far from established practice that management cannot easily relate activity costs to established accounting records.

In some cases, the business may already be organized into functions which closely parallel suitable activity groupings; then the team needs only to make minor realignments to produce a workable activity formulation. This situation occurred in a bank study where management had previously recognized the need for better controls and was planning revenue and cost centers for functions such as commercial checking, special checking, installment loans, commercial loans, mortgage loans, savings, and personal trusts. Since the revenue and cost centers were already related to functions which serviced individual markets and could be identified with particular goals of the business, they provided a basic activity definition for the study team. Further, the bank's management was accustomed to thinking in terms of these centers, and it required little reorientation for them to consider and appraise costs in terms of activities. Even though the revenue and cost center plan had not yet been fully implemented, the personnel of the bank were able to compile very quickly much of the activity cost data for the study team. The report of the present organization of this bank was completed well ahead of schedule.

Although initial activity formulation is performed during the study of the present business, the study team will have an opportunity to modify the preliminary results while determining the requirements of the new system. For example, in the Butodale Electronics case study, the first attempt to define activities produced the following results:

1. Prepare quotations and accept orders
2. Procure material
3. Manufacture general purpose analog computers
4. Provide other end items
5. Sell spare parts
6. Develop engineered products

Later, the team made some adjustments to this list and arrived at this set of activities:

1. Provide product demand
2. Provide material
3. Provide components
4. Provide end products
5. Provide engineered products and spare parts
6. Provide management, personnel, and facilities

The scope of the first activity (to prepare quotations and accept orders) was increased to cover all demand-related functions, rather than just the acceptance of orders and preparation of quotations. In other activities, a distinction was made between custom-designed and so-called standard products. The revised definitions also improved balance in size among the various activities.

There will always be an element of trial and error in achieving balance, identity, and boundaries. Experience has shown that several approximations are usually required before satisfactory results are obtained.

7.5 EXAMPLE OF ACTIVITY FORMULATION

It can be helpful to examine some of these activity formulation concepts by looking at a real organization. The model of the resource usage sheet (Figure 7–1) which shows the relation between the current organization and the activities with their associated costs is useful here. The resource usage sheet consists of three principal sections—an organization chart, a summary of costs by organizational areas for each resource, and a breakdown of costs for each identified activity detailed by organizational component and resource category. Figure 7–1 shows the completed resource usage sheet for Butodale Electronics.

Unfortunately this is too detailed an example to use in explaining the construction of a resource usage sheet, so an oil company illustration is used to provide an overview of the activities in a business. Because of the oil company's large size, the example does not represent the typical situation encountered by systems analysts. But the various steps taken in formulating its activities indicate the kind of thinking and interpretation involved in this process.

The purposes of the study of the large oil company were to resolve duplications in function and organization and to provide more effective overall control of operations. The company's structure is shown in Figure 7–2; in the following discussion the names in the bottom six boxes will be used for simplicity of reference.

Initially, the analysts studied the parent and subsidiary organizations to see what could be set apart as self-contained activities. They originally thought that Exploration and Production could be separated because its responsibility ended when crude oil was supplied to Pipeline. However, its operation was found to be interrelated with both Pipeline and Crude Oil Purchase and Sale. Pipeline exerted a great influence on the company information system, since it served as the linkage between Exploration, Crude Oil, and Refining. In contrast to these complex connections, Petrochemical was found to be a highly independent business. Its only interrelationship with other organizations was the purchase of material from Refining (which it supplemented through its own purchasing department); so Petrochemical, with its own manufacturing and distribution departments, was set aside as a preliminary activity.

Formulation of activities from the standpoint of organization, therefore, yielded only one — Petrochemical. The next step was to consider other points of view:

1. Did any of the subsidiaries have self-contained functions?
2. Was the key to the definition of activities in product lines, markets, or services?
3. How about activities defined by types of raw materials or kinds of resources?
4. Was there a clue in corporate goals?

A study according to function and product seemed to be a reasonable approach for this company, since every concern that manufac-

Figure 7–2 Structure of a large petroleum company used as an example of the formulation of activities.

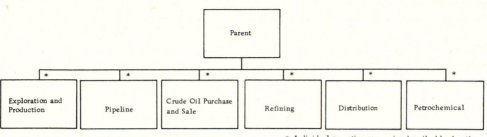

* Individual operating companies described by functions.

tures products uses materials and then processes them through a facility to manufacture the products.

The analysts discovered that Exploration, Pipeline, and Crude Oil were all concerned with providing material to the company; Refining was basically the manufacturing function that used the materials. Consequently, two more preliminary activities were established: (1) provide materials and (2) manufacture products.

Next, Distribution was studied and found to serve three different types of markets:

1. Internal combustion engine fuels (gasoline)
2. Accessories (mainly tires)
3. Heating fuels

Each market had decidedly different characteristics and required different marketing practices and organization. For this reason the analysts decided to establish three activities for Distribution to parallel these markets. Finally, the management and control functions of the parent company were assigned to an activity called *provide management.*

Because this company represented a very large organization, the initial activity definition served primarily to clarify the role of each separate organizational component. The outcome was the activity formulation shown in Figure 7–3. At the top of the diagram is the parent company with the six previously defined functional subsidiaries directly below.

On the left are shown the seven activities defined by the analysts. The shaded areas under each function indicate the activities carried out by functional unit. The three left functional units are engaged in the activity of providing materials. The parent unit provides the

Figure 7–3 An example of activity formulation for a large petroleum company. The shaded areas show the activities carried on by the various parts of the total organization.

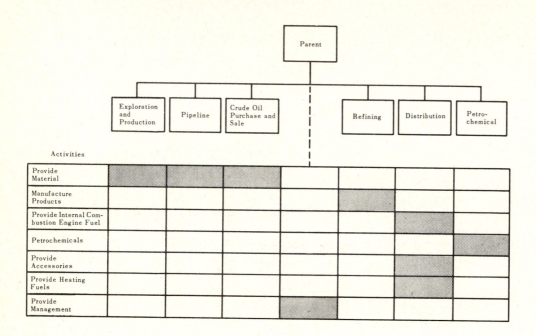

overall management activity. The activity of the refining unit is to manufacture products. The distribution unit is engaged in three activities: providing internal combustion engine fuel, providing accessories, and providing heating fuels. Finally, the petrochemical unit provides petrochemicals.

The resource usage sheet in Figure 7–1 is similar to this format; it is one of the foundations for understanding the present business structure.

7.6 ACTIVITY DESCRIPTION

An activity was first defined in terms of the goals it was intended to satisfy and then by its relations to the various organizational components. Now it must be clarified by describing the operational sequence needed for its realization and the associated volume and timing statistics.

The activity sheet (one for each activity) can be an effective way to associate visually the operation sequence with the quantitative data. A complete form from the Butodale case study is shown in Figure 7–4.

Two principal elements appear on the activity sheet. The first is a flow diagram which shows the logical flow among the operations which comprise an activity. The second is a tabular section to display related information on volumes, frequency of occurrence, elapsed time, and accuracy data. This activity sheet provides an integrated view of each activity, showing its component elements. After the activity is described and its costs determined, these can be posted on the resource usage sheet. Analysis of costs will be covered after the discussion of activity sheet formulation.

The study team has two principal alternatives in gathering data for the purpose of showing the flow, sequence, cost, and time of events. These alternatives relate closely to the methods followed in activity formulation.

Where few study restrictions have been specified, the team will probably begin with an examination of operations throughout the business (or in one or two major activities) before activity definitions and boundaries are set. After activities have been formulated, they are put on flow charts, and the operational documentation is completed by estimating the costs of the activities (the inductive method of data collection).

In studies with more restraints, such as improvement or conversion studies, or where management has stipulated the areas to be investigated and the steps to be followed, the costs of the separate activities may be estimated, the activities diagrammed for sequence, and finally, the operations documented as necessary. The method just outlined is the deductive method of data gathering.

7.7 THE FLOW OF OPERATIONS

One tool that analysts often use in giving management a clear idea of the operations that make up an activity and the sequence in which the operations are performed is the flow diagram. The typical flow diagram begins with a trigger that starts the activity. The diagram then traces the operations that the trigger activates, incorporates references to important information resources used in particular operations, and ends with the output from the activity.

In practice, analysts have found it particularly useful to affix to the flow diagram the tables showing elapsed times and volumes. This arrangement permits a composite picture of each operation, the time

Figure 7–4 Operation times and resource volumes and times for the "provide product demand" activity.

Activity Name

FUNCTION : QUOTATIONS
INPUTS : 2000, 2010

KEYS	AVG	PEAK	NOTE
1-2	1H	1D	
3-4	2H	6D	1200
4-6	1D	2D	
7-8	1H	4H	
8-11	1D	6D	1200
12-13	2D	5D	
13-14	1D	2D	
14-15	1D	2D	
15-16	12D	30D	1210
16-17	3D	10D	1200
17-18	2D	5D	
20-23	2D	5D	
7-11	2D	5D	
14-16	14D	30D	
23-25	14-D	90-D -MAX	
		20-D -MIN	

FUNCTION : ORDERS
INPUTS : 2020

KEYS	AVG	PEAK	NOTE
25-28	4D	10D	
28-29	2D	4D	
29-31	1D	3D	
25-31	7D	20D	1220

INPUTS

KEY	NAME	SOURCE	AVG VOLUME	PEAK VOLUME	NOTE
2000	QUOTE REQUEST	CUST	50/w	70/w	1020
	FREQUENCY		46 W/YR	4 W/YR	1030
2010	BID REQUEST	CUST	10/w	12/w	
	FREQUENCY		42 W/YR	10 W/YR	1040
2020	ORDER	CUST	16/w	20/w	1030
	FREQUENCY		44 W/YR	6 W/YR	

OUTPUTS

KEY	NAME	DEST	AVG VOLUME	PEAK VOLUME	NOTE
3000	QUOTATN	CUST	15/w	20/w	1030
	FREQUENCY		40 W/YR	10 W/YR	
3050	ACKNOW	CUST	16/w	—	1050

FILE USAGE

KEY	NAME	MSGS AVG	MSGS PEAK	ACCESS	USAGE TIME	NOTE
4000	PRICING	240K	300K	RANDM	8H/D	1100
4010	COST	1,000K	—	RANDM	—	1110
4020	RATE	2500	2800	RANDM	8H/D	
4030	INSTALLED SYSTEMS	400K	—	RANDM	4H/D	1120
4050	CONTRACT REGISTER	1500	2100	SEQ	8H/D	1130
4060	CUSTOMER INDEX	4000	5500	SEQ	2H/D	
4070	PROJECT INDEX	1500	2100	SEQ	1H/D	
4080	ASSIGN'T SHEET	20	80	RANDM	10H/D	1140

NOTES
1100 - PRICING FILE IS USED IN BOTH END ITEM AND SYSTEMS QUOTATIONS.
1110 - COST FILE IS PRESENTLY MAINTAINED IN 3 DIFFERENT AREAS. NO CARDS HAVE YET BEEN DISCARDED.
1120 - INSTALLED SYSTEMS FILE HAS NOT YET BEEN PURGED.
1130 - CONTRACT REGISTER IS MASTER OPEN CUSTOMER ORDER FILE. WHEN ORDERS ARE COMPLETED, THE RECORDS ARE MOVED TO THE INSTALLED SYSTEMS FILE.
1140 - MUST BE AVAILABLE FOR SECOND SHIFT.
1200 - WIDE VARIATION DUE TO SYSTEM VARIATION. THERE IS NO SUCH THING, STRICTLY, AS "STD SYSTEM"
1210 - MULTIPLE DESIGN "PASSES" (SEE NOTE 1000)
1220 - TIME ALLOWED BY CUSTOMERS TO ACKNOWLEDGE ORDER VARIES FROM 1D TO MAX. OF 30D.

NOTES
1020 - BREAKDOWN OF REQUESTS FOR QUOTATION:

	STD SYSTEMS	807-217	OTHER	STD END ITM	PLOTTER	OTHER
AVG	36/w	32/w	4/w	14/w	10/w	4/w
PEAK	51/w	40/w	11/w	19/w	14/w	5/w

1030 - PLANT CLOSES DOWN FOR 2 WEEKS EACH YEAR, SO THERE ARE 50 WEEKS /YR FOR THIS INPUT. PEAKS OCCUR JUST BEFORE AND JUST AFTER THE 2-WEEK CLOSED PERIOD.
1040 - ENGINEERING DOES NOT CLOSE DOWN ALONG WITH THE PLANT, SO THIS INPUT OCCURS 52 WEEKS PER YEAR. PEAKS OCCUR AT BEGINNING OF EACH FISCAL QUARTER.
1050 - ESSENTIALLY NO PEAKS IN THIS OUTPUT.

Figure 7–4 (contd.) Operation flow for the "provide product demand" activity.

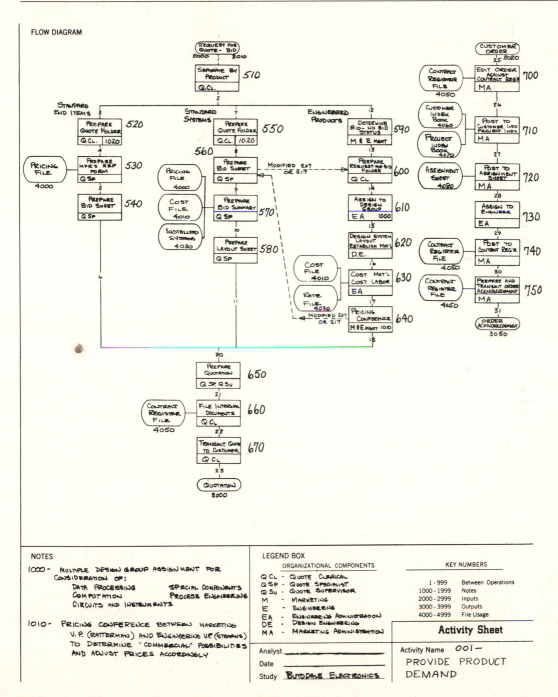

Figure 7–5 Flow diagram for product bidding.

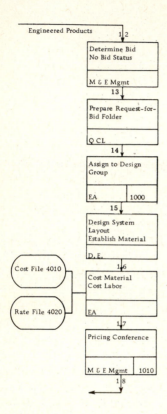

required for it, and the volume of documents, records, or messages involved in the operation.

Figure 7–5 gives an illustration of a flow diagram for a part of an activity concerned with product bidding; it is a portion of Figure 7–4. Each box in the flow diagram represents an operation with the name of the performing organization also shown in the box. The various numbers on or in the boxes represent codes for cross reference to tables on timing and volumes. Major files are shown as in the operation **Cost Material, Cost Labor.**

The flow diagram shows the current sequence of operations. Backing up each operation will be an operation sheet and appropriate message and file sheets. During this first phase the study team must trace each activity through the various organizational components so that the flow diagram can be correctly drawn.

There is a direct analogy between an information systems flow diagram and a critical path method (CPM) network used for physical operations. Industrial engineers have developed a series of tools and techniques like CPM for describing and analyzing the sequence of physical processes, the materials used, and the resulting products. Certainly, one of the objectives of this book is to introduce and show how to use similar formal descriptive and analytic tools for understanding and presenting information systems. Some of the connections between the physical and information systems become obvious through such examination.

7.8 ESTIMATING ELAPSED TIME

Important features of any information management system are the time it takes to perform any given operation and the time that items stand in a line or queue waiting to be serviced. Developing the second part of the activity sheet requires collecting and organizing data about the timing and volumes associated with the operations. These two kinds of time data provide a measure of the dynamics of the system. Moreover, analysts often must use estimates of time to obtain estimates of cost. A discussion of the problem of estimating time data is clearly indicated.

Time data should normally be collected by sampling and analysis, and not by interviews. The main reason is that people do not seem as accurate with time estimates as they are with costs. When recalling time in relation to events, most people remember the difficult, time-consuming situations or the exceptionally easy and fast ones, but rarely can they identify the average. For this reason, analysts usually find it necessary to determine directly the time required to perform each operation and the time that elapses between operations.

The time that items wait to be operated on should be recorded within operations and also should be summarized for the entire activity. Within operations, this elapsed time is usually defined as the time between the arrival of the first input and the availability of an output. Elapsed time is influenced by such factors as volume of transactions, day of the month (banking), and month of the year (retailing). Therefore, data must always be gathered for the peak as well as for the average situation.

Where good time data is not available, sampling methods have to be considered. For example, a batch of papers can be time-stamped at successive processing stations as they are being sent out. Stamping documents *after* people have worked on them avoids the implication that the person is being studied by time-and-motion methods. This is important in sampling; people must feel that their work, not their worth, is being studied. Time relationships can also be reconstructed from file data, correspondence, memos, and other information which fixes time directly or indirectly. Mailroom personnel can also be used to record time. In sampling, peak values can be determined by conducting tests during periods when peaks are most likely to occur.

To show how to record elapsed time we will look at the *Assign to Design Group* operation from Figure 7–5. Part of this process is shown on the operation sheet in Figure 7–6.

This operation is triggered when a *quote folder* arrives at the desk of the supervisor of the operation. (A quote folder is a manila file folder containing a request from a customer for a bid on some product he or she wishes to purchase.) When the quote folder arrives at a desk, the supervisor may not have the time to look it over immediately. Eventually, the folder is examined and given to the group or groups in the design part of the engineering services department that can complete the bid. The third process the supervisor performs is to determine that the group which gets the folder understands the request and the specifications in the customer request. For the waiting and actual work done by the supervisor, one sees in the elapsed time box of the form that one to two days (1–2D) elapse from the time the quote folder is received from the quotation section until the supervisor gives it to the design engineering group.

There are a few other points of interest in Figure 7–6 which can be examined. First, the operation sheet notes that the average volume of customer quotation requests is forty per month. This figure will be useful to the analysts in estimating the cost of operations for this activity (which is the **Provide Product Demand** activity of Butodale) and also for the second and third phases of the study, when the requirements of the system are determined and the new system is designed.

A second point of interest is that the resource used is engineering administration, also called engineering services. The total time required is shown as thirty-one hours per week.

The next time process to be reviewed is the recording of the amount of time that resources are used.

Analysts frequently have to use unit and total resource usage time as a basis for determining resource costs. To estimate the amount of time it takes each person in the organization to do one particular operation in transforming inputs into an output, analysts can often use preliminary data from supervisory interviews. Such data can be

Figure 7–6 A partial picture of an operation.

OPERATION			TRIGGERS, INPUTS AND OUTPUTS											
NO.	PERFORMED BY	ID. NO.	NAME AND QUALIFICATIONS	RECEIVED FROM OR SENT TO	VOLUME AVG	VOLUME PER	ELAPSED TIME							
010-001	Eng.Adm.	T1	RECEIPT OF I1											
KEY NOS. 14-15		I1	QUOTE FOLDER (SPEC, REQUEST FOR BID FOLDER, IDENT. CARD)	QUOTE SEC.	40	M	O							

Operation Sheet

	RESOURCES					
FREQ	ID. NO.	TYPE	UNIT TIME	TOTAL TIME AVG	TOTAL TIME PER	
½I1	X1	ADM. ENG. (1)		3½H	W	

R1	QUOTE FOLDER (WITH ALL PAPERS)	DESIGN ENG.	40	M	1-2D
	BIDDING			
P2	DETERMINE WHICH GROUP OR GROUPS IN ENG. DESIGN WILL COMPLETE BID	½I1		
P3	DETERMINE WITH PROPER GROUP THAT THEY UNDERSTAND REQUEST AND SPEC.	½I1		

verified by comparing them to the total work hours available for the selected period. In estimating the usage of nonhuman resources (such as machines, equipment, and information records), the amount of time they are used for each operation in an activity is probably best calculated by sampling or estimating. One method is to find the length of time a resource is actually used in the operation, then extend it by operation volume and frequency over a time period. For example, in the process of selecting a vendor from a stock record file, an average look-up and selection may require ten minutes. At one hundred orders a week, the resource usage time of the file becomes a thousand minutes per week, which may be recorded as seventeen hours per week.

After the analysts have obtained the resource usage data, they should have a convenient form on which to record the information. A simple table is often best. An example is found in Figure 7–4. The reader's attention is directed to the headings: Inputs, Outputs, and File Usage. To clarify the concept, one entry under each information heading will be explained.

Under Inputs, the key, 2000, is the analyst's code to refer to the input called *quote request.* This input is received from customers at the rate of about fifty per week during forty-six weeks per year and at the rate of seventy per week for four weeks during the year. Under Outputs it is noted that fifteen quotations a week are sent to customers for forty weeks per year and twenty are sent for ten weeks during the year. The last item concerns the information resource— files and records. The first entry under File Usage reveals that there are 240,000 pricing records in the file during normal periods, but this rises to 300,000 records in peak periods. The user can arrive at the particular price record needed by using a random access method (a search much like finding a word in a dictionary). Finally, this file is used eight hours per day.

These summary data are combined with the time required for operations and the elapsed time between operations to aid the analysts in arriving at the cost figures for the activity. There is such a variety of methods for making these final estimates that no single form can be prescribed. The main necessity is that analysts indicate clearly the method they use in making estimates.

7.9 VOLUME AND FREQUENCY DATA

Most management systems are characterized by an uneven combination of events and operations. For example, in the activity that was triggered by the arrival of a customer's request for a quotation, the trigger was operated fifty times a week during a normal week and seventy times during a peak week.

To obtain such input and output volumes and fluctuations above and below averages, an analyst must search the organization's records for these events over representative periods. But a historical approach has the disadvantage of producing flat distributions when representative time periods are extended over the entire year (for example, average vouchers per week, shipments for August, orders received for one year). This defect can be compensated for by pinpointing peaks and studying them individually (in a bank, for example, check-processing peaks occur on the day that factory and office payrolls are distributed). Another disadvantage to the historical approach is that the kinds of records the analyst would like to use often do not exist or are unsatisfactory. Consequently, when historical records are not productive, the analyst must conduct volume tests of inputs and the outputs created by the inputs.

Volume information, of course, is not meaningful unless related to frequency of occurrence. Noting that the average volume is 300 orders per day and peak volume 400 per day gives no idea of how significant the order peak is; if it occurs twice a week or lasts for three months, the peak obviously has greater impact than if it occurs only two days a year.

Clues on peaking times of cyclical and seasonal data are best obtained from people familiar with the business. In various parts of a study, an analyst should ask supervisors questions such as: What are customer invoicing days in a billing routine? Are most withdrawals from stock or inventory made during certain hours of the day? In accounting, what is the cutoff day for monthly interdepartment transfers?

7.10 ACTIVITY COST DATA

In their search, analysts have to obtain two kinds of data. First, they need to obtain data that reveal the nature of the organization's activities. Second, they must determine the cost of carrying on these activities. One might expect an obvious relationship between the activities and their costs. Unfortunately, this relationship is not always simple to establish, and in the typical situation one must seek data in several ways.

The objective of the activity data is to show management what operations are being performed for each activity, whereas the objective of the cost data is to inform management on the cost of performing each activity. The overall forms of operational data must therefore include both kinds of information. Their combined purpose is to show the cost, time, flow, and sequence of the events that take place in an organization. While many people presume that accounting records can readily establish the needed cost information, the truth is that accounting records typically identify cost by type of expense and the organization incurring the expense. They do not readily lend themselves to multi-organization activity flows.

Activity costs usually have to be compiled by indirect methods. During interviews, the analysts may find that some department heads and supervisors will respond to a direct question, such as: "How much of your budget and your resources are involved in this specific activity?" If this question cannot be answered with a fairly precise estimate, the question can be rephrased: "How much effort or money would you save by eliminating this activity from your department?" Still another approach is to ask: "How much money or effort would it take for you to set up this activity as an independent operation?" Sometimes none of these approaches works, and the analysts and top management must make the best estimates they can, based on their own knowledge of the business.

In a complete business study, estimates can be checked by comparing the total costs allocated to the defined activities with the total costs of the functional departments. In partial studies where only one or two activities are being investigated, the estimated costs allocated to activities should always be checked with the cost supervisor or with other managers.

Some types of useful cost summaries that provide input to the cost allocation done during the Phase I study are:

1. Department or product line costs by personnel, equipment, and other categories
2. Resource costs by operational usage

Inasmuch as activity costs generally cut across conventional accounting classifications, a study team will often run into difficulties preparing cost estimates; this need not cause surprise or dismay.

Each industry or field of endeavor (manufacturing, education, insurance, banking, government) has evolved its own accounting practices. Furthermore, considerable variation among businesses exists even within one industry. Before conducting cost studies, an analyst can save time and effort by consulting qualified financial personnel and learning about the special characteristics of the accounting system of the organization under consideration.

Figure 7–7 illustrates a typical manufacturing cost classification scheme. Such a classification is suitable for making departmental cost distributions, but data normally must be reclassified to produce costs by activities or product lines. Unit costs (the cost of a unit of production within a department) are relatively easy to compile under a direct costing system where all expenses are separated between fixed and variable costs. With the more prevalent allocation or burden cost systems, however, an analyst is faced with the problem of allocating expenses and overhead (or burden) to arrive at unit costs.

In the Butodale case study, the team initiated the activity cost allocation from a consolidated overhead statement. After they had obtained the labor and expense totals for each account (supplies, freight, taxes, wages) within each department, they successively interviewed department heads to determine what share of these accounts applied to each of the several activities. When the interviews were completed, they had sufficient information to show how the costs of the company could be presented both by nineteen departmentalized functions and by six defined activities. The total distribution was then reconciled to the consolidated overhead statement. After some adjustments and further consultation with management, the two sets of figures were brought into agreement. This kind of adjustment is normally required at this point in the study. The cost data are shown in Figure 7–1.

Figure 7–7 A typical cost system for a manufacturing organization, showing how costs may be classified for accounting purposes.

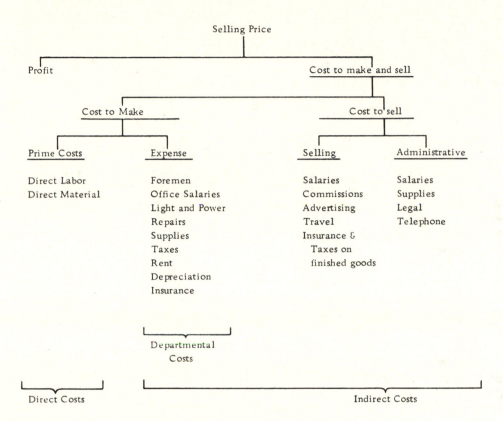

7.11 PRODUCT OR UNIT COSTS

In some situations, analysts find it useful to determine the cost of producing a given product, either as a whole or per unit. However, many companies do not establish product cost accounts and do not publish reports by product lines. Such information is usually confidential, and it also requires increased accounting expense to prepare and maintain such information.

The experience of one study team illustrates how product costs may be developed where records for this category do not exist. Working in a manufacturing business ($56 million annual sales), a four-person team was investigating marketing and engineering functions for several selected product lines representing roughly 15 percent of the total sales volume. Since management was specific in stating the objectives and scope of the study, the team employed the deductive method for estimating costs. The company had little reliable information on costs by product line. Instead of guessing at the costs, a method that compelling circumstances sometimes force on analysts, the team carefully selected a representative month and studied the flow of all orders and inquiries from the time they were received in sales offices until they reached a manufacturing schedule. This method entailed searches of order files in the engineering, marketing, and cost departments. Average unit costs were supplied by the accountants. Then the team assigned overhead costs to these direct engineering and labor costs. After extending the sample to an annual basis, they compared the totals based on the sample with the total sales figures obtained from the marketing department. Some minor adjustments were needed but both the analysts and management agreed that the cost estimates for the products were sound.

7.12 RESOURCE COSTS

Resources are defined as physical and informational elements used in performing various operations. They include items such as files, machine tools, data processing and communications equipment, and personnel. Dividing the costs of these resources among operations and activities is made difficult by the characteristics of most cost accounting systems. However, as a guide, data processing facilities can be allocated to each activity according to the amount or percent of time the facilities are used for the activity. Personnel expense can be distributed by multiplying the number of people in a department by the proportion of time they work on the activity and, then, by an average wage for the labor class. Files expense can be apportioned roughly by assigning first-cost and upkeep charges to the section requiring their maintenance. In general, this method must be tempered by weighing the costs of obtaining data by alternative methods against the desired levels of accuracy. Results should always be checked for reasonableness.

SUMMARY

Formulation of activities is an important part of present system studies which requires consideration of business goals, objectives, and purpose. The three activity formulation methods are deductive, inductive, and composite. An activity is a set of related operations. The degree of difficulty in determining activity boundaries is related to the functional structure of the organization being studied. An activity sheet is a useful tool for expressing activity relationships to the organization. Gathering cost data about each activity can be difficult, and care must be exercised so that costs are correctly allocated to each activity. A resource usage sheet shows the organization divided into its functional departments. The cost of each of the functions is determined as a step in grouping costs by activity. Useful cost data include department or product line cost, other activity costs, and resource costs by operation. In studying a system, it is important to determine the time required to perform an operation and the time the items stand in line waiting to be serviced. Peak periods must be recognized and volumes recorded for such periods. A flow chart is a useful tool for presenting relationships among the operations of an activity.

QUESTIONS AND PROBLEMS

7-1 Define an activity. How does an activity differ from a system?

7-2 Why is it impractical to structure an organization solely on the basis of activities?

7-3 Characterize the basic methods of activity formulation.

7-4 Explain the meaning of *area of application*.

7-5 In formulating activities, systems analysts continually use the word *data*. Explain its meaning.

7-6 During their activity formulation work, what are some areas that a team should examine when studying the information for a telephone company?

7-7 During activity formulation work, what might be the subteam assignments of a team which is to study an information system for a telephone company?

7-8 A study team has been assigned the task of formulating the activities for the information processing system of a large university. Suggest areas which may be assigned to the members of the team for study as separate units. For each area list the data, documents, and reports which should be studied.

7-9 With reference to Figure 7-4:
a) What do Points 12, 13, 14, etc., represent?
b) In the cost file, what does the *4010* represent?
c) What are the names of two information resources?

CHAPTER 8
DOCUMENTATION FOR THE STUDY OF AN EXISTING SYSTEM

8.1 PRESENT SYSTEM DOCUMENTATION

We envision three phases in designing a system: (1) understanding the existing system, (2) determining the requirements of the system, and (3) designing and describing a new system to fulfill these requirements.

In the first phase, the aim of the analyst or systems engineer—whoever is observing and analyzing the system—is to understand what the business or system does, and to a degree how it is done, in terms of activities that thread through the business. In the second phase, the observer analyzes what is logically necessary (or, alternatively, what is specified as necessary by the controlling management) to accomplish the goals of the specific activity under study. In the third phase, a system which can meet those requirements is designed and described.

The specific aim of this chapter is to detail the use of a set of five basic recording forms that can be used for documenting the first phase—understanding the existing system.

The documents and forms, together with guides for filling them out, are in effect a language for describing systems. They are vital for full-scale studies, and they were developed for this purpose. But they can be equally useful for quick, short-term surveys of existing systems, for system analyses, for describing new systems, or for case studies of advance applications.

The recording forms and the techniques for using them work together. They provide a clear, formal description of what is involved in a system or an application. The fields in the various descriptive forms guide the observer in making a logical review of existing practices and procedures.

These documents are aimed at easing the problem of communicating the characteristics of a system. If the forms are completed correctly, anyone familiar with their use can determine what the system does as a preliminary step to further study, whether the purpose is improvement or modification.

The level of detail to which an existing or planned system is studied varies at the discretion of the user of these techniques. This book covers the full use of all forms, but that level of detail is often unnecessary and undesirable. The analyst should go only as far as necessary to do the job at hand.

The amount of detail to be entered on these forms depends on what level of understanding is needed as well as on the time allotted for the survey. Information can be omitted; the observer can single out critical operations from the activity sheet and avoid making up operation sheets for every operation. Many of the fields on the message sheet can be left blank, since a sample of the completed message form is customarily attached. Qualification of content may not be needed on the file sheet, nor even a description of content. However, analysts should avoid the trap of assuming they can remember all details. Systems built on memory often collapse disastrously.

For reference purposes, we present Figure 8–1, which names the five forms and shows their logical interrelationship. Readers may also refer to the discussion of forms in Chapter 4.

8.2 DEVELOPING AN UNDERSTANDING OF A BUSINESS ACTIVITY

In using the five basic forms, the analyst may well think in terms of sets of machinery or blocks on an organization chart. The implicit characteristics of an activity are that it is self-contained and goal-directed. In other words, an activity is a set of operations aimed at a single goal or small number of related goals, with few connections to any other activity. Three or four paths aimed at a single goal may be grouped into a single activity, but branching paths with multiple goals are seldom single activities. Activities may vary widely in size or complexity. A materials management system in a manufacturing enterprise may be considered an activity. In this case, the system may include everything from the procurement of raw materials to the disposal of the finished article. On the other hand, invoicing—a small subsystem which is logically a part of department store sales—can also be considered an activity.

The procedure for developing a survey of an activity starts and ends with the preparation of a resource usage sheet, representing the structure of the business into which the activity fits. The first step is

Figure 8–1 Relationship among the five basic documents used in studying an existing organization.

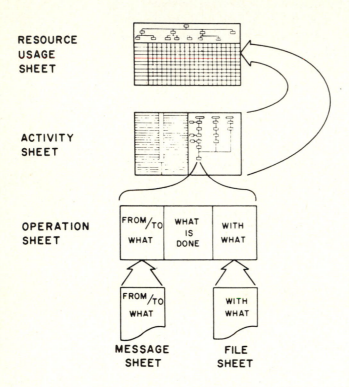

RESOURCE
USAGE
SHEET

ACTIVITY
SHEET

OPERATION
SHEET

| FROM/TO WHAT | WHAT IS DONE | WITH WHAT |

FROM/TO WHAT

WITH WHAT

MESSAGE
SHEET

FILE
SHEET

①

to lay out on the sheet the organization chart for the whole business, or for that part of the business which includes the system or activity under study.

The second step is to acquire the summary cost figures for each organizational component on the bottom tier of the chart. Cost figures for the preceding fiscal period are often available in the accounting department of the company. In many companies, fairly precise budget figures for the current fiscal period may be available; these are sometimes more valid than historical cost figures, especially if one section of the business is growing at a different rate than others.

If neither accurate budget figures nor historical cost figures are readily available, reasonable estimates by department managers are used. Interviews with department managers may be necessary in any case to apportion departmental budgets among personnel, machines and equipment, materials, training, and other costs called for in the tabulation on the resource usage sheet.

Imp info.

The next series of steps is critical to a successful study. The analyst must trace the activity through the organization to find all the departments affecting it, determining exactly what each department contributes to the end result. Here again, interviews with operating personnel and managers in each department will be necessary. Analysts must be particularly alert to unravel from the rest of the business those operations and processes connected with the activity of interest to the team. For example, a department store sales audit department purges charge-sale records and develops control totals. It also may handle time sales and other transactions. It is necessary to determine precisely how much time and effort this department expends on charge sales, and exactly what the department does for the charge account activity.

The processing steps in each operation are recorded on operation sheets. The associated inputs, outputs, and triggers are recorded; and the effort expended by the department is apportioned as accurately as available information will allow. Messages and files are given special attention on the message and file sheets that support each operation sheet. Fields on these three working documents guide the observer in his search for and collection of data.

The operations are next assembled in logical sequence. A flow diagram prepared from these operations in sequence is then laid out on the activity sheet; the process of preparing the flow diagram will disclose any skips in the operation sequence. Information on volumes, times, elapsed times, operation cycles, characteristics of inputs and outputs, and file usage is then entered in the grid section of the activity sheet from the data on the various operation sheets. The information on the operation sheets regarding the apportionment of departmental resources, equipment, materials, and manpower is next used to fill in the blocks on the resource usage sheet where activity costs are summarized. The refinement and summing of these figures and the addition of notes to explain peculiarities of the system are the final steps in the procedure.

As operations are grouped into activities, it may become apparent that some are too large and need to be subdivided or that several operations are actually a series of processes which could be efficiently combined. It is not unusual for initial documentation plans to be modified in the light of subsequent appraisals and evaluation. It is tempting at this stage to consider merging processes or operations for reasons of economy, or mechanizing them, or eliminating them because of their redundancy. *The purpose of studying an existing system, though, is to understand, not to solve; the report should be a descrip-*

tive document, not a proposal. Merging operations, eliminating them, or otherwise reorganizing the system may appear in the form of notes for subsequent phases of study and design or as incidental recommendations to management in the report introduction. As the team sees opportunities for improvement, it must avoid getting involved in their implementation at this point, since to do so can only cause delay.

Experience shows that a team diverted from its main objectives, trying to carry out short-range improvements, rarely returns to complete the original study; if one analyst leaves for the same reason, he or she probably will not rejoin the team. Thus, opportunities to improve the system should be brought to management's attention, but suggestions on how they may be implemented should utilize persons other than those on the team. Possibly, the conditions may be corrected with the introduction of the new system at a later date, or the condition may not even exist once the new system is in full operation. Since the impact of a new system cannot be predicted by the end of the study of an existing system, effort spent on implementation of short-range improvements can be totally wasted.

The end product of the study should be a coherent description of the system as it exists. Its basic dynamics are displayed on the resource usage and activity sheets, and the details of the processing steps are described on the operation sheets; message and file sheets provide close-ups of information inputs, outputs, and resources.

Once this description is completed and refined, it becomes possible to proceed with analysis of the requirements for a new system. This is the second phase of Stage I in the life of a business system, and is the subject of Part Three of this book.

8.3 RESOURCE USAGE SHEET

The purpose of the resource usage sheet is to present on a single page the organizational framework and cost analysis of that segment of the business into which the activity under study fits. It is filled in at two points in the first phase: the organization chart and overall costs are prepared early in the study, while the activity cost figures, which emerge only during the study, are recorded in the latter part of the study.

For specific reference, Figure 8–2 shows a partly filled-in sheet from an actual study of Associated Retailers, Inc. On this form are written encircled key numbers ranging from 1 to 8. For each of the

Figure 8–2 A portion of the resource usage sheet from the
Associated Retailers company used as an example.*

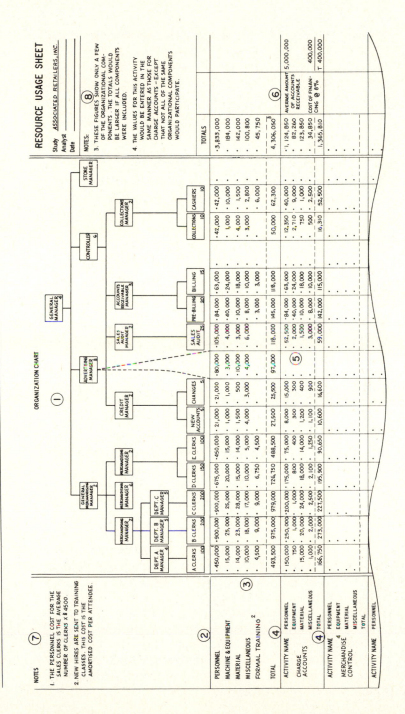

*Key numbers 1 to 8 are explained in Section 8.3.

keys there is an explanation of the concept or feature for the reader's assistance.

Notes for the key numbers on the resource usage sheet in Figure 8–2.

1. The structural organization is shown in an organization chart. This chart can be constructed from a company organization table or chart, or it can be developed from interviews. The area allotted dictates a three- to five-level chart. Organizational components of the bottom level are aligned over the vertical cost-columns. Hierarchic equivalence of the bottom-tier boxes is valuable but not necessary; if a group of units has little effect on the activity, those units can be lumped together on the next higher management level shown. Where it is necessary but topologically difficult to associate higher-tier units·with a cost column, we draw two dotted lines from the box to the sidelines of the column. Where possible, the command lines of the organization structure should be traced back until they join in a single management box. In Figure 8–2 the organization chart is not complete.

2. The first horizontal band under the organization chart is used to enter inclusive resource costs, summing the costs for each department that affects the activity or activities being studied. There should be a cost tabulation for every box in the bottom tier of this part of the chart. The figures can be historical costs, budgeted cost for the current year, or management estimates. Personnel costs should represent all salaries (including that of the head of the department) and direct fringe benefits. Machine and equipment costs include total annual machine rentals except where machines or equipment are purchased; in this case an annual cost is computed by amortizing or using approved write-off procedures. If machines are both purchased and rented, the sum of both costs must be developed. Material costs include annual expenditures for office supplies such as forms, paper, and punch cards.

3. The miscellaneous classification allows for unusual and significant costs not otherwise classified. These include personnel training, money costs in a financial enterprise, warehousing costs in a wholesaling organization, and overhead costs if significant and available. Totals in each box are the sum of these inclusive resource costs.

4. In the other horizontal bands, below the inclusive summaries, are entered activity resource costs for each activity under scrutiny, which are developed during the study. The definitions of the entries are the same. The values reflect only that portion which applies to the activity named in the identifying box at the left. For example, in Figure 8–2, all the equipment and material costs of the billing and prebilling departments result from the charge account activity and are so entered; 38 percent of the total costs of the new accounts department are ascribable to charge accounts, resulting in an entry of $10,600 in that column. The $10,600 is increased from $10,450 for adjustment purposes.

5. Costs are not entered for organizational components that have nothing to do with the activity, as in the case for the advertising manager.

6. Two unlabeled columns at the far right are used for miscellaneous items and for costs which are difficult to classify or not assignable to organizational units. The first of these columns identifies the item and the second displays the best cost figure available. These entries may fall into the top cost band (for inclusive or departmental summary figures) or into activity bands. Costs of inventories, including raw materials, in-process goods, or finished goods; costs of money, including collection costs and bad debts; costs of accounts receivable — these are among the items to be listed in these columns.

   Totals are developed horizontally for the inclusive departmental costs and the various activity costs. Miscellaneous items in the special columns on the right are summed into the grand totals. If all activities involving the departments in the bottom tier of the organization chart are presented on the activity cost breakdowns, the sum of the activity totals should be the inclusive departmental total.

7,8. Notes may be written in either the upper left or upper right corners of the resource usage sheet.

8.4 MESSAGE SHEET

A message may be defined as any communication of information. A message sheet is a form designed as a convenient document on which analysts can record the key information of any input or output message. Thus, entries in the various fields of a message sheet describe and define the characteristics of the input or the output conveyed by the message. There usually are a large number of message sheets for a study. Also, as indicated in Figure 8–1, analysts use the message sheets in the preparation of operation sheets.

Figure 8–3 is a general example of a blank message sheet developed for the above purposes. In it are sixteen key numbers that have been circled for ease in studying the form. Immediately following are the explanations of these key points. It is usually advantageous to attach a sample copy of the business form described in the message, preferably filled in with sample data.

Notes for the key numbers on the message sheet in Figure 8–3

1. **Message Name** This is a unique name for the message.
2. **Message No.** This is the unique identifying number for the message, with prefix indicating message type (R for report and S for signal) and suffix numerals indicating copies. Thus, the designation R 131.3 identifies the third copy of message 131.
3. **Other Names Used** Frequently used alternate names and synonyms are listed.
4. **Layout No.** Layout is the physical format of a message: each format is identified by a layout number. The layout is independent of both the messages using the format and the data within the format. Several message types may use the same layout number, with the fields differently interpreted on each. Layout defines physical locations of fields and field characteristics, permitting relatively flexible form design for a series of messages having the same layout number.
5. **Form No.** This number is assigned to identify the message form; it is usually printed on the form.
6. **No. of Copies** This figure includes both the number of copies prepared with the original and the number of copies later reproduced.
7. **Media** This entry displays the media employed in original and later reproduction.
8. **How Prepared** This pertains to reports, and describes the means by which basic fields are entered on the original message (by hand, typewritten, card-punched, and so on).
9. **Operations Involved in** This is the identifying number of each operation using the message as input or output.

Figure 8–3 A blank message sheet.*

Message Sheet

MESSAGE NAME ①			MESSAGE NO. ②
OTHER NAMES USED ③			LAYOUT NO. ④
			FORM NO. ⑤
			NO. OF COPIES ⑥
MEDIA ⑦	HOW PREPARED ⑧		
OPERATIONS INVOLVED IN ⑨			
REMARKS ⑩			

CONTENTS

NO. ⑪	DATA NAME ⑫	FREQUENCY ⑬	CHARACTERS ⑭	A/N ⑮	ORIGIN ⑯

DATE   ANALYST   SOURCE   PAGE

STUDY

*The 16 key numbers are explained in Section 8.4.

10. **Remarks** Enter here all supplemental data on message definition or handling (security, access, and so forth).

11. **No.** The identifying number of the data element can be any number; usually 01 to 99 are used. The message number and this number uniquely identify the data element for later reference.

12. **Data Name** This is the title for the data element.

13. **Frequency** Three types of entries appear here. If the data do not appear on every message carrying this message number, the frequency of appearance is entered as a decimal fraction. If the data appear once on each message, the entry is 1: if more than once, the number of appearances, or the possible range and average, is entered. Whenever a range is entered, the average should also be noted.

14. **Characters** This field shows the maximum number of characters in the data element.

15. **A/N** Enter A for alphabetic, N for numeric, and AN for alphameric (including special symbols).

16. **Origin** Enter the operation number for the operation that either initially accepts the data element into the system, or originates the data. Operations that merely post the data to the message are not entered.

8.5 FILE SHEET

The file sheet is used to display the detail concerning information resources, such as cost records, price records, and rate records. Normally, there are many file sheets for each study. It is generally helpful to management and to the analysts themselves if examples of actual records from each file are attached to the file sheets. The analysts use the collection of file sheets (together with the message sheets) to complete the operation sheets.

Figure 8–4 contains an example of a blank file sheet. In the figure are 18 key numbers which refer to the notes immediately following.

Notes for the key numbers on the file sheet in Figure 8–4

1. **File Name** There is a unique name for each file.
2. **File No.** There is also a unique number for the file, with prefix

Figure 8–4 A blank file sheet.*

File Sheet

FILE NAME ①		FILE NO. ②
LOCATION ③	STORAGE MEDIUM ④	
ACCESS REQUIREMENTS ⑤		
SEQUENCED BY ⑥		
CONTENT QUALIFICATIONS ⑦		
HOW CURRENT ⑧		
RETENTION CHARACTERISTICS ⑨		
LABELS ⑩		
REMARKS ⑪		

CONTENTS

SEQUENCE NO.	MESSAGE NAME	VOLUME		CHARACTERS PER MESSAGE	CHARACTERS PER FILE	
		AVG	PEAK		AVG.	PEAK
⑫	⑬	⑭	⑮	⑯	⑰	⑱

DATE   ANALYST   SOURCE   PAGE

STUDY

*The 18 key numbers are explained in Section 8.5.

F and suffixes indicating copies. The designations F 131.2 and F 131.4.2 identify copies 2 and 4 of file 131; copy 4 is located at a site "2" remote from the main file.

3. **Location** The name or number is given for the organization housing the file (or portion of the file) and the physical location if pertinent.

4. **Storage Medium** This is the type of housing for the file, such as tub file, tape storage cabinet, three-ring binder, etc. This entry is indirectly related to the medium of the information itself.

5. **Access Requirements** Several types of information appear here: who is or is not permitted access to the file, classified by job titles or by such entries as "Military—Top Secret" or "Company Confidential"; the availability of the file, in terms of what hours and how long the file is open daily; and access characteristics, including how often and how quickly reference must be made.

6. **Sequenced by** File sequence keys are described in this field. File sequence is described by minor key *within* intermediate keys *within* major key. A file of open purchase orders might, for example, be sequenced by transaction date within purchase order number within part number. Sequence keys are sometimes not contained in the messages themselves, yet must be described in this field. In the case of the purchase orders, transaction date might be missing from the messages; new transactions would be filed in back of existing transactions within the purchase order number and part number sequences.

7. **Content Qualifications** Details are displayed on file contents if file name is not sufficiently descriptive. A file named "Purchase Order File" might, for example, be qualified as "purchase orders for vendors within 25 miles."

8. **How Current** This gives the age of transactions when entered in the file.

9. **Retention Characteristics** Removal rules for each type of message in the file are entered here.

10. **Labels** These identify the file, carrying a code or phrase, such as "Master Payroll" to uniquely establish the file identity. Other information, such as date, number of records, is often carried as well. This field is particularly useful for tape or disk files.

11. **Remarks** Noted here are miscellaneous data and problems such as rapidly expanding size, excessive or inadequate retention cycles, or need for duplicate files differently sequenced.

12. **Sequence No.** This gives the relative sequence number for order of messages within the sequence keys of the file (for files in which multiple records are filed together). If report A and report B are to be processed for a common master report C, and report A must be filed in front of report B, then it is given sequence number 1 and report B is given sequence number 2.

13. **Message Name** This shows name and number of messages appearing in the file. The name should correspond to the name on a related Message Sheet.

14. **(Volume) Avg.** The average number of this type of message in the file is shown.

15. **(Volume) Peak** The peak number of this type of message in the file is shown.

16. **Characters per Message** This field displays the size of an average message. The number entered here is the total of each data element's character count multiplied by frequency; if a range and average appear, the average is used.

17. **(Characters per File) Avg.** The average file size for this message is given. Multiply the character count per message by the volume average to arrive at this figure.

18. **(Characters per File) Peak** The peak file size for this message is given. Multiply character count per message by volume peak to arrive at this figure.

8.6 OPERATION SHEET

The operation sheet is used by the analysts to describe the processing steps that make up one or more operations, together with the triggers, inputs, outputs, and the resources used in each operation.

In preparing this form, the analyst draws heavily from the information in the message and file sheets and combines that information with information about the process obtained by observing, interviewing, and sampling.

Figure 8–5 contains the top portion of a blank operation sheet. In

Figure 8-5 The top portion of a blank operation sheet.*

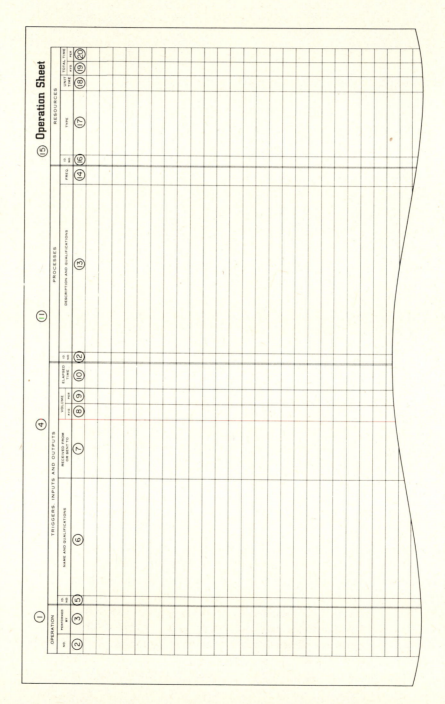

*The key numbers are explained in Section 8.6.

it are twenty encircled key numbers which refer to the notes given immediately below.

Notes for the key numbers on the operation sheet in Figure 8–5

1. **Operation** This field consists of two subfields.

2. **No.** This is a six-digit operation number. The first three digits refer either to the department which performs the operation, or to the activity which includes the operation. The last three digits form the unique operation number. Operation numbers need not be consecutive.

3. **Performed by** The name or number of the organizational component responsible for performing the operation is entered here.

4. **Triggers, Inputs, and Outputs** This field consists of five subfields.

5. **ID. No.** This differentiates among triggers, inputs, and outputs. T1 identifies the trigger for each operation. Inputs are identified by a series starting with I1. Outputs are identified by a series starting with R1 (for *result*).

6. **Name and Qualifications** The name of an input or output must correspond to that appearing on a related message sheet. Copies or parts of copies involved are indicated in parentheses after the name. If only a selected group of a named input or output is involved, the group qualifications are entered; the qualifying statement specifies constraining values. Normally only one trigger will be defined for each operation. Triggers may fall into many categories: receipt of an input, a time of day, week, or month, or a frequency per unit time; receipt of multiple inputs; or a combination of inputs and times.

7. **Received from or Sent to** Enter here the name or the number (or both) of the organizational component from which the input is received or to which the output is sent. If outside the activity under scrutiny, indicate the sender or receiver in general terms; customer, vendor, salesperson, government, etc.; if inside, use the lowest-level component involved. If an output is sent solely for filing, indicate destination file by name.

8,9. **Volume** Indicate the average quantity for each input, output, and multiple-input trigger during any given time period.

8. **Avg.** Use the arithmetic mean of the volume figures.

9. **Per** In defining time periods, choose a meaningful length of time. Since these data may help determine costs, the time period should be consistent, if possible, across the operations and with costing and accounting policies. Consider cylic concepts in making entries for such cases as file processing.

10. **Elapsed Time** This is determined as follows: A zero is entered for the input which normally arrives first; if more than one type of input is needed to start the process, average elapsed time between availability of the first input and availability of subsequent inputs is shown for each subsequent input. For each output, list the average elapsed time between time zero (the availability of the first input) and the arrival of the output at its destination. Where practical, elapsed time should be given in working days or fractions of a working day.

11. **Processes** This field includes three subfields.

12. **ID. No.** The identification number segregates the processes that make up the operation. Processes are identified by a number series starting with P1.

13. **Description and Qualifications** This subfield consists of a verb and its object, plus occasional qualifying phrases. Verbs should be broad enough to obviate the need for details, clear enough to avoid ambiguity. Such verbs as *determine, prepare, reproduce, insert, attach, select, post, arrange, edit, adjust, reject, destroy* have been adequately defined and exemplify the type of verb to use. The object of the verb should refer to inputs, outputs, or resources, and should tell what information is affected or transformed by the action implicit in the verb. Additional phrases *(to . . . , for . . . , into . . . , using . . . , etc.)* are entered as needed to explain the process. Conditional clauses *(if . . . , when . . .)* are also employed.

14. **Freq.** This field gives the frequency of performance in terms of the number of executions per input, output, or operation. Frequency may also be expressed as unit operating time, or

as a statement of the cycle: MC could indicate an operation performed on a monthly cycle.

15. **Resources** This field includes four subfields.

16. **ID. No.** This segregates the various resources used in the operation. Resources for each operation are identified by a separate number series starting with X1.

17. **Type** Here are shown the classifications of operating personnel and machines or equipment, with the numbers of each in parentheses. Names and classifications of materials are entered, with appropriate volumes; raw materials, work in process, forms, finished goods, all are listed. Resource data include files; these are identified by name and type of message, using names and numbers corresponding to entries on message and file sheets.

18. **Unit Time** Resource usage per operation is defined here. For a given resource, unit time may be separately defined for each process and again for the whole operation. The figure should represent average time for the total resource named. Thus, ten minutes from each of three clerks would demand an entry 1/2 H/OP under UNIT TIME opposite the entry CLERKS (3) in the TYPE subfield. Unit time is not given for materials, nor, in most instances, for files.

19,20. **Total Time** This defines the total resource usage per process or operation over a selected time period. The entry represents the average time that the total resource is employed; unit of time selected should be compatible across operations and with the accounting policies.

19. **Avg.** The quantity and time unit are shown.

20. **Per** List the selected time period.

8.7 ACTIVITY SHEET

The activity sheet is used by both management and analysts to provide an insight into the dynamics of an activity and a measurement of the magnitude of the processing problems in the activity. It is developed in part at the same time that the operation sheets are prepared, and in part from the data on the operations sheets. The activity sheet covers five major topics: A flow diagram on the right shows the operational flow of the activity. A tabular section on the left covers the characteristics of inputs, the characteristics of outputs, the characteristics of file usage, and the elapsed times involved in the activity.

The activity sheet shows the operations within an activity, whereas its corresponding major band on the resource usage sheet shows the cost of carrying on the activity.

Figure 8–6 is an example of an activity sheet taken from an actual case, Atlantic Distributors, Inc. The seven circled key numbers relate to the notes below.

Notes for the key numbers on the activity sheet in Figure 8–6

1. The flow diagram charts the mechanism of the activity in action. Operation boxes identify each related set of processing steps which can be defined as an operation. Local jargon or more formal operative verb phrases may be used to describe the operations. Space at the bottom of the operation box is used for indicating, in abbreviated form, the organizational component which performs the operation, and for footnote reference numbers. Inputs are flagged in small oval balloons in which are entered the key number and name of the input; outputs are similarly treated. All files referenced during, or used in, the various operations are flagged in the larger oval balloons. Key numbers are assigned to inputs, outputs, and files for cross reference to the tabular grid that takes up the left half of the activity sheet. Between-operations key numbers are also assigned for cross reference. The number series used for cross referencing is printed in the **Legend** box (6) on the activity sheet.

   The four other major areas covered by the activity sheet—characteristics of inputs, outputs, and file usage, and definitions of elapsed time—are all entered on the tabular grid. Since the space requirements for the four uses vary from one activity to another, no subdivisions or headings are preprinted; the analyst subdivides the grid in the manner most suitable to his purposes. Detail level of any and all entries in the grid can vary; only those details which point up significant operating conditions should be entered.

2,3. Entries describing input and output characteristics should define the inputs and outputs; the two classes of entries are grouped separately. Key number series for inputs is from 2000

Figure 8–6 An example of an activity sheet taken from an actual case study.*

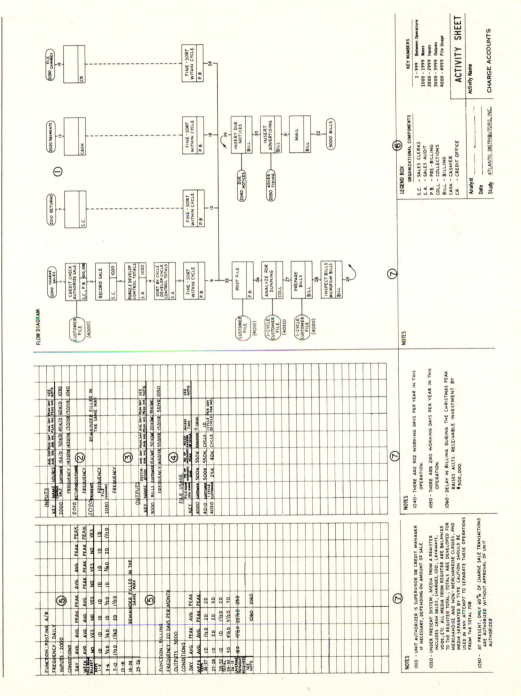

*The seven key numbers are explained in Section 8.7.

to 2999; for outputs, 3000 to 3999. Name of input or output should correspond to the name on a message sheet. Sources of inputs and destinations of outputs shown on the activity sheet are always in the environment external to the activity sheet. Volume of each input or output is expressed as quantity per unit time; if there are significant variations in the volume over the course of a year, these are spelled out. Causes of volume variation (calendar cycles or seasonal fluctuations) are shown. Frequency per year is shown for each volume level given. If batching is an input or output characteristic, batch size and batch-size variations are shown. If any of these items require additional explanation not easily entered in the grid, footnotes are added.

4. File usage is defined in terms of the size of the file and its access characteristics. The key number references the specific usage in the activity flow diagram; the same physical file may be used in several ways. File name may also change from use to use. Quantity of messages in the file is given for average and peak conditions if the difference is significant; quantity shown may be for all messages in the file or for just the type of message involved in the operation. Type of access (random or cyclic) is shown for each operation which is keyed to the file. Access time may be given as a maximum allowable figure, as a minimum attainable figure, or as a mean operating figure.

5. A tabular format is used to display elapsed time: in the table, combinations of the several controlling conditions are laid out, and the elapsed time for each set of conditions is then entered for every critical operation. Conditions include average and peak days during both average and peak weeks or seasons under various operating conditions. Where elapsed time is not appropriate, the fact that another event takes place may be entered; under certain volume conditions, for example, subcontracted assistance may be sought. Function name for the elapsed-time tabulation describes a sequence of operations. Frequency is given for the operations within this subset. Key-number designations for inputs or outputs cross-reference the definitions of the inputs and outputs. A table for the various operations is set up and the elapsed times entered; these may be totaled for long-operating sequences.

6. The **Legend** box on the activity sheet provides space to define the organizational components abbreviated in the

operation boxes, and to give the physical locations if pertinent. Key number series specifications are preprinted in this box. Here too, the analyst enters his or her name, the date the activity sheet was completed, and the identifying name of the activity.

7. Footnotes are entered in the three **Notes** boxes. Numbers are assigned to footnote references from the series 1000 to 1999 as the necessity to use footnotes arises.

8.8 DOCUMENTATION IN A NONMECHANIZED SYSTEM

The charge account system of a department store is typical of activities that are almost independent of other parts of the related business. The sale of goods is the department store's chief activity, with stock buying, advertising, inventory management, and personnel as other typical activities. Within the sales activity, charge accounts may be considered a major subdivision, with cash sales and time purchases as other subdivisions.

The charge account activity in some department stores remains a nonmechanized clerical system; the first example of documenting a study will deal with such an activity. For illustration, a case study called Associated Retailers, Inc., is used.

The section of the business which includes the charge account system is displayed on the resource usage sheet shown earlier in Figure 8–2. This basic form shows the economics of the system and of its immediate environment.

In the resource usage sheet the organizational structure of a major section of the department store is graphically illustrated in the organization chart. Each box on the chart shows the total number of people directly employed in the organizational component represented by the box. Employees in any lower-level components not shown on the chart are totaled into the proper lowest-level box on the chart. Upper-level boxes show only their own immediate employee totals not including components subordinate to them.

The lower section of the resource usage sheet is a cost tabulation. Costs of personnel, machines, equipment, materials, and so forth are summarized for each organizational component in the bottom tier of boxes in the chart. Higher-level components may also be summarized in this tabulation, as is the advertising manager's component in Figure 8–2. Costs for the higher-level organization components are usually prorated among the departments under the jurisdiction of the higher-level manager. Thus, the personnel costs tabulated on the resource usage sheet are comprehensive for the entire organization table as drawn. Unusual items of significant cost—such as an insurance policy carried on the president's life—would not be prorated, but would be separated out in the unlabeled columns at the right side of the sheet.

Costs used in this tabulation may be budget figures for the current year, actual figures from the previous year, or estimates. Note that in Figure 8–2 the formal training of personnel was important enough to be separated as a cost factor in the summary tabulation. Total costs for each organizational component are tabulated immediately below the related box on the organization chart, and grand totals for the section of the business covered by the resource usage sheet are developed in the **Totals** column at the right.

The costs are then allocated to activities. In Figure 8–2 the specific activity that this study is considering, the charge account system, is broken out in a separate tabulation. The costs shown for each activity are part of the summary costs listed in the top section of the cost tabulation. Thus the total cost budgeted for Department A and 100 clerks is $493,500; of this, $166,750 is the cost included in the charge account activity.

Merchandise control and cash sales are other activities that might be examined in the same manner as charge accounts; the same organizational components would not necessarily participate. Conversely, note that the advertising department does not directly participate in the charge account system, and so no costs are entered in this block.

Two unmarked columns at the right of the tabular section can display various data, such as the average amount of money invested in inventories or accounts receivable. Where possible, the cost of having the money invested would also be shown. In this case, the first of the two unheaded columns describes the item, and the second shows the amount. The average investment in accounts receivable and the cost of maintaining this investment are tabulated in Figure 8–2.

By summing horizontally, the analyst can develop the total costs for each activity. In Figure 8–2, the totals indicate that charge accounts involve $1.37 million in annual costs, about 31 percent of the total cost of $4.3 million.

The resource usage sheet permits a rapid analysis of the structure into which the system fits and of the costs of the activities that make up the system. Its principal function is to document the organizational and economic information from a study. In the example of the charge account system of a department store, it provides a quick look at the way in which the charge account activity fits into the department store organization.

The activity sheet, shown in Figure 8–6, includes a flow diagram which shows the sequence of operations performed by the various departments to provide the charge account service and a tabular section in which amplifying information is listed. The flow diagram starts with an action from the external environment—the customer's purchase of merchandise on his charge account—and carries through the mailing of bills.

To keep the flow path narrow, Figure 8–6 shows only operations on charge sales. Returns, payments, and file changes are parallel paths in the charge account activity, feeding into the posting and billing sequence. Details are omitted from this example; in a full study, these three sequences would be entered in the same detail as charge sales.

The tabular section at the left of the activity sheet displays amplifying information about the operations that make up the activity. This grid is unlabeled, without reserved spaces for specific information. Use of the grid is therefore at the discretion of the analyst. In Figure 8–6, the far left section displays elapsed times, volumes, and frequencies for critical operations. Elapsed time is shown for each of eight sets of conditions. The other section is used to show detailed information on volumes and frequencies of the inputs and outputs.

Special attention is given to information resources, the files that are referenced or changed during the various operations. The flow diagram shows which operations use which files; specifics of file usage are then detailed in the grid section. In Figure 8–6, the details on file usage include pertinent statistical information on the average and peak activity of the file and its access time.

The file name (usage name) describes the file in its specific usage. Thus, in Figure 8–6, the same physical file is referenced in keys 4000, 4010 and 4020. In the first case it is subject to random reference in less than a minute for checking credit limit and authorizing the sale. It is next referenced sequentially every day for posting the day's business. In key 4020, one-twentieth of the file is pulled out each day for the monthly billing cycle.

In the legend box at the lower right-hand corner of the activity sheet, the observer enters the names (and locations, if important) of the departments involved in the activity; the full-name entries explain the abbreviations used in the flow diagram. A numbering system is specified in this box which is useful for cross-referencing the flow diagram to the tabular grid section and to footnotes. Boxes marked **Notes** (below the grid) provide space for footnotes to amplify and explain peculiarities of the activity being described. In Figure 8–6, for example, the analyst has noted the various media emerging from the **Record Sale** operation (note 1020) and the number of working days for sales (note 1040) and preparing bills (note 1050).

One of the operation sheets for the charge account activity of Associated Retailers, Inc., is shown in Figure 8–7.

The operation sheet is the principal means for collecting and displaying operational data. It expands the operation boxes on the activity sheet to describe in more detail what is done, from or to what, with what.

Included in the information entered on the operation sheet are triggers, inputs, and outputs; the description and qualifications of the processing steps; and the resources used in the various steps. When a single sheet is used for more than one operation, as is frequently the case, all the material for each operation is segregated from the one following by a horizontal line drawn across the page.

The operation sheet in Figure 8–7 is thus subdivided. Note, too, in this illustration that there need not be any connection between a trigger, input, or output on the one hand and a process or resource entered on the same line; the three major sections of the sheet are tabulated without horizontal reference to each other except within heavy lines separating operations.

Inputs and outputs are identified by sequences of numbers starting respectively with I1 and R1 (for *result*). Inputs to an operation are items entering from the external environment or transferred from a previous operation. Outputs are items that are produced by the operation to go into the external environment or to a subsequent operation. The name of an information input or output must correspond to an identifying name on a corresponding message sheet which further describes the item.

Triggers are identified by the letter T. An operation is usually started by one trigger. A trigger may be the arrival of an input item or items, it may be a time of the day or day of the month; or it may be a combination of a time plus the availability of input items. In the operation sheet in Figure 8–7, it is the accumulation of ten customer sales records that triggers the file-posting operations; although ten documents are required, they are still considered one trigger.

The organization component from which an input is received, or to which an output is sent, is also listed. The volume figures on inputs and outputs are listed, together with the time elapsing from the ar-

Figure 8−7 The operation sheet for the charge account activity of the Associated Retailers company.

Operation 04 010 BILLING (T1) — (KEY NOS. 27–28)

OPERATION			TRIGGERS, INPUTS AND OUTPUTS		VOLUME		ELAPSED	
		IO NO	NAME AND QUALIFICATIONS	RECEIVED FROM OR SENT TO	AVG	PER	TIME	
04 010	BILLING	T1	RECEIPT OF IO I1					
(KEY NOS. 27–28)		I1	CUSTOMER RECORD	COLLECTIONS	20K	D	0	
		I2	TRANSACTION SLIP		160K	D	0	
		R1	CUSTOMER RECORD	ANALYSIS SECTION OF BILLING	20K	D	7MIN	
		R2	BILL		20K	D	7MIN	
		R3	TRANSACTION SLIP		160K	D	7MIN	
		R4	ERROR SHEET	COLLECTIONS SUPVR	5	D	8H	

PROCESSES

IO NO	DESCRIPTION AND QUALIFICATIONS	FREQ
P1	COUNT TRANSACTION SLIPS	$1/I1$
P2	COMPARE COUNT TO NUMBER OF TRANSACTIONS ON CUSTOMER RECORD	$1/I1$
P3	RETURN CUSTOMER RECORD AND TRANSACTION SLIPS TO COLLECTIONS DEPT FOR ERROR TRACING AND CORRECTION.	$1/150I1$
P4	ENTER ACCOUNT NUMBER AND NATURE OF ERROR ON ERROR SHEET.	$1/150I1$
P5	COPY BILL FROM CUSTOMER RECORD	$1/I1$
P6	ATTACH TRANSACTION SLIPS TO BILL	$1/I1$
P7	ENTER INITIALS ON CUSTOMER RECORD	$1/I1$
P8	SEND CUSTOMER RECORD, BILL, AND TRANSACTIONS SLIPS TO ANALYSIS SECTION	$1/10I1$
P9	SEND ERROR SHEET TO ANALYSIS SUPVR.	$1/D$

RESOURCES

	TYPE	UNIT TIME	TOTAL TIME AVG	PER
X1	CLERKS (5)	30 MIN		OP
X2	XEROX COPIER (2)		13H	D

Operation 04 020 BILLING (T1) — (KEY NOS. 28–29)

OPERATION			TRIGGERS, INPUTS AND OUTPUTS		VOLUME		ELAPSED	
		IO NO	NAME AND QUALIFICATIONS	RECEIVED FROM OR SENT TO	AVG	PER	TIME	
04 020	BILLING	T1	RECEIPT OF IO I1					
(KEY NOS. 28–29)		I1	CUSTOMER RECORD	FILE SECTION OF BILLING	20K	D	0	
		I2	BILL		20K	D	0	
		I3	TRANSACTION SLIP		160K	D	0	
		R1	CUSTOMER RECORD	COLLECTIONS			1H	
		R2	BILL	MAILING SECTION OF BILLING	(NOTE 1)		5MIN	
		R3	TRANSACTION SLIP				5MIN	
		R4	ERROR SHEET	FILE SECTION SUPVR	2	D	8H	

PROCESSES

IO NO	DESCRIPTION AND QUALIFICATIONS	FREQ
P1	INSPECT BILLS FOR LEGIBILITY AND ATTACHED TRANSACTION SLIPS	$1/I1$
P2	RETURN CUSTOMER RECORD, BILL, AND TRANSACTION SLIPS TO FILE SECTION.	$1/700I1$
P3	ENTER FILE CLERK INITIALS AND NATURE OF ERROR ON ERROR SHEET.	$1/700I1$
P4	MICROFILM BILL	$1/I1$
P5	SEND BILL AND TRANSACTION SLIPS TO MAILING SECTION.	$1/10I1$
P6	SEND CUSTOMER RECORD TO COLLECTIONS	$1/50I1$
P7	SEND ERROR SHEET TO FILE SECTION SUPVR	$1/D$

RESOURCES

	TYPE	UNIT TIME	TOTAL TIME AVG	PER
X1	CLERKS (2)	2MIN		OP
X2	MICROFILM CAMERA		4H	D

① VOLUME HAS CYCLIC FLUCTUATION:

FREQ.	166D/YR.	55D/YR	15D/YR	5D/YR
VOLUME	15K/D	30K/D	20K/D	35K/D

BILLING DEPT. − SCHULTZ   ASSOCIATED RETAILERS INC.   CHARGE ACCOUNTS   6

rival of the first input to the arrival of each output at its destination. In the example in Figure 8−7, the outputs go to the next department and so arrive all at the same time. In some cases, one output may be required locally while another may be used in a remote location; elapsed times for the various outputs include transfer periods embodying the average time required for delivery by messenger, mail, and so forth.

The **Description and Qualifications** field lists the processing steps that make up each operation. The process description consists of a verb and its objects plus necessary modifiers. Verbs broad enough to make details unnecessary and clear enough to avoid ambiguity should be selected. The object of each verb should answer the question "What?" in reference to inputs, outputs, and resources. Each process is assigned a number prefixed by P.

The frequency with which the process is performed is also displayed; where possible, it should be expressed in terms of the number of executions per input, output, or operation. Where this means of expression is not feasible, the frequency per unit of time is valid for processes occurring cyclically; but in these cases the cycle period should be shown (monthly cycle, weekly cycle, and so on).

The resources section of the operation sheet is concerned with people, equipment, information, and facilities which are used in the various process steps that make up the operation. Resources are identified by a sequence of numbers starting with X1. Classifications of operating personnel and the number of each class are entered; names or classifications, or both, of raw materials, blank forms, and so forth, are listed with the approximate volume of each.

Entries under **Unit Time** show how much of a particular resource is used per operation, or per input or output. Unit time is not specified for materials, nor generally for files; it is commonly shown for equipment and personnel. When it is specified, it should cover the total resource named even if a multiple-unit resource; thus five clerks who each contribute four minutes make a total contribution of twenty minutes of unit time. This figure is clarified by an entry **Clerks** (5) that appears in the **Type** column of the resources section.

Entries under **Total Time** show the average usage of the resource per process or per operation. Unit of time selected should be consistent with cost information. This column should be left blank for material resources and generally for files as well. An example of a message sheet from the charge account activity of the Associated Retailers company follows. The details of information inputs and outputs are recorded on message sheets. A message is considered to be any notice or communication entering or leaving an activity, regardless of the medium of transmission. It may be recorded or unrecorded. Signals, for instance, are unrecorded messages of a transitory nature; an example would be a telephone call. The contents of a formal message, on the other hand, are fixed in nature, order, and relative length, and the message is recorded on some more or less permanent medium, like paper.

The message sheet displays the name or names by which the message is identified. In Figure 8–8, the message sheet for the customer record indicates that this form is also called a customer master or a billing master. The message medium and the method by which it is prepared are shown. The message sheet displays both the operations which originate data in the message and the operations that merely use the message. The form in Figure 8–8 supports the two operations—prepare bills, and inspect and microfilm bills—displayed in Figure 8–7. In both these operations the customer record is involved, but neither operation originated data on the record. Consequently the numbers of these operations appear in the field **Operations Involved in** but not in the field **Origin.**

Figure 8–8 An example of a message sheet and an attached sample of a customer record to which the message sheet refers. The activity concerns charge customers in the Associated Retailers company.

MESSAGE NAME: CUSTOMER RECORD
MESSAGE NO.: R0030
OTHER NAMES USED: CUSTOMER MASTER; BILLING MASTER
LAYOUT NO: 12
FORM NO: GRC 172
NO. OF COPIES: 1
MEDIA: 8½ x 5½ MANILA CARD
HOW PREPARED: TYPED - BOOKKEEPING MACHINE
OPERATIONS INVOLVED IN: 005-001, 005, 010; 010-005, 010; 012-010, 015, 075; 014-010, 020.

REMARKS: THIS MESSAGE IS THE MASTER FOR COPIED BILL. AMOUNT REMITTED IS ENTERED ON THE BILL BY THE CUSTOMER, BUT THE FIELD IS NOT USED ON THIS RECORD.

CONTENTS

NO.	DATA NAME	FREQUENCY	CHARACTERS	A/N	ORIGIN
01	COMPANY NAME	1	25	AN	ON FORM
02	COMPANY ADDRESS	1	33	AN	ON FORM
03	TELEPHONE NUMBER	1	8	AN	ON FORM
04	CUSTOMER NAME	1	50	AN	012-075
05	CUSTOMER ADDRESS	1	150	AN	012-075
06	ACCOUNT NUMBER	1	7	N	012-075
07	AMOUNT REMITTED	1	6	N	SEE REMARKS
08	FIELD LABELS	1	35	AN	ON FORM
09	DATE	1-22 AVG 8	6	N	010-005
10	TRANSACTION NUMBER	1-22 AVG 8	2	N	010-005
11	CHARGE AMOUNT	1-22 AVG 7	6	N	010-005
12	PAYMENT / RETURN AMOUNT	1-22 AVG 1	6	N	010-005
13	BALANCE AMOUNT	1-22 AVG 8	6	N	010-005
14	PAYABLE INFORMATION	1	79	AN	ON FORM

DATE ______ ANALYST ______ SOURCE: COLLECTIONS PAGE: 1 OF 1
STUDY: ASSOCIATED RETAILERS INC.

ASSOCIATED RETAILERS INC.
1107 FOURTH STREET
HARTFORD CONN.
WG 5 1045

JOHN W. CUSTOMER III
7212 E. PLAZA COURT
HARTFORD, CONN.

173-4201

$ ______
AMOUNT REMITTED

DATE	T	CHARGES	PAYMENTS/RETURNS	BALANCE
02-29-61	B			27.00
03-01-61	1	12.77		39.77
03-05-61	2	3.09		42.86
03-06-61	3		27.00	15.86
03-09-61	4	3.79		19.65
03-14-61	5	8.45		28.10
03-23-61	6	2.04		30.14
03-25-61	7	5.27		35.41
03-26-61	8	2.80		38.21

PAYMENT DUE WITHIN 30 DAYS OF INVOICE RECEIPT
MAKE CHECKS PAYABLE TO
"ASSOCIATED RETAILERS"

Data elements and arrangement of fields are tabulated in the **Contents** section of the message sheet.

To further illustrate this display, a copy of the actual customer record in Figure 8–8 is associated with the message. In many cases, the attachment of the source forms eliminates the need for filling in the **Contents** section of the message sheet; the analyst can satisfy the survey requirements by identifying the message, describing the medium and preparation method, listing the operations which supply information for the message, and attaching a sample copy.

Signals are displayed on message sheets when they are critical inputs to an operation. For a customer-service or telephone-order department, incoming telephone calls are typical input signals that would require description on a message sheet.

The last document we shall consider in this example is a file sheet. An example from the charge account activity of the Associated Retailers Company is shown in Figure 8–9. A file sheet is used to identify,

Figure 8-9 An example of a file sheet from the charge account activity from the Associated Retailers company.

FILE NAME							FILE NO.			
CUSTOMER FILE							F 0400			

LOCATION: COLLECTIONS DEPT. **STORAGE MEDIUM:** TUB FILE

ACCESS REQUIREMENTS:
① ≤ 1 MIN (CREDIT CHECK); ② ≤ 1 DAY (POSTING); ③ CYCLE:
1 CYCLE / DAY , 20 CYCLES / MO. (BILLING)

SEQUENCED BY: ACCOUNT NUMBER

CONTENT QUALIFICATIONS: CUSTOMER RECORDS HAVING ACTIVITY WITHIN LAST 6 MONTHS.

HOW CURRENT: DATA UP TO 1 DAY OLD WHEN ENTERED.

RETENTION CHARACTERISTICS: CUSTOMER RECORDS NOT HAVING ACTIVITY WITHIN LAST 6 MONTHS ARE MOVED TO INACTIVE FILE.

LABELS:

REMARKS: FILE USED FOR 3 PURPOSES : CREDIT CHECK , POSTING , BILLING .

CONTENTS

SEQUENCE NO.	MESSAGE NAME	VOLUME		CHARACTERS PER MESSAGE	CHARACTERS PER FILE	
		AVG	PEAK		AVG	PEAK
01	CUSTOMER RECORD	500K	550K	553	276,500K	304,150K

DATE _____ **ANALYST** _____ **SOURCE:** COLLECTIONS - ALDRICH **PAGE:** 1 OF 1

STUDY: ASSOCIATED RETAILERS INC.

locate, and describe each ordered collection of messages that is needed as an information resource in an operation.

The upper sections of the file sheet identify the file by name, number, location, and storage medium; display access requirements; describe the type of material in the file; and outline the retention characteristics. If pertinent, they show who is and who is not allowed access to the file, tell how long the file is open and how often, or how quickly, it must be used, and similar operating characteristics.

The file sheet in Figure 8-9 describes the customer file of the charge account activity. This file serves three purposes in the charge account operations: (1) It must be quickly checked for credit authorization when the customer is in the store to buy, (2) it must be posted daily with new charges (and also with credits from payments and returns), and (3) one-twentieth of the total file must be billed daily for a monthly billing cycle. These details are entered in the **Access Requirements** field. In other fields are entered content qualifications (further explained by the entry in **Retention Characteristics**) and information on the immediacy of the file data and the method of sequencing the records in the file. Entries regarding file growth or peculiarities of usage appear under **Remarks**.

The lower section, **Contents**, provides space for identifying and characterizing the documents stored in the file. Data are entered both for average and peak volumes of documents and for average and peak volumes of characters. The latter are of only incidental importance in a manually-maintained file (as in the charge account activity) but become critically important in mechanized filing systems.

The five descriptive forms work together to enable an analyst to document the critical characteristics of an existing system. In the charge account activity previously discussed, the resource usage sheet provides graphic illustration of the way the activity fits into a section of the department store and of the cost of that activity. The activity sheet displays the flow of operations that make up the servicing of charge accounts. The operation sheet permits closer analysis of two operations selected for their critical effect on the activity. The message and file sheets permit a close-up of inputs to and outputs from the activity and the information resources used by it.

8.9 DOCUMENTATION IN A MECHANIZED SYSTEM

This section gives the reader a chance to see some of the basic forms used to document information in a study of a mechanized system.

The forms are taken from a case study of the system of a wholesale distributor, Atlantic Distributors, Inc. The particular activity under investigation was defined as *order-processing*.

The order-processing activity of a wholesale distributor provides a good example of a mechanized business system. The fact that machinery is used to perform many operations in the activity does not alter the requirements of the study in any substantial way, although it does place greater restrictions on certain types of information — records contained on punched cards, for instance, may need to be more rigorously described. But the main purpose of the study is to gain a coherent understanding of the system. The same basic five data collection forms are used.

The use of these forms to describe a mechanized system makes it easy to arrive at a clear understanding of the dynamics of system operation. The mass of detail data which conventionally emerges from a study of a mechanized system is considered only as supporting documentation. The structure and dynamic flow of the activity are clearly exposed in the five recording forms.

The information entered in the resource usage sheet is the same in both the mechanized and nonmechanized cases. The top part contains an organization chart of the business structure (in this case, the wholesale distributor) which contains all components affecting the activity of interest. The bottom part contains a summary tabulation of costs for each organizational component, with costs broken out and itemized for each activity and summed for an activity total. The resource usage sheet for Atlantic Distributors is not shown because the material is so similar to that already given in the nonmechanized system example. The activity sheet, however, differs.

The activity sheet in Figure 8 – 10 traces the mechanism of the order-processing activity. There are three main sequences: preparation of orders for shipment; preparation of will-call orders; and preparation of invoices, into which sequence both of the others feed. The orders-for-shipment sequence can be triggered by a salesman's order, received by mail or telephone, or by customer purchase orders, however received. In the case of a telephoned salesman's order or customer purchase order, a preliminary step is needed to prepare the sales order before the main sequence is begun with a credit check. The straight-line flow of the main sequence is not interrupted by what in some documenting or programming systems would be considered an exception loop, the preparation of a back order. The operation is included in the main path; if a back order is necessary, it is prepared as a normal tabulating room operation. If it is not needed,

Figure 8–10 An example of an activity sheet for a mechanized system. This particular sheet documents the order processing activity of Atlantic Distributors.

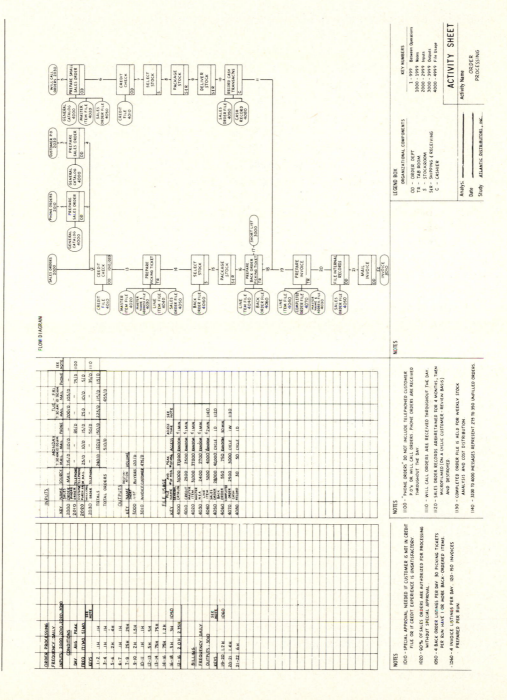

the step is skipped. Volume for the *short list* indicates frequency of execution.

In such an activity as order processing, the condition and frequency of inputs, and the elapsed times for various processes under average and peak loads, are critical parameters. These are listed in detail in the grid section on the activity sheet. Peculiarities of the system and amplifying data are displayed under **Notes**.

Two outputs from the activity are the invoice to the customer and the short list which guides the buyers. The merchandise can reasonably be considered an output, but for the purpose of this information-system example, it has not been covered.

Files are of paramount importance in the order-processing activity. File usage data are displayed in great detail. Five of the files must be randomly accessible in less than two minutes. A comparison of input volumes with these file access requirements quickly discloses whether the file arrangement is creating a bottleneck in the activity. This comparison also permits an estimate of when processing limitations may be reached.

The connection between activity sheets and operation sheets was mentioned earlier. The operation sheet shown in Figure 8–11 supports two operations: (1) the **Prepare Picking Ticket** operation occurs between Points 13 and 14 of the flowchart and (2) the **Prepare Invoice** operation between Points 19 and 20.

The picking ticket is used in the stockroom to select the merchandise for packing and shipment. The invoice is one of the two outputs to the activity's external environment. Both operations are mechanized sequences using tab room facilities which are listed in the **Resources** field on the Operation Sheet.

Although the whole order-processing activity has two outputs (the customer invoice and the short list), each processing step has its own inputs and outputs. There are five outputs, for example, from the operation **Prepare Picking Ticket:** (1) the picking ticket itself, sent to the order department, (2) line item cards and (3) name and address cards, to be filed for use in the invoice-preparation sequence, (4) a control sheet used by the order department for picking ticket control, and (5) the sales order—not prepared in this operation, but rather the input to it—which is sent back to the order department.

The sales order is the only input to this operation, and the trigger is its arrival. This is an example of a single-input trigger; it indicates that the operation is performed for each input. The analyst should be alert for such a trigger, since possible increases in efficiency may be

Figure 8–11 An example of an operation sheet for two operations in a mechanized activity. The form was taken from the Atlantic Distributors case study.

OPERATION		TRIGGERS, INPUTS AND OUTPUTS					PROCESSES			RESOURCES			
NO	PERFORMED BY	ID NO	NAME AND QUALIFICATIONS	RECEIVED FROM OR SENT TO	VOLUME AVG/PER	ELAPSED TIME	ID NO	DESCRIPTION AND QUALIFICATIONS	FREQ	ID NO	TYPE	UNIT TIME	TOTAL TIME AVG/PER
030 001	TAB ROOM	TI	RECEIPT OF SALES ORDER				P1	SELECT MASTER ITEM CARD FOR EACH	$15/11$	X1	KEYPUNCH OPR. (3)	24H/OP	
(KEY NOS. 13-14)		II	SALES ORDER	ORDER DEPT.	475 D	O		LINE ITEM ON SALES ORDER		X2	TAB MACHINE OPR.	4½H/OP	
		RI	PICKING TICKET	STOCKROOM	475 D	$1/10$ D	P2	PREPARE LINE ITEM CARD	$15/11$	X3	KEYPUNCH WITH CARD	24H/OP	
		R2	LINE ITEM CARDS	FILE	7125 D	$1/12$ D	P3	REFILE MASTER ITEM CARD	$15/11$		INSERTION DEV. (3)		
		R3	NAME AND ADDRESS CARDS	FILE	1425 D	$1/12$ D	P4	SORT LINE ITEM CARDS TO STOCKROOM	$1/101$	X4	SORTER	1H/OP	
		R4	CONTROL SHEET	ORDER DEPT.	48 D	$1/10$ D		LOC'N WITHIN CUSTOMER NO.		X5	ACCTG. MACH.	1H/OP	
		R5	SALES ORDER	ORDER DEPT.	475 D	$1/10$ D	P5	SELECT NAME AND ADDRESS CARDS	$1/11$	X6	PANEL	1H/OP	
							P6	INSERT NAME AND ADDRESS CARDS	$1/11$	X7	MASTER ITEM		24H D
								IN FRONT OF LINE ITEM CARDS			CARD FILE (3)		
								FOR EACH CUSTOMER.		X8	MASTER N&A FILE		2½H D
							P7	PREPARE PICKING TICKET AND	$1/11$	X9	LINE ITEM FILE		4H D
								CONTROL SHEET					
							P8	FILE NAME AND ADDRESS CARDS	$1/11$				
								AND LINE ITEM CARDS					
030 010	TAB ROOM	TI	RECEIPT OF PICKING TICKET				P1	SELECT NAME AND ADDRESS CARDS AND	$1/11$	X1	TAB MACHINE OPR.	4½H/OP	
(KEY NOS. 19-20)		II	PICKING TICKET	STOCKROOM	475 D	O		LINE ITEM CARDS		X2	CALCULATOR	1H/OP	
		RI	INVOICE	ORDER DEPT.	475 D	½H	P2	COMPUTE INVOICE AMOUNT AND COST	$1/11$	X3	PANEL	1H/OP	
		R2	PICKING TICKET	ORDER DEPT.	475 D	1H		AMOUNT AND GROSS PROFIT		X4	PUNCH	1H/OP	
							P3	PREPARE INVOICE	$1/11$	X5	PANEL	1H/OP	
							P4	SELECT NAME AND ADDRESS CARDS	$1/11$	X6	ACCTG. MACH.	1H/OP	
							P5	FILE NAME AND ADDRESS CARDS	$1/11$	X7	PANEL	1H/OP	
							P6	FILE LINE ITEM CARDS	$1/11$	X8	LINE ITEM FILE		4H D
										X9	MASTER N&A FILE		2½H D
										X10	COMPLETED		2½H D
											ORDERS FILE		

DATE   ANALYST   TAB ROOM – PANELLI (SOURCE)   ATLANTIC DISTRIBUTORS INC. (STUDY)   ORDER PROCESSING (ACTIVITY)   3 (PAGE)

obtained by batching input items and using a multiple-input trigger of six or ten orders or more. Noticing these conditions during the preliminary survey sometimes eases subsequent design problems.

In the invoice-preparation operation, again a single input—the picking ticket, received after use in the stockroom—triggers the sequence. The sole output besides the picking ticket is the invoice itself; both are sent to the order department.

The process descriptions include the individual steps which the machines perform and the multiple references to files. These process steps are described by verbs much like the language of a computer programmer: *sort, prepare, compute.* The steps of a tabulating room procedure are similar to computer subroutines of the type used during the execution of a program.

Frequency data listed as process qualifications should be fairly precise estimates, as should the times required of the various mechanical, material, and informational resources.

Figure 8–12 An example of a two-page message sheet describing the layout of a punched card for a mechanized system. (The second page is shown in the second part of this figure.)

MESSAGE NAME		MESSAGE NO.	
LINE ITEM CARD		R 3008	
OTHER NAMES USED		LAYOUT NO.	
PARTS CARD		02	
		FORM NO.	
		D 17130	
		NO. OF COPIES	
		1	

MEDIA	HOW PREPARED
PUNCHED CARD	KEYPUNCHED – FROM MASTER ITEM CARD [1]

OPERATIONS INVOLVED IN

030-001, 030-007, 030-010, 030-017, 030-020, 030-021,

AND ACCOUNTING DISTRIBUTION

AND STOCK ANALYSIS

REMARKS

[1] ORIGINALLY PREPARED FROM MASTER ITEM CARD (OPERATION 030-001).

LATER ENTRIES ARE KEYPUNCHED OR CALCULATED.

		CONTENTS				
NO.	DATA NAME		FREQUENCY	CHARACTERS	A/N	ORIGIN
01	ITEM NUMBER		1	6	N	030 - 001
02	ITEM NAME		1	10	AN	030 - 001
03	DEPARTMENT CODE		1	1	AN	030 - 001
04	COMMODITY CODE		1	1	AN	030 - 001
05	UNIT OF MEASURE		1	2	A	030 - 001
06	QUANTITY ORDERED		1	5	N	030 - 001
07	QUANTITY FILLED		.20	5	N	030 - 007
08	QUANTITY BACK ORDERED		.20	5	N	030 - 007
09	UNIT COST		1	5	N	030 - 001
10	TOTAL COST		1	6	N	030 - 010
11	UNIT GROSS MARGIN		1	4	N	030 - 001
12	TOTAL GROSS MARGIN		1	5	N	030 - 010
13	UNIT SELLING PRICE		1	5	N	030 - 001
14	TOTAL SELLING PRICE		1	6	N	030 - 010
15	CUSTOMER NO.		1	4	N	030 - 001

DATE	ANALYST	TAB ROOM	1 OF 2
		SOURCE	PAGE

ATLANTIC DISTRIBUTORS INC.
STUDY

Figure 8–12 (contd.)

MESSAGE NAME			MESSAGE NO.	
–CONTINUED–			R 3008	
OTHER NAMES USED			LAYOUT NO. 02	
			FORM NO. D 17130	
			NO. OF COPIES	
MEDIA		HOW PREPARED		
OPERATIONS INVOLVED IN				

REMARKS

CONTENTS

NO.	DATA NAME	FREQUENCY	CHARACTERS	A/N	ORIGIN
16	SALESMAN NO.	1	2	N	030 – 001
17	STOCKROOM LOCATION	1	4	AN	030 – 001
18	TRANSACTION CODE	1	1	AN	030 – 010
19	DATE PICKED	1	3	N	030 – 010

DATE   ANALYST   TAB ROOM   2 OF 2

SOURCE   PAGE

ATLANTIC DISTRIBUTORS INC.

STUDY

The supporting documentation illustrated for this mechanized example consists of the line item card described in the message sheet in Figure 8–12 and the file in which these messages are stored, described in the file sheet in Figure 8–13.

In Figure 8–12, the fields of the line item card (R2 from the first operation in the operation sheet) are delineated in the **Contents** section of the message sheet; a second page is required to list the information. The descriptive data in the upper half of the sheet display the operations with which the unit record is involved; typically, a punched card will be used in multiple operations.

In Figure 8–13, the reader should review every item and note the retention characteristics of the file. During the order-processing activity, the line item card and its associated customer name and address cards constitute a transient record, needed only until the picking ticket is returned to the tab room after the stockroom has filled the order. This information is shown on the file sheet, plus the added information that the file is purged in a special machine run every two weeks to make sure that no order or back order has been overlooked.

Message characteristics are taken off the message sheet, multiplied by average and peak character volumes per file. In the case of a multiple-record file (as in the present example), the total volumes and character counts should be recorded in order to display the overall characteristics of a mechanized file.

The reader should not forget that there will normally be a separate operation sheet for each operation in the activity and as many message and file sheets as needed to provide the information required on significant reports or signals.

As in the preceding example of a nonmechanized system, the basic reporting forms permit a clear picture to be developed of the workings of a business system. They answer the question: What is being done? To a great extent, they also permit the analyst to find out how it is done, in terms of the activities and operations that thread through the business system

SUMMARY

A system study requires documentation so that information is recorded and available for later use. Forms can facilitate documentation but must be used as needed, with design flexibility dictated by the functions of the enterprise. Five basic documents for recording infor-

Figure 8–13 An example of a file sheet from a mechanized system.

FILE NAME							FILE NO.		
LINE ITEM FILE							F 3404.1		

LOCATION TAB ROOM **STORAGE MEDIUM** IBM CARD TUB FILE

ACCESS REQUIREMENTS
DATA FOR ORDER MUST BE AVAILABLE WITHIN 2 MINUTES.

SEQUENCED BY
STOCKROOM LOCATION WITHIN CUSTOMER NUMBER

CONTENT QUALIFICATIONS
NAME AND ADDRESS CARDS AND LINE ITEM CARDS FOR PICKING
TICKETS IN PROCESS OR BACK-ORDERED.

HOW CURRENT
I TO 5 HOURS OLD WHEN ENTERED. REMAIN IN FILE UNTIL
STOCKROOM HAS ATTEMPTED TO FILL PICKING TICKET.

RETENTION CHARACTERISTICS
DATA NORMALLY REMOVED UPON RECEIPT OF PICKING TICKET,
SPECIAL PURGE RUN ONCE EVERY 2 WEEKS.

LABELS ——

REMARKS

CONTENTS

SEQUENCE NO.	MESSAGE NAME	VOLUME		CHARACTERS PER MESSAGE	CHARACTERS PER FILE	
		AVG	PEAK		AVG	PEAK
01	CUSTOMER NAME CARD	320	400	61	19,520	24,400
02	CUSTOMER ADDRESS CARDS	640	800	65	41,600	52,000
03	LINE ITEM CARDS	2250	2800	52	117,000	145,600
	TOTALS	3210	4000	178	178,120	222,000

DATE ___   **ANALYST** ___   **SOURCE** TAB ROOM   **PAGE** I OF I

ATLANTIC DISTRIBUTORS INC. **STUDY**

mation during the analysis of an existing system are the resource usage sheet, the activity sheet, the operation sheet, the message sheet, and the file sheet. The resource usage sheet fits each system under study into its larger organizational context. The activity sheet traces the flow of a single activity and breaks it down into its major operations. The operation sheet records the related processing steps that form a logical operation. The message sheet and the file sheet support the operation sheet. The message sheet describes the inputs and outputs of an operation. The file sheet shows with what stored information an operation works.

QUESTIONS AND PROBLEMS

8–1 What primary purpose do the documentation forms serve?

8–2 Would it be of any value to management to have available a resource usage sheet (as shown in Figure 8–2) for each year, six months, or quarter?

8–3 Why is it that so many departments of a company can be interested in the same source document?

8–4 What might be the purpose of a company administrative blueprint?

8–5 Explain the difference between a routine document and a management report.

8–6 In addition to the message and file sheets described in the text, would a *field description sheet* be of any value? What information might such a sheet include?

8–7 Examine Figure 8–12. If Atlantic sells a quantity of eleven of a given item at $999.99 each, will the line item card be able to hold all the data?

8–8 Based on the information contained in Figure 8–12, what is the highest possible unit price for an item sold by Atlantic Distributors?

8–9 Based on the information contained in Figure 8–12, what is the greatest number of departments that the Atlantic Distributors could have?

8–10 On the average, how many active customers does Atlantic Distributors have?

CHAPTER 9
PREPARING AND PRESENTING THE REPORT OF THE EXISTING SYSTEM

9.1 PURPOSE OF THE REPORT

The final task for analysts studying an existing system is to organize and present results to management in a written report called the Present Business Description.

The report includes a letter of transmittal; an introduction; general, structural, and operational sections; and an appendix where necessary. In evaluating what should be included and how much, study teams should ask themselves: Why do we have a report and what useful purposes does it serve? Among other objectives, the report must:

1. Demonstrate an understanding of the existing business
2. Develop a new view of the business in terms of activities
3. Establish benchmarks in time, cost, and accuracy
4. Serve as an adequate base for conducting later phases of the study
5. Present in one place a complete description of the business (for people who know certain parts well but lack the total picture)
6. Provide a dictionary of terminology and language unique to the business
7. Communicate the description for consistent interpretation by a diverse audience

9.2 THE REPORT

Introduction to the Report The introduction sets the climate for the report and gives the ground rules for performing the study as they were agreed to initially by management and the team.

The purpose of the study is stated, and the study scope defined. Was the study undertaken to create a wholly new system, or to improve the existing system? Was the objective to obtain dollar savings by improving operating efficiency, or was it to raise the quality of performance of the business? Whatever the purpose of the study, it should be explained in the introduction to the report, even if it is already widely known. The principal points covered in stating the scope are:

1. Areas of the business included (and excluded) in the study
2. Level of detail to be applied to what activities and departments
3. Modifications of the original agreement or study plan

Closely related to a discussion of scope are those special extensions of authority (or restrictions on authority) which apply to the conduct of a study. This statement includes rules on access to confidential information, restrictions on the release of operating data, contacts with employees and managers for interviews, permission to investigate special situations, use of processing facilities, and other matters that pertain to sound business practice and the maintenance of good relations.

The purpose of each major report section is briefly discussed. The purposes may be stated as:

Section	Purpose
General	Describe the environment in which the business operates and the position of that business in the environment
Structural	Amplify the description of the business in terms of inputs, outputs, and resources
Operational	Define activities and relate them to the established framework of the business
Appendix	Present more detailed documentation on the activities of the business

The final part of the introduction is a summary of the team's overall results and recommendations. What are the key facts on each of the activities in regard to size, volume, cost, and time? What suggestions does the team have on possible immediate improvements? What other insights of possible value to management were gained in the study? This last part of the introduction is vital. It gives management some idea of the value of the study, even though it is devoted mainly to a description of the present system.

9.3 REPORT MECHANICS

At the conclusion of data gathering, the study team usually has a large collection of notes, exhibits, flowcharts, and miscellaneous documents representing the sum of their efforts over the time of the study. Now the problem is to sort wheat from chaff — combine, condense, and edit the material, converting it to a report that has balance, continuity, and flow. Examples from earlier chapters can be used as guides for preparing individual parts of the three major report sections. Once the preparation of these sections has been accomplished, the total report is evaluated once more for completeness, sequence, and relationships among the several parts. Data processing equipment can be used to enter, edit, lay out, and print the report.

The general section, with its emphasis on narrative, is directed mainly to the top management audience, as is the structural section. However, the presentation of structural information shifts from a concentration on narrative to a more extensive use of visual aids employed to achieve maximum data coverage in a minimum of reading time. Where possible, data are displayed in line charts, bar graphs, pictures, layouts, floor plans, lists, and summaries. Some narrative is required for transition, explanation, and interpretation, and for a sense of pace and flow of ideas.

The operational section is aimed principally at the systems engineer or analyst, and resource usage and activity sheets can be included here without annotation. However, a number of study teams have found that managers show considerable interest in these forms (particularly the resource usage sheets and summaries of volumes and elapsed times), and some verbal explanation may be helpful to point out significant data and results.

When they are part of a study, operation sheets, message sheets, file sheets, and special detail exhibits are located in the appendix without further notation.

The length of the report depends largely on the size and complexity of the business to be described. In Butodale, for example, the general section runs six pages, and the structural section contains twenty-seven pages. Worthington Hardware has twelve and twenty-three pages, respectively; National Bank of Commerce contains sixteen and twenty-five pages to cover these two sections. The inclusion of a great deal of data on manufacturing equipment lengthened Butodale's facilities section and added little to an understanding of the business. The same can be said for the four pages of notes appended to the financial statements in the Worthington report.

9.4 AUDITING THE REPORT

As the study team assembles data into a final report, individual sections are tested against accepted standards for good business reports. Considering the importance of time and economy, the information content should be adequate for its immediate purpose, but not too detailed. The parts of the report should demonstrate coherence and unity, so that each part evolves sequentially from the preceding parts. Consistency implies that events of the same importance will be treated generally in the same way, or to the same level of detail, so that the report audience need not switch frames of reference from subject to subject.

The study team can ask a few specific questions that help appraise the report.

1. *Are there any gaps?* Are operations missing from the documentation of any activity? Do the activities traced out in the operational section adequately represent the business or business sector that is in the scope of the study? Any omitted activities should be noted to show their impact on the activities described in the study.

2. *Do the descriptions at each of the various levels give the same kinds of information, in the same detail, and in the same form?* Coherence and consistency within each of the three sections is important for comprehension. Detailed descriptions of products and markets in the structural section, for example, should be matched in tone, form, and detail by the descriptions of materials and suppliers if both are equally important. Two equally important activities traced out in the operational section should be documented to the same depth; if message sheets are prepared for one activity, they should be prepared for the other; if input and output operations are omitted from one, they should be omitted from the other. An audience is affected by the proportion and balance of a report, and if an unimportant process is omitted from the documentation of one activity and not from another, the process will assume unwarranted importance in the second case.

3. *Is the environment consistent across the entire present business description?* Environment includes the surroundings which are directly outside the scope of the study. In the study of a complete business, consistent environment is no problem: It is everything not in the organization studied. But if one part of a company has been set off as the business (the subject of the study), then other departments of the company that influence the study become part of the environment.

4. *Is the level of detail adequate for the phases to follow?* A subsequent phase of requirements analysis follows, as does the phase in which a new system is designed and communicated. Before the study of the present system is finished, the analyst should determine whether or not the information serves as a *foundation* for determining requirements of the system and for designing the new system. If not, the team should seek further operational data.

9.5 DYNAMIC ASPECTS OF THE REPORT

So far the study has been referred to as describing and understanding the present business, but it has other important purposes. The general and structural sections portray static elements of the business; but in the operational section, the business is described by activities which contribute to goals and objectives, a recasting which views the enterprise from a new angle. Starting from the broad base of organization and costs on a resource usage sheet, the description moves into a display of individual activities on activity sheets, supplemented where necessary by operation, message, and file sheets. Thorough understanding of the business must be demonstrated as the documentation includes progressively more detail and as it builds upward from file, message, and operation sheets to activity and resource usage sheets. Each of the documentation forms contributes data to other forms. If operation sheets are weak in time and cost information and strong on the sequence of events, then flowcharts of activities can be drawn up accurately, but without sufficient factual data for a cost allocation on the resource usage sheets or for the tabular section of the activity sheet. The team analysts must be sensitive to the total data requirements and continually think about the impact of each file studied in relationship to broad data requirements.

Description of a communications network from the complete system to its elemental parts and back to its whole again is an example of how description interacts from section to section. The capacity is set for the network in the structural section, while utilization and operations variability are covered in the operational section. Failure to inject flow and relationship among the several sections will produce a total description of the business, but it will be static, not dynamic.

9.6 PRESENTATION OF THE REPORT

When the report is finished, a cover letter of transmittal is prepared even though the recipient may be the analyst's own management. The principal function of this letter is to transmit the report formally; it need not be long or detailed. Since this is a well-recognized document, it needs little comment, except that key officials are thanked for their interest and cooperation, and a request is made for an audience to review the findings in the near future.

The report should be presented to management far enough in advance of a formal review session to permit knowledgeable discussion when the analysts make their oral summary.

An oral presentation is sometimes more effective with the use of enlarged exhibits to illustrate general and structural data and the resource usage sheet. Narrative from the general section can be converted to flipcharts. Under no circumstances should the report be read as written. Nor should the presentation cover the data exactly as written. The presentation will be most effective if it is somewhat extemporaneous with well-prepared charts used for emphasis and support.

9.7 A TYPICAL PROCEDURE

Figure 9-1 contains a diagram illustrating a typical procedure for collecting data and for preparing a report of an existing organization.

In studying the flow of the chart, readers can put themselves in the place of an analyst, or the leader of the study team. As a matter of fact, a modification of this diagram could be useful in the preliminary part of the study in which the analysts explain to management what they propose to do during their work in studying the business. Another use of this diagram could be in estimating times for the study. As analysts go through a study, they can keep a record of their time for

Figure 9–1 A procedure for collecting data and preparing a report of an existing organization.

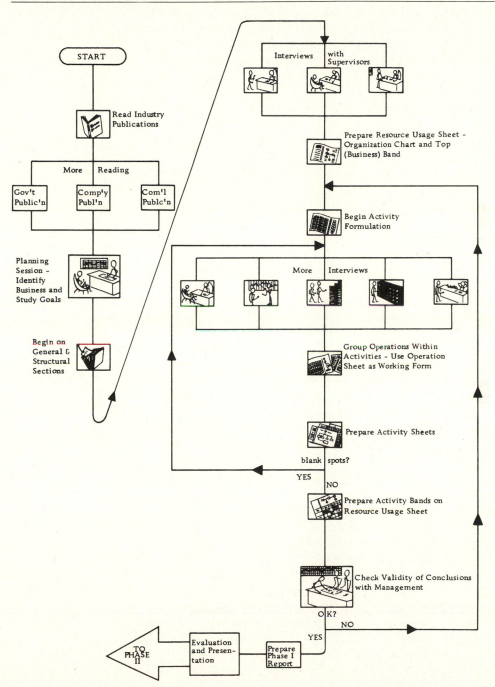

each aspect shown in the diagram. After a few studies, they will have an idea of the time required for each kind of search and preparation. Then, when entering a new study, they will have some data for making time estimates from start to completion.

9.8 LOOKING AHEAD

After the report on the existing system has been prepared, audited, presented, and accepted by management, Phase I is complete. In actual practice, though, there is no abrupt demarcation among the three phases, since the transition is progressive and some of the work overlaps. While studying the present business, analysts always look ahead to the requirements of system specifications and design, and in later phases they look back to recall earlier results and conclusions.

Concurrently with Phase I report preparation, some team members will be refining goal and activity definitions and analyzing system requirements. In this work, many different analytical techniques will be applied to devise a system specification.

SUMMARY

The report of the existing system consists of a letter of transmittal; an introduction; general, structural, and operational sections; and an appendix when necessary. The introduction includes definitions of the purpose and scope of the study and a summary of the team's overall results and recommendations. The general section describes the environment in which the business operates. The structural section amplifies the description of the business in terms of input, output, and resources. The operational section defines activities and relates them to the established framework of the business. The appendix presents more detailed documentation of the activities of the business. Before it is presented to management, the report must be carefully audited for correctness and completeness. The report is reviewed with management and an oral presentation made, using visual aids to supplement the report. The information in the report of the existing system is used in the next phase of the study: System Requirements Specification.

QUESTIONS AND PROBLEMS

9-1 The text states that the report of Phase I is useful in Phases II and III, during which systems requirements are defined and a new system is designed. Which sections (general, structural, operational, appendix) would be most useful in Phase II? in Phase III?

9-2 Describe the key purposes of each of the sections of the present business description.

9-3 Briefly outline the various parts of a "Present Business Description" for a major league baseball team.

CHAPTER 10
THE EXISTING SYSTEM
FOR BUTODALE

10.1 GUIDE TO STUDY OF THE BUTODALE CASE

Chapter 10 presents extracts from a report for a real organization. The purpose is to provide some tangible results of the methodology covered thus far. The Butodale Electronics Company is a fictitious name given to a real company.

Examination of the material will help the student achieve a general impression of the total content. A guide to the report in the next section serves to emphasize main points in the report. This is a detailed case study, whose very length may provide special opportunities for analysis and evaluation projects.

For convenient reference and for consistency with the numbering system of the book, the figures that appear in the case study are re-numbered. Designations I, II, and so on for the original report are now numbers 10−1, 10−2, and so on. The actual years for the company's data have been coded as 0, 1, . . . , 8, 9.

First, the reader should merely examine the main sections of the report in order to compare its contents with the general outline described in Chapter 4. This overall perusal provides a chance to see the report as a totality. Management personnel normally examine a report in much the same way when they first receive it.

As far as the technical aspects of report writing are concerned, style and arrangement vary with the organization and the circumstances in which the report is prepared. Consequently, what the reader sees in the following section could be arranged in various formats. Here style and arrangement are not the subject; only content is. The principal requirement of arrangement is that it be convenient to use and suitable for the purpose of conveying information.

The main topic in the introduction to the report is the scope. Only a brief statement is needed because management should see immediately what the study has covered.

The general section contains topics that one would ordinarily expect management to know well. However, in a dynamic business most members of management are busy with their functional specialties and seldom get to see the overall picture. Also, the analysts have talked to many people in the company and have examined many records. Even in a large company, such a study may never have been done before; and this composite picture is of interest to most people in management as a unique collection of data.

From the history, background, and policies sections of the Butodale report, one gets the impression of a young, dynamic company. One can almost see the early beginning, with a small group of energetic people succeeding in starting a company and then working hard to expand it. The statistical summaries were included primarily to give management a better picture of the growth and the distribution of sales among their products.

The structural section opens with a figure which contains Butodale's business model. The environment is called the market, and it comprises both vendors and customers. The number and type of items Butodale purchases, and their outputs, are also designated. The analysts listed four types of resources — two of them given with dollar amounts, one with numbers of people, and one with the number of facilities. Here, it might also be good to include dollar figures. This model is intended to attract management's attention. In most organizations it is the first diagram to be discussed at length during the oral presentation. It helps to focus management's attention on the nature of their business.

The next significant exhibit is Figure 10–3, which shows the growth of sales for each major product. At a glance, management can get an accurate picture of performance for the last five years. The other financial statements may be of less interest as they are routine financial documents, yet they are necessary inclusions for completeness of the report. Figure 10–9 is of greater interest, for it shows the dynamic growth in sales and net worth. Note that the profit picture is not so strong. If these exhibits are frequently used by management, they form an important input to the study team beginning to synthesize the requirements statement covered later.

The organization chart in Figure 10–12 is often of interest because in many organizations this kind of chart may not exist or may be out of date.

Perhaps the main single exhibit of interest to management would be Figure 10–13. In addition to the routine presentation of functional departments and their costs are the six activities that the study team discovered, defined, and described. This method of viewing the company is unusual for most organizations. At a glance one finds that it costs Butodale about $1.5 million to carry on the activity of providing the demand for the company's products. The other activity of providing end products excited this particular management. In fact, their evaluation of these two activities, in conjunction with their study of the corresponding activity sheets, brought them to the conclusion that the study team should concentrate its efforts on these two activities during the second phase of the study.

This type of exhibit is particularly important in decentralized companies functionally organized (marketing, manufacturing, engineering, and the like) under a general manager. Each functional element optimizes its own function with respect to data handling. But this usually creates problems in managing the interfaces among functions. Identification of these interfaces through horizontal activity formulation and the accumulation of total activity costs can often lead to the identification of fundamental problems of concern to a general manager. It further leads to key requirements for data processing.

Ordinarily, top management does not spend much time on the appendix. Some members of the junior levels of management and supervision, however, will possibly be more concerned with this information. In reviewing the material, the reader may wish to examine R–2000. This message sheet contains the description of the typical customer request for a quotation from Butodale. This message serves to trigger the activity. This single trigger starts the whole left side of the activity of providing product demand.

Message R–3000 is the output of the left side of the activity shown in Figure 10–15. It is the document that Butodale sends to the customer in response to the request for a quotation. The document shown immediately after message R–3000 is a photograph of a blank quotation sheet that Butodale uses.

The reader will also note file sheets and operation sheets such as F-4050.1 (the description of a quote folder—an ordinary manila folder—into which the customer's request for a quotation has been placed) and 001-540 (where the arrival of the quote folder triggers the start of this operation). In the flow diagram in Figure 10–15 one sees that Operation 540 is **Prepare Bid Sheet.** Operation 001–540 has four processes in the operation, P1 to P4; and there are four resources, X1 to X4. From this sheet, one can easily envision the quote specialist (X1) performing the four processes by using the operational reference manuals, the cost file (F–4010), and the price catalog.

Thus, one personnel resource uses three information resources to perform four processes in accomplishing the **Prepare Bid Sheet** operation of the **Provide Product Demand** activity.

The cost file is described in the file sheet numbered F–4010. An actual example of the kind of record in the file is shown on the next page after F–4010. In the flow diagram (Figure 10–15) one notes that the cost file is attached to the 630 operation, **Cost Material and Cost Labor,** and to the 570 operation, **Prepare Bid Summary.** However, it could also have been attached to Operation 540 because it also uses the file.

We now present the case study itself.

10.2 BUTODALE'S PRESENT BUSINESS DESCRIPTION

INTRODUCTION

Purpose and Scope

Purpose The management of Butodale Electronics Company requested that a study be made of the complete organization and its procedures. It was anticipated that the study would be conducted in three phases, namely:

1. Review the existing company.
2. Establish requirements for a new system.
3. Design and propose a new system employing automated procedures as much as possible.

The first phase has been completed and the purpose of this report is to present the results of that phase. Similar reports will be prepared as each of the two remaining phases are completed.

Project Scope The complete company has been studied in accordance with the original understanding. It was expected that during the study the team would search out those areas which could be automated with cost reduction. We believe that we have determined which areas meet those requirements and we explain them in this report.

Ground Rules

It was agreed that Butodale Electronics would authorize access to whatever data the team deemed necessary for the study.

The study team agreed to treat all information as confidential, and to obtain approval prior to removing documents, forms, and other company records from the normal storage locations.

Butodale management agreed to the request for interview facilities and time. Furthermore, the team was provided two offices, a conference room, and a supply room for use throughout the study. In addition, a secretary was to be assigned to the team full time and a clerk-assistant part time.

Thus far the study team has had excellent cooperation from all employees and we should like to express our appreciation. Further, to the best of our knowledge, the study team has acted within the initial requirements agreed to.

Content

The report consists of four sections: general, structural, operational, and appendix. The content of each section is:

General The general section describes Butodale's history, its industry background, its policies and practices, its objectives and goals, and the government regulations that affect it.

Structural The structural section provides a business model view of Butodale in terms of its vendors, inputs, outputs, customers, company operations, and its resources.

Operational The operational section presents the structure of Butodale both from the point of view of nineteen departmental functions and six operational activities.

Appendix The appendix contains the main documents that support the data presented in the operational section. Also, the methods and formulas the team used in arriving at the cost estimates are shown.

Summary and Findings

The study team was able to define six major activities for Butodale. These are:

1. Provide product demand
2. Provide material
3. Provide components
4. Provide end products
5. Provide engineered products and spare parts
6. Provide management, personnel and facilities

Now that the first phase of the study has been completed, it appears that the balance of the study should place emphasis on two activities: provide product demand and provide end products. We should like to review this report with Butodale management and explain why we recommend that our efforts be concentrated on these two activities.

GENERAL SECTION

History and Framework

The Butodale Electronics Company was established in 1961, incorporated in the State of Massachusetts. It was founded by four engineers and scientists who had worked together for a number of years in a large corporation on advanced government project work. Their main objective was to aid research laboratories and manufacturers in design and production of the latest radar, radio, and other electronic equipment.

It is significant that the corporation sales have increased from $170,000 to $15.9 million since its founding. Some of the major milestones in the last five years were:

1. Established the Worcester Computation Center to develop new fields of application for the analog computer (for example, heat transfer, nuclear engineering, process control engineering).
2. Established the Long Beach and Rio de Janeiro Computation Centers to extend what was started at Worcester and to educate prospective customers in the use of analog computer techniques.
3. Opened additional sales offices in Chicago and Forth Worth.
4. Greatly expanded and modernized the original plant in Danvers.
5. Instituted a major drive to secure overseas business, particularly in South America.

Industry Background

Butodale is in the electronics industry and specifically in the analog computer area. Analog computers are widely used industrial tools which fall into two categories, general purpose and special purpose computers. There is considerable competition in this industry; some of the biggest competitors are ABC Instrument, Jones Instrument, and National Systems, Inc. Many investment analysts feel there will be continued growth for the general-purpose computer, but this growth may not be at the same rate as in the past. The company agrees with the conclusions and, therefore, there is considerable stress put on finding new markets and new products. In order to uncover these areas and products, the company has set up a New Products Committee and a Market Analysis Section. It is the specific purpose of these groups to plan future growth and to direct engineering efforts towards this growth in order that the company may maintain a planned growth pattern of 20% per annum, or greater.

Some of the product areas under scrutiny are instruments, special purpose computers, and process control equipment. Likewise, industry statistical analyses by marketing areas are developed in order to concentrate effort in the proper industries. There has been no designed plan to integrate this company through component manufacture; however, it is not opposed to this type of growth if necessary to insure a reliable source of supply, and if excess capacity can be sold profitably. Recently, the company absorbed the Premium Capacitors Company and is now building high-quality capacitors.

Policies and Practices

Some of the major policies instituted by Butodale have unquestionably helped the company attain its position of eminence in the analog computer industry. One of these policies is the corporation's attitude towards its employees. Butodale has developed a labor philosophy in which it endeavors not to infringe on the private lives of its people, while offering liberal employee fringe benefits, including educational opportunities. The company makes a strenuous effort to keep layoffs to an absolute minimum. This policy has resulted in a fine labor-management atmosphere. This has made itself felt in pride of workmanship and company loyalty which are hard to equal in modern industry.

Another policy is building a superior product. Rigid quality control is a key to manufacturing ascendancy and, together with the labor policy, has produced an outstanding product with significant stature in the industry.

A third policy bears on market penetration. Butodale does not attempt to compete directly with giants in the industry, but rather to supplement them and their products and not engage in direct competition with their long-established lines.

Objectives and Goals

A major objective of this corporation is to expand sales and profits which will guarantee a proper return to stockholders and offer continued opportunity to employees.

The present sales goal is to increase gross by at least 20%; a net profit goal of 7% of sales and 15% of net worth has been established.

Government Regulations

Government regulations do not play a major role in company plans. However, a very high percentage of sales, perhaps 60%, is subject to renegotiation. Since the government sets profit objectives as a percent of sales, this has an effect on company plans and strategy.

Statistical Summary

Personnel and Space

Past 10 Years	Number of Individuals	Factory and General Office Square Footage
0	116	37,500
1	203	37,500
2	341	61,500
3	426	61,500
4	565	61,500
5	717	113,000
6	789	113,000
7	844	126,000
8	856	126,000
9	1069	130,000 (expandable to 250,000)

Products Sales for the Current Year

	Dollars (000)
General purpose analog computers	10,480
Large plotters	910
Data plotters	870
Computer Centers	725
Engineering and special fabrication	1,062
Small plotters	515
Multichannel recorders	347
Special purpose analog computers	320
Repair and service	180
Small general purpose analog computers	333
Instruments	173
	15,915

STRUCTURAL SECTION

Markets and Products

The domestic sales organization breakdown is as follows:

	Personnel
A. General Office	
Sales administration and clerical	8
Advertising and sales promotion	6
Development engineering sales	4
Service engineering	25
Standard parts sales	10
B. Branch Offices	
Eastern Region	11
Central Region	3
Southwestern Region	4
Western Region	7
Manufacturers' representatives	1

Standard Products Market

The market for the General Purpose Analog Computer, which makes up almost three fourths of Butodale's sales dollar, is quite difficult to identify. Applications, to date, have been in the research departments of large corporations; the customer list includes a generous portion of top American industry. Note, however, that although the term "General Purpose" implies a catalog or standard product, each computer is engineered to precise customer specifications.

The company merchandises the large computers through its own sales force, having four branch offices in the United States and one in South America. It also uses its computer centers to good advantage in the selling effort. Prospective customers can solve sample problems at these centers to gain a better appreciation of the equipment. The centers are also used for demonstrations and presentations.

Because the general purpose analog market is difficult to ascertain, the company has diversified its line to include a smaller computer and several sizes of plotting boards, as well as instruments. This diversification of products has presented additional distribution problems. Butodale has resolved these problems by having manufacturers' representatives handle the smaller, diversified lines. These new products and the method of merchandising them have only been in operation for a year, so it is difficult to forecast their full impact on sales.

Spare Parts Marketing Another source of revenue is the sale of spare parts to existing customers. These parts may be used as replacements, as spares, or to increase the capacity of the system. The market is approximately $1.5 million annually, and it is handled primarily on a

Figure 10–1 A business model for Butodale.

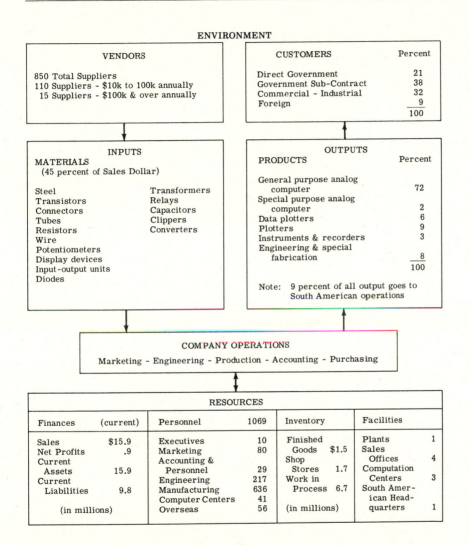

ENVIRONMENT

VENDORS

850 Total Suppliers
110 Suppliers - $10k to 100k annually
 15 Suppliers - $100k & over annually

CUSTOMERS	Percent
Direct Government	21
Government Sub-Contract	38
Commercial - Industrial	32
Foreign	9
	100

INPUTS

MATERIALS
 (45 percent of Sales Dollar)

Steel	Transformers
Transistors	Relays
Connectors	Capacitors
Tubes	Clippers
Resistors	Converters
Wire	
Potentiometers	
Display devices	
Input-output units	
Diodes	

OUTPUTS

PRODUCTS	Percent
General purpose analog computer	72
Special purpose analog computer	2
Data plotters	6
Plotters	9
Instruments & recorders	3
Engineering & special fabrication	8
	100

Note: 9 percent of all output goes to South American operations

COMPANY OPERATIONS

Marketing - Engineering - Production - Accounting - Purchasing

RESOURCES

Finances	(current)	Personnel	1069	Inventory		Facilities	
Sales	$15.9	Executives	10	Finished		Plants	1
Net Profits	.9	Marketing	80	Goods	$1.5	Sales	
Current		Accounting &		Shop		Offices	4
Assets	15.9	Personnel	29	Stores	1.7	Computation	
Current		Engineering	217	Work in		Centers	3
Liabilities	9.8	Manufacturing	636	Process	6.7	South Amer-	
		Computer Centers	41			ican Head-	
(in millions)		Overseas	56	(in millions)		quarters	1

telephone or correspondence basis. It certainly will continue to grow in direct proportion to the sales of major equipment.

Engineered Products Marketing The third major source of revenue is design and manufacture of specially engineered products in response to bids accepted. The present market is slightly more than $1 million and has been rising at a rate of approximately 20% per year since the company's

Figure 10–2 Comparative sales by product for Butodale for the last five years (years 5–9 of the past decade). All figures are in millions of dollars.

	Year				
	5	6	7	8	9
General purpose analog computers	4.0	6.6	8.1	7.9	10.5
Special purpose analog computers	.3	.5	.9	.6	.4
Large & small plotters	.5	.8	1.7	1.4	1.4
Data plotter	.1	.2	.3	.3	.9
Engineering	.4	.6	.8	.5	1.1
Recorders	.2	.3	.3	.3	.4
Computer centers	.3	.4	.5	.4	.7
Small general purpose computers	.2	.2	.2	.2	.3
Repair service	—	.1	.1	.1	.2
	6.0	9.7	12.9	11.7	15.9

founding. Profit is substantially lower than on standard products and spare parts, so Butodale does not actively market engineered products. It is significant that almost all basic engineering for standard products has been done when designing engineered products; thus, Butodale bidding depends on interest in the engineering design work required.

Materials and Suppliers Approximately 45% of the sales dollar at Butodale is the cost of material. Some of the major purchased materials include:

Steel	Capacitors
Transistors	Connectors
Tubes	Relays
Potentiometers	Wire
Display Devices	Resistors
Transformers	

At present Butodale controls this material by a procedure based on relative annual parts cost. It is important to note that the time lag for material purchased varies from two weeks to four months. An Order Record Card is sent to the buyer, who originates the purchase authorization. Different buyers handle different classes of items. Fifty percent of the time the buyer inspects the Order Record Card; selection is automatic the rest of the time. Ninety percent (90%) of the items handled through the inventory control section have Butodale part numbers, which makes processing very fast. When part numbers are missing or not assigned, it is difficult to determine if there is such an item, or if it is ordered directly by name and charged to a project.

Figure 10–3 Comparative sales by product for the past five years for Butodale Electronics.

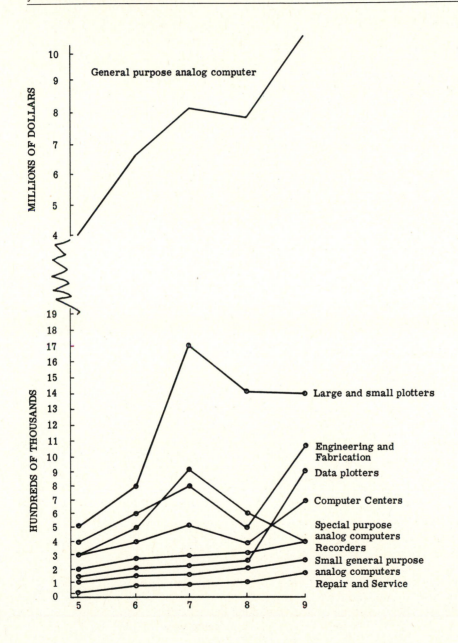

**Figure 10–4 Sales by customer group and region for
Butodale Electronics.**

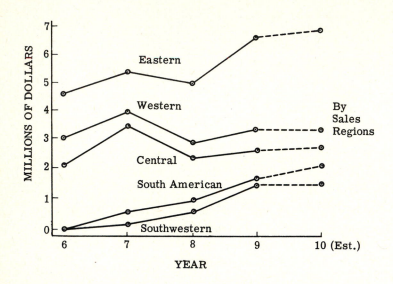

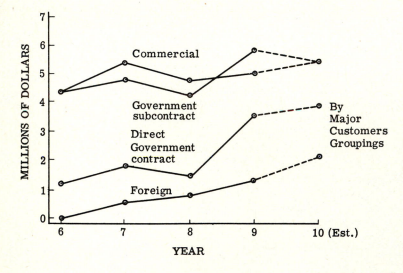

Figure 10–5 Financial summary for Butodale Electronics for the
past ten years.

		9	8	7	6	5	4	3	2	1	0
Thousands $	Net Sales	15,915	11,670	12,944	9,745	6,037	4,570	4,261	2,174	1,265	753
	Net Earnings before Taxes	1,763	709	2,226	2,184	1,138	547	258	268	175	49
	Net Earnings after Taxes	887	355	1,075	1,070	561	258	129	138	89	27
	Working Capital	6,154	5,691	4,938	3,612	1,733	1,030	726	568	284	150
	Long Term Debt	610	1,658	1,276	975	25	25	65	40	40	40
	Net Worth	7,548	5,277	4,206	3,046	2,057	1,452	909	685	427	261
	Stockholders (number)	3,143	2,170	1,485	921	717	527	418	314	151	77
	Earnings per share	.98	.80	2.48	2. 61	3.00	1.58	.79	.83	.42	.11
	Dividends - Common Stock	100% stock	3% stock	3% stock .50	100% stock .50	.25	.25	.10	--	--	--

Forms Flow	Annual Volume
Purchase Orders	13,500
Debit Memo or Shipping Notices	3,250
Individual Receipts of Material	34,000
Stores Requisitions	23,000
Material Requisitions	3,500
Work Orders Packaged	1,500

The company has about 850 suppliers, 125 of whom could be
considered major suppliers. Of these, 110 receive $10,000 to $100,000 of
business annually and the remaining 15 receive $100,000 or over. The
company endeavors to have multiple sources, but because of the high
quality of Butodale equipment, this is not always possible. A limited
number of very expensive attachments for systems input and output are
required; the purchase of these units is forecasted and an agreement
negotiated with the supplier giving an annual requirement with quantities
to be delivered at specified dates. This arrangement seems to work
satisfactorily. In view of the high-quality standards set by Butodale, all
incoming material must go through a stringent quality-control check. This,
on occasion, causes material shortages if inferior material is received.
Records are maintained to reflect these conditions and to eliminate
recurrence of such conditions.

Figure 10–6 Butodale's consolidated balance sheet.

ASSETS	9	8	7	6	5
Current Assets					
Cash and Receivables	1,436,711	781,346	834,790	185,488	133,847
Billings Receivable	4,916,245	4,139,861	2,946,381	2,573,222	1,862,585
Employee Receivables	10,761	9,278	5,004	3,614	2,005
Subscriptions Receivable	240,843	235,189	391,244	170,285	36,243
	6,604,560	5,165,674	4,177,419	2,932,609	2,034,680
Inventories					
Work-in-process	6,743,617	4,410,855	4,586,238	4,529,811	2,586,715
Less Partial Delivery	607,320	901,438	810,104	585,316	953,764
	6,136,297	3,509,417	3,776,134	3,944,495	1,632,951
Finished Goods	1,526,334	590,007	310,842	151,725	138,749
Shop Stores	1,675,381	1,163,425	1,210,777	1,117,663	553,892
	9,338,012	5,262,849	5,297,753	5,213,883	2,325,592
Total Current Assets	15,942,572	10,428,523	9,475,172	8,146,492	4,360,272
Fixed Assets					
Plant and Equipment	3,371,493	2,355,864	1,874,386	1,576,334	925,747
Depreciation Reserve	1,106,285	881,469	631,491	521,820	376,210
	2,265,208	1,474,395	1,242,895	1,054,514	549,537
Miscellaneous Charges	165,007	142,916	101,247	67,289	61,309
Overseas Investment	137,500	110,000	----	----	----
TOTAL ASSETS	18,510,287	12,155,834	10,819,314	9,268,295	4,971,118
LIABILITIES & SURPLUS					
Current Liabilities					
Notes due banks	7,710,000	3,565,000	3,410,000	2,700,000	1,324,500
Accounts Payable	758,391	421,769	210,479	503,781	327,604
Reserve for Federal tax	659,244	249,653	846,215	1,058,342	558,912
Other	633,871	551,090	493,246	505,038	196,214
TOTAL	9,761,506	4,787,512	4,959,940	4,767,161	2,407,230
Long-term notes & mortgages	567,249	1,658,379	1,276,501	975,500	25,350
TOTAL LIABILITIES	10,328,755	6,445,891	6,236,441	5,742,661	2,432,580
Contingency Reserve	100,000	100,000	100,000	100,000	100,000
Subscriptions on common stock	268,286	263,744	463,808	181,387	46,213
Common stock - $1.00 par value	908,617	447,391	436,755	409,371	187,246
Stock Premiums	2,943,812	1,476,819	1,083,499	808,679	728,439
Earned Surplus	3,960,817	3,421,989	2,498,811	2,026,197	1,476,640
TOTAL CAPITAL & SURPLUS	7,813,246	5,346,199	4,019,065	3,244,247	2,392,325
TOTAL LIABILITIES & CAPITAL	18,510,287	12,155,834	10,819,314	9,268,295	4,971,118

Figure 10—7 Butodale's consolidated overhead statement.
See Figure 10—8 for notes.

	Labor	Expense	Distribution/Remarks
Salaries	$2,453,800		
Overtime & Fringe Benefits	786,000		
Indirect Materials		$627,500	Purchasing
Shop Supplies		430,300	Note 1
Freight - Inbound		68,300	Purchasing
General Engineering	450,400	95,600	Expense to Prod. Eng'g.
Field Engineering	52,500	342,000	Expense to Sales & Serv.
Engineering Administration	68,400	21,000	Expense to Prod. Eng'g.
Drafting & Photo Supplies		72,600	Engineering Service
Plant Eng'g. Supplies		162,900	Maintenance
Terminated Contracts	26,000	9,100	Expense to Management
Rent		21,000	Management
Utilities (Power, Heat, Water, Sewer)		101,200	Management
Taxes - Real Property		39,200	Management
Taxes - Miscellaneous		13,000	Management
Depreciation - Buildings		83,200	Management
Depreciation - Equipment		201,800	Note 2
Repairs - Equipment (Mat'l)	13,700	34,500	Note 1 (Exp. only)
Vehicles (Rent, Operation, Depreciation)		20,200	50% Sales & Serv: 50% Supply
Insurance		67,000	Management
Travel & Entertaining		251,600	Sales & Service
Advertising		167,300	Sales Admin. & Adv.
Foreign Operations & Taxes		101,400	- Excluded -
Office Supplies		96,000	Note 3
Office Equipment (Rental & Depre.)		60,300	Note 4
Telephone & Telegraph		101,600	Management
Professional Fees		19,100	Management
Interest		303,700	Management
Miscellaneous Expense		13,000	Management
Totals	$ 3,850,800	$ 3,524,500	
Add Direct Labor	2,601,700		
Exclude Computer Center & Overseas	-562,600	-205,200	
Total Salaries & Wages	$ 5,889,900	$ 3,319,300	Net Indirect Expense

Figure 10–8 Supplement to Butodale's consolidated
overhead statement.

NOTE #1 - Distribution of Shop Supplies & Equipment Repair

- Shop Supplies
  - Shop Supplies $253,900
  - Material Writeoff $176,400 to purchasing
- Equip. Repair Mat'l.   34,500
  -                  288,400

           Distribution Base: Number employees in user
                               departments

Allocation

Supply Rec'g. & Shipping	$ 21,000
Manufacturing Process	46,000
Components Assembly	75,000
Final Assembly	46,000
Special Components	32,000
Production Tooling	10,000
Quality Control	58,400
	$288,400

NOTE #2 - Depreciation of Mfg. Equipment

       TOTAL CHARGES $201,800

       Distribution Base: By acquiring department or current
             usage as determined by maintenance manager.

Allocation

Management	$ 22,000 (Air Cond.)
Mfg. Process	18,000
Components Assembly	6,000
Quality Control	31,000
Maintenance	15,000
Eng'g. Services	6,000
Computer Centers	103,800 (Excluded)
	$201,800

Figure 10—8 (contd.)

NOTE #3 - Office Supplies

        TOTAL CHARGES $ .96,000

        Distribution Base: Number employees in user departments.

Allocation:

Management (postage & misc.)	$ 26,000
Accounting	14,000
Personnel	6,000
Spare Parts	7,000
Sales Admin. & Adv.	11,000
Purchasing	12,000
Mfg. Admin. & Subcontr.	20,000
	$ 96,000

NOTE #4 - Office Equipment Rent & Depr.

        TOTAL CHARGES $ 60,300

        Distribution Base:
           Rentals - As used
           Depreciation - Number employees in user depts.

Schedule:

Accounting	$ 22,000
Personnel	1,000
Spare Parts	2,000
Sales Admin. & Adv.	3,000
Purchasing	3,000
Mat'l. Control	24,300
Mfg. Admin. & Subcontr.	5,000
	$ 60,300

Figure 10–9 Ten-year growth pattern for Butodale Electronics.

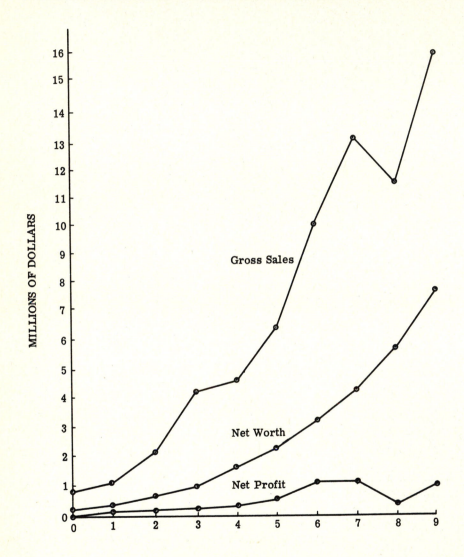

Figure 10–10 Profit relationships for Butodale Electronics.

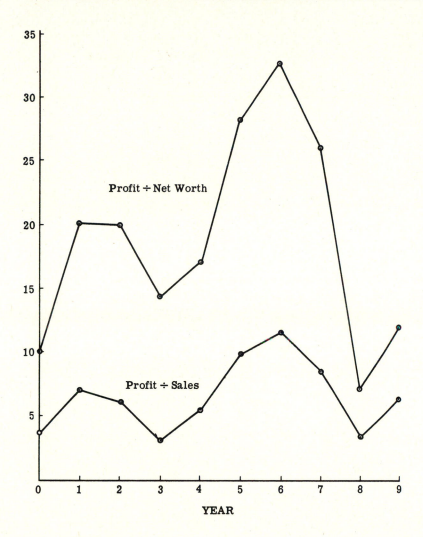

Figure 10–11 Profit as a percent of net worth and as a percent of sales for the past ten years.

Year	$\dfrac{\text{Profit}}{\text{Net Worth}}$ %	$\dfrac{\text{Profit}}{\text{Sales}}$ %
0	10	3.5
1	20	7.0
2	20	6.0
3	14	3.0
4	17	5.6
5	28	9.3
6	33	11.0
7	26	8.3
8	7	3.0
9	12	5.5

Personnel

Butodale employs skilled personnel in the electronic, mechanical, and clerical fields. The wage rate is competitive with its neighbors. Butodale hires its service and development engineers on a national basis and moves them to the required area. While little difficulty is encountered in hiring clerical and mechanical personnel, there is stiff competition among other companies in the surrounding area for those with electronics skills; Butodale has gained a slight edge on the market with its past record of treating employees fairly and equitably.

The company has a broad (mostly company-paid) employee benefit program including:

Life Insurance
Hospitalization
Retirement
Tuition Reimbursement
Stock Option
Annual Bonus (dependent on profit results)
Professional Society Dues (75%), plus Initiation Fee.

The manufacturing and clerical people are on an hourly basis with time and one-half for over eight hours per day or 40 hours per week. The company-employee relationship is carefully cultivated and, as a result, turnover, even in the clerical group, is quite low.

The personnel breakdown of the company's 1069 employees and managers is as follows:

President and Top Management		9
Public Relations		1
Personnel and Accounting		29
Personnel and Industrial Relations	8	
Accounting	21	
Marketing		80

Engineering		217
Product Engineering	73	
Services	97	
All Other	47	
Manufacturing		636
Materials	71	
Quality Control	109	
Operations	394	
Subcontracting	3	
Maintenance	28	
Administration	31	
Other Operations (but excluded from this study)		97
Computer Centers	41	
Overseas Operations	56	
	Total: 1069	

Personnel Classified by Function

Department		Total	Supervisor	Clerical	Other	Skilled	Semiskilled	Unskilled
Administration	39							
Exec. Off. & P.R.		10	10	0	0	0	0	0
Personnel		8	2	6	0	0	0	0
Accounting		21	3	18	0	0	0	0
Marketing	80							
Sales & Ser.		56	8	8	40	0	0	0
Parts Sales		10	2	8	0	0	0	0
Sales Admin.		14	4	4	6	0	0	0
Engineering	217							
Product Eng.		73	5	12	56	0	0	0
Eng. Ser.		97	6	11	80	0	0	0
Other Eng.		47	5	2	40	0	0	0
Manufacturing	636							
Purchasing		22	1	14	7	0	0	0
Material Control		15	1	10	4	0	0	0
Supply-R&S		34	4	7	0	0	13	10
Qual. Control		109	11	7	6	21	53	11
Production Tool'g		19	1	1	17	0	0	0
Comp. Ass'y		152	8	0	0	2	14	128
Final Ass'y		81	4	1	0	0	39	37
Special Components		61	3	0	0	1	10	47
Mfg. Process		81	5	7	0	9	23	37
Sub-contracting		3	1	2	0	0	0	0
Maintenance		28	3	0	0	6	8	11
Mfg. Admin.		31	11	11	9	0	0	0
		972	98	129	265	39	160	281
Excludable Sections								
Computer Centers		41						
Overseas		56						
		1069						

Inventory

Since a major portion of the end product is customized, it is not desirable to manufacture to inventory. However, because a large number of standard components is used, Butodale endeavors to forecast sales and stock a number of them for immediate support to production schedules. This means that work-in-process inventory is made up of both this preplanned stock and project stock where a system is being assembled and tested for a specific customer's order. It should be noted that general and administrative expense is applied to this work-in-process inventory.

The inventory is divided into the following major categories:

Shop Stores. Purchased parts and some fabricated mechanical parts used to support preplanned and project stock.

Work-in-Process Inventory. Material and labor already expended against preplanned and project stock (including components completed except for final quality control).

Finished Goods Inventory. End products and components ready for sale or on customers' orders. Note—**Indirect Material** includes low-cost purchased parts and fabricated mechanical parts commonly used in components, and end products not carried as inventory.

Direct Material. Includes materials purchased directly for preplanned or project stock but not placed in Shop Stores inventory; it goes directly to work-in-process.

Inventory Breakdown at December 31:

	Number of Parts	Value (in dollars)
Shop Stores	3120	1,675,381
Finished Goods	850	1,526,334
Work-in-Process	350	
Preplanned Stock		2,750,000
Project Stock		3,182,894
In-Process Stores		810,723
*Indirect Material	5000	410,385

*Not included in inventory; consists of 3000 purchased parts and 2000 fabricated parts.

Shop Stores Inventory Annual Usage—(divided into three classes):

Class A—$10,000 or more annual use
Class B—Less than $10,000 annual use, including items with long lead
       time and new items that may develop into Class A
Class C—Items of low unit cost with common usage
Total annual use (issues from Shop Stores)—$4,637,000

	Items	Percent of dollar
Class A	90	65
Class B	240	11
Class C	2790	24

Direct Material & Shop Stores—$6,384,000

Figure 10–12 Butodale's organization chart.

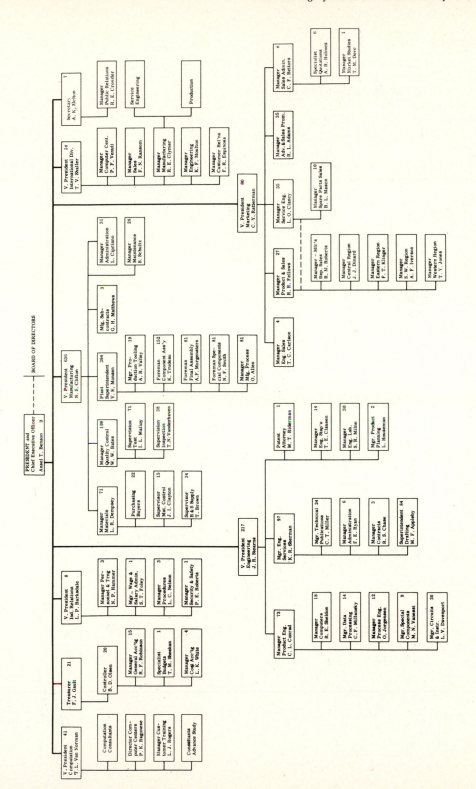

Analysis of Shop Stores Inventory, December

Number of Items	Price Category (in dollars)	Total (in dollars)
1830	Under 2.00	463,319
717	2.00 to 5.00	285,008
238	5.00 to 10.00	178,916
156	10.00 to 25.00	265,312
97	25.00 to 50.00	182,694
33	50.000 to 100.00	64,371
49	100.00 and over	235,761
3120		1,675,381

Facilities

Building: 130,000 square feet expandable to 250,000 square feet; Butler type building, party prefabricated 80′ spans north and south, 20′ spans east and west.

Roof: Sheet metal with 1½″ Fiberglas insulation.

Light: Provide 65 ft. candles at bench level.

Heat: Combination gas and oil, hot air. Gas operated until outside temperature drops to 32°, then switched to oil.

Fire Protection: Overhead sprinkler system with 100,000 gallon underground water tank. Fire hoses throughout the plant. Roof vents fused at 212° to open.

Area of Grounds: 40 acres.

Parking: 500 cars, expandable to 1500.

Air Conditioning: Two systems; front office area has a central compressor and chiller. Plant area has 50 individual units, each rated at 7½ tons. Water is circulated thru a water tower to exchange the heat before it is returned to the individual systems. Each unit is individually thermostatically controlled to maintain a temperature 10° below outside temperature with 50% to 60% relative humidity.

Shipping Area: Wirebound crates to reduce weight for shipping by air.

Finished Goods Stores: Completed units for replacement parts and field expansions of systems.

Receiving Section: All incoming material counted, checked and distributed.

In-Process Stores: Material fabricated at plant. Completed components ready for final assembly.

Supply: Purchased material inventory. Packaging area. (Parts packed to work-order quantity.) Printed Circuit assembly area. Automatic insertion equipment, eyelet machine.

Ultrasonic Cleaner: Completely cleans, rinses and dries printed circuit boards. Used to remove flux and other contamination after dip-soldering.

Solder Dipping Operations: Completely solders all connections in one operation.

Harness Fabrication: For installation at Butodale or in the field.

Wire Preparation Area: Automatic wire stripper, automatic taper pin installing machines. 1600 miles of wire used a year.

Finished Amplifiers:
Quad amplifiers, printed circuit
Dual amplifiers, printed circuit
Dual amplifiers, wired version to meet high specs
LK-5 printed circuit components
    Completed LK-5's: 1100 Plotters

D.A.S. & D.D.F.G.: Display comparing old design (mechanical) to new design (electrical).

PZC: Winding sine cards and mandrels (wire size .0017). Cleaning and checking mandrels (microscope). Displays of arms for plotters.

Network Final Wiring: Ovens for temperature cycling resistors networks checked for .002% accuracy. New phase shift checker to insure operation of networks in any oven position.

Plotter Test: Several types of plotters, vertical or horizontal plotters operated on signals from radar or other computing devices. Horizontal data and line plotters operated from information on cards or punched tape.

Plotter Assembly: Display of data plotter drawer wiring sequence including harness boards.

Special Wiring Group: Assembly and wire non-standard items.

Accessory Rack Assembly and Wiring: Any combination of single bay racks bolted together and equipped with standard modules to accommodate additional computing elements for the 207 Computing System.

207–217 Assembly and Wiring Group: Computer built as a basic unit with 18 harnesses. Possible maximum expansion equals 58 harnesses.

Systems Test: All elements of the computing system brought together and tested out by a team of test technicians and engineers. Final cleanup and preparation for packing.

Final Test: Computing systems operated on typical customer problems.

Other Facilities

Office Equipment	Owned	Rented	Total
Typewriters	47	57	104
Adding mach. & calc.	23	10	33
Bookkeeping mach.		3	3
Dictating mach.		5	5
Cars	10	7	17
Trucks	5		5
Keypunch	3	3	6
Verifier	3	2	5
Collator	1	1	2
Sorter	1	1	2
Acct. machine	2	2	4
Document orig. mach.	1	1	2
Calculating punch	1	1	2
Interpreter	1	1	2

OPERATIONAL SECTION

Resource Usage Sheet

Activity Sheets

Provide Product Demand

Provide End Products

Figure 10–13 Butodale's cost of functions and cost of activities.

NOTES

1. ORGANIZATION CHART DOES NOT INCLUDE COMPUTER CENTERS OR FOREIGN OPERATIONS, A TOTAL OF 97 PERSONS.

ORGANIZATION CHART

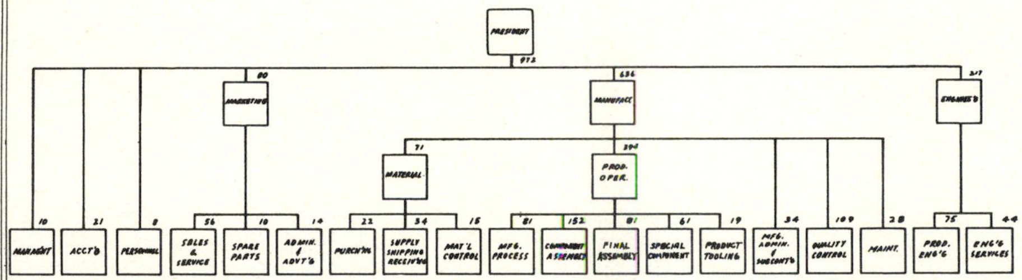

Resource Usage Sheet

Study BUTODALE ELECTRONICS
Analyst R. L. CASEY
Date

NOTES:

(BALANCE SHEET)

Activity	Item	MANAG'NT (10)	ACCT'G (21)	PERSONNEL (8)	SALES & SERVICE (56)	SPARE PARTS (10)	ADMIN. & ADVT'G (14)	PURCH'NG (22)	SUPPLY SHIPPING RECEIVING (34)	MAT'L CONTROL (15)	MFG. PROCESS (81)
PERSONNEL		230,000	115,500	48,800	448,000	41,000	84,000	149,600	183,600	61,500	421,200
MACHINE & EQUIPMENT			22,000	1,000	10,100	2,000	3,000	3,000	10,100	24,300	
MATERIAL			14,000	6,000	342,00	7,000	11,000	12,000	21,000		46,000
MISCELLANEOUS		515,400			251,600		167,300	872,200			18,000
		303,700						6,384,000			
TOTAL		1,049,100	151,500	55,800	1,051,700	50,000	265,300	7,420,800	214,700	85,800	485,200
ACTIVITY NAME PROVIDE PRODUCT DEMAND (001)	PERS.	24,000	25,260		448,000		84,000				
	EQUIP.		2,800		10,000		3,000				
	MAT'L.		4,100		342,000		11,000				
	MISC.				251,600		167,300				
	TOT.	24,000	32,160		1,051,700		265,300				
ACTIVITY NAME PROVIDE MATERIAL (002)	PERS.		21,760					36,000	70,400	32,600	421,200
	EQUIP.		4,800					1,000	3,300	8,400	
	MAT'L.		1,600					5,000	9,300		46,000
	MISC.							2,940,400			18,000
	TOT.		28,160					2,982,400	83,000	41,000	485,200
ACTIVITY NAME PROVIDE COMPONENTS (003)	PERS.		8,500					37,600	12,800	3,000	
	EQUIP.		510					1,000	2,000	4,100	
	MAT'L.							4,000	6,000		
	MISC.							1,003,900			
	TOT.		9,010					1,046,500	20,800	7,100	719,400
ACTIVITY NAME PROVIDE END PRODUCT (004)	PERS.		7,500					42,000	51,500	3,900	
	EQUIP.		1,000						3,300	1,100	
	MAT'L.		510						3,200		
	MISC.							984,000			
	TOT.		9,010					1,026,000	58,000	5,000	
ACTIVITY NAME PROVIDE ENGINEERED PRODUCTS AND SPARE PARTS (005)	PERS.		8,700			91,000		34,000	48,900	22,000	
	EQUIP.		310			2,000		1,000	1,500	10,700	
	MAT'L.					7,000		3,000	2,500		
	MISC.							2,327,900			
	TOT.		9,010			50,000		2,365,900	52,900	32,700	
ACTIVITY NAME PROVIDE MANAGEMENT, PERSONNEL, AND FACILITIES (006)	PERS.	206,000	43,780	48,800							
	EQUIP.		12,580	1,000							
	MAT'L.		7,790	6,000							
	MISC.	819,100									
	TOT.	1,025,100	64,150	55,800							

Activity	Item	COMPONENT ASSEMBLY (152)	FINAL ASSEMBLY (81)	SPECIAL COMPONENT (61)	PRODUCT TOOLING (19)	MFG. ADMIN. & SUBCONT'G (34)	QUALITY CONTROL (109)	MAINT. (28)	PROD. ENG'G (75)	ENG'G SERVICES (44)	TOTALS	ASSETS	LIABILITIES
PERSONNEL		638,400	356,400	268,400	134,900	326,400	632,200	142,800	642,400	964,800	5,889,900	CASH & RECEIV. 6,604,560	CURRENT NOTES 7,710,000
MACHINE & EQUIPMENT						5,000					80,500	INVENTORIES	OTHER
MATERIAL		75,000	46,000	32,000	10,000	20,000	58,400	162,900	116,600	72,600	1,052,600	9,338,012	2,051,506
MISCELLANEOUS		6,000					31,000	15,000		6,000	1,882,500	FIXED ASSETS 2,265,208	LONG TERM 567,249
											6,384,000		OWNERSHIP 7,813,246
TOTAL		719,400	402,400	300,400	144,900	351,400	721,600	320,700	759,000	1,043,400	15,593,200	18,207,780	18,142,001
ACTIVITY NAME PROVIDE PRODUCT DEMAND (001)	PERS.								126,400	148,300	855,960		
	EQUIP.										15,900		
	MAT'L.									2,200	359,300		
	MISC.									700	419,600		
	TOT.								126,400	151,200	1,650,760		
ACTIVITY NAME PROVIDE MATERIAL (002)	PERS.				34,900	84,600	108,100			44,500	854,060		
	EQUIP.					1,700					19,200		
	MAT'L.				1,500	5,000	18,000			2,800	89,200		
	MISC.						4,500			500	2,963,400		
	TOT.				36,400	91,300	130,600			47,800	3,925,860		
ACTIVITY NAME PROVIDE COMPONENTS (003)	PERS.	638,400		268,400	66,500	112,800	294,800			43,500	1,486,300		
	EQUIP.					2,700					10,310		
	MAT'L.	75,000		32,000	5,500	8,000	6,700			3,800	141,000		
	MISC.	6,000					13,000			500	1,023,400		
	TOT.	719,400		300,400	72,000	123,500	314,500			47,800	2,661,010		
ACTIVITY NAME PROVIDE END PRODUCT (004)	PERS.		356,400		33,500	129,000	229,300			91,300	944,400		
	EQUIP.					600					6,000		
	MAT'L.		46,000		3,000	7,000	33,700			13,900	107,310		
	MISC.						13,500			2,800	1,000,300		
	TOT.		402,400		36,500	136,600	276,500			108,000	2,058,010		
ACTIVITY NAME PROVIDE ENGINEERED PRODUCTS AND SPARE PARTS (005)	PERS.								516,000	637,200	1,307,800		
	EQUIP.										15,610		
	MAT'L.								116,700	49,900	179,100		
	MISC.									1,500	2,329,400		
	TOT.								632,700	688,600	3,831,810		
ACTIVITY NAME PROVIDE MANAGEMENT, PERSONNEL, AND FACILITIES (006)	PERS.							192,800			441,380		
	EQUIP.										13,580		
	MAT'L.							162,900			176,690		
	MISC.							15,000			834,100		
	TOT.							320,700			1,465,750		

Figure 10–14 Operation times and resource volumes and times
for the Provide Product Demand activity.

					Activity Name					

FUNCTION : QUOTATIONS
INPUTS : 2000, 2010

KEYS	AVG	PEAK	NOTE
1-2	1H	1D	
3-4	2H	6D	1200
4-6	1D	2D	
7-8	1H	4H	
8-11	1D	6D	1200
12-13	2D	5D	
13-14	1D	2D	
14-15	1D	2D	
15-16	12D	30D	1210
16-17	3D	10D	1200
17-18	2D	5D	
20-23	2D	5D	
7-11	2D	5D	
14-16	14D	30D	
23-25	14-D	90-D	-MAX
		20-D	-MIN

FUNCTION : ORDERS
INPUTS : 2020

KEYS	AVG	PEAK	NOTE
25-28	4D	10D	
28-29	2D	4D	
29-31	1D	3D	
25-31	7D	20D	1220

INPUTS

KEY	NAME	SOURCE	AVG VOLUME	PEAK VOLUME	NOTE
2000	QUOTE REQUEST	CUST	50/w	70/w	1020
	FREQUENCY		46 W/YR	4 W/YR	1030
2010	BID REQUEST	CUST	10/w	12/w	
	FREQUENCY		42 W/YR	10 W/YR	1040
2020	ORDER	CUST	16/w	20/w	1030
	FREQUENCY		44 W/YR	6 W/YR	

OUTPUTS

KEY	NAME	DEST	AVG VOLUME	PEAK VOLUME	NOTE
3000	QUOTATN	CUST	15/w	20/w	1030
	FREQUENCY		40 W/YR	10 W/YR	
3050	ACKNOW	CUST	16/w	—	1050

FILE USAGE

KEY	NAME	MSGS AVG	MSGS PEAK	ACCESS	USAGE TIME	NOTE
4000	PRICING	240K	300K	RANDM	8H/D	1100
4010	COST	1,000K	—	RANDM	—	1110
4020	RATE	2500	2800	RANDM	8H/D	
4030	INSTALLED SYSTEMS	400K	—	RANDM	4H/D	1120
4050	CONTRACT REGISTER	1500	2100	SEQ	8H/D	1130
4060	CUSTOMER INDEX	4000	5500	SEQ	2H/D	
4070	PROJECT INDEX	1500	2100	SEQ	1H/D	
4080	ASSIGN'T SHEET	20	80	RANDM	10H/D	1140

NOTES
1100 – PRICING FILE IS USED IN BOTH END ITEM AND SYSTEMS QUOTATIONS.
1110 – COST FILE IS PRESENTLY MAINTAINED IN 3 DIFFERENT AREAS. NO CARDS HAVE YET BEEN DISCARDED.
1120 – INSTALLED SYSTEMS FILE HAS NOT YET BEEN PURGED.
1130 – CONTRACT REGISTER IS MASTER OPEN CUSTOMER ORDER FILE. WHEN ORDERS ARE COMPLETED, THE RECORDS ARE MOVED TO THE INSTALLED SYSTEMS FILE.
1140 – MUST BE AVAILABLE FOR SECOND SHIFT.
1200 – WIDE VARIATION DUE TO SYSTEM VARIATION. THERE IS NO SUCH THING, STRICTLY, AS "STD SYSTEM"
1210 – MULTIPLE DESIGN "PASSES" (SEE NOTE 1000)
1220 – TIME ALLOWED BY CUSTOMERS TO ACKNOWLEDGE ORDER VARIES FROM 1D TO MAX. OF 30D.

NOTES
1020 – BREAKDOWN OF REQUESTS FOR QUOTATION :

	STD SYSTEMS	207-217	OTHER	STD END ITM	PLOTTER	OTHER
AVG	36 /w	32 /w	4 /w	14 /w	10 /w	4 /w
PEAK	51 /w	44 /w	11 /w	19 /w	14 /w	5 /w

1030 – PLANT CLOSES DOWN FOR 2 WEEKS EACH YEAR, SO THERE ARE 50 WEEKS / YR FOR THIS INPUT. PEAKS OCCUR JUST BEFORE AND JUST AFTER THE 2-WEEK CLOSED PERIOD.
1040 – ENGINEERING DOES NOT CLOSE DOWN ALONG WITH THE PLANT, SO THIS INPUT OCCURS 52 WEEKS PER YEAR. PEAKS OCCUR AT BEGINNING OF EACH FISCAL QUARTER.
1050 – ESSENTIALLY NO PEAKS IN THIS OUTPUT.

**Figure 10–15 Operation flow for the Provide Product
Demand activity.**

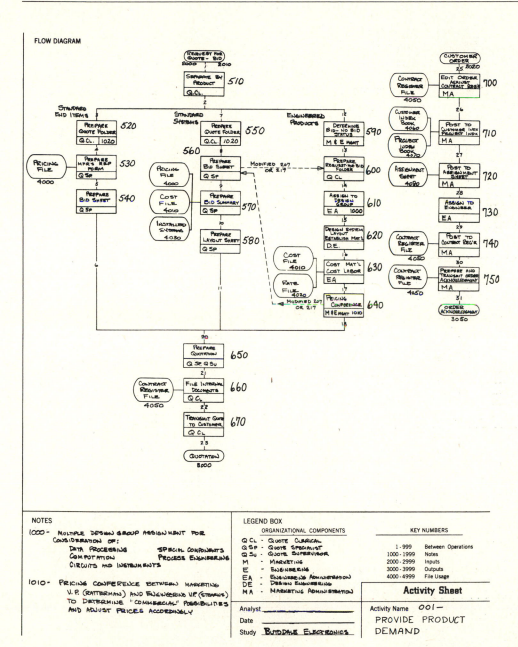

FLOW DIAGRAM

Figure 10–16 Operation times and resource volumes and times for the Provide End Products activity.

Activity Name **PROVIDE END PRODUCTS (004)**

FUNCTION: ASSEMBLY AND TEST

INPUTS: 3050

KEY	AVG	PEAK	CYCLE	NOTE
1-2	2 D	5 D	DAILY	
2-3	60 D	90 D	—	1100
3-4	30 D	45 D	—	1100
1-4	90 D	140 D		

FUNCTION: COSTING AND INVOICING

INPUTS: 3010

KEY	AVG	PEAK	CYCLE	NOTE
6-7	1 D	3 D	WEEKLY	
7-8	1 D	3 D	WEEKLY	
9-10	½ D	—	DAILY	
11-12	2 D	5 D	Daily	1120
12-13	1 D	3 D	WEEKLY	
13-14	2 D	3 D	DAILY	
14-15	½ D	1 D	DAILY	
15-16	1 D	3 D	DAILY	
6-8	2 D	5 D	—	
13-16	3 D	7 D	—	
1-16	100 D	150 D	—	

INPUTS

KEY	NAME	SOURCE	AVG VOLUME	PEAK VOLUME	NOTE
3010	MAT'L COST	MAT'L CONT'L	100/D	140/D	1000

FREQUENCY

3050	ORDER ACKNOW	MKTG. ADMIN	16/W	—	1010
			NO	PEAKS	

OUTPUTS

KEY	NAME	DESTIN	AVG VOL.	PEAK VOL.	FREQ.	NOTE
3020	JOB PROGRESS	SUPT.	65 JOBS	110 JOBS	DAILY	
3030	HOT LIST	SEE NOTE	30 PARTS	50 PARTS	DAILY	1020
3040	QUAL. REPORT	Q/C	5 ITEMS	20 ITEMS	DAILY	
3060	PAYROLL REPORT	GEN'L ACCTG	300 MEN	335 MEN	WKLY	
3070	SHIP'S REPORT	SUPT	4 ITEMS	12 ITEMS	DAILY	
3080	PERF'CE REPORT	SUPT.	200 ITEMS	400 ITEMS	WKLY	
3090	COMPL PROJECT	SUPT.	15 ITEMS	45 ITEMS	WKLY	
3100	INVOICE	CUST.	15/W	20/W	DAILY	
3110	PACKING LIST	CUST.	15/W	20/W	DAILY	

FILE USAGE

KEY	NAME	MSGS AVG	MSGS PEAK	ACCESS	USAGE TIME	NOTE
4050	CONTRACT REGISTER	1500	2100	RANDM	2 H/D	
4070	PROJECT INDEX	1500	2100	RANDM	2 H/W	
4080	ASSIGN- MENT	20	80	RANDM	10 H/D	1030
4090	ROUTING FILE	250	350	RANDM	8 H/D	
4100	JOB TICKETS	2000	3200	SEQ	3 H/W	
4110	STAND'D FILE	5000	5500	SEQ	12 H/W	
4120	WORK IN PROCESS	400	750	SEQ	8 H/W	
4130	ACCT'S REC'BLE	4000	5500	SEQ	8 H/W	

Activity Sheet

NOTES

1000 FROM PROVIDE MATERIAL ACTIVITY, OPERATION 002-800

1010 FROM PROVIDE DEMAND ACTIVITY, OPERATION 001-750. NO PEAKS.

1020 HOT LIST DISTRIBUTED TO:
MGR.- COMPONENT ASSEMBLY
MGR.- FINAL ASSEMBLY
MGR.- MANUFACTURING PROCESS

1030 MUST BE AVAILABLE FOR SECOND SHIFT AND OVERTIME WORKERS.

NOTES

1100 - MANUFACTURING CYCLE TIME VARIES FROM 3 MONTHS TO 5 MONTHS

1110 - TESTING CYCLE TIME VARIES FROM 1½ MONTHS TO 2½ MONTHS.

1120 INCLUDES LOOKUP, POSTING, COMPUTING VARIANCE.

Figure 10–17 Operation flow for the Provide End Products activity.

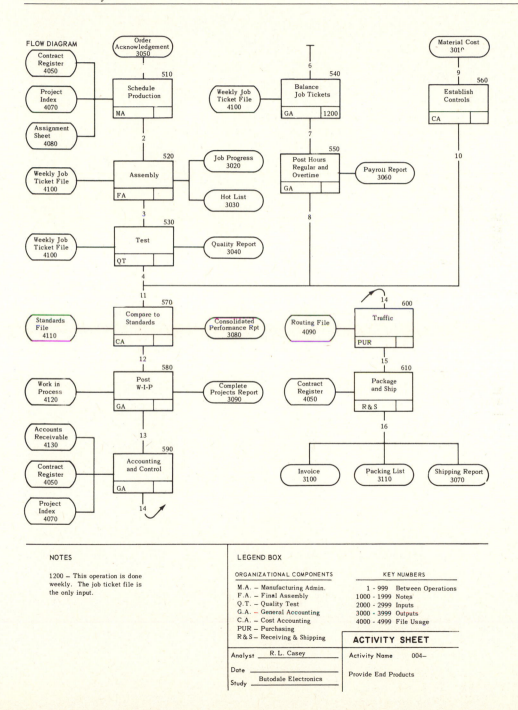

APPENDIX

Selected Operation Sheets

Selected Message Sheets

Selected File Sheets

Figure 10–18 Operation sheet for operation 001-540.

OPERATION: 001-540 Quote Section

Triggers, Inputs and Outputs

ID NO	Name and Qualifications	Received From or Sent To	Volume AVG	Volume PER	Elapsed Time
T1	Receipt of I1 (F-4050.1)				
I1	Quote Folder (all papers)	Quote Secn Clerk	1/2	D	O
R1	Quote Folder (F-4050.1)	Quotation Supvr.	1 1/2	D	1-2 D

NOTE: 2 out of 3 quotations are standard and take approx 1/2 – 1 hr. Modified orders take 4-6 hrs. Excess time (in elapsed time compared to resource time) is due to quote specialist performing other duties and letting end item quotes wait.

Processes

ID NO	Description and Qualifications	Freq
P1	Select preprinted end item and component sheets to align with quote request in quote folder.	1/I1
P2	Modify component groups as necessary to agree with quote request by entering:	1/3I1
	• "Partial" to reduce plug in components	
	• "Modify" to substitute components or parts	
	• "Special" to change entire group	
	• Full description as necessary	
P3	Prepare cost and price sheet.	1/I1
P4	Add all items to quote folder.	1/I1

Resources

ID NO	Type	Unit Time	Total Time AVG	PER
X1	Quote Specialist	2H/6P		
X2	Operational Reference Manuals	1H/OP		
X3	Cost File (F-4010)	1H/OP		
X4	Price Catalog (F-4000)	1H/OP		

Analyst	Source	Study	Activity	Page
R.L. Casey	A.R. Holmes	Butodale	001 – Provide Demand	1 of 1

DATE

Figure 10–19 Operation sheet for operations 001-580 and 001-650.

OPERATION 001-580 — Performed by: Quote Section

ID. NO.	TRIGGERS, INPUTS AND OUTPUTS — Name and Qualifications	Received From or Sent To	Vol. Avg.	Per	Elapsed Time	ID. NO.	PROCESSES — Description and Qualifications	Freq.	RESOURCES ID. NO.	Type	Unit Time Avg.	Total Time Per
T1	RECEIPT OF I1					P1	SELECT STANDARD RACK DIAGRAMS FOR COMPONENTS	1/I1	X1	QUOTE SPECIALIST(3) IN/OP OPERATIONAL DATA	8H	D
I1	QUOTE FOLDER (F-4050.1)	Quote Specialist	10	D	0				X2	REFERENCE MANUALS		
I2	QUOTE FOLDER (F-4050.1)	Quotation Supvr.	10	D	1 D	P2	ENTER APPROPRIATE ASSEMBLY NUMBER IN EACH RACK POSITION USED	1/4 1/I1				
						P3	SELECT FLOOR LAYOUT SHEET (207-217 ONLY. OTHER STD. SYSTEMS DO NOT REQUIRE FLOOR LAYOUT)	7/8 I1				
						P4	ENTER COMPONENT AND/OR END ITEM DESCRIPTION IN FLOOR LAYOUT DIAGRAM	7/8 I1				
						P5	PLACE LAYOUT SHEETS IN QUOTE FOLDER	1/I1				

OPERATION 001-650 — Performed by: Quote Section

ID. NO.	TRIGGERS, INPUTS AND OUTPUTS — Name and Qualifications	Received From or Sent To	Vol. Avg.	Per	Elapsed Time	ID. NO.	PROCESSES — Description and Qualifications	Freq.	RESOURCES ID. NO.	Type	Unit Time Avg.	Total Time Per
T1	RECEIPT OF I1 OR I2					P1	REVIEW OF QUOTE OR BID BY QUOTE SECTION SUPERVISOR	1/I1	X1	QUOTE SECTION SUPV'R		
I1	QUOTE FOLDER (COMPLETED) (F-4050.1)	Quote Specialist	12	D	0	P2	TYPE QUOTATION FROM BID SHEET	1/I1	X2	QUOTE CLERK		
I2	BID FOLDER (COMPLETED) (F-4050.2)	Marketing V.P.	2	D	1-2 D	P3	PREPARE IDENTIFICATION CARDS (3)	1/I1	X3	TYPEWRITER		
R1	QUOTATION (5 PARTS)	Quote Clerk	14	D	1-2 D	P4	SELECT ADVERTISING LITERATURE	1/I1				
R2	IDENTIFICATION CARDS(3)	"	14	D	1-2 D	P5	ASSEMBLE QUOTATION AND INTERNAL DOCUMENTS.	1/I1				
R3	QUOTE/BID FOLDER	"	14	D	1-2 D							
R4	DRAWINGS, PRINTS, ETC.	"	10	D	1-2 D							
R5	ADVERTISING LITERATURE	"	14	D	1-2 D							

Analyst: R. L. CASEY — Source: A. R. HOLMES — Study: BUTODALE — Activity: 001—PROVIDE DEMAND — Page: 1 of 1

Figure 10–20 Operation sheet for operation 001-630.

OPERATION							PROCESSES			RESOURCES			
NO. 001-630	**PERFORMED BY** ENGINEERING ADMIN.												
	TRIGGERS, INPUTS AND OUTPUTS												
ID. NO.	**NAME AND QUALIFICATIONS**	**RECEIVED FROM OR SENT TO**	**VOLUME AVG**	**PER**	**ELAPSED TIME**	**ID. NO.**	**DESCRIPTION AND QUALIFICATIONS**	**FREQ.**	**ID. NO.**	**TYPE**	**UNIT TIME**	**TOTAL TIME AVG**	**PER**
T1	RECEIPT OF I 1					P1	Determine if proper entries of Time and material are entered in Bid Folder by Design Engineering groups.	1/I1	X1	ADMIN. ENGR. (2)	8H	D
I1	BID FOLDER (WITH ALL PAPERS PLUS PRINTS, DRAWINGS, LAYOUTS, MATERIAL SPECS, TIME ESTIMATES, ETC.) (F-4050.2)	DESIGN ENG'RG	10	W	0				X2	COST FILE (4010)	8H	D
									X3	RATE FILE (4020)		
R1	BID FOLDER (COSTED) (F-4050.2)	ENGINEERING V.P.	10	W	1-8W	P2	Modify estimates based on experience with individual engineer.	1/I1		NOTE: 2 ADMINISTRATIVE ENGINEERS FULL TIME FOR LIAISON BETWEEN DESIGN GROUPS AND QUOTE SECTION.		
						P3	Compute costs for material	1/I1				
						P4	Compute labor cost	1/I1		NO TIME ESTIMATES PER BID; USE ELAPSED TIME.		
						P5	Set Bid Price. Confirm with Design Engineering group manager.					
						P6	Send bid folder to V.P. Eng'g.	1/I1				

R.L. CASEY — ANALYST   F.E. RYAN — SOURCE   BUTODALE — STUDY   001- PROVIDE DEMAND — ACTIVITY   1 of 1 — PAGE   DATE

Figure 10–21 Message sheet for quotation request.

MESSAGE NAME							MESSAGE NO.	
REQUEST FOR QUOTE							R-2000	
OTHER NAMES USED							LAYOUT NO. NONE	
							FORM NO. NONE	
							NO. OF COPIES 1	
MEDIA LETTER OR NOTE				HOW PREPARED HAND OR TYPEWRITTEN				
OPERATIONS INVOLVED IN 001 – SIX, 001-52 X, 001-55 X								
F - 4050.1								
REMARKS COVERS ONLY CATALOG, STANDARD AND MODIFIED STANDARD PRODUCTS. SEE ALSO R 2010								

NO.	DATA NAME	FREQUENCY	CHARACTERS	A/N	ORIGIN
1	DATE	1	MAX 6	N	CUST/SALES
2	CUSTOMER NAME	1	MAX 30	A	"
3	CUSTOMER ADDRESS	.9	MAX 40	A/N	"
4	CUSTOMER NUMBER	.1	5	N	"
5	PRODUCT SPECIFICATIONS	1	AVG. 350	A/N	"
6	QUANTITY	1	3	N	"
7	REQUEST QUOTE BY DATE	.5	MAX 6	N	"
8	REQUEST DELIVERY DATE	.3	MAX 6	N	"
9	SPECIAL INSTRUCTIONS	.2	AVG. 150	A/N	"
	ESTIMATED TOTAL		460		

R.L. CASEY   A.R. HOLMES   1 OF 1

DATE   ANALYST   SOURCE   PAGE

BUTODALE
STUDY

Figure 10–22 Message sheet for bid request.

MESSAGE NAME				MESSAGE NO.		
REQUEST FOR BID				R-2010		
OTHER NAMES USED				LAYOUT NO.		
				FORM NO. ●		
				NO. OF COPIES 1		

MEDIA	HOW PREPARED	
LETTER	NORMALLY TYPEWRITTEN	

OPERATIONS INVOLVED IN

001-51X, 001-59X, 001-60X

F-4050.2

REMARKS

COVERS ONLY ENGINEERED PRODUCTS

		CONTENTS				
NO.	DATA NAME		FREQUENCY	CHARACTERS	A/N	ORIGIN
	SAME AS R 2000					
	EXCEPT					
5	PRODUCT SPECIFICATIONS		1	AVG. 1000	A/N	
	ESTIMATED TOTAL			1110		

R.L. CASEY	A.R. HOLMES	1 OF 1	
ANALYST	SOURCE	PAGE	

DATE

BUTODALE

STUDY

Figure 10–23 Message sheet for a customer order.

MESSAGE NAME CUSTOMER ORDER						MESSAGE NO. R-2020	
OTHER NAMES USED PURCHASE ORDER						LAYOUT NO. ✳ QO 561	
						FORM NO. ✳ QO 561-2 OR -3	
						NO. OF COPIES 1	
MEDIA ✳			HOW PREPARED ✳				
OPERATIONS INVOLVED IN 001 – 70X							
F-4050							
REMARKS ✳ TWO COPIES OF QUOTATION SHEET (R-3000) ARE SENT TO THE CUSTOMER. MORE THAN 95% OF CUSTOMER ORDERS USE ONE OF THESE COPIES TO PLACE A FIRM ORDER AND ACCOMPANY IT WITH A PURCHASE ORDER. THE REMAINING CUSTOMER ORDERS CONSIST OF A PURCHASE ORDER REFERENCING THE QUOTE SHEET.							
NO.	DATA NAME CONTENTS			FREQUENCY	CHARACTERS	A/N	ORIGIN
	✳ SAME AS R-3000						
	NOTE:						
	IF R-3000 IS NOT USED AS CUSTOMER ORDER, FILE COPY IS REPRODUCED TO CREATE R 2020.						

R.L. CASEY   C.F. BETTORS   1 OF 1

DATE   ANALYST   SOURCE   PAGE

BUTODALE
STUDY

Figure 10–24 Message sheet for a quotation.

MESSAGE NAME						
QUOTATION			MESSAGE NO. R- 3000			

OTHER NAMES USED						
QUOTE, QUOTE SHEET, BID			LAYOUT NO. QO-561			

FORM NO. QO-561-1 THRU-5

NO. OF COPIES 5

MEDIA 5 - PART FORM	HOW PREPARED TYPEWRITTEN

OPERATIONS INVOLVED IN
001-65X, 001-66X, 001-67X, 001-70X

F 4050.1 IF QUOTE;
F 4050.2 IF BID

REMARKS
THE MESSAGE ISSUED IS A QUOTATION, WHETHER IN RESPONSE TO A REQUEST FOR QUOTATION (R-2000) OR REQUEST FOR BID (R-2010). TWO COPIES ARE SENT TO CUSTOMER; ONE COPY IS USUALLY RETURNED AS R-2020

CONTENTS

NO.	DATA NAME	FREQUENCY	CHARACTERS	A/N	ORIGIN
1	CUSTOMER ORDER # AND DATE	1/PG	AVG. 12/18 MAX 12/16	4-A /16-N	001-650
2	OUR ORDER # AND DATE	1/PG	16	N	
3	VIA AND TERMS	1/PG	10/30	A/N	
4	BILL TO (3-5 LINES)	1/PG	100/150	A/N	
5	SHIP TO (1-5 LINES)	1/PG	50/150	A/N	
6	ITEM #	.4/PG	1/2	N	
7	QUANTITY	1.9/PG	4/5	A/N	
8	DESCRIPTION	1/PG	1500/2000	A	
9	UNIT PRICE	2.3/PG	3/6	N	
10	PRICE (TOTAL)	.4/PG	5/7	N	
11	DELIVERY DATE	1/PG	6	N	
12	MISC.	.5/PG	70/100	A/N	
	(TOTAL PER PAGE)	✕	1746/2447		
	PAGES: MIN - 1 AVE - 6				
	MAX - 17	(SEE ATTACHED SAMPLE)			

R.L. CASEY	A.R. HOLMES	1 OF 1
DATE ANALYST	SOURCE	PAGE

BUTODALE
STUDY

Figure 10–25 Blank quotation form.

BUTODALE ELECTRONICS CO. ■ DANVERS, MASSACHUSETTS

TO:

DATE _____

VALID UNTIL _____

REFERENCE _____

ITEM	QTY.	DESCRIPTION	UNIT PRICE	PRICE	DELIVERY

see reverse side hereof for terms and conditions

quotation

BY: _____

BUTODALE ELECTRONICS CO.
ROUTE 128
DANVERS, MASSACHUSETTS

Figure 10–26 Message sheet for material cost.

MESSAGE NAME								
MATERIAL COST				MESSAGE NO. R-3010				
OTHER NAMES USED COST CARD				LAYOUT NO. _____				
				FORM NO. _____				
				NO. OF COPIES 1				
MEDIA 3×5 CARD			HOW PREPARED MANUAL (002-800)					
OPERATIONS INVOLVED IN								
002 - 800								
004 - 56X								
004 - 57X								
004 - 58X								
REMARKS								

		CONTENTS					
NO.	DATA NAME		FREQUENCY	CHARACTERS	A/N	ORIGIN	
	SIMILAR FORMAT TO SAMPLE ATTACHED TO F-4010						

_____ DATE   R.L. CASEY ANALYST   L.K. WHITE SOURCE   1 OF 1 PAGE

BUTODALE STUDY

Figure 10–27 Message sheet for a job progress report.

MESSAGE NAME JOB PROGRESS REPORT				MESSAGE NO. R- 3020	
OTHER NAMES USED				LAYOUT NO.	
				FORM NO.	
				NO. OF COPIES 3	
MEDIA PAPER		HOW PREPARED HAND WRITTEN			
OPERATIONS INVOLVED IN 004 - 520 , USED AS A PRODUCTION AND SCHEDULING MANAGEMENT AID.					
REMARKS PREPARED DAILY BY PRODUCTION FOREMAN . ONE OR TWO COMMENTS ON EACH JOB HANDLED THAT DAY.					
		CONTENTS			
NO.	DATA NAME	FREQUENCY	CHARACTERS	A/N	ORIGIN
	PERCENT COMPLETE (ESTIMATE)	1	2	N	
	ESTIMATED COMPLETION DATE	1	4	N	
	COMMENTS ON QUALITY, PROBLEMS SCHEDULE ETC.	1	100	A	
	JOB # (ORDER #)	1	6	N	

R.L. CASEY   L. CIPRIANO   1 OF 1

DATE   ANALYST   SOURCE   PAGE

BUTODALE

STUDY

Figure 10–28 Message sheet for the hot list.

MESSAGE NAME HOT LIST				MESSAGE NO. R-3030		
OTHER NAMES USED				LAYOUT NO.		
				FORM NO.		
				NO. OF COPIES 3		
MEDIA PAPER		HOW PREPARED MANUALLY				
OPERATIONS INVOLVED IN 004-520						
REMARKS USED TO PROMPT PART AND MATERIAL EXPEDITING						
		CONTENTS				
NO.	DATA NAME		FREQUENCY	CHARACTERS	A/N	ORIGIN
	ESTIMATED DAYS BEHIND SCHEDULE		1	2	N	
	PART #		1	6	N	
	JOB (ORDER #)		1	6	N	

DATE	R.L. CASEY	L. CIPRIANO	1 OF 1
BUTODALE	ANALYST	SOURCE	PAGE
STUDY			

Figure 10–29 Message sheet for the quality report.

MESSAGE NAME QUALITY REPORT			MESSAGE NO. R-3040		
OTHER NAMES USED REJECT SHEET			LAYOUT NO.		
			FORM NO.		
			NO. OF COPIES 2		
MEDIA PAPER (TABULAR)		HOW PREPARED MANUALLY			
OPERATIONS INVOLVED IN 004 - 530					
REMARKS					

		CONTENTS			
NO.	DATA NAME	FREQUENCY	CHARACTERS	A/N	ORIGIN
	LOT SIZE	1	3	N	
	SAMPLE SIZE	1	3	N	
	# REJECTED	1	3	N	
	JOB # (ORDER #)	1	6	N	

DATE	ANALYST R.L. CASEY	SOURCE I.L. MALLOY	PAGE 1 OF 1
BUTO DALE STUDY			

Figure 10–30 Message sheet for the order acknowledgment.

MESSAGE NAME ORDER ACKNOWLEDGMENT				MESSAGE NO. R-3050		
OTHER NAMES USED				LAYOUT NO. _____		
				FORM NO. _____		
				NO. OF COPIES 3		
MEDIA LETTER		HOW PREPARED TYPEWRITTEN				
OPERATIONS INVOLVED IN						
001 – 75 X						
004 – 51 X						
F – 4050						
REMARKS						
ORIGINAL TO CUSTOMER						
FIRST COPY TO F – 4050						
SECOND COPY TO T.R. FELLOWS (SALES MGR.)						
		CONTENTS				
NO.	DATA NAME		FREQUENCY	CHARACTERS	A/N	ORIGIN
1.	TODAYS DATE		1	AVE 6 max	N	
2.	CUSTOMER NAME AND ADDRESS		1	30/70	A	
3.	REFERENCE #'s		1	6/18	A/N	
4	DELIVERY DATE		1	6	N	
5	PRICE		1	5/7	N	
6	MISC. COPY		1	120/400	A	
7	AUTHORIZED SIGNATURE		1	12/30	A	
	ESTIMATED TOTAL			179/531		

R.L. CASEY	C.F. BETTORS	1 OF 1
ANALYST	SOURCE	PAGE

BUTODALE
DATE
STUDY

Figure 10–31 Message sheet for the payroll report.

MESSAGE NAME						
PAYROLL REPORT			MESSAGE NO. R- 3060			
OTHER NAMES USED HOURS LIST			LAYOUT NO.			
			FORM NO.			
			NO. OF COPIES 3			
MEDIA STOCK TAB PAPER	HOW PREPARED		ACCOUNTING MACHINE			
OPERATIONS INVOLVED IN 004 - 550 P/R ACCOUNTING						

REMARKS

	CONTENTS				
NO.	DATA NAME	FREQUENCY	CHARACTERS	A/N	ORIGIN
	DEPARTMENT		3	N	
	MAN		5	N	
	SHIFT		1	N	
	CODE ("X" OVER SHIFT FOR O.T.)				
	REGULAR HOURS (XXO)	✳	3	N	
	OVERTIME HOURS (XXO)	✳	3	N	
	TOTAL HOURS	✳	3	N	
	CARD COUNT	✳	2	N	
	MAN TOTAL COUNTS EXCEPT MINOR	✳	3		
	MINOR TOTALS OF ✳ BY MAN	325	11		
	INTERMED. TOTALS " " " SHIFT	36	21		
	MAJOR " " " " DEPT.	27	21		
	FINAL " " " OVERALL	1	22		

R.L. CASEY   ANALYST   R.F. ROBINSON   SOURCE   1 OF 1   PAGE

DATE

BUTODALE   STUDY

Figure 10–32 Message sheet for the shipping report.

MESSAGE NAME			MESSAGE NO.	
SHIPPING REPORT			*R-3070*	
OTHER NAMES USED			LAYOUT NO.	
			FORM NO.	
			NO. OF COPIES	
MEDIA		HOW PREPARED		
OPERATIONS INVOLVED IN				
REMARKS				
NOT REVIEWED				

		CONTENTS				
NO.	DATA NAME		FREQUENCY	CHARACTERS	A/N	ORIGIN

R.L. CASEY
DATE   ANALYST   SOURCE   *1 oF 1* PAGE

BuTo DALE STUDY

Figure 10–33 Message sheet for the consolidated
performance report.

MESSAGE NAME CONSOLIDATED PERFORMANCE REPORT.		MESSAGE NO. R-3080
OTHER NAMES USED		LAYOUT NO.
		FORM NO.
		NO. OF COPIES 3

MEDIA STANDARD TAB PAPER	HOW PREPARED TAB EQUIPMENT

OPERATIONS INVOLVED IN
004 - 570

COMPLETE PREPARATION PROCEDURE DOCUMENTED
IN COST ACCOUNTING D P SECTION

REMARKS
SHOWS % DEVIATION FROM STANDARD
BY OPERATION.

	CONTENTS				
NO.	DATA NAME	FREQUENCY	CHARACTERS	A/N	ORIGIN

R.L. CASEY   L.K. WHITE   1 OF 1
DATE ANALYST   SOURCE   PAGE

BUTODALE
STUDY

Figure 10–34 Message sheet for the completed projects report.

MESSAGE NAME	COMPLETED PROJECTS REPORT.		MESSAGE NO.	R-3090
OTHER NAMES USED			LAYOUT NO.	
			FORM NO.	
			NO. OF COPIES	2

MEDIA	STANDARD TAB PAPER	HOW PREPARED	TAB EQUIPMENT

OPERATIONS INVOLVED IN

004 – 580

COMPLETE PROCEDURE DOCUMENTED IN GENERAL ACCOUNTING D.P. SECTION

REMARKS

LISTS COMPLETED (WEEKLY) PROJECTS WITH SCHEDULED AND ACTUAL COMPLETION DATES

CONTENTS

NO.	DATA NAME	FREQUENCY	CHARACTERS	A/N	ORIGIN

R.L. CASEY — ANALYST   R.F. ROBINSON — SOURCE   1 OF 1 — PAGE

BUTODALE — DATE
STUDY

Figure 10–35 File sheet for the pricing file.

FILE NAME			FILE NO.	
PRICING FILE			F-4000	

LOCATION	STORAGE MEDIUM
QUOTATION SECTION	3 × 5 TRACK-INDEX ROLLER CABINETS

ACCESS REQUIREMENTS
MANUAL, RANDOM — 10 SECOND SEARCH;
RECORD STAYS IN FILE

SEQUENCED BY
END ITEM OR PART #

CONTENT QUALIFICATIONS
STANDARD SELLING PRICE IS SHOWN.

HOW CURRENT
DAILY

RETENTION CHARACTERISTICS
UNTIL ITEM/PART DISCONTINUED
OR PRICE CHANGED

LABELS
USED IN 001-53X, 001-57X,

REMARKS
FILE CARD FORMAT IS SHOWN BELOW; THERE IS NO
MESSAGE SHEET TO DESCRIBE "PRICING FILE CARD".

SEQUENCE NO.	MESSAGE NAME	VOLUME		CHARACTERS PER MESSAGE	CHARACTERS PER FILE	
		AVG.	PEAK		AVG.	PEAK
1	ITEM OR PART #	240K	300K	7	1,680K	2,100K
2	DESCRIPTION			6/30	1,440K	9,000K
3	EFFECTIVE DATE			6	1,440K	1,800K
4	PRICE			3/7	720K	2,100K
5	UNIT OF MEASURE			2	480K	600K
	TOTAL			24/52	5,760K	15,600K

R.F. CASEY	A.R. HOLMES	1 OF 1
ANALYST	SOURCE	PAGE

DATE
BUTODALE
STUDY

Figure 10–36 File sheet for the cost file.

FILE NAME COST FILE				FILE NO. F - 4010		
LOCATION QUOTATIONS SECTION			STORAGE MEDIUM 3X5 TRACK-INDEX ROLLER CABINETS			
ACCESS REQUIREMENTS						
SEQUENCED BY DATE WITHIN BUTODALE PART NUMBER.						
CONTENT QUALIFICATIONS						
HOW CURRENT						
RETENTION CHARACTERISTICS NO CARDS HAVE YET BEEN DISCARDED.						
LABELS USED IN 001-57X, 001-63X,						
REMARKS FILE CONTINUES TO GROW, AS NO DISCARD RULES EXIST. OLDEST CARDS ARE AGE OF COMPANY'S RECORDING SYSTEM.						

CONTENTS

SEQUENCE NO.	MESSAGE NAME	VOLUME		CHARACTERS PER MESSAGE	CHARACTERS PER FILE	
		AVG.	PEAK		AVG.	PEAK
	HISTORICAL COST DATA CARDS	1,000 K UPWARDS. FILE INCREASES AT RATE OF 4200 CARDS PER MONTH.				
	(SEE ATTACHED SAMPLE CARD)					

DATE	R. L. CASEY ANALYST	QUOTATIONS SOURCE	1 OF 1 PAGE

BUTODALE STUDY

Figure 10–37 Sample of a record from the cost file.

Type No.		HISTORIAL COST DATA *Sample*					Item	
5.001.ANC.3							Pre–Patch Panel	

Proj No.	Qty.	Std. Cost	Unit Direct L.	Unit O/H	Unit Material	Actual Cost	Unit Time
6843	253	122.^{78}	12.^{91}	36.^{92}	T/i + 24.89 / 44.86	119.^{58}	
6083	150	80.^{00}	11.^{60}	40.^{14}	T/o + 2.13 / 72.61	122.^{22}	
5533	800	66.^{67}	9.^{45}	12.^{84}	T/i + 3.76 / 48.81	74.^{86}	*

* Cost Less G. A

Figure 10–38 File sheet for the rate file.

FILE NAME				FILE NO.	
RATE FILE				F - 4020	

LOCATION		STORAGE MEDIUM	
ENGINEERING ADMIN.		3 × 5 CARDS	

ACCESS REQUIREMENTS
MANUAL, RANDOM

SEQUENCED BY
OPERATION TYPE SEQUENCE FOR FIRST SECTION
MATERIAL CODE " " " SECOND " "

CONTENT QUALIFICATIONS

HOW CURRENT

RETENTION CHARACTERISTICS

LABELS

REMARKS
USED IN 001-63X (COSTING SPECIAL PARTS ETC.)

CONTENTS

SEQUENCE NO.	MESSAGE NAME	VOLUME		CHARACTERS PER MESSAGE	CHARACTERS PER FILE	
		AVG.	PEAK		AVG.	PEAK
	FLEXIBLE FORMAT SIMILAR					
	TO F-4010					
	APPROX. 4000 CARDS IN FILE					
	OPERATION OR MATERIAL #					
	RATE/COST FOR: DIRECT LBR					
	O/H					
	MATERIAL					
	MISC. NOTES AND REFERENCES					

DATE	R.L. CASEY	F.E. RYAN	1 OF 1
BUTODALE STUDY	ANALYST	SOURCE	PAGE

Figure 10–39 File sheet for the installed systems file.

FILE NAME						FILE NO.	
INSTALLED SYSTEMS						F- 4030	

LOCATION		STORAGE MEDIUM	
MARKETING ADMIN.		MANILA FOLDERS	

ACCESS REQUIREMENTS

SEQUENCED BY

BUTODALE ORDER NUMBER WITHIN
SYSTEM TYPE

CONTENT QUALIFICATIONS

HOW CURRENT

RETENTION CHARACTERISTICS

NEVER BEEN PURGED

LABELS

USED IN 001 – 57X

REMARKS

INTENT OF FILE SEEMS VAGUE; A DIFFERENT
SEQUENCE MAY MAKE INFO READILY USABLE.

SEQUENCE NO.	MESSAGE NAME	VOLUME		CHARACTERS PER MESSAGE	CHARACTERS PER FILE	
		AVG.	PEAK		AVG.	PEAK
	SAME AS					
	F- 4050					
	15 FILE CABINETS (4-DRAWER)					
	ESTIMATED 4,500 FOLDERS					

CONTENTS

R.L. CASEY	A.R. HOLMES	1 OF 1
DATE	SOURCE	PAGE
ANALYST		

BUTODALE
STUDY

Figure 10–40 File sheet for the contract register file.

SEE ALSO F-4050.1 AND .2

FILE NAME			FILE NO.	
CONTRACT REGISTER FILE			F-4050	

LOCATION	STORAGE MEDIUM
MARKETING ADMINISTRATION	MANILA FOLDERS

ACCESS REQUIREMENTS

SEQUENCED BY

CONTENT QUALIFICATIONS
F-4050.1 AS QUOTE IS PROCESSED; F-4050.2 AS BID IS PROCESSED. DESIGNATION OF .1 AND .2 IS DISCONTINUED AS ORDER IS PROCESSED.

HOW CURRENT

RETENTION CHARACTERISTICS
WHEN DELIVERY TO CUSTOMER IS MADE, FOLDER IS MOVED TO F-4030

LABELS

REMARKS
001-66X, 001-70X, 001-74X, 001-75X, 004-51X
004-59X, 004-61X

CONTENTS

SEQUENCE NO.	MESSAGE NAME	VOLUME		CHARACTERS PER MESSAGE	CHARACTERS PER FILE	
		AVG.	PEAK		AVG.	PEAK
—	F-4050.1 QUOTE FOLDER	50/w	70/w	460	23,000	32,200
—	F-4050.2 BID FOLDER	10/w	12/w	1,110	11,100	13,320
—	OPEN ORDERS					
	TOTAL	1500	2100			

R.L. CASEY	A.R. HOLMES	1 OF 1
ANALYST	SOURCE	PAGE

BUTODALE
STUDY
DATE

Figure 10–41 File sheet for the quote folder.

FILE NAME						FILE NO.		
QUOTE FOLDER						F-4050.1		

LOCATION		STORAGE MEDIUM						
		MANILA FOLDER						

ACCESS REQUIREMENTS

SEQUENCED BY

CONTENT QUALIFICATIONS

HOW CURRENT

RETENTION CHARACTERISTICS

LABELS

REMARKS

CONTENTS

SEQUENCE NO.	MESSAGE NAME	VOLUME		CHARACTERS PER MESSAGE	CHARACTERS PER FILE	
		AVG.	PEAK		AVG.	PEAK
1	R-2000 REQUEST FOR QUOTE	50/w	70/w	460	23,000	32,200

R.L. CASEY	A.R. HOLMES	1 OF 1
ANALYST	SOURCE	PAGE

DATE
BUTODALE
STUDY

Figure 10–42 File sheet for the request-for-bid folder.

FILE NAME						FILE NO.		
REQUEST – FOR – BID FOLDER						F–4050.2		

LOCATION	STORAGE MEDIUM	
—	MANILA FOLDER	

ACCESS REQUIREMENTS

SEQUENCED BY

CONTENT QUALIFICATIONS

HOW CURRENT

RETENTION CHARACTERISTICS

LABELS

REMARKS

CONTENTS

SEQUENCE NO.	MESSAGE NAME	VOLUME		CHARACTERS PER MESSAGE	CHARACTERS PER FILE	
		AVG.	PEAK		AVG.	PEAK
1	R-2010 REQUEST FOR BID	10/W	12/W	1110	11,100	13,320

R.L. CASEY	A.R. HOLMES	1 OF 1
ANALYST	SOURCE	PAGE

DATE

BUTODALE
STUDY

Figure 10–43 File sheet for the customer index book.

FILE NAME		FILE NO.
CUSTOMER INDEX BOOK		F-4060

LOCATION MARKETING ADMIN.
STORAGE MEDIUM Post Binders (4 Volumes) Columnar Paper

ACCESS REQUIREMENTS

SEQUENCED BY CUSTOMER NAME

CONTENT QUALIFICATIONS ACTIVITY IN PAST 10 YEARS

HOW CURRENT DAILY

RETENTION CHARACTERISTICS

LABELS

REMARKS HAND ENTRIES POSTED ON ORDER RECEIPT
001 – 71X

CONTENTS

SEQUENCE NO.	MESSAGE NAME	VOLUME		CHARACTERS PER MESSAGE	CHARACTERS PER FILE	
		AVG.	PEAK		AVG.	PEAK
	CUSTOMER NAME					
	CUSTOMER #					
	REFERENCE #'s AND DATES					
	BUTODALE ORDER # AND DATE					
	APPROXIMATELY 4,000 CUSTOMERS					
	MINIMUM ENTRIES – 1					
	AVERAGE ENTRIES – 4					
	MAXIMUM ENTRIES – 50					

R.L. CASEY	C.F. BETTORS	1 OF 1
DATE ANALYST	SOURCE	PAGE

BUTODALE
STUDY

Figure 10–44 File sheet for the project index book.

FILE NAME	PROJECT INDEX BOOK				FILE NO. F-4070			
LOCATION				STORAGE MEDIUM POST BINDER, COLUMNAR PAPER				
ACCESS REQUIREMENTS								
SEQUENCED BY BUTODALE ORDER #								
CONTENT QUALIFICATIONS ORDER RECEIVED OR PROJECT INITIATED								
HOW CURRENT DAILY								
RETENTION CHARACTERISTICS WHEN BINDER IS FULL, SHEETS BEARING PROJECTS CLOSED 6 MONTHS ARE PUT IN DEAD STORAGE.								
LABELS								
REMARKS HAND ENTRIES ARE POSTED AS PROJECT IS INITIATED (001-71X) AND COMPLETED (004-59X)								

CONTENTS

SEQUENCE NO.	MESSAGE NAME	VOLUME		CHARACTERS PER MESSAGE	CHARACTERS PER FILE	
		AVG.	PEAK		AVG.	PEAK
	PROJECT IN BINDER (30 PROJECTS/PAGE)	1,500	2,100			

R.L. CASEY   C.F. BETTORS   1 OF 1

DATE — ANALYST   SOURCE   PAGE

BUTODALE STUDY

Figure 10–45 File sheet for the assignment sheet.

FILE NAME		FILE NO.
ASSIGNMENT SHEET		F-4080

LOCATION	STORAGE MEDIUM
MANUFACTURING ADMIN.	"SCHEDUGRAPH" BOARD

ACCESS REQUIREMENTS
DAILY — PHOTO COPIES DISTRIBUTED TO MARKETING
AND MANUFACTURING DAILY

SEQUENCED BY
DUE DATE

CONTENT QUALIFICATIONS
ACCEPTED ORDER OR ACTIVE PROJECT

HOW CURRENT
BOARD SHOWS PREVIOUS 2 WEEKS AND
FUTURE 28 WEEKS —

RETENTION CHARACTERISTICS
PHOTO COPIES SHOW CLOSING DAILY STATUS
BOARD CHANGES CONTINUALLY

LABELS

REMARKS
001-72X,   004-51X

CONTENTS

SEQUENCE NO.	MESSAGE NAME	VOLUME		CHARACTERS PER MESSAGE	CHARACTERS PER FILE	
		AVG.	PEAK		AVG.	PEAK
	PROJECT OR ORDER #					
	PRODUCT TYPE					
	SCHEDULE DATES					
	DUE DATE					

R.L. CASEY	L. CIPRIANO	1 OF 1
DATE / ANALYST	SOURCE	PAGE

BUTODALE
STUDY

QUESTIONS AND PROBLEMS

10–1 Of what value would a present business description report, such as the Butodale report, be to organizations in their search for management personnel?

10–2 Use your local library or write to an appropriate brokerage house to obtain an annual report on three selected companies. See if you can obtain a history of one of the companies and its industry. Prepare a narrative description by following the format of the general section for Butodale.

10–3 There are many fine source books on certain basic industries such as insurance, banking, transportation, etc. Classify businesses and institutions into approximately twenty-five categories and identify source items which give industry history, government regulations, etc. for three of these categories.

10–4 Of what value are case studies, such as Butodale Phase I, for introducing students to business?

10–5 What kind of frequency curve is suggested by the data for suppliers in Figure 10–1? Is this unexpected?

10–6 In Figure 10–13, is the selection of the words *provide product demand* reasonable to define the activity described by the phrase?

10–7 What is the average time for answering a quotation on a standard analog computer at Butodale? Why does it take so long if the product is standard?

10–8 What are some of the components that make up the miscellaneous costs in Figure 10–13?

10–9 What triggers the costing operation (630) shown in Figure 10–15?

10–10 In the Butodale system, how large a record will be needed to contain the information on a customer's request for a quotation? for a bid?

10–11 If one were to classify both message sheets and file sheets under a single name, what might be the term?

10–12 Figure 10–25 shows a blank form described on the message sheet in Figure 10–24. How could the analysts improve their reported information relative to this form?

10–13 What critical information is contained in file sheet number F–4010?

10–14 In file sheet F–4030, the analysts noted that the retention characteristic of the file is, NEVER BEEN PURGED. What does this mean?

PART THREE
DETERMINING SYSTEM REQUIREMENTS

The purpose of Part 3 is to present the philosophy and methodology involved in determining system requirements. After completion of the study of the present business and before designing the new system, analysts must determine what the system is required to do and how its performance will be evaluated.

Part 3 covers the methodology involved in establishing systems requirements and the preparation of a report called the System Requirements Specification. Part 3 discusses how the information gathered during the study of the existing system assists in determining the requirements for the new system. In this second phase, it is necessary to look beyond present relationships to establish the logical requirements needed to meet future goals and objectives.

Additional documentation methods are explained as they apply to this phase, and Part 3 concludes with the System Requirements Specification for two activities of the Butodale case study.

CHAPTER 11
SYSTEM GOALS AND ACTIVITY ALIGNMENT

11.1 DEFINING GOALS AND REQUIREMENTS

In determining the requirements of a system, the analysts must answer three questions:

1. What is the system required to do?
2. How well is it to do it?
3. How is the system's performance to be evaluated?

In understanding an existing organization, a study team must first concentrate on gaining understanding and insight into a business as it presently operates and reacts to its environment. After that, it is necessary to look beyond present relationships to determine what the system is logically required to do to meet future business goals and objectives.

The Goal Statement A goal statement is valuable as a definition of purpose and intent; it acquires larger significance when it is related directly to the activities of a business. An activity is a series of logically related operations which support and fulfill a specific business goal. Since an activity is goal-directed in nature, it inherently demonstrates by its functions a justification for existence. This characteristic is often absent in contemporary organizational alignments.

The Importance of Activities Activities are defined by the analysts as they study the existing organization and, along with the statement of present and future goals, they are the basis for requirement definitions. The goal statement and activity formulation are vital inputs to the study since it is possible to analyze what is required of a system only if it is first known what useful purpose the system will serve.

Determining System Requirements System requirements cannot be determined solely from an understanding of present conditions; future plans and growth have perhaps an overriding influence if one intends to implement systems with long lives. Analysts must gauge the future by forecasting the impact of new products and services, changes in mix, volume trends, design and process innovations, enactment of regulatory laws, and introduction of competitive products. In doing this work, a study team hypothesizes, analyzes, synthesizes, and simulates to establish balanced systems requirements reflecting both the present and the future.

The objective toward which the team works is a report on system requirements, activity by activity. The report shows operations that must be performed, inputs that must be accepted, outputs that must be produced, resources that should be employed, and factors for measuring the value of alternative system designs.

Imp.

The goal statement; the definition of activities; and time, cost, and accuracy data for individual operations within an activity and in summary are principal inputs to the requirements specification. The Phase I report describing the present business furnishes a substantial share of the information for requirements specification, but data about the future must still be obtained. Often the goal statement and activity formulation are not sufficiently precise; sometimes they must be revised in the light of new study findings. These possibilities must be appraised early in Phase II before definitive requirements specifications are established.

11.2 STUDY SCOPE

The formal study of requirements begins after the report of the existing organization has been accepted by management and approval is given to continue. This second part of the study ends with management approval of the system requirements specifications. Between these two points, the study team engages in the diverse tasks of specifying the requirements for the new system. These tasks include:

1. Analyzing, defining, and modifying present and future objectives to produce a realistic statement of business goals
2. Modifying present activities or creating new ones to align with these redefined business goals; specifying activity scope and boundaries
3. Analyzing each activity to establish required inputs, operations, outputs, and resources
4. Refining these requirements through several iterations

5. Constructing measures of effectiveness for each activity
6. Documenting system requirements

Requirement complexity varies from activity to activity. Since activities initially are defined as relatively self-contained, analysts can reduce complexity by analyzing each activity individually. When designing the new system, the multiple activities can be integrated, and any inconsistencies or incompatibilities worked out. Analysis by activity may disclose certain overall constraints, technical or managerial, which may limit the study team's range of possible solutions. Recognition of these constraints is necessary for successful systems design. After requirements have been determined, acceptable and desirable performance levels are identified. This sets up a series of performance targets to be met in systems design.

The development of requirements can be a straightforward process. It can also involve difficult and complex analysis. In many instances, interviews and data analysis provide satisfactory information for specifications. In others, technical competence in the use of management science techniques will be required.

11.3 THE REPORT OF SYSTEMS REQUIREMENTS

The System Requirements Specification (SRS) is the output report from Phase II. Analysts begin the report with a summary section describing the present and future business goals, the general considerations of the overall system, and pertinent information on the several activities as they affect the business.

1st three steps of the report.

System Requirements Specification Format The balance of the report can be a series of packets, one for each activity, each composed of three sections: general, operations, and measurement. Figure 2–3 shows the structure of a report assembled according to this plan.

The *general section* customarily outlines activity goals and objectives, scope and boundaries, and other information, such as policies and costs, not examined in the more specialized sections.

The *operations section* should state what is required of an activity in terms of inputs it must accept, operations it must perform, outputs it must produce, and resources (such as personnel, equipment, facilities, inventories, information) it must use to support the operations. These elements can be summarized at the beginning of the section in the *activity requirements model*.

The *measurement section* specifies factors and rating scales for evaluating a system designed to perform the activity under a variety of conditions.

The specification report defines requirements at the problem level, contrasting them in the solution description to the proposed design for the new system. This definition forms the base that makes the flexibility of a solution possible, and it is the base on which new systems can be built as the organization changes.

11.4 GOALS IN THE SRS

Goals of the present business were defined in Phase I, and activities were formulated to meet these goals. In Phase II, goal and activity statements are reviewed and refined to accommodate changes that occur as a business plans for the future. The goals directly considered are those within the scope of the study. After the analysts and management have reached a mutual understanding on a balanced set of goals for the present and future business, activity definitions can be reshaped, and activity scope realigned to conform to the new goal statement.

In an established business, the pronounced emphasis on daily work demands and pressures often results in insufficient regard for future events. A billing date arrives and statements must go out; sales decline, and a promotional scheme must be devised to boost orders; productive capacity is exceeded, and work must be subcontracted. Operating personnel usually have little time to consider the goals of a business; this is more usually the responsibility of those who plan for the future of the business. Top managers or business owners decide goals, but product planners and systems analysts must know and understand these goals if systems designed to support the business are to be effective.

No matter how well the goals of an enterprise have been formulated by management, they are seldom expressed in a form useful to the systems analyst. The problem in goal analysis is to change broad, generalized statements into direct, specific definitions of what a business is to do. Where goals exist only in the minds of management, they must be extracted and written down—and must be based on interviews and discussions. The more clearly and precisely goals are expressed, the more valid the specification of system requirements will be.

Goals reveal purpose in a business; they state what a business is to do, both now and in the future. A business goal is stated in terms of:

1. Business results to be achieved
2. Products and services to be supplied
3. Maintenance of resources, both physical and informational
4. Improvement of relationships and communications with consumers, suppliers, governments, shareowners, and the general public

The degree of attention devoted to goals varies with the study. Precise goal definition, in a study aimed at creating a new system design for a large and complex business, provides adequate direction for the study team; precision becomes less important in improvement or mechanization studies, the assumption being that an adequate goal has already been stated. If the team cannot state the goal, then an adequately stated one must be developed and approved by management. This methodology is a useful tool for less than an entire business, and most studies are of this kind. In most businesses, a considerable amount of time elapses from the inception of an idea to its practical implementation as a finished product or service. To maintain competitive advantage, a business must continually look ahead and plan for new products and services, often years before they are brought to the market. These ideas both determine future goals and support management's plans.

The existence and availability of short- and long-range business plans provides the team with an important input for their study. A typical long-range plan contains a wide variety of data about the future business:

1. Characterization of current and future markets; user requirements for new and existing products
2. Economic and business environment
3. Types of new products
4. Development of new and present markets
5. Possible changes in product mix
6. Research and development projects
7. Plant expansions and new site selection
8. Projections of cash flow to finance corporate growth
9. Projections on sales and manpower

In some cases these plans exist only in part or even as ideas in the minds of managers. On these occasions, the study team must draw out the full plans in interviews. For example, in one large bank study, the future-planning documents revealed the imminent introduction of new services, such as no-check payroll processing, retail credit servicing, automatic loans, and utility bill payment and collections. Individual interviews with bank officers also revealed that nonreturn of checks, customer accounts payable processing, and a community credit reference service were under consideration for the future. These services were incorporated in the future-goal statement.

One study team, faced with poorly-defined plans, asked each manager to make a list of future goals for new services and growth for the next ten years as he or she would personally express them. The individual replies were correlated, and those judged most appropriate and those most frequently mentioned were compiled into a composite consensus report. The study team then used this report as a basis for discussion at a management meeting, where an acceptable future-goal statement was finally devised.

11.5 SOURCES OF INFORMATION FOR GOALS

Within a business, analysts can gather information about the future from many different sources. The marketing manager is cognizant of future plans on new markets and products, distribution channels, and market penetration; engineering and research managers are sources for new product and technology data; the manufacturing manager controls plans for the employment of new processes and materials that can affect current and future products.

Throughout Phase II, trend and projection data will be needed to establish a quantification of future system requirements. This information can also be usefully applied to goal definition, especially when long-range plans have not been documented in detail.

An organization's annual report often furnishes clues to future goals. The following excerpts are from the report of a large manufacturer:

On expansion

An aggressive plan of expansion and acquisition has been continued by management while increasing available sales and manufacturing capacity, and, at the same time, allied fields with exceptionally good earning potentials have been entered.

On distribution

Immediate and economical delivery is an especially strong competitive advantage of the company to both its commercial and industrial

Figure 11–1   Trends of cosmetic sales for an eleven-year period.

Sales Growth of Selected Cosmetics Items
(All sales figures expressed in millions of dollars)

	10	9	8	7	6	5	4	3	2	1	0
Rinses, Tints, Dyes	74	67	46	37	32	28	24	14	13	12	11
Spray Hair Fixatives	91	81	76	81	82	75	38	23	16	5	2
Shaving Cream-Aerosol	54	51	44	39	36	30	27	20	—	—	—
After-Shave Lotion	49	47	44	41	38	35	32	30	28	27	26
Liquid Facial Cleansers	29	29	26	26	26	25	21	8	—	—	—
Lipsticks	121	100	91	82	76	71	64	56	54	35	32
Mascara, Eyebrow Pencil, Eye Shadow	21	18	15	12	10	9	8	7	6	6	5
Toilet Water and Cologne	103	93	84	73	65	58	53	51	49	48	46

customers. Recognizing the trend of large industrial companies as well as the newer small technological concerns to locate their research and, in many cases, production facilities away from the traditional population centers, the company began systematically enlarging its market facilities with this in mind. Its branch warehouses from coast to coast are being improved with better inventories, automated billing and invoicing, and efficient stock control.

On capacity

An additional 240,000 square feet of facility will be ready for occupancy this summer, freeing (additional) space presently needed for manufacturing and product development.

Internal projections should be supplemented by forecasts from other sources. Trade associations and research consultants customarily predict industry trends, and multiclient studies are often available for purchase; government bureaus and brokerage houses develop analyses by industry and commodity; research foundations and centers have information on product and other technological changes. Export markets, consumer attitudes, requirements for presently unsupplied goods and services, and other external factors can affect the planning and should be studied.

Figure 11–1 indicates trends of cosmetic sales. The trends projected from these data helped management decide on future product mix and on where to concentrate marketing efforts.

Developments and trends in urban renewal, additional legislation on health and welfare, changes in leisure habits, and new patterns in income by family groups can be analyzed for their effect on future conditions.

Though an analyst can draw on considerable company, industry, and government material for future goal formulation, the raw data must be related directly to the future operations of the particular business. Until such data are translated into plans for facilities, manpower, and materials, they are not particularly useful. The systems analyst, working with this type of data, can serve as a catalyst to management thinking. The ultimate decision on appropriate goals for the future of a business rests with management.

11.6 AN EXAMPLE OF SETTING GOALS

The modification of a preliminary goals and objectives statement can be shown in the study of a large commercial bank. The study's initial statement emphasized present goals.

Goals and Objectives—Phase I

1. Maintain and increase time and deposit balances to provide lending and investment ability consistent with customer needs and bank profit planning.
2. Increase speed, accuracy, and control of operations without incurring increased costs.
3. Improve customer service by reducing teller and loan processing time.
4. Pay interest rates and establish interest policies that are competitive with the banking industry, and as prescribed by Federal Reserve regulations.
5. Maintain loans outstanding at a figure consistent with and prescribed by bank policy through the extension of credit to qualified applicants.
6. Strengthen and maintain dealer relationships through continued good service, fair policies and practices, and competitive plans.
7. Serve the financing needs of the community and provide a profitable return to the bank on investments.
8. Make each customer a total bank customer.
9. Protect the quality of the loan portfolio and produce accurate and timely records for the customer.
10. Fulfill the borrowing requirements of present and potential individual and business customers, in order to provide a safe and profitable return to the bank.
11. Portray the bank's image by presenting positive identification factors to the public.

The goal statement, developed while the analysts were studying the existing management system, was inclusive enough, but it contained a mixture of performance, system, and business goals; and many were tied to the general-purpose goal of profit. Early in Phase II, the goal statement was reappraised and modified to read:

Goals and Objectives—Phase II

1. Offer a balanced package of banking services to the community and surrounding areas which recognizes customer needs, complies with federal, state and local regulations and laws, and is competitive in cost, accuracy, and timeliness.
2. Maintain and increase time and demand deposit balances to provide lending and investment ability.
3. Maintain outstanding loan balances at a level consistent with established bank policy, and by accepting only qualified applicants.
4. Secure new and total bank account affiliations through promotional programs, and maintain the quality of bank-customer relationships and services.
5. Provide for the extension of bank services into newly developed surburban areas within the bank's established jurisdiction.
6. Explore and develop new banking financing practices and services for individual and business customers.
7. Strengthen and maintain community and employee relationships through continued good service, fair policies and practices, and forward planning.

A study of the two sets of goals reveals that the new set not only brings sharper focus, but also highlights the bank's strategy to achieve the goals.

11.7 ACTIVITY REFORMULATION

Activities are the means by which goals are accomplished. Formulated during the study of the existing organization, they undergo modification as future business goals are developed. Individual activities often correspond to individual goals in a one-to-one relationship, but there will be instances when a number of activities contribute to a single goal, or when a single activity will contribute to two or more goals.

The following example shows how an initial statement of activities was realigned to match a restatement of goals. The goals were those listed above for the commercial bank. For this bank, the analysts originally defined the activities as:

Activities – Phase I

 1. Commercial checking accounts
 2. Special checking accounts
 3. Commercial loans
 4. Mortgage loans
 5. Foreign banking
 6. Investments and stock transfer
 7. Marketing, advertising, and public relations
 8. Correspondent banking
 9. Legal and real estate
10. Savings accounts
11. Cashier and comptroller
12. Installment loans

Early in Phase II these activities were reviewed with bank management and compared with the new goal statement. It was clear that the early definitions could be realigned. Management and the analysts redefined the bank's activities as:

Activity Formulation – Phase II

1. Demand deposits
2. Time deposits
3. Installment loans
4. Mortgage loans
5. Commercial loans
6. Marketing

Commercial and special checking accounts, having similar characteristics, were combined into the demand deposits activity. Demand and time deposits were maintained separately for legal reasons. Correspondent banking was absorbed into each of these activities by type of service (demand deposit, time deposit). The three loan activities were, in effect, separate product lines, relatively self-contained, each one starting from and terminating in the outside environment. Advertising, public relations, international banking, legal, and real estate activities were set aside from the immediate study for lack of transaction volume, although some of their operations were picked up in the selected activities. Each of the six activities included certain elements of the bank's functional costs (for example, all activities were entered through teller operations and employed central files).

11.8 ACTIVITY SCOPE

The alignment process yields broad activity definitions. Generalized statements must now be sharpened to provide a scope and boundary for each activity. There is no other way to describe the content of a wholly new activity.

It is just as important to decide what is excluded from an activity as it is to decide what is included. Precise terminology avoids the uncertainty of ambiguous function names. A clear, complete, and understandable reference is necessary to prevent confusion between adjacent activities on the part of the study team. The scope and boundary statement describes both what is and what is not included; the format of the description is secondary.

The Provide Product Demand activity statement from Butodale Electronics illustrates these points by treating the activity scope in the following manner:

This activity is concerned with accepting customer orders and preparing bids and quotations for potential customers. Requests and orders are received from company salesmen, manufacturers' representatives, or are placed directly by the customer. They include orders for standard and custom-designed equipment and spare parts, but do not include requests for computation services. Standard equipment is processed routinely and the customer is furnished documents including price quotations, descriptive data, layouts, diagrams, and other information necessary to make the purchase decision.

The statement goes on to mention special cases:

Where the equipment is special, this activity includes management and engineering reviews, engineering design and layout, and the compilation of special cost data. After receipt of a formal order, the contract is edited and clarified for communication to engineering and manufacturing. Present volume of requests averages 15-20 weekly for standard products, and 3–4 for engineered products. This is expected to rise to a combined total of 25–30 weekly.

While it is not necessary to mention volumes in a scope statement, such information does indicate the activity size. The statement goes on to tell what is not included in this activity:

Provide product demand does not include market forecasting, determination of plant schedules (this is actually worked out in conference with manufacturing when available capacity does not conform with customer requirements in regard to requested shipping dates), or the calculation of costs and prices.

A final sentence summarizes the statement:

The principal inputs, then, to this activity are customer orders or requests for quotation, and the principal outputs are quotations and specifications to the customer and communication of accepted orders to manufacturing.

An alternative method to the sentence-style activity statement is simply to list the operations performed and the operations excluded. The study team for Custodian Life Insurance Company chose the latter technique, which is appropriate when operations are clear-cut and self-explanatory:

Operations performed by the New Business activity

Review application and related forms
Request medical and policyholder history
Prepare processing documents
Assemble application data
Underwrite application
Request additional information
Prepare declination letter
Calculate premiums
Prepare policy
Prepare internal records
Prepare external records
Provide new business statistics on current basis

Operations not performed by the New Business activity

Determine outside underwriting services
Determine underwriting standards
Set limits for policy size
Initiate new plans of insurance
Determine medical standards
Determine premium rates or dividend schedules

Recognition of exclusions as well as inclusions avoids making unwarranted assumptions about an activity. An integrated material control activity, for example, usually includes production scheduling and control, inventory control, traffic and transportation, receiving and shipping, purchasing, and other operations related to overall material flow. Sometimes, however, the purchasing activity is under accounting or is independent. The inclusion-exclusion coverage should also point out the presence or the absence of functional work. In purchasing, traffic may be an identifiable function or it may be performed by a buyer.

11.9 ACTIVITY VALIDATION

After the analysts have completed the alignment of activities, their statements are validated by comparing them with the activity sheets developed earlier or by having them reviewed by management.

When finished with the alignment, the analysts should review the activities as a whole to determine if they are complete and meet the established goals; whether they are relatively independent so that they can be installed separately if desired; and whether they are of a practicable size. Completeness of coverage can be determined by comparing the aligned statements with the activity sheets. The independence feature is determined by comparing the individual statements as a unit against each of the others within the activity and to other activities to check for conflicts and overlapping. This audit confirms that each activity is relatively independent and has few interactions with other activities so that any activity interaction will not prevent sequential activity implementation.

The review by management of activity formulation serves two purposes:

1. It advises management of the team's approach and progress.
2. It allows management to make known any preferences about the sequence in which activities are to be analyzed.

11.10 ASSIGNING ACTIVITY PRIORITY

Management may have several compelling reasons for assigning priority to activities for analysis and implementation, and their decision establishes the sequence of events for the study team. The total dollars expended in an activity frequently help decide which activity is selected for initial study: activities with a high potential for payoff will generally be accorded priority. For example, activities which can increase the profitability of an industrial enterprise by assisting management to control costs, increase revenues, improve productivity, decrease expenses, and shorten response time to fulfill user requirements, will obviously stand an excellent chance of being high on the list of priorities for early implementation. Further, those activities which not only satisfy user requirements but also return to the business the above benefits with relatively minor customer risk will rank higher on the list of those activities for initial implementation. The balance of projected benefits against implementation risks will have to be considered in arriving at a realistic set of activity requirements.

In some studies, activities having input from or output to the environment are analyzed first. In other studies, outputs from one activity serve as inputs to the following one. One output from a design engineering activity, for example, can be a bill of materials; the content of the bill of materials establishes the input to the manufacturing-planning activity. Unless there is a strong reason for conducting the manufacturing study first, the engineering analysis takes precedence. Single-activity studies, of course, pose no sequencing problem.

Once management approval has been secured on activity definitions and priorities have been assigned, schedules can be drawn up for the rest of the work the analysts must do to determine the requirements of the system.

SUMMARY

In determining system requirements, analysts must ascertain what the system is required to do and how the performance of the system is to be evaluated. System requirements cannot be determined solely from an understanding of present conditions; future plans and growth have an equally important influence. The goal statement, the definition of activities, and time, cost, and accuracy data for individual operations within an activity are principal inputs to the requirements specification. Requirement complexity varies from activity to activity. The System Requirements Specification (SRS) consists of a summary section and a series of packets, one for each activity. Each activity packet consists of three sections: general, operations, and measurement. Goals must be defined before activities can be isolated. Information about goals can be obtained from many sources, including the marketing, engineering, research, and production managers. Activities are reformulated and modified as future goals are developed. The scope and boundary of each activity must be determined, and it is important to specify what is included and what is excluded from each activity. Activity statements prepared by the analysts can be validated by managerial review or by comparison with previously devloped activity sheets. Management, of course, will ultimately approve these statements, through acceptance or rejection of the SRS.

QUESTIONS AND PROBLEMS

11–1 State three major kinds of goals that might apply to most organizations in general.

11–2 Public agencies often have a difficult time expressing their goals because they are not directly related to profit-making activities. For any three federal, state, or community agencies which you select, state what you consider are their principal goals.

11–3 Identify and define activities related to the goals stated in response to Question 11–2.

11–4 In establishing goals, what are some considerations that should be recognized?

11–5 What might be the future goals of a quality control system for a manufacturing process?

11–6 What might be the goals a state might use for designing a welfare information system?

11–7 What might be the major files in a university information system set up after the activities of the university have been reformulated to accommodate a computer system?

11–8 A study team has been requested to analyze the activities relative to order entry, billing, and accounts receivable. The team soon realizes that the organization has a very fine cost system for product costing, but has no costs recorded which may be useful in analyzing activities during their reformulation. Why might this be?

11–9 What goals might the analysts record for an information system involving the accounts payable activity of a company?

11–10 What are some of the goals that analysts might record for a production control activity?

11–11 What may be considered as goals for the purchasing activity of a company?

11–12 What might be the goals of a team which is studying an information system for a telephone company?

11–13 What might some of the goals of a plant maintenance management system be?

CHAPTER 12
SYSTEM REQUIREMENTS

12.1 REQUIREMENTS SPECIFICATION

The central theme in requirements specification is to determine what a system is required to do, activity by activity, in terms of:

1. Outputs it *must* produce
2. Inputs it *must* accept
3. Operations it *must* perform
4. Resources it *must* use

To define system requirements, a study team moves away from present operations as they were described for the current system and organization and develops a specification from the position of what is logically necessary, or imposed, to fulfill the goals of an activity.

It is important to specify only those inputs, outputs, operations, and resources which are required, since unnecessary specifications will constrain the new system design to be developed in Phase III. The flexibility permitted the system designers is inversely proportional to the tightness of the imposed requirements specification.

The logically required specifications are established first and then are adjusted to accommodate practical considerations. This produces a more valid specification than one devised by building only on present operations. Most activities contain so many variable and interacting factors and conditions that it is difficult to achieve a requirements specification in a single attempt; frequently several attempts are necessary to produce a satisfactory statement.

A study team normally begins by developing descriptive requirements for inputs, operations, outputs, and resources. They next add quantitative data, such as volume and time, to this description. Management science techniques, such as correlation analysis, sampling, trend projection, forecasting, and simulation, are applied where necessary to increase the validity of the specifications.

Figure 12–1   An abstract model used in specifying the requirements of an activity.

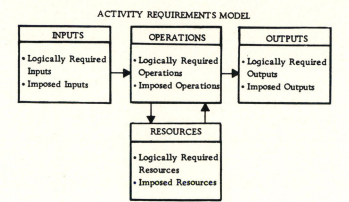

12.2 **ACTIVITY REQUIREMENTS MODEL**

Many analysts have found it useful to prepare a preliminary version of an activity requirements model, even though the model may be subsequently revised. Figure 12–1 shows an abstraction of the relationships in such a model.

Inputs and outputs are stated first, since they are usually more closely associated with the goals and objectives of the activity than are operations or resources. After specifying inputs and outputs, the study team progressively works through an activity to establish a logical sequence of operations required in its performance. Analysis of required resources results first in the identification of those that are imposed; logically required resources then emerge as relationships among inputs, operations, and outputs are developed.

12.3 **REQUIRED OUTPUTS AND INPUTS**

Activity outputs are often closely related to activity goals. Therefore, many outputs in an established organization are subject to constraints. For example, the form of an invoice may be so firmly fixed that management may not permit any change. In somewhat the same way, the method and form of paying employees may be set by a rigid union contract. Government reporting rules may fix the form and frequency of certain documents for regulated companies like utilities, banks, insurance, and transportation companies. These and other constraints usually make it easier for the analysts to establish an activity's output requirements than its input requirements. Administrative practices often reduce the room for creativity in designing a new system. Because of this, outputs are defined first by most study teams in analyzing an activity. Outputs from one activity that become inputs to another are defined in the form that is acceptable to the second activity. Once outputs are defined, the team can decide what information (inputs) is required to produce the outputs (and, in turn, what operations are required to transform the inputs into outputs) or what operations must be performed to produce the output (and what information is therefore required).

Customer acceptance controls the form and content of many outputs — particularly in a business competing in services, such as banking. Legal and audit stipulations either affect outputs or are outputs in themselves (insurance and banking reports, small business administration reports, Social Security and income tax reports, and similar forms). Industry practice, as recognized by individual companies or as published by trade associations, also affects output formats. An output may be required by another activity within the business; it may also be required as feedback for repetitive processing or recycling of the activity.

Required inputs have many of the characteristics of required outputs and similarly may be imposed by the environment or other activities. In addition, some inputs are logically required to furnish information for outputs and provide access to, or maintain, resources.

The determination of logically required inputs and outputs is illustrated in the Butodale study. The goals and objectives of the activity carried on to provide the demand for Butodale's products had been identified as:

1. Sell custom-designed and standard computer equipment and accessories
2. Communicate individual specifications and requirements for special computer models

This activity, according to the scope statement shown earlier, was concerned with accepting customer orders and preparing bids and quotations for potential customers. The analysts asked themselves what outputs were logically required to meet these objectives. The second goal suggested one output: equipment specifications. The activity covered both custom-designed and standard units; therefore, some customers ordered from a catalog, while others negotiated a specification and quotation through a series of conferences and letters with the engineering department. For the former, the order was acknowledged and a price and delivery schedule confirmed; for the latter, quotations of estimated price and delivery were prepared and supported by drawings and specifications outlining special equipment features and performance characteristics. Besides these outputs to the customer, the manufacturing department required customer order information to plan production schedules and determine shipping dates. A preliminary specification for outputs was developed from the following information:

1. Quotations
2. Acknowledgments
3. Bids
4. Letters of transmittal
5. Prints and drawings
6. Specifications
7. Audited firm orders
8. Communication of firm orders to shop

After examining the eight outputs, the study team had to decide whether to first establish inputs or the operations required to produce these outputs. From their earlier study of the activities, they knew that operations were extremely complex in engineering, sales, and manufacturing planning; so inputs were selected. The analysts then asked themselves, "What inputs are logically required?" Certainly, firm orders were a prime input; where a prospect was inquiring for information, his or her letter (or telephone call, wire, or any other suitable form) was also an input. The required inputs were described as:

1. Request for quotation
2. Request to bid
3. Formal orders
4. Telephone calls
5. Letters
6. Wires

With inputs and outputs thus defined, operations were then identified—as they were logically required to transform these inputs into outputs, not necessarily as they were presently performed.

12.4 **THE LOGIC OF OPERATIONS**

If a team can define cause-and-effect relationships which govern the transformation of inputs to outputs, it has established a sound basis for specifying required operations.

Actions do not just happen in a business; they are caused by some event or combination of conditions. The logic behind these operations must be identified before an analyst can see the connections among the events. This logic may take many forms:

1. There may be a specific, identifiable cause or condition which determines the action. ("If the credit rating is OK, approve the order; if not, reject it.")
2. It may be imposed as a directive. ("Response time on telephone calls may not exceed eighteen seconds." The reason for this ruling was a survey which found that people intending to place an order hang up after this length of time when the call is unanswered.)
3. It is the only practical alternative to a situation; or it is an industry-wide practice.
4. It is the selection of a series of sequential operations, all of which have to be performed, but not necessarily in a specific order (for example, auditing an invoice).

Any or all of these are used in the development of requirements. Sometimes there is a direct cause-and-effect relationship among events; at other times there is a process of selecting or combining practical alternatives.

Narrative form is often used to document simple operations. The following paragraph shows the basis for determining an insurance premium rate:

Premium rate for a policy depends on the status of an applicant's health, age, occupation and sex. When these conditions are not covered in the appropriate instructions, rate is established by the underwriting department.

Although narrative form is widely used to inform people about operations, practices, and procedures, it can be supplemented by two alternative methods that have considerable merit for the documentation of operations — flowcharts and decision tables.

Figure 12–2 Narrative form stating the logical decisions and operations involved in handling a customer's order.

---

a. If the order is for a stock item and the item is in stock, prepare its shipment and send it to the customer.

b. If the order is for a nonstock item and it is feasible to make the item, have it made, prepare its shipment, and send to the customer. Otherwise, examine the feasibility of purchasing the item.

c. If it is feasible to purchase the item, then order it. When it is received, prepare the shipment and send it to the customer. Otherwise, prepare a refusal notice and send to the customer.

d. If the order is for a stock item but the item is not in stock, follow the procedure for a nonstock item.

12.5 FLOWCHARTS

Where decision logic becomes too unwieldy for successful explanation through narrative, techniques such as flowcharts or decision tables can be used to demonstrate significant relationships among operations. As an example, the reader can consider the logical operations required in determining whether a customer's order can be filled or must be refused.

Figure 12–2 contains a narrative of the steps in the process. Figure 12–3 contains the same process in flowchart form. The symbols in the flowchart have been numbered, and the statements in the narrative lettered, to facilitate the explanation.

In the example, one of four results must occur. They are:

1. Fill the order from stock
2. Fill the order by making the item
3. Fill the order by purchasing the item
4. Refuse the order

In the narrative form Statement a is the procedure for obtaining Result 1 above. The same procedure is expressed in the flowchart through Symbols 1, 2, 9, and 10.

Figure 12–3 Flowchart exhibiting the logical decisions and operations in handling a customer's order.

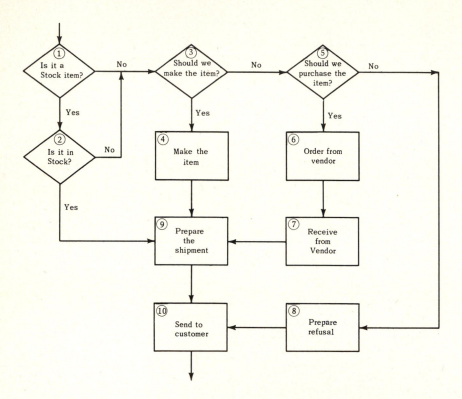

12.6 DECISION TABLES

The basic objective of decision tables is to arrange and present the logic of a set of operations in a form which will facilitate the understanding of the relationship between the conditions and the resultant actions. A decision table expresses logic in tabular form, just as a flowchart expresses logic in diagram form, and a Boolean equation uses symbolic representation for the same purpose. Figure 12–4 is an example of a *limited entry decision table*. It is called limited entry because the analyst can only use Y (for yes), N (for no) or X (for execute) as the entries. It expresses the same logic as the narrative in Figure 12–2 and the flowchart in Figure 12–3. An *extended entry decision table* would allow actual values or rules within the body of the table and not just in the stubs.

The decision table in Figure 12–4 consists of a condition stub, a condition entry, an action stub, and an action entry, as do all decision

Figure 12–4 Decision table containing the logical decisions and operations in handling a customer's order.

	Rule No.	1	2	3	4	5	6	7	
Condition stub	Is it a stock item	Y	Y	Y	Y	N	N	N	Condition entry
	Is the item in stock	Y	N	N	N				
	Should we make it		Y	N	N	Y	N	N	
	Should we purchase it			Y	N		Y	N	
Action stub	Make the item		X			X			Action entry
	Order & receive the item			X			X		
	Prepare shipment	X	X	X		X	X		
	Prepare refusal				X			X	
	Send to customer	X	X	X	X	X	X	X	

tables. In the decision table the decision rules are numbered. Each of these rules can be expressed in statement form. Thus, Rule 1 represents the statement, "Fill the order from stock." The complete equivalent descriptions of the rules are listed below:

1. Fill the order from stock
2. Make the item and send it to the customer
3. Order the item and send it to the customer
4. Send the customer a refusal notice
5. Make the item and send it to the customer
6. Order the item and send it to the customer
7. Send the customer a refusal notice

Perhaps the best way for the student to study the decision table is to trace each of the seven possible paths on the flowchart while at the same time following the entries in a single column in the decision table for each path followed in the flowchart.

12.7 COMMENTS ON THE METHODS

Each of the three methods of portraying decisions and operations has advantages and disadvantages.

Figure 12–5 is a table showing the statements of the narrative form and the corresponding symbols of the flowchart which are executed

Figure 12–5 Table showing the relation among the steps in narrative form (Figure 12–2), in flowchart form (Figure 12–3), and in decision table form (Figure 12–4).

Result (output)	Type of Item	Narrative Statements	Flowchart Sequence	Decision Table Rule
1. Fill the order from stock	Stock	a	①, ②, ⑨, ⑩	1
2. Fill the order by making the item	Stock	d, b	①, ②, ③, ④, ⑨, ⑩	2
	Nonstock	b	①, ③, ④, ⑨, ⑩	5
3. Fill the order by purchasing the item	Stock	d, b, c	①, ②, ③, ⑤, ⑥, ⑦, ⑨, ⑩	3
	Nonstock	b, c	①, ③, ⑤, ⑥, ⑦, ⑨, ⑩	6
4. Refuse the order	Stock	d, b, c	①, ②, ③, ⑤, ⑧, ⑩	4
	Nonstock	b, c	①, ③, ⑤, ⑧, ⑩	7

to obtain each of the above four possible results. Figure 12–5 also shows the equivalent rules of a decision table expressing the same basic logic as in the narrative and flowchart forms.

The narrative form is customarily used by management and supervisory personnel who usually find it the most convenient. However, narrative form can be misleading because of varying interpretations of the words and the complexity of multiple conditions.

The flowchart has the advantage of being explicit, but it may be rejected by management or occasionally by scientists because of its specialized expression of logic. Analysts should not be surprised if flowcharts and decision tables are met with lack of interest by some members of management. However, for computer programming purposes the flowchart form is advantageous. Programmers usually write computer programs from flowcharts or mentally picture the logic in flowchart form as they are writing the program. A problem with flowcharts is that they try to picture parallel cases with a serial method of representation.

The decision table form is also explicit. Decision tables generally have the advantage of requiring less space than flowcharts. Decision tables can be used for documenting decision logic at almost any level of complexity. They are particularly valuable as analytical tools, and are the preferred technique of some analysts, although flowcharts are far more widely used. Like flowcharts, decision tables help to insure logical completeness and accuracy.

The methods the analyst should use — narrative, flowchart, decision table, or other analysis and display techniques — depend on the complexity of the problem, the nature of the audience, the analyst's personal inclination, and the use that will be made of the logical expressions. Since multiple methods may be required in preparing the information for a study, it is important that members of the study team be able to use all of them. Space does not permit further discussion of the methods here, but the reader can find sources of further information in the bibliography.

12.8 REQUIRED OPERATIONS

Three ways that an analyst can represent the logic of a set of operations have been discussed. It is logical next to consider how analysts determine the operations required of an activity.

Required operations are those necessary to produce a required output, accept an input, maintain a resource, satisfy an activity goal, or satisfy audit or legal requirements.

Operations are determined through observation, by hypothesizing operation logic from required inputs or outputs, or by experimentation. Observations of present operations must always be analyzed in terms of future, rather than present, circumstances.

Several types of relationships are generally evident among operations. There can be *causal dependence* — an operation is required because of the outcome of another operation. In a charge-account activity, the recording of a sale and posting of the file are dependent upon the completion of a sale. *Sequential dependence* occurs when one operation must follow another. In an order-processing activity, the order is received; a picking ticket is prepared; stock is selected, packaged, and shipped; and an invoice is prepared and sent. Stock cannot be shipped until selected and packaged; the selection process must follow the preparation of the picking ticket. This is a sequentially dependent set of operations. When operations are required at periodic or fixed intervals, a *time dependence* relationship is established. For example, a retail store may bill A–F customers on the 10th day of the month, G–R customers on the 20th, and S–Z customers on the 30th; operations relating to charges for each group of customers must be performed at these times.

Certain operations in a series of sequential operations may not be carried out in parallel with others, while other operations can be overlapped to reduce total cycle time. Many retail businesses, for example, prepare a multiple-copy order for parallel processing by accounting (setting up the invoice and charge records), stockrooms (stock picking and packaging), and inventory control (reordering). Another example of the overlapping of operations is shown in processing a batch of 100 invoices; calculation of price times quantity is started for the first invoices in the batch, while price-lookup and posting is still going on for the bulk of the batch.

An effective approach in operations analysis is to start with required outputs and try to reconstruct the logical sequence back to the required inputs, or the reverse. In this way, the transformation pattern or logic between inputs and outputs is clearly identified. Systems planners using this approach have found that they tend to identify only necessary processing steps. Another approach is to decide how present system operations (displayed on activity sheets and detailed on operation sheets) need to be modified to accommodate the newly-stated required outputs and inputs. Only occasionally do unusually profitable systems evolve from this approach. However, for companies proceeding from manual to computer-assisted systems, mechanization of current operations may be one practical road to take. Unless there are some major logical inconsistencies in current practice, it is often a sensible starting point.

In specifying required operations for the **Provide Product Demand** activity at Butodale, the study team used the scope and boundary statement as a base for postulating operations. For standard orders, these operations were designated as logically required:

1. Assemble records relating to an individual order
2. Determine a delivery schedule
3. Edit the order in accordance with standard practices
4. Complete internal and external records
5. Enter the order on a shop schedule

For special orders, in addition to the above five, the following three operations were set forth:

1. Establish a design configuration as necessary to meet special customer requirements
2. Compile special costs and delivery data
3. Issue quotations and bids

For the activity requirements model, this statement of operations was documented as follows:

1. Classify incoming requisitions
2. Prepare quote folder
3. Prepare bid sheet
4. Compile cost and price
5. Establish system configuration on layout sheet
6. Complete internal and external records
7. Conduct engineering edit and management review
8. Issue quotations and bids
9. Audit and record firm orders
10. Describe and enter orders to shop schedule

After the logically required operations of an activity were developed through this analysis, results were compared with the information on the previously prepared activity and operation sheets. This comparison served as a check on the team's work to insure that requirements were not overlooked.

12.9 REQUIRED RESOURCES

Operations in an information system usually imply the use of resources. Analysts have found that resources are more likely to be subjected to constraints than are operations. When compiling their first list of requirements, analysts usually make sure to include those resources that will be imposed on the new design. Warehouses, teller windows, and branch offices, for example, are usually imposed even when a business is planning a major expansion or merger. However, to maximize their profitability, linear programming may be used to determine optimal location, size, and number. Likewise, computer simulations of operations may be used to determine the effect of changes in location, grouping, and utilization of imposed manufacturing resources such as machine tools and personnel.

The same situation exists for raw, in-process, and finished stock inventories. Inventories will usually be imposed, but their level (as the result of using different reordering rules) can be established by using computer simulations of inventory management.

The list of personnel requirements is usually confined to skill and job descriptions. The number of individuals employed by a business probably will not change (with the exception of normal hiring to fill vacancies and newly-created positions),but the positions and their work content may be altered considerably when the new system is installed. Therefore, personnel requirements carrying over to the new system are expressed in terms of what is presently known about position descriptions and costs.

Information resources, or files, should be described by the present name for the resources that already exist and a name that indicates content for those that do not. Some files are imposed, others are developed by reclassifying logically-required information (presently considered input) as a file. File content or accessibility may be more important than the file name and should also be described.

Generally, resources are left rather open in the report of requirements, except for those that are imposed. This permits the analysts greater freedom in designing the new system.

As an example, the required resources for the activity needed to provide product demand at Butodale were composed mainly of source files and personnel connected with the performance of the activity. They are:

1. Quotation specialists—engineers
2. Management—typists—clerks
3. Marketing specialists
4. Calculators—typewriters
5. Cost file—assignment sheets
6. Price catalog
7. Rate file
8. Installed systems file
9. Contract register
10. Customer index
11. Project index

12.10 ACTIVITY MODEL EXAMPLE

The activity requirements model for the **Provide Product Demand** activity at Butodale is shown in Figure 12–6. This activity did not exist as an entity except in the minds of the study team. The outputs, for example, were at the time produced by many different departments. Quotations, acknowledgements, and letters of transmittal were processed by the sales administration and engineering sales departments; bids were processed by engineering sales and product engineering; prints and drawings were handled by engi-

Figure 12–6 The Provide Product Demand activity requirements model for Butodale.

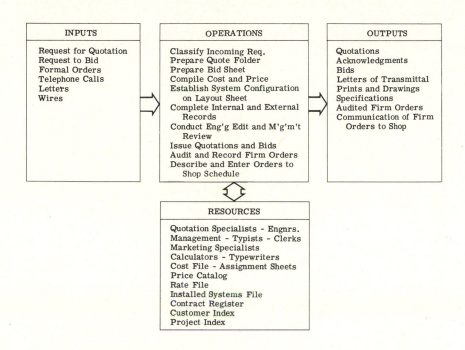

INPUTS	OPERATIONS	OUTPUTS
Request for Quotation	Classify Incoming Req.	Quotations
Request to Bid	Prepare Quote Folder	Acknowledgments
Formal Orders	Prepare Bid Sheet	Bids
Telephone Calls	Compile Cost and Price	Letters of Transmittal
Letters	Establish System Configuration	Prints and Drawings
Wires	on Layout Sheet	Specifications
	Complete Internal and External	Audited Firm Orders
	Records	Communication of Firm
	Conduct Eng'g Edit and M'g'm't	Orders to Shop
	Review	
	Issue Quotations and Bids	
	Audit and Record Firm Orders	
	Describe and Enter Orders to	
	Shop Schedule	

RESOURCES

Quotation Specialists - Engnrs.
Management - Typists - Clerks
Marketing Specialists
Calculators - Typewriters
Cost File - Assignment Sheets
Price Catalog
Rate File
Installed Systems File
Contract Register
Customer Index
Project Index

neering services; and firm orders were handled by the sales administration and manufacturing administration departments. Operations were scattered throughout an equally wide variety of departments.

Identification of required inputs, outputs, operations, and resources is not a simple, tunnel-like review of the existing system, organization, or activity structure to isolate extraneous tasks and reports. It requires a careful analysis of logical necessities that are often scattered throughout the business. Then it requires a creative definition of the system requirements necessary to meet activity goals. In addition, more than one pass through an activity is usually needed for the team to arrive at a balanced statement of valid requirements. After the first pass, subsequent iterations can be made in reverse to check requirements accuracy, starting with inputs and proceeding through operations before outputs or resources are established. For example, at the National Bank of Commerce, the study team worked from inputs to operations to outputs for the **Demand Deposit** activity, since inputs arrived directly from the outside environment (customers). The goal statement and definition of activity scope and boundaries again served as the starting point for analysis.

Inputs were specified as they were imposed (utility bill payments), and as they were logically required by the goal statement (deposits from customers). Operations were determined as they became necessary to process each of the inputs, and outputs were identified from the operations. During this analysis, the value of checking out requirements by reversing the analysis was graphically demonstrated. The operation **Calcuate Service Charges** was omitted on the first pass because there was no direct indication that such an operation was logically required from the input statement. However, in working back from outputs, this operation was recognized from the general ledger entries on depositor statements.

12.11 QUANTITATIVE REQUIREMENTS

After the descriptive model of requirements has been completed, analysts develop rate, frequency, and cost data for inputs, outputs, operations, and resources. Although the subject is treated independently here, in an actual study much of this task is performed concurrently with the building of the rough model of requirements.

Special documentation forms—input-output, operations and resource sheets—which are normally included in the report, are used to show certain details for each input and output within an activity.

Inputs and outputs should be analyzed for peak and average volumes and rates, cyclic and periodic properties, trends, and patterns to the degree of detail necessary. In classifying requirements, analysts find useful the methods of aggregation (putting like items together) and segregation (differentiating unlike items). If, for example, customer orders for specials, standards, and spare parts are processed under entirely separate controls at different time cycles, then each parts category should be treated individually.

Much Phase I data on peak and average volumes can be used here, expanded to reflect future requirements. Sales forecasts, operating budgets for future time periods, and management plans secured when analyzing goals are sources for this information. If forecasting data are not available, estimates of potential growth can be made from industry forecasts or from present averages extended into the future. Whenever trend projections are used, it is important to determine whether the assumptions made about the future environment are explicitly agreed to by management. Sampling techniques are used whenever possible in trend projection to reduce the volume of data.

Figure 12-7 is an input-output sheet filled out for the **Provide**

Figure 12—7 Input-output sheet for the Provide Product
Demand activity.

NO.	NAME	RATE	MEDIA	SOURCE DESTINATION	NO. OF FIELDS	NO. OF CHAR.	F O R M	C O N T	NOTES
I1	REQUEST FOR QUOTATION (R-2000)	50/W	WIRES TELEPHONE LETTERS	CUSTOMER					AVG. PEAK STD SYSTEMS 22 30 207 - 217 20 27 OTHER 8 13
I2	REQUEST FOR BID (R-2010)	10/W	LETTERS	CUSTOMER					PEAK VOLUME 12/W 10 WKS A YEAR
I3	CUSTOMER ORDERS (R-2020)	17/W	8½ x 11 4 PART	CUSTOMER					PEAK 20/WK 6 WEEKS A YEAR
R1	QUOTATIONS * (R-3000)	15/W	8½ x 11 4 PART	CUSTOMER				X	PEAK 20/WK 10 WEEKS A YEAR
R2	ACKNOWLEDGMENTS (R-3050)	17/W		CUSTOMER SHOP (PROVIDE END PRODUCTS ACTIVITY)			X	X	NO PEAKS
R3	NEW ORDER SCHEDULE (F-4080)	17/W		SHOP (PROVIDE END PRODUCTS ACTIVITY)				X	COMMUNICATES DATA ON FIRM ORDERS
R4	CUSTOMER ORDER (R-2020)	17/W		SHOP				X	DETAILS OF FIRM ORDER ARE ENTERED ON CONTRACT REGISTER

* INCLUDES LETTERS, DRAWINGS, SPECIFICATIONS, LAYOUTS
AS NECESSARY TO SUPPLEMENT QUOTATION

DATE	R.L. CASEY ANALYST	DEMAND ACTIVITY	BUTODALE STUDY	1 PAGE

Product Demand activity in Butodale Electronics. Information on inputs is located at the top; data on outputs is shown below. The input-
output sheet is a summary, not a detailed descriptive form; it shows
pertinent characteristics of messages that must be accepted or produced by the system designed for the activity. Amplification of data,

when useful, is placed in the appendix to the report. If, for example, the format or content is fixed (imposed), a message sheet, together with a sample of the message, can be included in the appendix. Summary data on traffic peaks appearing in the notes column of the input-output sheet may be cited by appendix displays of traffic distributions and variations, if significant enough.

Quantitative requirements for operations have to be considered from the present view and for the future. In Phase I, operations are described as they are presently performed; in Phase II, operations are characterized by indicating the kind and number of input factors they must accept, the kind and number of output factors they must produce, and how often they must be performed. In most cases, these numeric data are estimated from the same statistical projections used to establish volume and frequency of inputs and outputs.

An operation is further characterized by the nature and estimated number of processes involved in its execution. These data are particularly useful in systems design. For example:

1. How many arithmetical and logical processes must be performed?
2. How many relations (comparison of one factor with another) must be examined?
3. How many times will a resource be consulted for data (retrieval or lookup)?
4. How many edit or audit functions will be necessary in the operation?

A required operations sheet should be included in the report, and it can be applied as a working paper in analysis. When completed, this sheet contains a narrative description of each required operation, along with the number of input and output data fields used in the operation, the number of times the operation will be executed within a selected time span, and a summary of the types of processes making it up. Flowcharts and decision tables used for special analyses should be placed in the appendix. A required operations sheet for Butodale's **Provide Product Demand** activity is shown in Figure 12 – 8.

Finally, quantitative requirements for resources must be considered. Present and future physical and informational resources may be described on a resource sheet as shown in Figure 12 – 9.

Personnel, identified by occupational skill, are grouped wherever practical. Costs are projected from payroll registers and from the report of the present business. Equipment should be identified by

Figure 12–8 Required operations sheet for the Provide Product Demand activity.

NO.	OPERATION NAME	INPUT FACTORS	OUTPUT FACTORS	FREQUENCY OF EXECUTION	PROCESS SUMMARY
01	CLASSIFY INCOMING REQUESTS ALL REQUESTS FOR BID (R-2010) OR QUOTATION (R-2000) ARE SEPARATED INITIALLY INTO 3 GROUPS: STANDARD END ITEMS, STANDARD SYSTEMS, AND ENGINEERED PRODUCTS.	5	10	60/W	7 LOOKUP 3 EDIT 6 RELATIONAL
02	PREPARE QUOTE FOLDER (F-4050.1) A FOLDER IS PREPARED FOR EACH REQUEST TO HOLD CUSTOMER PAPERS AND DOCUMENTS GENERATED WITHIN BUTODALE TO FILL THE ORDER.	7	12	15/D	2 LOOKUP 4 EDIT 3 RELATIONAL
03	PREPARE BID SHEET (R-3000) A BID SHEET IS PREPARED FOR EACH REQUEST FROM PRICE, COST, AND INSTALLED SYSTEMS FILES DEPENDING ON THE TYPE REQUEST, EACH IS PROCESSED SOMEWHAT DIFFERENTLY. A GPAC* HAS APPROXIMATELY 13 MAJOR INTERCONNECTED COMPONENTS AVAILABLE IN DIFFERENT GROUPINGS. INPUT-OUTPUT DEVICES ARE OPTIONAL IN 6 MODELS. ALTHOUGH CONSOLE AND GROUPS DESCRIPTIONS ARE STANDARD, THEY MAY BE MODIFIED AT CUSTOMER REQUEST.	15	20	45/W	10 ARITHMETIC 50 LOGICAL 30 LOOKUP
04	DETERMINE SYSTEM LAYOUT A GPAC MAY HAVE ANY ONE OF SEVERAL CONSOLES, AND ANY ONE OF SEVERAL RACK CONFIGURATIONS. *GENERAL PURPOSE ANALOG COMPUTER	27	38	12/W	60 ARITHMETIC 32 LOGICAL 5 EDIT 15 LOOKUP

R.L. CASEY   DEMAND   BUTODALE   1 OF 8

DATE   ANALYST   ACTIVITY   STUDY   PAGE

name and type. Costs should be projected on a consistent base. Wherever practical, equipment is grouped by function to compress the list. Facilities are listed by name, location, size, and utility, with emphasis on those that may be affected by systems design.

Figure 12–8 (continued)

NO.	OPERATION NAME	INPUT FACTORS	OUTPUT FACTORS	FREQUENCY OF EXECUTION	PROCESS SUMMARY
05	DECIDE BID STATUS ON ENGINEERED PRODUCTS, A MANAGEMENT CONFERENCE IS HELD TO DETERMINE SPECIAL CONSIDERATIONS, PRICES, AND PROMISED DELIVERY.	40	70	40/M	30 LOOKUP 50 RELATIONAL 80 LOGICAL 10 ARITHMETIC
06	DESIGN SYSTEM LAYOUT ON ENGINEERED PRODUCTS, ENGINEERING DESIGN AND DRAFTING IS REQUIRED TO LAY OUT ALL SPECIAL REQUIREMENTS.	200	600	20/W	700 LOOKUP 200 LOGICAL 50 ARITHMETIC 40 RELATIONAL 300 EDIT
07	COST SPECIAL COMPONENTS FOR EACH SPECIAL ITEM, COSTS AND PRICES ARE ESTABLISHED TO SUPPORT THE FINAL QUOTATION.	10	18	150/W	4 LOOKUP 16 ARITHMETIC 10 RELATIONAL 8 EDIT
08	PREPARE QUOTATION (R-3000) THE CUSTOMER IS SUPPLIED A DOCUMENT DESCRIBING THE PRODUCT, ITS RACKS AND ATTACHMENTS, AND THE TOTAL PRICE, WITH OPTIONS.	75	100	20/W	30 LOOKUP 10 LOGICAL 100 EDIT 200 POSTING
09	ESTABLISH INTERNAL RECORDS DETAILS OF THE PROPOSAL ARE RECORDED ON INTERNAL DOCUMENTS AND IN THE CONTRACT REGISTER FILE. (F-4050)	200	800	20/W	10 LOGICAL 10 LOOKUP 500 POSTING 20 EDIT

R.L. CASEY   DEMAND   BUTODALE   2 OF 3
DATE   ANALYST   ACTIVITY   STUDY   PAGE

Figure 12 – 8 (continued)

NO.	OPERATION NAME	INPUT FACTORS	OUTPUT FACTORS	FREQUENCY OF EXECUTION	PROCESS SUMMARY
10	TRANSMIT QUOTATION (R-3000) THE QUOTATION IS MAILED TO THE CUSTOMER WITH SUPPORTING DATA INCLUDING A LETTER OF TRANSMITTAL, PRINTS, DRAWINGS, LAYOUT, SPECIFICATIONS, ETC.	10	10	20/W	25 LOGICAL 10 LOOKUP 10 EDIT
11	EDIT INCOMING ORDERS (R-2020) FIRM CUSTOMER ORDERS ARE EDITED AGAINST THE CONTRACT REGISTER FILE (F-4050) AND POSTED TO THE CUSTOMER (F-4060) AND PROJECT INDEX. (F-4070)	150	30	16/W	10 LOOKUP 150 EDIT 75 POSTING
12	PREPARE & TRANSMIT ACKNOWLEDGMENT (R-3050) THE CUSTOMER IS NOTIFIED OF THE ORDER RECEIPT, AND ACCEPTANCE AND DELIVERY DATES ARE RECONFIRMED.	30	30	16/W	10 LOOKUP 15 ARITHMETIC 30 EDIT
13	COMMUNICATE ORDERS TO SHOP THE CUSTOMER ORDER IS POSTED TO AN ASSIGNMENT SHEET (F-4080) AND PREPARED FOR SHOP RELEASE, OR TO ENGINEERING. SPECIAL CONDITIONS AND TERMS ARE COMMUNICATED TO INTERESTED PARTIES AT THIS TIME.	10	15	20/W	10 LOOKUP 20 POSTING 10 LOGICAL 10 EDIT

DATE   R.L. CASEY   ANALYST   DEMAND   ACTIVITY   BUTODALE   STUDY   3 OF 3   PAGE

Figure 12−9 Resource sheet for the Provide Product
Demand activity.

NO.	NAME AND DESCRIPTION	AMOUNT	COST	NOTES
P1	MANAGEMENT (PARTIAL)	2	$24,000	REVIEW QUOTATIONS
P2	SALES AND SERVICE			
	MANAGER, SALESMEN,			
	SERVICE ENGINEERS,			
	SECRETARIES, CLERKS	56	$448,000	
P3	ADMINISTRATION & ADVERTISING	14	84,000	
	MANAGER, MEDIA			
	SPECIALISTS, SECRETARIES			
	CLERKS, ANALYSTS,			
	SUPERVISORS			
P4	COST CLERKS	2	9,000	
P5	ACCOUNTS RECEIVABLE CLERKS	4	19,000	
P6	PRODUCT ENGINEERS	3	26,400	
P7	ADMINISTRATIVE ENGINEERS	2	13,400	
P8	PUBLICATIONS SPECIALISTS	3	20,100	
E1	VEHICLES		10,100	DEPRECIATION & RENTAL
E2	TYPEWRITERS	15		
E3	CALCULATORS	2		
E4	DICTATING MACHINES	2		

DATE   R.L. CASEY   ANALYST   DEMAND   ACTIVITY   BUTODALE   STUDY   1 of 1   PAGE

File resources are identified, established, and assigned costs from the results of the required-inputs analysis. File sheets can be used to describe the characteristics of each information file. Special attention should be placed on the characteristics of a file that may have been changed in requirements analysis. Consideration should be given to:

1. Size of the file in characters
2. Retention rules
3. Age of data
4. Peak and average message volume
5. Access requirements

Categories such as *Sequenced by*, *Labels*, *Storage Medium*, and *Location* should be omitted unless imposed, since these characteristics will be developed in new systems design. The resource sheet shows only a descriptive file name, application, and cost, wherever possible; the file sheet provides the definitive information. For studies involving communications facilities, the network diagram should be modified to show planned addition or deletion of trunk lines and terminals. The need for duplexing equipment, if these requirements are imposed or logically needed, should also be noted.

Finances become an important consideration in resource requirements analysis when a major change or expansion in an activity, such as those necessitating large outlays in capital equipment, is contemplated. Many companies have standard policies connected with the outlay of funds for new equipment purchases; these policies can be described in the appendix and cited by a note on the resource sheet.

An area often requiring special attention is the physical inventory for retail and manufacturing concerns. Inventory may be described either as a dollar inventory value for one or more forecasted sales and production levels or as a series of decision rules developed from simulation experiments. When the latter is the case, descriptions of the rules are included on a required operations sheet, and are summarized with anticipated results on a resource sheet. Inventory rules include:

1. Frequency of forecast
2. Frequency of stock level review
3. Required service level (safety stock requirements)
4. Application of special inventory practices such as item control according to the annual usage value of the item and the use of economic order quantity

5. Type of order system (fixed quantity per order or fixed interval of ordering)

The level of future inventories may also be estimated from an analysis of inventories in relation to sales, if inventories have been adequately controlled in the past.

Other methods of estimating the size and content of a required inventory include:

1. Computing inventory level at various levels of sales by summarizing average inventory level of all parts stocked
2. Comparing stock/sales ratios with those of others in the industry from analysis of balance sheets or published industry statistics
3. Classifying into raw, in-process, and finished stock by value, then computing average level
4. Analyzing high yearly value parts, models, or services in depth

12.12 REFINING THE REQUIREMENTS

At this point, the study team has produced system input, operation, output, and resource requirements for each of the activities within the scope of the study. The results may adequately state what the system is required to do, particularly in the case of improvement or mechanization studies. More likely there is a need to reconsider certain of these requirements and to refine them by one or more passes back through each activity, this time applying a different approach (that is, if outputs were determined from inputs, the analysts would now work in reverse). The need to refine requirements and resolve any apparent conflicts or problems usually is discovered when the activity is to be validated as an integrated whole.

In certain advanced studies it may be desirable to call upon other sophisticated techniques, such as management science—especially if the study team is involved in creating a unique new design, or if few constraints have been placed on their actions. For example, a computer program to simulate systems may be used to develop an understanding of true requirements through the simulation of the structure and action of complex, real-life situations. Vital information about the maximum and the average size of queues, response time, and percent use of selected resources may be obtained from each simulation run. The model must accurately reflect real conditions, and its output requires expert interpretation. There may be, however, no other way to secure this information at a reasonable cost.

SUMMARY

To define system requirements, the study team develops specifications for each operation from the position of what is logically necessary to fulfill the goals of an activity. Establishing logical requirements may necessitate several attempts because most activities contain variables and interacting factors. An activity requirements model, showing inputs, operations, outputs, and resources, is a useful framework for the analysis of requirements. After the study team has defined the relationships that govern the transformation of inputs to outputs, it has a sound basis for specifying required operations. Operations may be documented by narrative, flowchart, or decision table forms. Each of the three methods has advantages and disadvantages. Flowcharts and decision tables are particularly useful if the operations are to be programmed for a computer. Required operations are those that are necessary to produce an output, to accept an input, to maintain a resource, or to satisfy an activity goal. Types of relationships among operations include causal dependence, sequential dependence, and time dependence. Operations usually imply the use of resources, and the resources may be subject to management constraints.

QUESTIONS AND PROBLEMS

12–1   What is the principal purpose of Phase II?

12–2   Describe various ways in which information collected during Phase I can be used in Phase II.

12–3   In driving a car, what are some of the required inputs? What are the required outputs? Indicate some inputs and outputs which are not required. Indicate certain operations that must be performed on certain resources that must be used. Indicate some operations and resources which are optional.

12–4   What might be some of the questions that a study team should ask while defining an information retrieval system for an organization?

12–5   Prepare a narrative description of the operations involved in purchasing food from a supermarket. Cover all operations from entering the store until the groceries have been taken from the store. Show the same operation in flow chart form; use decision tables to express the decision logic used in making correct change.

12–6   The Slowburn Gas Company bills its customers according
to the following rate schedule:

First 500 cubic feet $1.00 minimum charge
Next 3,050 cubic feet @ .125 per hundred cf.
Next 35,000 cubic feet @ .120 per hundred cf.
Next 125,000 cubic feet @ .110 per hundred cf.
Next 125,000 cubic feet @ .095 per hundred cf.
Next 425,000 cubic feet @ .0825 per hundred cf.
Any additional cubic feet @ .0735 per hundred cf.

Prepare a flowchart to show the steps in calculating a
customer's bill.

12–7   An asset has a purchase price of X dollars and an estimated
scrap value of S dollars. Prepare a flowchart to show the
steps in each of the following procedures:
a. The asset is to be depreciated over Y years. Calculate
the reserve for depreciation and net value at the end of
each year of the life of the asset. Use the straight line
depreciation method.
b. The asset is to be depreciated over Y years. Calculate
the reserve for depreciation and net value at the end of
each year of the life of the asset. Use the sum of the
digits method of depreciation.

12–8   A study of a student information system for a university
proposes that five basic uses of student information are
counseling, admissions, academic, general student data,
and alumni. Prepare a list of the fields of information
which might be included in each record of such a file, and
indicate for each field which of the five uses listed above
the information will serve. A field may serve from one to
five uses.

12–9   a. Prepare a flowchart to show the steps necessary to
compute the value of a principal amount P at the end of
Y years if the principal earns simple interest at the rate
of X percent.
b. Prepare a flowchart to show the steps necessary to
compute the value of a principal amount P at the end of
each year from one year through Y years if a compound
interest rate of X is used.

12–10 A study team has been requested to define the contents of
a customer record in a file of a public utility company.
What information might the team recommend be included
in such a record?

12–11 Prepare a flowchart to show the steps necessary to calculate a twelve-month moving average for a set of sales data.

12–12 Assume that you are a member of a study team that is studying a system for maintaining the customer records of a commercial bank. You are assigned the task of investigating and documenting the present file maintenance techniques. What steps should you follow in completing this task?

12–13 A study team is examining the overall operations of a credit bureau. As one of the steps in the study the team wishes to define the prime purpose for automating the credit bureau operations. What might their statement be?

12–14 A large metropolitan hotel has decided to install a new online data processing system for recording all guest charges. What might be the inputs to such a system?

CHAPTER 13
MEASURING THE PERFORMANCE OF SYSTEMS

13.1 MEASUREMENT FACTORS

When analysts design a new system, they must have some criteria for choosing among designs. The factors to be included in making such an evaluation are established while the analysts are determining the new system requirements. In fact, the process of setting measurements goes on throughout Phase II of the study.

Measurement factors are the criteria by which the new system will be judged. Their values will determine the goodness of a proposed system. The identification of measurement factors and the development of appropriate measurement scales are usually performed simultaneously with the formulation of input, output, operation, and resource requirements. When peak and average volumes, frequency of execution, rate, elapsed time, and other numeric data are being compiled for inclusion in the study documents, measurement units and ranges can also be determined and recorded. Similarly, as each nonnumeric requirement is spelled out, its definition of different performance levels and range of acceptability should be set.

Uses of Measurement Factors There are three principal uses for these measurement factors in planning a new information management system. First, the analysis of factors can serve to determine which activities should be given priority treatment, which one or two should be pursued for maximum benefit to management. Second, the measurement factors can be the means for ranking the various requirements from the most important to the least; they also help decide whether any requirements can be eliminated. Third, the trade-off among the projected values for the different factors will be vital in guiding solution design and selecting the best proposal to recommend.

This chapter discusses the four key steps in identifying and evaluating measurements. The measurement factors have to be identified;

this is the *what* of evaluation. Next, the potential performance levels for each measurement factor are described, and a range of acceptability established; this is the *how much* of evaluation. These two steps are necessary in any system study.

However, in some cases, such as government studies or those involving very large expenditures, it is necessary to go even further in quantifying the solution selection process. In these instances the additional two steps are needed. Each measurement factor must have associated with it a *conversion* to a consistent value scale. Finally, each of these separate value scales must be weighted so that a total *score* can be determined for any proposed solution.

13.2 TYPES OF MEASUREMENT FACTORS

Three types of measurement factors are direct, indirect, and qualitative. Some measurements are direct and quantitative and can be shown on a numeric scale. Examples are the cost of computing an individual's weekly pay, the number of days from receipt of a customer order to product shipment, and the average number of errors in preparing each day's invoices. Measurements can also be indirect or derived from a combination of factors; these would still be quantitative. These measurements include items like budget variance, return on investment, productive efficiency, and inventory turnover. The third type of measurements consists of those that are qualitative or subjective, such as service effectiveness, customer goodwill, and product appearance. This third class is quite difficult to define; the measurement value is often expressed in abstract terms such as *outstanding*, *excellent*, or *fair*.

Each of these types of measurements must be examined in detail. Here is a list of potential measurement factors:

1. The elapsed time between two events, such as receipt of a customer order and its fulfillment
2. The processing time required to complete a specific transaction
3. The unit cost of certain supplies needed for invoicing
4. The frequency and duration of computer or terminal breakdowns
5. The number of rejects of input data
6. The number of records in a file
7. The number of unfilled product orders

All of these measurements are direct and record a current or previous event in the business. The recurrent themes are time (elapsed and processing), cost (investment and operational), accuracy (reliability and repeatability), and rate. These each indicate something one can record as an identified numeric value. Most factory and clerical measurement schemes fit into such a picture of direct measurement.

Dealing with direct measurements is reasonably straightforward. One identifies the nature of the event or events to be measured, then indicates the frequency of taking the measurement (each occurrence, each hour) and the time span of examination (over an hour, day, week). It is also useful to show the units of measure and expected range.

The second type of measurement is indirect, or derived:

1. Percentage of delivery promises kept
2. Computer usage budget variance
3. Return on data processing investment
4. Percentage of change in sales, year to year
5. Profit margin on a particular product line

Such measurements tend to be more complex than direct measurements, as they must be defined in terms of other direct measurements. They often require summation over some time period, with comparisons to preset standards, budgets, targets, or previous performance. Many accounting and statistical measurements fall into this category. One must insure that the ratios used in fact reflect cause/effect relations and reasonably describe system performance.

The third type of measurement covers those factors which are qualitative or subjective. Some examples are:

1. Employee satisfaction with job content
2. Potential for individual employee development
3. Customer goodwill
4. Product appearance
5. Sales forecasts

These are in many ways the most interesting factors; they tend also to be the most misused. Either they are literally discarded since they cannot be quantified, or else they are treated as paramount since their performance is simply good or bad—not along a measurement line.

Study teams have found that a representative number of measurements is needed for a balanced appraisal of system performance. To achieve this coverage, major measurement categories are analyzed so that precise factors can be defined for each activity. Time is certainly a major measurement in an airlines study; however, it must be refined to a precise measurement factor like customer inquiry response time or record update time. A total of ten to twelve specific measurement factors are often sufficient for the evaluation of an activity. Note that the measurement factors may be quite different from one activity to another.

Some of the kinds of measurements and illustrative measurement factors are:

1. Cost—operating, maintenance, unit
2. Time—response, access, elapsed, cycle, process, turnover
3. Accuracy—frequency and number of errors, significance of errors
4. Reliability—stability, durability, life, availability, serviceability
5. Security—legality, safety, secrecy, privacy, auditability
6. Quality—appearance, tolerance
7. Flexibility—variability, sensitivity
8. Capacity—average load, low load, peak load
9. Efficiency—productivity, performance
10. Acceptability—customer, employee, management, stockholder

This list shows many of the measurements by which a system's value can be judged. In a study for a brokerage house, measurements were first identified and described for the entire business as follows:

1. *Execution Response Time* Customer service must be as good as or better than the present system.
2. *Error Rate* Critical, since money errors are absorbed by the firm. Errors also affect customer and industry relations; they must not be greater than with the present system.
3. *Reliability* Ability to install new system with no service interruptions; ability to conclude posting before beginning business operations the next day.
4. *Capacity* Management requires system to operate at double present daily volume, while at the same time working efficiently under variable loads.
5. *Cost* Comparable to present system. Any increased cost must be paid for by additional fee services.
6. *Security* Certain procedures must meet industry regulations, audit practices, and provide data security.

7. *Update Response Time* An important factor, but dependent on the type of account inquiries.
8. *Inquiry Response Time* Again, this is a function of the class of inquiry, but it is important since inquiries result in trades.

Each of the descriptions gave an indication of the importance of the measurement factors to the business, but further work was still required to associate the detailed measurements with each activity.

The measurement factors developed for Custodian Life show a different pattern:

Custodian Life Insurance Company

New Business Activity

1. *Volume Increase Capability* The new system must be capable of handling double the present volume, without overtime.
2. *Accuracy* Defined as the degree of conformity and correctness in all documents and records. Measured by the total number of detected errors requiring reprocessing.
3. *Processing Time* The number of days it takes to process a life insurance application from its receipt at home office to issuance of policy, by policy type.
4. *Appearance* Prepared documents and reports will be judged for legibility, neatness and arrangement.
5. *Personnel Cost* Annual salaries and employee benefits allocated to the operation of the activity.
6. *Equipment and Supply Cost* Includes the costs of machine purchases and rentals, maintenance and parts charges, magnetic tapes, and service fees.
7. *Operational Efficiency and Control* The degree to which operational efficiency is controlled by management. (Is the status of an application always known? Are schedules maintained on time? Can the system handle anticipated peaks?)
8. *Conformity to Practices* The extent to which company policies and practices are complied with, and the degree to which the system provides statistical data for management information and action.

Some factors are defined only in general terms; others state exactly what performance level is required. A number of other factors, such as personnel training costs and flexibility change, were considered earlier and eliminated because of lack of significance and difficulty of measurement.

13.3 MEASUREMENT SCALES

For each measurement factor chosen, an appropriate measurement scale must also be selected. A manufacturer of automobile accessories is an example. Delivery cycle performance in the manufacturing enterprise will be used to evaluate any system proposals. First, the unit of measure of concern to the factor delivery cycle is established; in car manufacturing, it is days. Next, the range of performance with which the analysts are concerned is identified. One place to start is with a review of current performance. Orders received and delivery dates could be reviewed and the difference in days noted; this would give a good indication of the unit of measure range for this factor. The longest and shortest times taken from order to delivery date might be the upper and lower limits of the measurement.

The car manufacturing example used direct measurement factors. There are also indirect and qualitative factors, which use ratios or terms such as *excellent*, *good*, *fair*, and *poor*, rather than *10 days* or *7 days*. For nonquantitative measurements, descriptions of the various recognizable states of a factor are needed. How can a clear definition of something as intangible as customer goodwill be conveyed? Statements such as the following define the possible states of the measurement factor.

Customer goodwill: None, Moderate, Excellent.

None: There is no particular customer association with this gas station. Customers will go to other stations if their price is lower than this station's or if others offer any special feature.

Moderate: There is a moderate amount of customer goodwill: There are many repeat customers. To get a customer to change stations requires a substantial advertising expenditure, a significant price differential, or a positive dissatisfaction with service.

Excellent: There is extremely strong customer goodwill. Customers will not change stations even as a result of heavy advertising of major price differences.

A rating scale shows ranges of values for each measurement factor. Three sets of values are shown on the scale:

1. Present operating point

Figure 13–1 Present operating points for the incoming "orders per day" measurement in a brokerage house.

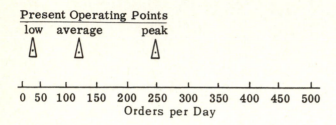

2. Acceptable performance range
3. Desirable performance range

Operating points for the present system are secured from the Phase I analysis and data gathered during Phase II. For example, in the brokerage house, present operating points for incoming customer orders were designated as shown in Figure 13–1.

An acceptable range covers the points at which activity performance satisfies future conditions. A desirable range is a statement of performance that will be more difficult to achieve through design, yet represents a more satisfactory level of attainment.

With values defined in this fashion, system designers are able to propose a range of solutions in Phase III and evaluate and adjust the cost versus response time trade-off.

Sometimes targets can be approached from a different viewpoint. This is illustrated by the measurement scale for an invoicing operation shown in Figure 13–2.

The present performance of the invoicing operation was not considered acceptable, because too much time (nine days, at least) elapses until shipping papers are forwarded to the billing section. However, what happens if a system can be designed to include the invoice with the shipment without holding up the shipment? This will not be resolved until system design takes place, but the performance targets are extended to evaluate the desirability of such a possibility.

There are other methods of displaying ranges of values for measurement factors. For example, values for elapsed time measurements can be shown in the form of cumulative curves. A specific illustration of this method is given in Figure 13–3, which shows what percent of the items take how much elapsed time. The point on the present system curve defined by the intersecting dotted lines reads: "Thirty

Figure 13–2 Present, acceptable, and desirable operating points
for an invoicing operation.

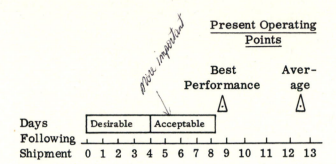

percent of the total number of items processed are handled in under
ten hours." The other points are read similarly.

Often, rating scales have significantly different ranges of values for
quite similar measurement factors. In these cases, a separate scale
should be constructed for each one. Unwarranted complexity would
be introduced by attempting to display too many factors simultaneously.

The physical appearance of a printed document is an example of a
qualitative factor. However, it can be measured on the same type of
scale as for quantitative variables. Figure 13–4 presents such an
example. In it the attribute is the appearance of an invoice. The scale
ranges from unsatisfactory to outstanding. Each point on a qualitative rating scale should be supported by a narrative definition. For
example, *Good* means that the invoice is uniform in printing dark-
ness, has no corrections, strikeovers, or smudges, and can be read
without difficulty. Line item entries should be in ascending part
number sequence for easy reference, and the totals should be quickly
identifiable.

If a study team can design a new system that operates within the
high range of desirable performance in most factors, it can be assured
that the design is at a near-optimum condition. If, however, costs
and other special considerations restrain performance of the design
to acceptable ranges in a number of categories, the study team can be
confident that system performance is still within satisfactory bounds,
since acceptable performance levels were reviewed and approved by
management.

The study team is responsible for selecting measurement factors
and constructing a rating scale for each one, but a final determination

Figure 13–3 "Less than" relation between (1) the number of hours an input received from a vendor sits on the receiving dock waiting to be taken to the inventory stock room and (2) the cumulative proportion of shipments. The bands indicate performance levels.

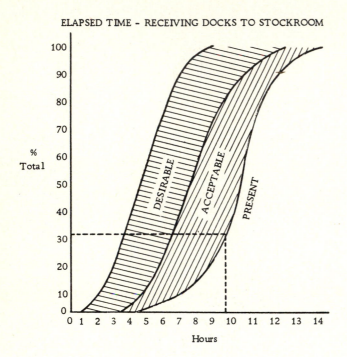

on acceptable and desirable values and ranges of value for each factor should be accomplished jointly with management. Before measurement data are reviewed with management, requirements analysis should be fairly well along, and a substantial amount of information developed to support each rating scale. When a computer is used to simulate the management of inventories, the results of a number of simulations can be gathered to show how several management decision rules influenced inventory investment for various sales forecasts. In this case, of course, management should be interviewed before the simulation to determine the inventory policies to be tested.

In the measurement review with management, systems analysts do not merely seek information; they try to discern how a manager feels about the business, what factors are important, and what the business expects to gain from a new system. During these reviews, it is useful to develop an insight into the feelings, opinions, biases, and pressures on an individual as well as to form an objective appraisal on a subject. A manager may have strong opinions on certain topics.

Figure 13–4 An example of the use of a scale for a qualitative
factor. Here the qualitative factor is the "appearance" of an invoice.

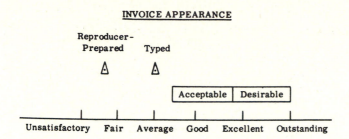

If the opinions are controversial, or pertain to business policies
which are not widely discussed, then it is important to find out how
these beliefs affect system requirements.

13.4 CONVERSION TO A COMMON VALUE SCALE

The techniques described in the previous sections are used in the
rest of this text to show how analysts have defined measurements
and established operating ranges. Through them, readers will
note that the same people will probably be involved in the design
phase as in the requirements phase.

However, there are cases where the study team will find it necessary to prepare more quantitative schemes for evaluating alternative
design solutions. These extra steps are described relatively briefly in
the next two sections. If it is essential to use these more formal criteria and trade-off procedures, then reference can be made to appropriate texts in the bibliography of this book.

The difficulty of converting from the natural units of measure for a
single measurement factor to a common value scale which allows one
factor to be compared to another is akin to the old problem of adding
up apples and oranges. The process breaks down into two steps:

1. Establishing a relative value scale for each measurement factor
2. Determining a weighting scheme to compare the various
   measurement factors

The first problem is to set up relative values for different performance levels for a single measurement factor. For instance, if one is
trying to evaluate inquiry response cycle, the objective is to decide
how much more valuable it is to respond in one day than in two; or

Figure 13–5 Value conversion graph.

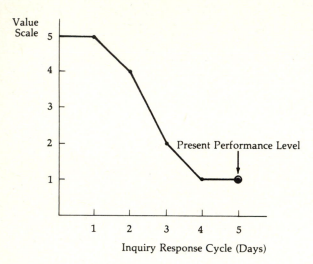

in two days instead of five; or, one hour rather than one day. Clearly, the analyst cannot assume that the relationship is linear (that is, five days is only ⅕ as valuable as one day) or even positive (for example, the higher the measurement, the more valuable the performance). The same general problem arises in regard to indirect and qualitative factors.

The most practical way to cope with this problem is to concentrate on setting value scales for fairly few measurement factors and treat the others on a *go – no go* basis (that is, acceptable/unacceptable). For each selected factor, the analyst must discuss with one or more management people the relative worth of different performance levels. How much would the business be willing to invest to reduce the present inquiry response cycle of five days to one day? Would it be worth $1,000 per year or as much as $10,000 per year? An amount must be agreed to. Suppose the cycle could be reduced to two days at half the value agreed to above; would it be worth the additional money to make the further reduction?

Through a series of these comparative questions, a measurement value conversion graph can be drawn as in Figure 13–5.

Notice that there is no difference in value between a four-day and a five-day response. In this case the business would pay twice as much as is being paid now to achieve a three-day response; four times as much for a two-day response; but only five times as much

Figure 13–6 Value conversion table.

Product Appearance	Outstanding	Superior	Good	Fair
Value Points	100	75	50	25
	Acceptable		Unacceptable	

for a one-day turnaround. There is no incremental value in achieving faster than a one-day response.

To determine these relative values for a measurement factor it is usually necessary to stick to a range reasonably close to the present performance level. It is also advisable to make the comparisons to well-understood linear criteria like money or volume of orders rather than to nonlinear factors. Finally, it is essential to get opinions from more than one person in order to smooth out any existing personal differences. It is convenient to always express the relationships in terms of a common units-free scale. Use of money or days as the value axis leads to misunderstanding and may be interpreted too literally. The initial objective is to determine the relative value for a single measurement, not to set the trade-off among measurements.

The value conversion can be shown in a graph or in a simple table or some combination of the two display forms.

Figure 13–6 shows a table which converts a qualitative measurement to a consistent value scale. In this example *outstanding* and *superior* are the only acceptable performances, while *good* and *fair* are unacceptable.

13.5 MEASUREMENT VALUE WEIGHTING

The value scale for the individual measurement factor indicates a great deal about that factor, but says nothing about how important one factor is with respect to the others. Individual ratings do not tell a complete story on system effectiveness; analysts must determine the relationship among the various value scales so as to weight the individual measurements for ranking requirements, guiding design, or selecting among solutions. This is probably the most difficult of the evaluative tasks. But weighting provides a structure and makes it possible to combine separate value scales.

One note of caution: The weights assigned are still relative values; the score is not an absolute. The number must never be interpreted too literally. This process should be used as an aid to decisions, not as a substitute for human logic and reasoning.

The idea of a weighting scheme is basically simple. If an analyst has properly reflected the relative significance of the measurement criteria, then the total score should lead to the best system solution. With this knowledge, the Phase III analyst can guide the solutions toward achieving high values for those measurement factors having the greatest weight. The process tends to focus and direct the design tasks.

The weighting process usually starts through an intuitive ranking of the measurements based on the need to meet the minimum acceptable performance. One asks which measurement would cause the most serious problem by falling below the acceptable level. The initial ranking can also be based on which measurement factor has the greatest opportunity for upside gain. This is equivalent to asking which measurement value improvement could produce the most additional profit.

After this initial ranking, the trade-off analysis is begun, using pairs of measurement factors near each other in the list. If possible, one chooses factors where there is a natural cause/effect relationship, such as that between cost of printing equipment and the appearance of the documents produced. But in other cases, factors will have to be compared on an abstract basis. This is sometimes called *indifference analysis*. The analyst asks various management people whether a unit of improved value in one factor would be worth more or less than an increase in another factor. One tries to find that trade-off level between values where the management consensus is that it doesn't matter; they are worth the same. This discovery would provide the weighting ratio.

There are a number of text books that describe in detail procedures for obtaining such trade-off ratios as the Kepner–Tregoe method, so that a weight can be assigned to each factor. The result in any event is a table listing the weights for each measurement.

To determine the total score for a particular system solution, the design analyst projects the rating for each measurement of significance; the rating is then converted into the appropriate numeric value from the value scale; finally, this number is multiplied by the assigned weight, and these figures are added up for all the measurement factors. The sum represents the total score for the proposed system solution. These scores can, of course, be used to select alternative configurations of people and machines.

But the analyst must always remember that numbers are not enough.

To diagnose the real reasons behind management decisions and opinions, a systems analyst not only has to be well prepared with factual data, but also adept at leading discussion on sensitive subjects and developing insight into the meaning behind statements made by the managers. What factors have a bearing on the subject: labor contracts? employee attitudes? satisfaction of a large and demanding customer? poor industry outlook? attitudes among consumers and suppliers? trade reciprocity? Many times it will be difficult to discover and interpret some of the deep-rooted problems which influence a management position; if they are not expressed openly, the study team has difficulty in deciding just what is desirable and acceptable in a business.

While these conditions have to be faced in most studies, the system analyst emphasizes first the need for evaluation based on objective data, then adjusts these decisions to accommodate subjective opinions and judgments when they must be recognized. This approach affirms that there must initially be an order, a logic, and a magnitude to events; when these are defined, results can be qualified by the experience, judgment, and even intuition of management.

An important aspect of the analyst's work has to do with interaction among the factors, for example, performance versus cost. The analyst cannot treat these factors as independent, but must use appropriate statistical methods for assigning weights to the factors and for measuring the amount of interaction.

SUMMARY

Measurement of acceptable and desirable performance levels is rarely an absolute process. The team must be aware of the need for measurement early in Phase II and constantly seek a series of particularly appropriate factors for the study. Appropriate factors adequately measure management objectives. Scales and values on the scales evolve simultaneously with requirements analysis, but become usable measures only after they have been thoroughly reviewed with, and approved by, management. Once they have been worked into a cohesive framework, the measures form the basis for judging the validity of various systems designs.

QUESTIONS AND PROBLEMS

13–1 Establishing rating scales and setting values is a difficult task. To gain insight into a formal process quite analogous to this procedure, read a chapter from any of the standard personnel text books on position evaluation. This is a method for defining and rating the various positions within an organization. After reading about the method, point out five similarities and differences between the position classification problem and the establishment of a rating procedure for a new management system. Note to instructor: As a group exercise you may wish to draw up position descriptions and rate them for various positions on a study team.

13–2 Identify and define briefly five measurement factors for local commercial enterprises like a drug store, restaurant, book store.

13–3 When are measurement factors and measurement scales established?

13–4 List ten major measurement categories and possible measurement factors.

13–5 What is the purpose of a rating scale?

13–6 Are measurement factors related to business goals?

13–7 What is the fundamental defect in simple business control ratios, which are often used as measuring factors?

13–8 What might be the goals in the design of a data processing system for work measurement?

13–9 Compare the concept of measuring the performance of a system to evaluating a new product which an organization is considering to replace an existing product.

13–10 From Figure 13–1,
  a) What are the desirable and acceptable ranges?
  b) Who sets and achieves the ranges in question a?
  c) How does the information revealed by the figure affect how the analysts plan the system?

13–11 For the information in Figure 13–3:
  a) What is the smallest proportion of shipments under

six hours that will permit the system to be classified as operating in the acceptable range?

b) If 10% of the shipments had to wait eight or more hours, what is the conclusion about the new system's performance?

c) If less than 50% of the shipments under the new system had to wait less than seven hours, how would one classify the system?

CHAPTER 14
DOCUMENTATION FOR SYSTEM REQUIREMENTS

14.1 PREPARING TO DOCUMENT REQUIREMENTS

The existing system is normally of interest to the analysts only as it can be used as a basis for improving the system and enlarging its capabilities. But the way from a completed study to a new system is not simply a matter of supplementing the present system study by intuition. The necessary intermediate step between a study of the present system and the design of a new system is a rigorous determination of the new system requirements. The procedure is not as clear-cut as the procedure for describing an existing system, but certain guideposts can be noted.

This chapter shows a related group of forms developed to help the observer recognize these guides and to help increase the effectiveness of the analyst's approach. These forms and the manner in which the previously discussed descriptive forms provide source data for the analysis of system requirements are the subject of this chapter. They help structure the process through which the requirements are defined to management.

Understanding an existing system is essential to the analysis of system requirements. If such a study has been performed, the five types of descriptive forms on which the system is documented compose a readily accessible, coherently organized body of known facts. Where such a study has not been performed, other conventional survey documents or equivalent information is necessary.

Other information to guide the system analyst may be found in forecasts and predictions of future markets, new products or services being planned by management, contemplated changes in design or product mix, or other changes in management policies and objectives. Such changes may include increased specialization or diversification or expansion of the enterprise along either horizontal or vertical patterns. Changes in the pattern of availability of labor or of raw materials may also influence the activity. Government regulations must be considered too; these include the rulings of regulatory agencies, the labor codes, health and welfare rulings, consent decrees governing the permissible operating areas of certain enterprises, and so forth. The rules of regulatory agencies frequently affect the form and content of certain reports, and obviously must be considered in the analysis of information system requirements.

The outputs from the system are a prime determinant for system requirements. The system functions to produce goods, services, or information, which are the system outputs. Outputs may be logically required, or they may be imposed by management; in either case, production of the output is a primary goal toward which the system is directed.

Outputs are not, however, the only factor which influences the requirements of the system. Processing steps leading to these outputs and even inputs to the processing steps may be imposed by the environment, as when a government ruling specifies the method of accounting for certain funds. These additional constraints may significantly affect the system requirements.

After all specified operations or inputs have been considered, the outputs can determine the operation and input requirements. Outputs in many cases imply specific operations. The characteristics of an invoice, for instance, are determined by management preference and the environment: It must be capable of being transmitted to the customer and being read and understood. These characteristics may identify many operations, inputs, and resources. When the output form or the content has not been explicitly determined, greater flexibility and creativity in system design are possible. The outputs, once determined, suggest classes or types of operations. They also determine or suggest resources. And working backward one more step, the operations, resources, and outputs often indicate input requirements.

To document the specification of the requirements for a system, three additional forms are presented in the chapter. They enable the analyst to summarize the requirements of inputs-outputs, operations, and resources (informational and material) and are called the input-output sheet, the required operations sheet, and the resource sheet. These forms differ from those described in Chapter 8 in that these describe requirements in addition to current operations. These forms are also used later in Phase III as guides to help structure system design.

14.2 **THE INPUT-OUTPUT SHEET**

The input-output sheet is a summary form for recording the characteristics of required inputs and outputs. It is not a detailed descriptive form; where needed, detailed descriptions are displayed on supporting message sheets. Fields on the input-output sheet are reserved for the name of the message, medium of transmission, source or destination, number of fields, number of characters, and so forth. If the characteristics of the input or output are imposed by management, or logically required, the fact is noted. Both external and internal messages are reported on the input-output sheet, and this record helps ensure that necessary connecting operations will not subsequently be overlooked. When analyzing a system at the operational level, the analysts should relate all the input and output items of a specific operation together in the same input-output sheet or on successive sheets; this is not necessary, of course, when analyzing the input, output, and resource requirements as related to the activity as a whole.

Figure 14–1 contains the headings of a blank input-output sheet. Ten circled numbers reference the main fields in the form. The use of each of the keyed fields is explained below.

Notes to explain key numbers on the input-output sheet

1. **No.** The identification number serves the purpose of reference and separates inputs from outputs; inputs are identified by a number series beginning with I1, outputs by a series starting with R1.

2. **Name** This should be descriptive and reflect contents, appearance, or purpose. In the case of messages, the message number should also be included.

3. **Rate** This figure should characterize arrival or departure frequency of the item in terms of volume for some unit of time. Typical entries might be 1,200 per day, 1,000 per hour, 20 per month; the figures reflect projected rates determined through analysis.

4. **Media** Includes punched cards, teletypewriter, telephone, index cards, cathode-ray tubes, letters, telegrams, and so forth. This field specifies the means by which the input or output is represented. If management has not specified the means for representing or transmitting the items, permissible alternatives

**Figure 14–1 The top part of a blank input-output sheet. See
Section 14.2 for the notes referenced by the ten encircled key numbers.**

Input–Output Sheet

NO.	NAME	RATE	MEDIA	SOURCE DESTINATION	NO. OF FIELDS	NO. OF CHAR.	F O R M	C O N T	NOTES
①	②	③	④	⑤	⑥	⑦	⑧	⑨	⑩

may be entered here; if the area is completely unspecified, a note to that effect is entered.

5. **Source/Destination** Pertains to sources of inputs and destinations of outputs. Source and destination are generally expressed in terms of an organizational component, an activity, or, in the case of a principal input or output, an organization or entity outside of the activity under scrutiny.

6. **No. of Fields** Represents the average number of data fields on the document being described.

7. **No. of Characters** Represents the average size of the message, measured in characters.

8. **Form** An X in this column indicates that the format has been specified by management. When the format of the message has been specified, a message sheet representing it should be included as supporting material. The column is left blank when the format is not fixed in advance.

9. **Cont.** An X in this column indicates that the content has been specified by management, which means that the fields which make up the input or output item have been determined. The entry is left blank when management specifies the function or purpose but not the contents.

10. **Notes** The notes column is used to indicate special situations regarding any of the preceding items, or other information which bears on input-output requirements. Batching characteristics, for instance, are spelled out here if they are significant; acceptable alternatives to management specifications are also noted.

14.3 **THE REQUIRED OPERATIONS SHEET**

The required operations sheet summarizes the input factors, output factors, and frequency of execution of each logically necessary operation. A narrative description of the operation describing what the operation does and what it logically must do is entered on this form. The analyst also estimates the number and kinds of processes that compose the operation. Kinds of processes include logical and arithmetical, table lookup, editing, relational (comparing one factor with another), and so forth.

Figure 14–2 contains the top part of a blank required operations sheet. Seven encircled numbers serve to reference the seven main fields in the form. Each of the seven keyed fields is explained immediately below.

Notes for key numbers on the required operations sheet

1. **No.** An identification number is assigned to each operation for reference.

2. **Operation Name** A descriptive name is given to each operation to describe either what the operation does or its end product.

3. **Input Factors** This field displays the total number of data fields in all input items used in, or files referenced by, the operation. The figure is not the total number of fields in the input media, but rather the total number processed in the operation.

4. **Output Factors** This field displays information of the same type, and adheres to the same rules as Field 3. Only data fields produced by the operation are entered.

5. **Frequency of Execution** This is determined by analysis. A convenient time span is selected and the total number of executions for this time period is displayed. Exceptional considerations, such as unusual workload distributions, are expressed in the narrative description (see Field 7).

6. **Process Summary** An estimate is made of the total number of process steps. Processes are classified into practical categories (arithmetical, logical, relational, editorial, and so forth) and summarized by these classifications to characterize the size and complexity of the operation.

7. **(Narrative Description)** This section of the required operations sheet is used to describe what the operation does (but not how

**Figure 14–2 The top part of a blank required operations sheet.
See Section 14.3 for the notes referenced by the seven circled
key numbers.**

Required Operations Sheet

NO.	OPERATION NAME	INPUT FACTORS	OUTPUT FACTORS	FREQUENCY OF EXECUTION	PROCESS SUMMARY
①	②	③	④	⑤	⑥
			⑦		
①	②	③	④	⑤	⑥
			⑦		

it is done). It is also used to point out special considerations
normally covered in the other categories. In characterizing the
operation, some indication of the inputs and outputs should be
given, as well as an indication of the transformations that must
take place in order to change inputs into outputs.

14.4 THE RESOURCE SHEET

The resource sheet summarizes the material and informational resources that are either logically necessary or imposed on the operation. Again, in an analysis at the operational level, all the resources
related to a specific operation should be summarized on one resource
sheet or on successive sheets. All resources are summarized: types of
people, present or projected equipment, facilities, and files.

Figure 14–3 contains the top part of a blank resource sheet. Five
circled numbers reference the main fields in the form. Each of the
keyed fields is explained below.

Notes for the key numbers on the resource sheet

1. **No.** Besides serving as a reference, the identification number
   specifies which of the four types of resources is being
   represented; P1, E1, F1, and V1 respectively are used for
   personnel, equipment, facilities, or inventories. (Identifying

Figure 14–3 The top part of a blank resource sheet. See Section
14.4 for the notes referenced by the five circled key numbers.

Resource Sheet

NO.	NAME AND DESCRIPTION	AMOUNT	COST	NOTES
①	②	③	④	⑤

numbers of any kind or length may be used, but for
convenience they should be kept short.)

2. **Name and Description** The name of the resource should
   represent what it is, as well as characteristics, such as capacity
   or capability, which help identify it. Personnel are generally
   described by occupational specialty. Equipment should be
   described by general type, purpose, or function, unless the
   make and model are specified by management. Facilities are
   defined by type and location; contents are not entered in this
   category. Thus a reservoir might appear, but not the water, or a
   filing cabinet, but not the file. Both material and informational
   inventories are listed; the water or the file would be listed in
   this latter category.

3. **Amount** This is usually represented by a quantity: number of
   people, number of pieces of equipment, and so forth. For
   facilities, amount is normally specified in terms of capacity, in
   square or cubic footage. If resources are available only
   partially or part-time, the actual amount is entered; seven
   people available half the time would indicate an entry of 3½
   people.

4. **Cost** Either cost-per-unit time or cost per unit is shown. Cost-
   per-unit time reflects the total cost of an item over a period of
   time multiplied by the number of items. Some fixed percentage
   should be added to personnel and salary costs to reflect fringe
   benefits. Other overhead costs should be included. Similar
   pieces of equipment are totaled before they are entered on the
   resource sheet. Yearly rental figures should be entered for
   equipment unless it is purchased; in this case, write-off or
   depreciation procedures should be used to amortize the
   purchase price into an annual figure. Certain materials—blank
   forms, for instance—are more practically defined by unit costs.

5. **Notes** This column is used to record special considerations, add

supplemental information, indicate alternate resources, and so forth. Other uses might be to indicate the capacity of machines or provide a detailed description of complex equipment.

14.5 SUMMARY CHARACTER OF THE THREE FORMS

The three forms just described implicitly require a systematic approach to determine the system requirements. Their general and summary character guides the analyst to look more closely at what is to be done than at how it is to be accomplished. The stress in this second phase of study and design is on the results the system must achieve; the third phase of system design considers the procedures by which and the equipment with which these results are to be achieved.

The analyst must understand that system requirements can be determined conceptually. A business system is approached as a single entity, existing for the purpose of achieving an imposed goal. The mechanisms required to achieve that goal are then inferred; and the resources, operations, and inputs defined. From this point on, the analyst can be concerned with how, in terms of hardware and equipment, the outputs are generated. Of course, imposed characteristics resulting from capital investment in existing equipment or materials must be considered, but when these limitations are not present, the analyst is free from considerations of method and materials until there is clear understanding of the requirements of the system implied by the activities.

This chapter demonstrates the use of the three summary forms to derive the requirements of a system by extending the nonmechanized and mechanized examples already covered in Chapter 8. This demonstration assumes that the reporting forms discussed in those sections are serving as information sources, as a body of known facts, to support the determination of system requirements.

14.6 REQUIREMENTS IN A NONMECHANIZED SYSTEM

The final output from the nonmechanized charge account activity, as shown on the activity sheet in Figure 8–6, was the mailed bill which left the activity to go to the customer. The preparation of this bill was one of the operations described on the operation sheet in Figure 8–7.

Figure 14–4 Example of a completed input-output sheet for a nonmechanized activity—charge accounts.

Input-Output Sheet

NO.	NAME	RATE	MEDIA	SOURCE DESTINATION	NO. OF FIELDS	NO OF CHAR	CONT	NOTES
I1	CUSTOMER RECORD	20 K/D ①	①	CUSTOMER FILE ②	49	409 ②	X	① NO SPECIFICATION
								② CUSTOMER RECORD HAS:
								4 "FIXED" FIELDS - 292 CHAR
								5 "TRANSAC'N" FIELDS - 13 CHAR
								PER TRANSACTION,
								AVG. 9 TRANSACTION
								PER RECORD PER
								MONTH
I2	TRANSACTION SLIP	7.8 M/YR ①	②	SALES FLOOR ③	18	535 ③	X	① RATE FLUCTUATION:
								FREQ. | RATE
								143 D/YR | 15 K/D
								143 D/YR | 30 K/D
								13 D/YR | 45 K/D
								13 D/YR | 60 K/D
								② NO SPECIFICATION
								③ TRANSACTION SLIP HAS:
								12 "FIXED" FIELDS - 485 CHAR
								4 "TRANSAC'N" FIELDS - 25
								CHAR PER TRANS'N.
								AVG. 2 TRANS PER
								SLIP.
R1	BILL	4.6 M/YR ①	②	CUSTOMER ③	45	481 ③	X	① RATE FLUCTUATION:
								FREQ. | RATE
								165 D/YR | 15 K/D
								55 D/YR | 30 K/D
								15 D/YR | 20 K/D
								5 D/YR | 35 K/D
								② NO SPECIFICATION
								③ BILL HAS:
								9 "FIXED" FIELDS - 364 CHAR
								4 "TRANSAC'N" FIELDS –
								13 CHAR PER TRANS,
								AVG. 9 TRANS PER
								BILL.

DATE	ANALYST	CHARGE ACCOUNTS ACTIVITY	ASSOCIATED RETAILERS INC. STUDY	1 PAGE

The bill can be considered a logically imposed output from the activity.

The input-output sheet in Figure 14–4 lists the bill as the output of an operation in the charge account activity. The rate figure shown, 4.6 million a year, flags this as a critical output in a nonmechanized activity. Other pertinent statistics are summarized: the number of fields and number of characters, with explanatory notes, and a breakdown of rate fluctuations over the course of a yearly cycle. The medium of preparation is noted as unspecified, allowing a fair degree of freedom in setting up an operation to produce the bill.

One input logically necessary under any circumstances to produce a bill is some kind of customer record, from which the bill is essentially an excerpt. Since customers prefer to see transaction slips supporting the data on the bill, these slips can also be considered as required inputs. Summary data on volumes, fluctuations, and so forth are given for these inputs. Note that the medium and form of all three messages are not specified; however, the X in the **Cont.** column indicates that the contents of all three are fixed.

As a matter of record, the study documentation showed that the bill is presently prepared by duplicating the customer record by a copy process. This does not constitute specification of either the form or the medium, and the analyst should pass this fact over as incidental unless management has stipulated a continuation of the copy process for preparation of bills. Similarly, the transaction slips are presently stapled to the bill prior to mailing; a redesign of format for either or both forms might save staples, paper, or both by leading to an equally secure alternative procedure (for example, putting the transaction slips in a pocket formed by folding the bill in a certain way).

These are later considerations, of course; they are mentioned here merely to reinforce the point that the analyst at this stage should consider only *what must be done* and should not yet become entangled in considerations of *how it is done*.

The required operations sheet in Figure 14–5 defines the operations required to produce a bill and two related operations. The first entry gives the name of the operation, using a verb phrase of the same type as used in the activity and operation sheets in the Phase I study. Input and output factors and frequency of execution are also shown in this identifying field.

Input factors are the different fields of data that must be accepted by the operation; this figure is the total of all input elements from all sources used by the operation. The 38 input factors used in prepar-

Figure 14–5 Example of a completed required operations sheet for a nonmechanized system — charge accounts.

Required Operations Sheet

NO.	OPERATION NAME	INPUT FACTORS	OUTPUT FACTORS	FREQUENCY OF EXECUTION	PROCESS SUMMARY
01	PREPARE BILLS	38	45	19K/D	25 LOGICAL
	DETERMINE BALANCE FROM CHARGES, PAYMENTS,				17 ARITHMETIC
	AND RETURNS; SPECIAL ARITHMETIC IS REQUIRED FOR				4 RELATIONAL
	DISCOUNT CALCULATION AND PAST DUE CARRYING				3 LOOKUPS
	CHARGES. PRINT A BILL AFTER EXTENSIVE EDITING.				25 EDITS
02	MICROFILM BILLS	4	4	19K/D	4 LOGICAL
	PHOTOGRAPH BILLS WITH MICROFILM EQUIPMENT.				3 LOOKUPS
	CODE FILM FOR INFORMATION RETRIEVAL.				
03	INSERT DUE NOTICES	12	17	1800/D	8 LOGICAL
	DETERMINE PAST DUE STATUS ON BILL BALANCE.				3 ARITHMETIC
	SPECIAL HANDLING IS REQUIRED ON 3 OR MORE				4 EDITS
	MONTHS PAST DUE ITEMS. INSERT DUE NOTICE IN				
	BILL ENVELOPES AS REQUIRED.				

DATE ___ ANALYST ___ CHARGE ACCOUNTS / ACTIVITY — ASSOCIATED RETAILERS INC. / STUDY — 01 PAGE

ing bills include customer name and address, merchandise-identi-
fying fields and charges from transactions slips, data on returns and
payments, factors for calculating discounts and carrying charges, and
so forth. The same rules apply to the entry which shows the number
of output factors. In both cases, the entry gives the number of elements used in or produced by the operation, not the number of characters or fields on the input or output documents.

The steps involved in the operation are then described in a brief
sequential narrative. The narrative will implicitly suggest certain of
the processing steps and many of the inputs and information resources. Unusual characteristics are noted; the analyst who prepared
the description in Figure 14–5 noted that "extensive editing" was
required before the bill was printed.

The number and kinds of process steps are estimated and entered
in the process-summary field. Supporting the previous remark about
extensive editing in Figure 14–5 is the estimate of 25 editorial steps
required to prepare a bill.

Operation 02, **Microfilm Bills,** is required to maintain records
of the bills sent out. The microfilm process would not normally be
mentioned specifically; it was, we may assume, made a requirement
because of storage-space considerations and the department store's
capital investment in microfilm equipment. The **Due Notice** exception routine is obviously imposed as a requirement by the collection department.

The object of the summary on the required operations sheet is to
solve this problem: Given necessary (or imposed) outputs and inferred (or imposed) inputs, what are the steps in between? The narrative description helps define the process steps. The process summary
gives an estimate of the magnitude and complexity of the operation.

Working with the description and summary, the analysts can make
a preliminary estimate of what resources will be needed to achieve
the goals. This first approximation includes all required resources —
people, facilities, equipment, files — and is summarized on the resource sheet. The resource sheet for the analysis of the bill-preparing
operation is shown in Figure 14–6.

Four classes of resources are generally required: personnel, equipment, facilities, and inventories. Files are included as information
inventories. Description, amount, and cost are listed for each resource. Personnel resources are usually identified by occupational
skill. Equipment resources should, at this stage, be identified by
broad purpose or function rather than by name or type. Facilities are
identified by name and location; the contents of the facility — equip-

Figure 14–6 Example of a completed resource sheet for a nonmechanized system—charge accounts.

NO.	NAME AND DESCRIPTION	AMOUNT	COST	NOTES
				Resource Sheet
PO1	CLERK	5	$40,000/YR	
PO2	SUPERVISOR	1/2	$5000/YR	
PO3	TYPIST	1/8	$700/YR	
E1	COPIER	2	$3100/YR ①	① FIXED CHARGE OF $40 PER MO ; VARIABLE USE CHARGE OF .01 PER COPY.
E2	TYPEWRITER	1/3	$90/YR	AMORTIZED ON 5-YR BASE.
V1	CUSTOMER RECORD CARDS	5M/YR	$.02/UNIT	4 IDEN. FIELDS , 5 TRANSACTION FIELDS— AVG. 409 CHARACTERS PRINTED.
V2	CUSTOMER FILE	1	$145 K/YR	

DATE	ANALYST	CHARGE ACCOUNTS ACTIVITY	ASSOCIATED RETAILERS INC. STUDY	01 PAGE

ment, merchandise, and so forth— are described in other categories on the resource sheet. Inventories and files are described in terms of their intrinsic properties, such as name, location, file medium, volume, number of fields, and characters per message.

Resources are apportioned to the task under analysis. Thus, in Figure 14–6, half of the supervisor's time and an eighth of a typist's time are taken by the preparation of the charge account bills; but five full-time clerks are required. The total cost is shown in the cost field when the number or quantity of the resource in the amount field is greater than one. In this instance, the sum of the annual salaries of the five clerks is recorded. Actual costs are also shown for the supervisor's and the typist's time and for use of the typewriter a third of the time. It should be noted that these specified resources are estimates of what is *required* in the new system. Unless they are *imposed* on the new system design, however, they should not be stated explicitly because this implies that the concept and procedures must be used.

Necessary materials—in this case blank-form customer record cards or some such recording device—are also summarized. Information resources are listed on the resource sheet; Figure 14–6 lists the customer file, with its annual cost.

A close analysis of this resource sheet, supported by the resource usage sheet from Phase I, may lead the analyst to refine this first approximation of the resources required to achieve the activity goal. For example, preparing the customer record in duplicate in the first place might cut the equipment and clerical costs for only a slight increase in material costs. Since the copiers by which the customer record is presently prepared are rented, such a move, if it did present savings, would not meet management resistance because it would require no capital investment.

In general, the resource sheet summarizes the characteristics of resources without mentioning actual equipment—unless the equipment has been imposed as a requirement. Only during the design of the system does the analyst consider actual equipment.

The form and content of critical inputs and outputs, or of those input and output items whose characteristics are predetermined, may be described in message sheets, which then become supporting documentation for the input-output sheet. Similarly, the resource sheet may be supported by descriptive file sheets wherever the operational characteristics of the file are imposed or otherwise known in advance. Supporting documents for required operations sheets include the operation sheets from Phase I; additional support may be provided by displays of operations logic to show the interconnection

Figure 14-7 Example of a completed input-output sheet for a mechanized activity—order processing.

NO.	NAME	RATE	MEDIA	SOURCE DESTINATION	NO OF FIELDS	NO OF CHAR	FORM	CONT	NOTES
I 1	SALES ORDER	2330/WK	8½×11 FORM	SALESMAN	① 112	① 1010	X	X	① SALES ORDER HAS: 22 "FIXED" FIELDS-500 CHAR. 6 "ITEM" FIELDS- 34 CHAR. PER ITEM - AVG. OF 15 ITEMS PER ORDER.
R 1	PICKING TICKET	2500/WK	①	STOCKROOM	103	900			① NO SPECIFICATION.
I 1	PICKING TICKET	2500/WK	①	STOCKROOM	118	950			① NO SPECIFICATION.
I 2	NAME AND ADDRESS CARDS	1700/WK	IBM CARD	N & A FILE	7	73			MEDIA MAY BE CHANGED.
I 3	LINE ITEM CARD	25.5K/WK	IBM CARD	SALES ORDER	19	80			MEDIA MAY BE CHANGED.
R 1	INVOICE	2400/WK	8½×11 FORM	CUSTOMER	① 132	① 1070			① INVOICE HAS: 12 "FIXED" FIELDS-320 CHAR. 8 "ITEM" FIELDS- 50 CHAR. AVG. OF 15 ITEMS PER INVOICE.

Input-Output Sheet

ORDER PROCESSING ATLANTIC DISTRIB. INC. 1

DATE   ANALYST   ACTIVITY   STUDY   PAGE

of inputs, outputs, and resources, and decision logic to show what happens in the operation. Flowcharts and decision tables are useful tools for these displays.

The three summary forms, plus supporting documentation, guide the analyst to a valid determination of what the system will be required to do to produce a required output. Operational requirements, and the necessary inputs and resources, are inferred. Conditions imposed by logical necessity, the environment, or management are duly considered; where no preference exists, a new operational path is designed, or the most efficient existing path is selected.

14.7 REQUIREMENTS OF A MECHANIZED SYSTEM

Two operations — preparing the invoice and preparing the picking ticket in the mechanized order-processing system from Chapter 8 — are logical candidates for analysis, if only because of the volume of work involved. The operation sheet, prepared while the analysts were studying the existing activity, tells us that both are processed at the rate of 475 a day (see Figure 8–11). Besides, the expeditious movement of orders is critical to the business because of the importance of rapid service to the customer; the preparation of the picking ticket is the necessary intermediate step between receiving the order and getting the merchandise together for shipment. The invoice-preparation step is important also because customers normally do not pay for the goods they receive until they have the invoice.

The input-output sheet in Figure 14–7 summarizes the input and output requirements associated with the preparation of the picking ticket and the invoice. We can assume that some external influence — probably the habitual preference of either the company or its customers — has dictated an $8\frac{1}{2}'' \times 11''$ form as the medium for the invoice, just as the fixed format and content of the input sales order dictates the characteristics of its medium. The present mechanization level indicates punched cards as the medium for name-and-address and line-item cards, but flexibility of approach is permitted by the note that the medium may be changed. Only the picking ticket is of unspecified medium. Again, the volumes, sources and destinations, and other required characteristics are entered.

On the required operations sheet, Figure 14–8, the narrative description for the **Prepare Invoice** operation suggests that a proportionately large amount of calculation is performed in this operation. This is borne out by the estimate of processing steps in the

Figure 14–8 Final page of a completed required operations sheet for a mechanized activity—order processing.

					Required Operations Sheet
NO.	OPERATION NAME	INPUT FACTORS	OUTPUT FACTORS	FREQUENCY OF EXECUTION	PROCESS SUMMARY
22	PREPARE PICKING TICKET	47	60	2500/WK.	18 RELATIONAL
	USING ITEM NUMBER, DETERMINE STOCK LOCATION.				25 LOOKUPS
	USING CUSTOMER NAME, DETERMINE CUSTOMER				40 EDITS
	ADDRESS. SEQUENCE BY LOCATION AND PRINT				
	PICKING TICKET.				
23	PREPARE INVOICE	105	135	2400/WK.	70 ARITHMETIC
	USING ITEM NUMBER AND QUANTITY SHIPPED,				12 RELATIONAL
	DETERMINE UNIT AND TOTAL COST, UNIT AND TOTAL				10 LOGICAL
	GROSS MARGIN, UNIT AND TOTAL PRICE, AND INVOICE				30 LOOKUPS
	PRICE. USING INVOICE PRICE AND CUSTOMER				35 EDITS
	NUMBER, DETERMINE DISCOUNT, EDIT AND PRINT				
	INVOICE.				

DATE	ANALYST	ORDER PROCESSING ACTIVITY	ATLANTIC DISTRIB. INC. STUDY	04 PAGE

process summary. The invoice preparation sequence also works from a relatively large number of inputs and resources, as suggested by the entry of 105 under **Input Factors**. By comparison, the preparation of the picking ticket is fairly simple.

The resource sheet in Figure 14–9 summarizes the equipment, personnel, facilities, materials, and files required by the two operations undergoing analysis. It lists the costs projected by the whole-sale distributor for three card punches and an accounting machine with six wiring panels, plus the salaries of their operators and a full-time supervisor. Location and rental cost of the single facility are noted. Materials—blank line-item cards, picking tickets, and sales orders—are listed, as are the two files which are referenced by the operation. The constraints on resources implicit in the resource sheet in Figure 14–9 indicate that the company has stipulated the means for performing this operation.

The sales catalog is shown as an additional reference or information resource. It is used in preparation of sales from telephoned orders or customer purchase orders and is occasionally referenced in other operations.

14.8 DYNAMIC USE OF FORMS

In the first approximation of the analysis of system requirements, the summary forms serve as recording sheets for the logical collection and organization of data. As the flow of the activity emerges during the information gathering and manipulating process, the analyst gains insights into what the requirements actually are and frequently rewrites the forms to summarize the requirements from a new point of view. The technique of successive approximation and the willingness of management and the analysts to try new approaches are vital to the dynamic process that determines the actual requirements of the system.

It is neither easy nor straightforward to develop the true requirements of a business system. Rigid rules and step-by-step procedures are impossible. Since information gained at one point will almost invariably necessitate reevaluation of a previously acquired conclusion, a series of successive approximations is necessary.

Several general procedures have been evolved through experience to guide the analyst in making these successive passes at the system. In these procedures, the three summary forms are used to define the requirements as they are deduced. The five descriptive forms from

**Figure 14–9 Example of a completed resource sheet for a
mechanized activity — order processing.**

Resource Sheet

NO.	NAME AND DESCRIPTION	AMOUNT	COST	NOTES
P01	KEY PUNCH OPERATOR	3	$16000/YR	
P02	TAB MACHINE OPERATOR	2	$14500/YR	
P03	SUPERVISOR	1	$10,200/YR	
E01	KEYPUNCH WITH CARD INSERTION DEVICE	3	$195/MO	
E02	ACCOUNTING MACHINE MOD A2	1	$835/MO	
E03	ACCOUNTING MACHINE PANEL	6	$84/YR	$70/PANEL DEPRECIATED ON 5-YR BASIS
F1	TAB ROOM	430 SQ.FT. ①	$95/MO RENT	① IN OFFICE BLDG. 272 WILLOW ST
			$170/MO UTILITIES	
V1	LINE ITEM CARDS	1.35 M/YR	$3.10/K	
			$4200/YR	
V2	PICKING TICKET	125 K/YR	$.05/UNIT	
			$7000/YR	
V3	MASTER ITEM FILE	3	$21000/YR	32000-37000 ITEMS
V4	NAME AND ADDRESS FILE	1	$1275/YR	1700 CUSTOMERS
V5	SALES ORDER	120 K/YR	$.07/UNIT	
			$8400/YR	
V1	CATALOG① – 32000 TO 37000 ITEMS 700 TO 820 pp.	2000/YR ②	$4.20/UNIT	① INTERNAL CATALOG MAY BE SUPPLANTED BY OTHER TYPE OF FILE.
			$8400/YR	② SUPPLEMENT ISSUED QUARTER-LY 40 pp. PER SUPPLEMENT @ $1400 PER ISSUE TOTAL $5600/YR.

DATE ___ ANALYST ___ ORDER PROCESSING
ACTIVITY ___ ATLANTIC DISTRIB. STUDY ___ 1 PAGE

the Phase I survey, or equivalent information sources, serve as the initial inputs to the analytical phase; two of them—message and file sheets—are valuable supporting documents to the Phase II summary forms since they describe newly evolved inputs, outputs, and files.

Principal inputs and outputs are those related to the external environment. Others are those which are logically imposed or specified by management. These inputs and outputs are a logical starting point for the analytical process.

In first sketching out the requirements of the system, a rough requirements model is valuable. This model first displays all the imposed activity characteristics and their necessary interrelationships. From these can be inferred other activity requirements. A customer service department, for example, must accept telephone calls; for this, telephones can be inferred as a required resource. An order processing activity normally must calculate costs; a merchandise catalog or file can be inferred as a necessary information resource.

From the model of the system, the observer can begin to specify requirements. The activity output is defined first and after that, the operations that are required to produce it. These operations are listed and described along with their required resources and inputs. When these definitions are made, they may dictate or suggest changes in operation logic; a new approximation will suggest further changes, and so on.

In aggregating operations into larger groups to be defined in the subsequent system as activities, logical grouping is of prime importance. Operations can be related causally, sequentially, or chronologically.

Causal dependence refers to operations required because of the outcome of another operation. In the charge account activity, the recording of the sale and the posting of the file are causally dependent on the sale.

Sequential dependence is fixed when one operation must follow another. In the order processing activity, the order is received; the picking ticket prepared; the stock selected, packaged, and shipped; and the invoice prepared. The invoice is generally not prepared before the other steps are completed; stock cannot be shipped until selected and packaged; and the selection process must follow the preparation of the picking ticket. This is a sequentially dependent set of processes.

Chronological dependence requires performance of several operations either simultaneously or at fixed intervals. In the select stock operation of the order-processing activity, the back order, if one is required, can be generated only at the time the stock selection process discloses inadequate stock. At no other time is the information available to enter the system.

If the team is analyzing a single activity, the interrelationships among the operations will be clearly established. However, in determining the requirements of larger segments of a business, or of a whole business, the analyst must be alert to the various types of operational dependence and must group the operations logically. In studying system characteristics, the possibility of being misled by merely incidental relationships must be avoided.

There are two ways to develop the decision logic of a system. The more important involves the use of imposed inputs, outputs, and resources as limiting factors as well as the construction of a logic to connect them, with inputs and resources added where needed. This procedure places great demands on the resourcefulness and imagination of the analyst, but may in the long run produce a more valid statement of true requirements. The second way is to extract the basic decision logic from present operations, as displayed on the activity and operation sheets from the Phase I survey, then modify it by interviews with management.

The decision logic evolved through the process of inference within imposed restraints must be tested in operational models. The test procedure can be as simple as tracing an input rigorously through the system as inferred; missing operations and resources will be disclosed in the process. The procedure is not unlike debugging a computer program.

At each step, or for each of the several successive approximations, the requirements are summarized on input-output, required operations, and resource sheets. At the final analysis, the sheets are grouped together in their logical relationship and then recast. The supporting documentation is then prepared from preliminary sketches, in the case of flowcharts and decision tables; and message and file sheets are drawn up for critical inputs, outputs, and resources.

The summary of requirements present in the three forms and supporting documents now becomes the guide to the design and description of the new system. This is the third phase in the study and design stage of the life of a business system, which is discussed in Part 4 of this book. Part 3 ends with a discussion of the construction of the report of requirements, followed by the continuing Butodale case study, in which the forms described in this chapter are illustrated.

SUMMARY

Three forms may be used to document the specification of the requirements of a system—input-output sheet, required operations sheet, and resource sheet. The input-output sheet is a summary form for recording the required characteristics of inputs and outputs. Detailed descriptions, where needed, are displayed on supporting message sheets. The required operations sheet summarizes the input factors, output factors, and frequency of execution of each logically necessary operation. A narrative description outlining what the operation logically must do is entered on the form. The resource sheet summarizes the material and informational resources that are either logically necessary or imposed on the operation. All resources are summarized: types of people, present or projected equipment, facilities, and files. The general and summary character of the three documents guides the analyst to look more closely at what is to be done than at how it is to be accomplished.

QUESTIONS AND PROBLEMS

14–1   What is the purpose of the input-output sheet?

14–2   What does the required operations sheet summarize?

14–3   What does the resource sheet summarize?

14–4   How are inventories and files described on a resource sheet?

14–5   What is the prime determinant for system requirements?

14–6   What is the most important source of information for analysts when they try to establish the requirements of a system?

14–7   How much freedom do the analysts have in designing the format of the customer record in the input-output sheet in Figure 14–4?

14–8   For how many days a year must the charge account activity of Associated Retailers be operational?

14–9   Explain the five types of processes the analysts have established for the **Prepare Bills** operation shown in Figure 14–5. How do they affect the system design?

14–10 In Figure 14–9 we see that management has imposed a unit record installation on the system. Comment.

CHAPTER 15
PREPARING THE REPORT OF REQUIREMENTS

15.1 GENERAL CONSIDERATIONS

A report of requirements should document Phase II results, activity by activity, under three major headings: general, operations, and measurement. A summary is used to tie the individual activity packets together.

When requirements analysis is complete, the remaining tasks are to prepare summary statements and cost analyses and then draw the data into a cohesive requirements report. There is no established rule on how many passes are necessary to develop a satisfactory statement of system requirements. One or two may be sufficient for mechanization or improvement studies; as variability increases and constraints are fewer, analysis is more complex and more passes are required. Even in more complex studies, however, a number of activities may be fairly straightforward and consist only of a single chain of decision logic. For example, in automated manufacturing planning, the study team must develop the logic chain between parts characteristics and operator or machine instructions. Complexity arises from the individual analysis of the many thousands of parts there can be in a product line.

A common procedure for preparing a report of requirements is to start with activity packets, then compile the summary section. A number of important considerations that can materialize during Phase II, however, do not fall in any activity. These relate usually to policy statements and management decisions about implementation of the system and are shown in a section of the summary entitled "General Considerations." Included can be such topics as rental or purchase of data processing facilities, financial limitations on overall system implementation and operating costs, location of equipment, and how the changeover is to be performed.

The statement of general considerations, noted below, is taken from the Custodian Life report:

Figure 15–1 Gantt chart showing a tentative schedule of work for a study team designing a new system. Time is shown by month from June to January.

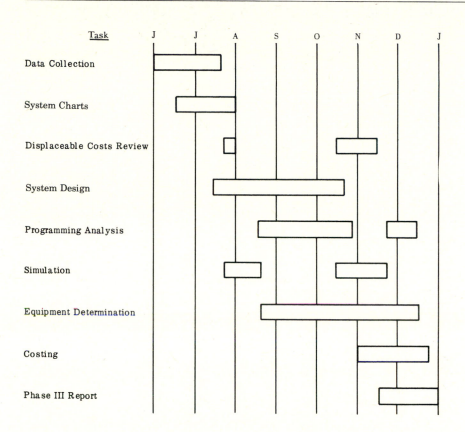

Cost

The present total cost for each activity is a tentative upper cost limit for any new design applying to that activity. This includes personnel, equipment, and facilities used to perform the work normally associated with data processing.

Policies

The standards used by the underwriters in determining the acceptability of an applicant are defined by the management of the company. These standards are the guideposts in the selection of risks, and must be adhered to in the underwriting decision.

Custodian Life both leases and purchases data processing equipment; the plan most advantageous at the time is selected.

Location

Data processing is performed at the home office. Any new system would utilize the facilities and resources at this location, rather than possible facilities at the general agencies.

Conversion and Implementation

Any proposed system will be run in parallel, as much as possible, and results compared in detail with the existing system output. The period of parallel operation will last only so long as needed to prove out the results of the new system but in no case will be less than one accounting period.

It is important that any new system provide for information on the status of a customer application at all times as it goes through the new-business processing.

The study team can also show for management's approval a tentative schedule for designing the new system. The estimated start, elapsed time, and completion dates can be displayed on a Gantt chart similar to that shown in Figure 15–1.

15.2 THE GENERAL SECTION OF THE REQUIREMENTS REPORT

The general section of each activity packet describes business goals and objectives as they relate to that activity, its scope and boundaries, and any applicable general considerations.

Phase I goals are refined and documented early in Phase II in order to direct the requirements analysis properly. While a complete narrative goal statement for the entire business is included in the summary section of the report of requirements, individual goals appropriate to single activities are placed in the general section of each activity packet.

Activity definitions, having been resolved as the goal statement was prepared and revised during Phase II analysis, are reviewed and entered in the general section in the form as described in Chapter 11.

Most of the general considerations have impact on the entire business and therefore are contained in the summary section as described earlier. General considerations applying only to one activity should be placed in the general section for that activity.

15.3 THE OPERATIONS SECTION

The operations section specifies what each activity is required to do: what inputs must be accepted, what operations must be performed, what outputs must be produced, and what resources must be employed.

All four elements — inputs, outputs, operations, and resources — are described briefly in an activity requirements model similar to that shown in Figure 12 – 1. This model, used throughout Phase II as a working paper to portray activity elements, is subject to revision as changes occur during analysis. Now these changes are introduced and the model produced in final form to show both imposed and logically determined requirements.

The input-output sheet, used earlier as a working paper, is now revised to summarize important features of required inputs and outputs emerging from requirements analysis.

The required operations sheet describes transformations which convert inputs to outputs. In documenting operations, emphasis is placed on identifying the decision logic rather than on describing the operation with a procedure statement. Any internal relationships, time dependencies, and required sequencing are noted in the description. Decision logic shown on decision tables and flowcharts is contained in the appendix of the report. Special studies conducted to test operational validity, such as simulation runs, may also be described there.

The resource sheet shows personnel, equipment, facilities, information, and physical inventories required by the activity. Resources may remain relatively unchanged if management imposes many constraints. More frequently, there will be important changes in resource requirements.

When positions and jobs of personnel are altered in content, the new work elements are outlined to show how they differ from previous job descriptions. Where the job title suggests the work content (computer programmer, transactions auditor, and so on), this is sufficient explanation. Position guides for new and revised jobs are prepared while the new system is being designed.

A map of an existing communications network could be placed in the appendix after it is revised to show network requirements resulting from Phase II traffic analysis.

15.4 **THE MEASUREMENT SECTION**

Measurement factors and scales for evaluating the effectiveness of alternative Phase III system designs are shown in each activity packet's measurement section. Factors are displayed graphically, with verbal definitions of each factor placed in the appendix. In addition to determining the worth of alternatives in system design, measurement factors are also used in evaluating the final system through the implementation and operation stages. Finally, the individual weights used to compare and note the measurement factors are included here, if appropriate.

15.5 **APPENDIX AND SUMMARY SECTIONS OF THE REQUIREMENTS REPORT**

The content, layout, and forms of the report of requirements are aimed at stating system requirements clearly and briefly. Any analysis which cannot be readily condensed is put in the appendix. The appendix includes items such as simulation details, extensive equipment lists, message and file sheets (where they are needed to describe imposed inputs, outputs, and resources), definitions of measurement factors, and the like.

The summary section integrates the activity packets and appraises the impact of the study on the entire business.

General considerations affecting more than one activity (for example, management policy, new systems cost, and location) appear here. The statement of the overall goals for the business is located in this section.

Although activities are somewhat independent in structure and content, outputs from some activities serve as inputs to others. There may be points of overlap, particularly in the use of common facilities. Interactive relationships are described in this section.

A preface introduces the objectives and content of the report and the sequence in which information is presented. The following paragraphs are excerpts from the introduction to the National Bank of Commerce report:

This report is a specification of system requirements which describes the present and future requirements for a business system at the National Bank of Commerce and establishes the measurements by which the performance of the new system is to be evaluated.

Several changes have taken place since the Present Business Description report was published. The goal statement has been expanded to reflect the anticipated growth of this institution and introduction of many new customer services. The activities (activities are sometimes referred to as subsystems) have been clarified both in definition and scope. Management also decided to include only those activities which have good growth potential and high transaction volumes in the new system. Consequently, five activities were selected and these five constitute the major sections of the requirements report.

The introduction continues by pointing out that management wanted the most advanced system design possible and therefore had placed very few constraints on the study team. The team leader devotes several paragraphs to an explanation of why requirements analysis is critical to system design, and also discusses the difference between an existing and a required system. The main report of requirements is then introduced.

SUMMARY

A requirements report documents Phase II results, activity by activity, under three major headings: general, operations, and measurement. An overall summary entitled "General Considerations" can introduce the complete report and may include such topics as financial limitations on overall system implementation and operating costs, location of equipment, rental or purchase of data processing facilities, and how the changeover is to be accomplished. A tentative schedule of Phase III may also be included. The general section of each activity packet describes business goals and objectives as they relate to that activity, activity scope and boundaries, and applicable general considerations. The operations section specifies what each activity is required to do in terms of the inputs that must be accepted, operations that must be performed, outputs that are produced, and resources employed. All four elements are related in an activity requirements model. The measurement section shows measurement factors and scales for evaluating the effectiveness of various systems designs. The report sometimes includes an appendix with simulation details, equipment lists, message and file sheets, and definitions of measurement factors.

QUESTIONS AND PROBLEMS

15-1   According to Figure 15-1, what three tasks require the greatest amount of time of a study team designing a new system?

15-2   What does the general section of each activity packet of the system requirements specification describe?

15-3   What is included in the operations section of the system requirements specification?

15-4   What is the purpose of the summary section of the system requirements specification report?

15-5   What is the relationship between the information in Figure 15-1 and the implementation of the system once the new system plan is approved?

CHAPTER 16
SPECIFYING REQUIREMENTS
FOR BUTODALE

16.1 GUIDE TO THE SYSTEM REQUIREMENTS REPORT

This chapter presents a continuation of the Butodale case study. Chapter 10 showed an adaptation of the actual report prepared by the systems analysts who studied Butodale as an existing organization. The report was accepted by management, who, in authorizing the study team to probe deeper into Butodale, ordered them to concentrate on two activities—**Provide Product Demand** and **Provide End Products.**

After an overview of this report on requirements, the reader will probably concentrate study on these points:

1. Comparison of goals and objectives as modified since Chapter 10.
2. Time and money constraints in the section on general considerations.
3. The goals the **Provide Product Demand** activity is to satisfy and the scope of the activity. These statements are important, having been set by a series of conferences between the analysts and those concerned with the activity. They become the criteria against which the requirements are matched.
4. The model exhibiting Butodale's requirements for the activity of providing product demand.
5. The input-output sheet, required operations sheet, and resource sheets for the **Provide Product Demand** activity and their relations with the Appendix.
6. The exhibits in the measurement section, especially the expectations that the new system will perform as well as, or better than, the existing system.
7. The explanation of measurement factors for the **Provide Product Demand** activity in the appendix. This matter shows how the analysts arrived at figures for their measurement scales, pro-

viding the formula for an unambiguous measurement of time and cost in the future.

16.2 SYSTEM REQUIREMENTS SPECIFICATION: A REPORT FOR BUTODALE

SUMMARY SECTION

Introduction

This report, the System Requirements Specification, describes the present and future requirements for a business system at Butodale Electronics Company, and establishes the measurements by which the performance of the new system is to be evaluated.

Several changes have taken place since the Present Business Description report was published. The goal statement has been expanded to reflect anticipated growth and modification of the business and introduction of new products. Activities have been sharpened and clarified both in definition and scope. A decision was reached with Butodale management during this redefinition process to analyze only the Provide Product Demand and Provide End Products activities at this time, since these are the critical activities in the main-line operation of the business.

Prime emphasis has been placed by Butodale management on considerations of the future so that the new system will have sufficient flexibility for development and manufacture of new products and product lines and still react quickly to customer needs. Present policies and practices, therefore, are to have a minimum influence.

Goals and Objectives

Goals and objectives of the Butodale Electronics Company are as follows:

1. Manufacture and sell standard computer equipment and accessories.
2. Design and manufacture special computer models and accessories to satisfy individual specifications and requirements.
3. Offer computation services and engineering consultation on a fee basis to industry, commerce, and schools, among others.
4. Manufacture spare parts and components for sale to the trade.
5. Repair and maintain installed equipment.
6. Conduct research on new products and services to support present lines and initiate new ones within Butodale's area of knowledge and proficiency.
7. Compensate employees and suppliers for services, and provide a satisfactory return for investors.

8. Demonstrate competence and quality in every product to clearly show advantage over competitive equipment.

General Considerations

Technological advances in the computer industry are rapidly developing needs for new products and new product characteristics. Manufacturing processes and skills will probably follow existing trends but the physical nature and end usage of products may shift radically. A system to perform Provide Product Demand and Provide End Products activities must be flexible enough to control more complex and more highly specialized products for a wider range of customers. For example, developments in microminiaturization and vibration engineering will alter manufacturing and testing techniques, and the space industry has specified severe environmental requirements.

Expansion and specialization of products means that a higher percentage of orders will require engineering design. To remain competitive, the cycle times for bid/quote, design, and manufacturing must improve over current cycle times.

Cost The combined data processing costs for operation of the new system (Provide Product Demand and Provide End Products activities) should not exceed 110% of current costs. Implementation and conversion costs are to be analyzed on the basis of a seven year amortization plan. Current system costs, based on current volumes, and new system costs, based on future volumes, are to be used.

Analysis must include purchase versus rental options available.

Conversion and Implementation All actions and plans shall be based on 80% of available workload to be operational under the new system within twenty months after implementation begins.

Source language for programming the equipment designated for any new system will be PL/I.

Activity Definitions and Relationships

Provide Product Demand is the interface with Butodale's customer market. Inputs from this part of the environment enter directly (requests for quotation and bids, inquiries, orders, etc.) and outputs from Provide

Product Demand directly enter the environment (quotations, bids, acknowledgments, and so on). Provide Product Demand interfaces with Provide End Products through the new order schedule. Provide Product Demand furnishes customer orders to the master scheduling operation of Provide End Products; this operation furnishes delivery dates to Provide Product Demand. Interfaces with other activities are limited to commonly-used files of basic product, customer, and order information.

Provide End Products is the product assembly function of Butodale. This activity interfaces with the environment through outputs of finished products and invoices, but does not follow up on these outputs through control of receivables. Significant interfaces with other Butodale activities (and areas not presently classified into activities) are:

Provide Product Demand, through the master scheduling operation and supplying of order status data as requested.

Provide Material through inputs of material cost records, subassemblies and parts and outputs of production schedules and work in process reports.

Engineering, through inputs of production standards, quality control and testing standards and procedures, and facilities planning data; outputs of standards and variances, testing results, and modification requests.

Accounting (Management Control) through inputs of work-in-process controls and outputs of certified labor records, work-in-process data, disbursements for additional (subcontracted) facilities, and invoices.

Other interfaces are only through shared files and file data.

PROVIDE PRODUCT DEMAND ACTIVITY GENERAL SECTION

Goals and Objectives

The prime goal of the Provide Product Demand activity is to communicate customer requirements and specifications for the manufacture of end products and spare parts. This is to be accomplished by meeting the following objectives:

1. Satisfy customer information requests.
2. Determine need for and carry out engineering design.
3. Supply information for cost accounting and management control.
4. Inform customers of order disposition and schedules.
5. Arrange for manufacturing.

Scope and Boundaries

This activity is concerned with accepting customer orders and preparing bids and quotations for potential customers. Requests and orders are received from company salesmen, manufacturers' representatives, or are placed directly by the customer. They include orders for standard and custom-designed equipment and spare parts, but do not include requests for computation services. Standard equipment is processed routinely, and the customer is furnished documents including price quotations, descriptive data, layouts, diagrams, and other information necessary to make the purchase decision.

Where the equipment is special, this activity includes management and engineering reviews, engineering design and layout, and the compilation of special cost data.

After receipt of a firm order, the contract is edited and clarified for communication to engineering and manufacturing. The present volume of requests averages 15–20 weekly for standard products, and 3–4 for engineered products. In the near future this could rise to a combined total of 25–30 per week.

Provide Product Demand does not include market forecasting, determination of plant schedules (this is actually worked out in conference with manufacturing when available capacity does not conform with customer requirements in regard to requested shipping dates), or the calculation of costs and prices.

The principal inputs, then, to this activity are customer orders or requests for quotation, and the principal outputs are quotations and specifications to the customer and communication of accepted orders and product specifications to manufacturing.

PROVIDE END PRODUCTS ACTIVITY GENERAL SECTION

Goals and Objectives

Goals and objectives of the Provide End Products activity are:

1. Develop and control production schedules to achieve at least current customer satisfaction level. In event of conflicting orders, preference is given to:
   a. standard products orders
   b. order acceptance date
   c. prime customers
2. Manufacture end products and components in accordance with Butodale quality standards.
3. Provide basic information for control of work-in-process, receivables, direct labor payroll, and end product shipping.

Scope and Boundaries

Provide End Products includes the functions of:
Production scheduling and dispatching

Component assembly and test
End product assembly and test
Maintenance of production and quality standards (material and labor)
Control of work-in-process
Providing certified labor records for direct payroll
Routing, packing, and shipping
Invoicing

Functions not included in Provide End Products are:

Establishing production standards
Establishing testing standards or procedure
Fabrication
Accounts payable (or disbursement)
Accounts receivable (or cashier)
Purchasing or subcontracting
Personnel or payroll administration
Transportation claims or administration
Facilities planning

Prime inputs are the Order Acknowledgment (R-3050) and New Order
Schedule (F-4080); prime outputs are end products and components,
Invoice (R-2100), and Shipping Report (R-3070).

General Considerations

Complexity of the production schedule is expected to increase as a
result of technological advances leading to more complex products.
System flexibility to handle a broader general-purpose product line and
(simultaneously) a more specialized product line is therefore mandatory.

Figure 16–1 The Provide Product Demand activity requirements model for Butodale.

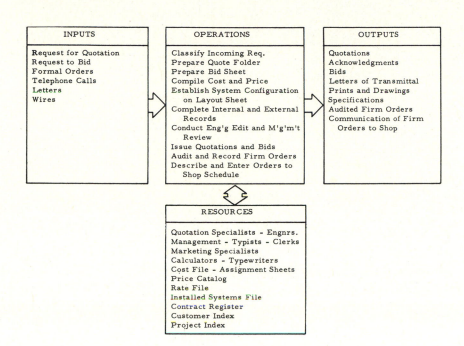

INPUTS	OPERATIONS	OUTPUTS
Request for Quotation	Classify Incoming Req.	Quotations
Request to Bid	Prepare Quote Folder	Acknowledgments
Formal Orders	Prepare Bid Sheet	Bids
Telephone Calls	Compile Cost and Price	Letters of Transmittal
Letters	Establish System Configuration	Prints and Drawings
Wires	on Layout Sheet	Specifications
	Complete Internal and External	Audited Firm Orders
	Records	Communication of Firm
	Conduct Eng'g Edit and M'g'm't	Orders to Shop
	Review	
	Issue Quotations and Bids	
	Audit and Record Firm Orders	
	Describe and Enter Orders to	
	Shop Schedule	

RESOURCES

Quotation Specialists - Engnrs.
Management - Typists - Clerks
Marketing Specialists
Calculators - Typewriters
Cost File - Assignment Sheets
Price Catalog
Rate File
Installed Systems File
Contract Register
Customer Index
Project Index

Figure 16–2 Input-output sheet for the Provide Product
Demand activity.

NO.	NAME	RATE	MEDIA	SOURCE DESTINATION	NO. OF FIELDS	NO. OF CHAR.	F O R M	C O N T	NOTES
I1	REQUEST FOR QUOTATION (R-2000)	50/W	WIRES TELEPHONE LETTERS	CUSTOMER					AVG. PEAK STD SYSTEMS 22 30 207-217 20 27 OTHER 8 13
I2	REQUEST FOR BID (R-2010)	10/W	LETTERS	CUSTOMER					PEAK VOLUME 12/W 10 WKS A YEAR
I3	CUSTOMER ORDERS (R-2020)	17/W	8½ x 11 4 PART	CUSTOMER					PEAK 20/WK 6 WEEKS A YEAR
R1	QUOTATIONS * (R-3000)	15/W	8½ x 11 4 PART	CUSTOMER				X	PEAK 20/WK 10 WEEKS A YEAR
R2	ACKNOWLEDGMENTS (R-3050)	17/W		CUSTOMER SHOP (PROVIDE END PRODUCTS ACTIVITY)			X	X	NO PEAKS
R3	NEW ORDER SCHEDULE (F-4080)	17/W		SHOP (PROVIDE END PRODUCTS ACTIVITY)				X	COMMUNICATES DATA ON FIRM ORDERS
R4	CUSTOMER ORDER (R-2020)	17/W		SHOP				X	DETAILS OF FIRM ORDER ARE ENTERED ON CONTRACT REGISTER

* INCLUDES LETTERS, DRAWINGS, SPECIFICATIONS, LAYOUTS
AS NECESSARY TO SUPPLEMENT QUOTATION

R.L. CASEY	DEMAND	BUTODALE	1
DATE ANALYST	ACTIVITY	STUDY	PAGE

Figure 16–3 Required operations sheet for the Provide Product
Demand activity.

NO.	OPERATION NAME	INPUT FACTORS	OUTPUT FACTORS	FREQUENCY OF EXECUTION	PROCESS SUMMARY
01	CLASSIFY INCOMING REQUESTS	5	10	60/W	7 LOOKUP
	ALL REQUESTS FOR BID (R-2010) OR QUOTATION (R-2000)				3 EDIT
	ARE SEPARATED INITIALLY INTO 3 GROUPS: STANDARD				6 RELATIONAL
	END ITEMS, STANDARD SYSTEMS, AND ENGINEERED				
	PRODUCTS.				
02	PREPARE QUOTE FOLDER (F-4050.1)	7	12	15/D	2 LOOKUP
	A FOLDER IS PREPARED FOR EACH REQUEST				4 EDIT
	TO HOLD CUSTOMER PAPERS AND DOCUMENTS				3 RELATIONAL
	GENERATED WITHIN BUTODALE TO FILL THE				
	ORDER.				
03	PREPARE BID SHEET (R-3000)	15	20	45/W	10 ARITHMETIC
	A BID SHEET IS PREPARED FOR EACH REQUEST				50 LOGICAL
	FROM PRICE, COST, AND INSTALLED SYSTEMS FILES				30 LOOKUP
	DEPENDING ON THE TYPE REQUEST, EACH IS PRO-				
	CESSED SOMEWHAT DIFFERENTLY. A GPAC* HAS				
	APPROXIMATELY 13 MAJOR INTERCONNECTED				
	COMPONENTS AVAILABLE IN DIFFERENT GROUPINGS.				
	INPUT-OUTPUT DEVICES ARE OPTIONAL IN 6 MODELS.				
	ALTHOUGH CONSOLE AND GROUPS DESCRIPTIONS				
	ARE STANDARD, THEY MAY BE MODIFIED AT				
	CUSTOMER REQUEST.				
04	DETERMINE SYSTEM LAYOUT	27	38	12/W	60 ARITHMETIC
	A GPAC MAY HAVE ANY ONE OF SEVERAL CON-				32 LOGICAL
	SOLES, AND ANY ONE OF SEVERAL RACK CONFIGURATIONS.				5 EDIT
	*GENERAL PURPOSE ANALOG COMPUTER				15 LOOKUP

	R.L. CASEY	DEMAND	BUTODALE	1 OF 3
DATE	ANALYST	ACTIVITY	STUDY	PAGE

Figure 16–3 (continued)

NO.	OPERATION NAME	INPUT FACTORS	OUTPUT FACTORS	FREQUENCY OF EXECUTION	PROCESS SUMMARY
05	DECIDE BID STATUS ON ENGINEERED PRODUCTS, A MANAGEMENT CONFERENCE IS HELD TO DETERMINE SPECIAL CONSIDERATIONS, PRICES, AND PROMISED DELIVERY.	40	70	40/M	30 LOOKUP 50 RELATIONAL 80 LOGICAL 10 ARITHMETIC
06	DESIGN SYSTEM LAYOUT ON ENGINEERED PRODUCTS, ENGINEERING DESIGN AND DRAFTING IS REQUIRED TO LAY OUT ALL SPECIAL REQUIREMENTS.	200	600	20/W	700 LOOKUP 200 LOGICAL 50 ARITHMETIC 40 RELATIONAL 300 EDIT
07	COST SPECIAL COMPONENTS FOR EACH SPECIAL ITEM, COSTS AND PRICES ARE ESTABLISHED TO SUPPORT THE FINAL QUOTATION.	10	18	150/W	4 LOOKUP 16 ARITHMETIC 10 RELATIONAL 8 EDIT
08	PREPARE QUOTATION (R-3000) THE CUSTOMER IS SUPPLIED A DOCUMENT DESCRIBING THE PRODUCT, ITS RACKS AND ATTACHMENTS, AND THE TOTAL PRICE, WITH OPTIONS.	75	100	20/W	30 LOOKUP 10 LOGICAL 100 EDIT 200 POSTING
09	ESTABLISH INTERNAL RECORDS DETAILS OF THE PROPOSAL ARE RECORDED ON INTERNAL DOCUMENTS AND IN THE CONTRACT REGISTER FILE. (F-4050)	200	800	20/W	10 LOGICAL 10 LOOKUP 500 POSTING 20 EDIT

DATE   R.L. CASEY   ANALYST   DEMAND   ACTIVITY   BUTODALE   STUDY   2 OF 3   PAGE

Figure 16–3 (continued)

NO.	OPERATION NAME	INPUT FACTORS	OUTPUT FACTORS	FREQUENCY OF EXECUTION	PROCESS SUMMARY
10	TRANSMIT QUOTATION (R-3000) THE QUOTATION IS MAILED TO THE CUSTOMER WITH SUPPORTING DATA INCLUDING A LETTER OF TRANSMITTAL, PRINTS, DRAWINGS, LAYOUT, SPECIFICATIONS, ETC.	10	10	20/W	25 LOGICAL 10 LOOKUP 10 EDIT
11	EDIT INCOMING ORDERS (R-2020) FIRM CUSTOMER ORDERS ARE EDITED AGAINST THE CONTRACT REGISTER FILE (F-4050) AND POSTED TO THE CUSTOMER (F-4060) AND PROJECT INDEX. (F-4070)	150	30	16/W	10 LOOKUP 150 EDIT 75 POSTING
12	PREPARE & TRANSMIT ACKNOWLEDGMENT (R-3050) THE CUSTOMER IS NOTIFIED OF THE ORDER RECEIPT, AND ACCEPTANCE AND DELIVERY DATES ARE RECONFIRMED.	30	30	16/W	10 LOOKUP 15 ARITHMETIC 30 EDIT
13	COMMUNICATE ORDERS TO SHOP THE CUSTOMER ORDER IS POSTED TO AN ASSIGNMENT SHEET (F-4080) AND PREPARED FOR SHOP RELEASE, OR TO ENGINEERING. SPECIAL CONDITIONS AND TERMS ARE COMMUNICATED TO INTERESTED PARTIES AT THIS TIME.	10	15	20/W	10 LOOKUP 20 POSTING 10 LOGICAL 10 EDIT

DATE _____ ANALYST **R. L. CASEY** ACTIVITY **DEMAND** STUDY **BUTODALE** PAGE **3 OF 3**

Figure 16—4 Resource sheet for the Provide Product
Demand activity.

Resource Sheet

NO.	NAME AND DESCRIPTION	AMOUNT	COST	NOTES
P1	MANAGEMENT (PARTIAL)	2	$24,000	REVIEW QUOTATIONS
P2	SALES AND SERVICE			
	MANAGER, SALESMEN,			
	SERVICE ENGINEERS,			
	SECRETARIES, CLERKS	56	$448,000	
P3	ADMINISTRATION & ADVERTISING	14	84,000	
	MANAGER, MEDIA			
	SPECIALISTS, SECRETARIES			
	CLERKS, ANALYSTS,			
	SUPERVISORS			
P4	COST CLERKS	2	9,000	
P5	ACCOUNTS RECEIVABLE CLERKS	4	19,000	
P6	PRODUCT ENGINEERS	3	26,400	
P7	ADMINISTRATIVE ENGINEERS	2	13,400	
P8	PUBLICATIONS SPECIALISTS	3	20,100	
E1	VEHICLES		10,100	DEPRECIATION & RENTAL
E2	TYPEWRITERS	15		
E3	CALCULATORS	2		
E4	DICTATING MACHINES	2		

R.L. CASEY   DEMAND   BUTODALE   1 of 1

DATE   ANALYST   ACTIVITY   STUDY   PAGE

Figure 16–5 Average order processing cost.

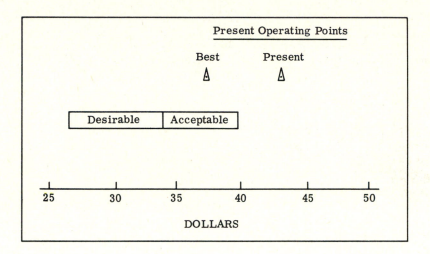

Figure 16–6 Order acknowledgment.

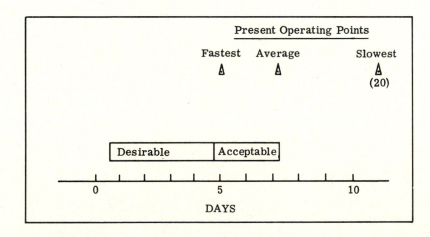

Figure 16–7 Response time for quotation.

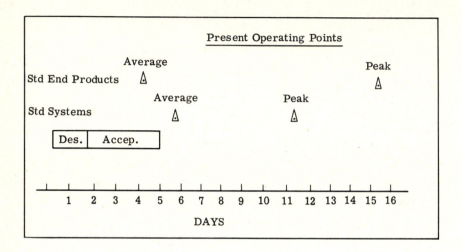

Figure 16–8 Response time for bid.

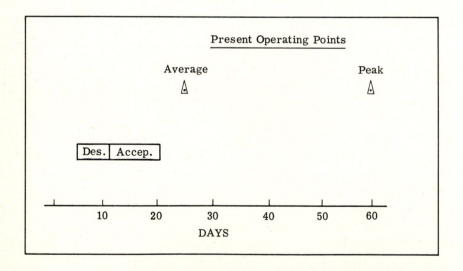

Figure 16–9 Quotation (bid) appearance.

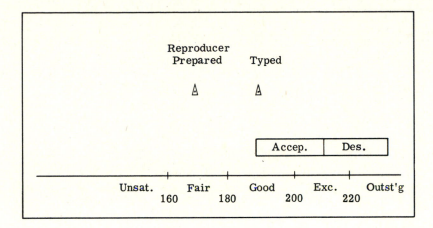

Figure 16–10 Processable request for bid/quotes.

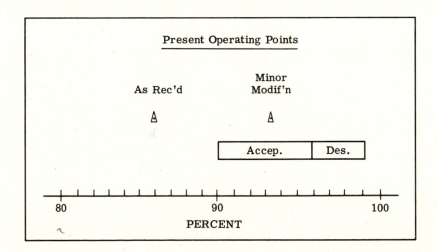

Figure 16–11 Standard products requested
(compared to total requests).

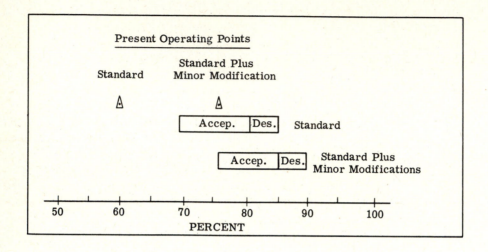

Figure 16–12 Percent relating dollars of standard product orders
to dollars of total orders.

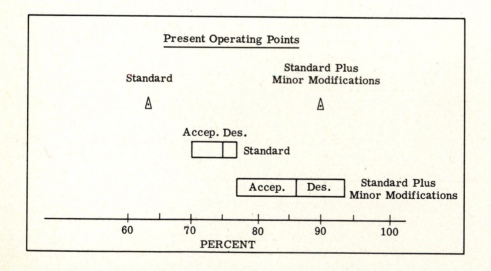

Operations Section

Figure 16–13 The Provide End Products activity requirements model for Butodale.

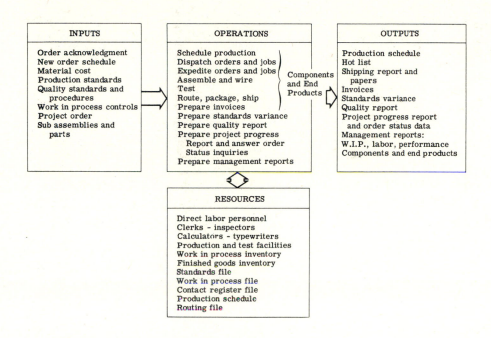

INPUTS	OPERATIONS	OUTPUTS

Order acknowledgment
New order schedule
Material cost
Production standards
Quality standards and
  procedures
Work in process controls
Project order
Sub assemblies and
  parts
	Schedule production
	Dispatch orders and jobs
	Expedite orders and jobs
	Assemble and wire
	Test
	Route, package, ship
	Prepare invoices
	Prepare standards variance
	Prepare quality report
	Prepare project progress
	  Report and answer order
	  Status inquiries
	Prepare management reports
		Production schedule
		Hot list
		Shipping report and
		  papers
		Invoices
		Standards variance
		Quality report
		Project progress report
		  and order status data
		Management reports:
		W.I.P., labor, performance
		Components and end products

Components and End Products

RESOURCES

Direct labor personnel
Clerks - inspectors
Calculators - typewriters
Production and test facilities
Work in process inventory
Finished goods inventory
Standards file
Work in process file
Contact register file
Production schedule
Routing file

Figure 16–14 Input-output sheet for the Provide End
Products activity.

Input-Output Sheet

NO.	NAME	RATE	MEDIA	SOURCE DESTINATION	NO. OF FIELDS	NO. OF CHAR.	F O R M	C O N T	NOTES
I1	ORDER ACKNOWLEDGMENTS (R-3050)	17/ω	LETTER	PROVIDE DEMAND ACTIVITY			X	X	NO PEAKS
I2	NEW ORDER SCHEDULE (F-4080)	1/ω		PROVIDE DEMAND ACTIVITY				X	MASTER SCHEDULE FOR END PRODUCT SHIPMENTS
I3	MATERIAL COST (R-3010)	100/D		PROVIDE MATERIAL ACTIVITY				X	COSTED MATERIAL WITHDRAWALS
I4	PRODUCTION STANDARDS	25/ω		ENG'G STDS PRODUCT'N TOOLING					ENGINEERING AND MFG MEMORANDA
I5	QUALITY STANDARDS	5/ω		ENG'G STDS					ENGINEERING MEMOS
I6	QUALITY PROCEDURES	5/MO		QUALITY CONTROL			X	X	ENTERED INTO QUALITY SECTION OF STANDARDS FILE
I7	W.I.P. CONTROLS	1/M		COST ACCT'G					
I8	PROJECT ORDERS	17/ω		MARKETG					SALES AND BUILD ORDER FOR END PRODUCTS AND COMPONENTS
R1	PRODUCTION SCHED.	1/ωᴛ	TAB LISTING	PRODUCT'N DEPTS			X	X	DETAIL BY PRODUCT. DEPT. AND PROJECT
R2	HOT LIST (R-3030) 30-50 LINES	1/D –	TYPED	PRODUCT'N DEPTS			X		

R.L. CASEY — DATE / ANALYST   END PRODUCTS ACTIVITY   BUTODALE STUDY   1 of 2 PAGE

Figure 16–14 (continued)

Input–Output Sheet

NO.	NAME	RATE	MEDIA	SOURCE DESTINATION	NO. OF FIELDS	NO. OF CHAR.	FORM	LOT	NOTES
R3	SHIPPING REPORT (R-3070)	1/DAY 4-12 ITEMS	TYPED	SUPT				X	
R4	INVOICE (R-3100)	20/ω		CUST & ACCTG				X	INCLUDES SHIPPING PAPERS
R5	STANDARDS VARIANCE	10/D		PRODUCT ENG'G					INSPECTION AND TEST MEMOS
R6	QUALITY REPORT (R-3040)	1/D 5-20 ITEMS	TYPED	Q/C					ACTION REPORT
R7	PROJECT PROGRESS REPORT	1/D 100 JOBS*		SUPT					COMBINED R-3020 AND R-3070 * EXPECTED TO GROW
R8	WORK IN PROCESS REPORT	1/ω		GEN'L ACCTG					DATA AVAILABLE IN F4120
R9	LABOR REPORT	1/ω		SUPT					ANALYSIS OF F4100
R10	PERFORMANCE REPORT (R-3080)	1/D		SUPT					
R11	ORDER STATUS INQUIRY DATA	3/D	PHONE	MKTG					FURNISH WITHIN 1 HOUR

M08-4606-1

| DATE | R.L. CASEY ANALYST | END PRODUCTS ACTIVITY | BUTODALE STUDY | 2 of 2 PAGE |

Figure 16–15 Required operations sheet for the Provide End
Products activity.

Required Operations Sheet

NO.	OPERATION NAME	INPUT FACTORS	OUTPUT FACTORS	FREQUENCY OF EXECUTION	PROCESS SUMMARY
01	SCHEDULE PRODUCTION	420	1200	1/W	750 LOOKUP
	BASED ON NEW ORDER SCHEDULE (F-4080)				1500 ARITHMETIC
	PREPARE DETAIL PRODUCTION SCHEDULE				150 LOGICAL
	FOR ASSEMBLY, WIRING, AND TEST AREAS. DETAIL				1500 RELATIONAL
	BY PRODUCT, DEPARTMENT, AND PROJECT				2400 POST
	(TWO TYPES OF PROJECTS ARE IN THE NEW				
	ORDER SCHEDULE: SALES PROJECTS, WHICH				
	HAVE A CUSTOMER ORDER, AND BUILD				
	PROJECTS, WHICH DO NOT).				
	DECISION RULES FOR PRIORITY IN				
	PRODUCTION SCHEDULING:				
	1. SALES PROJECT				
	2. STANDARD PRODUCT				
	3. PRIME CUSTOMER				
02	DISPATCH ORDERS	2700	4500	1/D	700 LOOKUP
	REQUISITION SUB ASSEMBLIES, PARTS, AND				250 ARITHMETIC
	TOOLS. RELEASE PROJECTS TO ASSIGNED ASSEMBLY				450 LOGICAL
	AREAS. ADVANCE ASSEMBLED AND WIRED PROJECTS				80 RELATIONAL
	TO TEST. MOVE COMPLETED PROJECTS TO FINAL				400 EDIT
	CLEAN UP AREA.				300 POST
03	EXPEDITE ORDERS	1600	200	30/D	1000 LOOKUP
	CHECK PROGRESS TO SCHEDULE. RE-ALLOCATE				300 ARITHMETIC
	MANPOWER, EQUIPMENT, AND SPACE AS NECESSARY				400 LOGICAL
	TO MEET COMPLETION DATES.				120 RELATIONAL
	EXPEDITE PARTS SHORTAGES.				200 POST

DATE   R.L. CASEY ANALYST   END PRODUCTS ACTIVITY   BUTODALE STUDY   1 of 3 PAGE

Figure 16–15 (continued)

Required Operations Sheet

NO.	OPERATION NAME	INPUT FACTORS	OUTPUT FACTORS	FREQUENCY OF EXECUTION	PROCESS SUMMARY
04	ASSEMBLE AND WIRE PROJECTS USING STANDARDS DATA, PROJECT ORDER, AND SPECIAL ENGINEERING INSTRUCTIONS, PERFORM REQUIRED ASSEMBLY AND WIRING OPERATIONS. INSPECT FOR QUALITY OF PHYSICAL CONFORMANCE TO SPECIFICATIONS.	1800	300	1/D	3100 LOOK UP 600 ARITHMETIC 3100 LOGICAL 1600 RELATIONAL
05	TEST PROJECTS USING STANDARD TEST DATA, PROGRAMS, AND SPECIAL TESTING EQUIPMENT, CHECK OUT PROJECTS TO PERFORMANCE SPECIFICATIONS AND MAKE NECESSARY ADJUSTMENTS TO MEET OR EXCEED STANDARDS.	2700	400	1/D	3100 LOOK UP 2000 ARITHMETIC 3100 LOGICAL 1500 RELATIONAL 600 EDIT 600 POST
06	FINAL CLEAN UP, ROUTING, PACKING AND SHIPPING. PERFORM HOUSEKEEPING ON COMPLETED PROJECTS. LOOK UP TRAFFIC ROUTES AND CARRIERS. PACK ACCORDING TO CARRIER INSTRUCTIONS. PREPARE SHIPPING PAPERS. MOVE EQUIPMENT TO TRANSPORT.	120	350	17/W	250 LOOK UP 170 ARITHMETIC 550 LOGICAL 250 RELATIONAL 170 EDIT 350 POST
07	PREPARE INVOICES USING PROJECT ORDER, SHIPPING PAPERS, AND CONTRACT REGISTER (F-4050), PREPARE INVOICE (R-3100). POST UNIT AND TOTAL PRICE, TRANSPORTATION PRICE, PAYMENT TERMS. COMPUTE DISCOUNT. EDIT INVOICE.	300	300	17/W	100 LOOK UP 50 ARITHMETIC 30 LOGICAL 200 POST 300 EDIT

R.L. CASEY   END PRODUCTS   BUTODALE   2 of 3

DATE   ANALYST   ACTIVITY   STUDY   PAGE

Figure 16–15 (continued)

Required Operations Sheet

NO.	OPERATION NAME	INPUT FACTORS	OUTPUT FACTORS	FREQUENCY OF EXECUTION	PROCESS SUMMARY
08	PREPARE STANDARDS VARIANCE USING STANDARDS DATA (F-4110), INSPECTION AND TEST DATA, AND ACTION MEMOS. PREPARE STANDARDS VARIANCE MEMOS (ON DEVIATIONS FROM CONFORMANCE AND PERFORMANCE SPECIFICATIONS) FOR ENGINEERING. INCLUDES VARIANCES AUTHORIZED BY ENGINEERING.	2100	600	10/D	800 LOOK UP 50 ARITHMETIC 1200 LOGICAL 300 RELATIONAL 600 POST
09	PREPARE QUALITY REPORT REPORT ON QUALITY PERFORMANCE WITH DETAIL ON REASONS FOR REJECTIONS.	350	175	1/D	350 LOOK UP 700 LOGICAL 200 POST
10	PROGRESS REPORTING PREPARE PROGRESS REPORTS ON PROJECT STATUS, WITH DETAIL ON UNITS AHEAD OR BEHIND SCHEDULE. ANSWER STATUS INQUIRIES AS RECEIVED.	1800	600	1/D	600 LOOK UP 1800 ARITHMETIC 1800 RELATIONAL 300 EDIT 900 POST
11	PREPARE MANAGEMENT REPORTS COMPILE WORK-IN-PROCESS, LABOR, AND PERFORMANCE REPORTS, INCLUDING EXPENDITURES OF TIME AND MATERIAL AS ALLOCATED TO PROJECTS.	3600	1200	1/W	300 LOOK UP 3600 ARITHMETIC 1800 EDIT 2400 POST

DATE _____ ANALYST R.L. CASEY   ACTIVITY END PRODUCTS   STUDY BUTODALE   PAGE 3 of 3

Figure 16–16 Resource sheet for the Provide End Products activity.

Resource Sheet

NO.	NAME AND DESCRIPTION	AMOUNT	COST	NOTES
P1	DIRECT LABOR	450	$2.6 MILLION/YR.	*SHOULD REMAIN CONSTANT
P2	CLERKS	30	$135,000	@ $4,500/YR.
P3	INSPECTORS	85	$425,000	@ $5,000
E1	CALCULATORS	3	$100/MO	RENTED
E2	TYPEWRITERS	25	$1,200	DEPRECIATED VALUE
F1	PRODUCTION AND TEST FACILITIES	130,000 SQ. FT.		
V1	WORK-IN-PROCESS INVENTORY		*$2,830,000	PORTION OF W-I-P INVENTORY COMMITED TO END PRODUCTS ACTIVITY. TRANSFERRED TO FINISHED GOODS INVENTORY AT END OF TEST.
V2	FINISHED GOODS INVENTORY		*$1,210,000	ON-THE-SHELF PRODUCTS LIQUIDATED THROUGH CUSTOMER BILLING

*DEVELOPED BY USING SHOP DECISION RULES IN SIMULATION AT SALES VOLUME OF $22,700,000.

DATE — ANALYST R.L. CASEY — ACTIVITY END PRODUCTS — STUDY BUTODALE — PAGE 1 of 2

Figure 16–16 (continued)

Resource Sheet

NO.	NAME AND DESCRIPTION	AMOUNT	COST	NOTES
V3	DECISION RULES			
	(1) PRODUCTION SCHEDULING			
	END PRODUCTS ARE BUILT TO NEW ORDER SCHEDULE			
	(F-4080) WHICH INCLUDES BOTH SALES AND BUILD			
	PROJECTS. INCOMING CUSTOMER ORDERS ARE			
	ASSIGNED TO BUILD PROJECTS USING PRIORITY RULE			
	(BELOW).			
	(2) PRIORITY			
	a. STANDARD PRODUCTS ORDERS			
	b. ORDER ACCEPTANCE DATE			
	c. PRIME CUSTOMER			
	(3) DISPATCHING			
	DISPATCHED ACCORDING TO DEPT. COMPLETION DATE.			
	SALES PROJECTS RECEIVE PRIORITY OVER BUILD			
	PROJECTS. WITHIN SALES PROJECTS, PRIORITY RULES			
	(ABOVE) APPLY.			
V4	STANDARDS FILE (F-4110)	6000 ITEMS		
V5	WORK-IN-PROCESS FILE (F-4120)	600 TO 800 ITEMS		
V6	CONTRACT REGISTER (F-4050)	2100 ITEMS		
V7	PRODUCTION SCHEDULE			KEPT BY EACH DEPT. CLERK
V8	ROUTING FILE (F-4090)	4 VOLS	$1200/YR	COMMON CARRIER SUBSCRIPTION REFERENCE MANUALS

DATE	R.L. CASEY	END PRODUCTS	BUTODALE	2 of 2
	ANALYST	ACTIVITY	STUDY	PAGE

APPENDIX

Measurement Factors for the Provide Product Demand Activity

1. Average Order Processing Cost

   Total of costs attributable to processing an order divided by number of orders per year.

   Costs for order processing are based on sales salaries, field administration expense, and central marketing and engineering costs.

   Present system—
   Average of 16 orders/week; 800/year.

   Departments directly affected are Marketing Administration (Sales Administration, Quotations, Engineering Sales) and Engineering Administration.

   Present costs—
   12% of Marketing Administration.
   10% of Product Engineering costs in Provide Product Demand activity.

2. Order Acknowledgment

   Elapsed time *from* receipt of a customer order by Marketing Administration (by mail, telephone, wire, and so on) *to* mailing of a written acknowledgment to customer.

   Statistics directly obtainable.

3. Response Time for Quotation

   Elapsed time *from* receipt of a request for quotation by Marketing Administration (by mail, telephone, wire, and so on) *to* mailing of a written quotation to customer.

   Wide variation between shortest, average, and longest performance on standard end items and on standard systems due to nonstandard nature of product.

4. Response Time for Bid

   Same as for quotation.

   Note: Bid cycle, in the opinion of Butodale management, must not lengthen under any new system; due to increased competition in Butodale's broadened future market, a cycle decrease is desirable. Since future products are expected to be significantly more complex, the engineering design portion of the bidding cycle will probably lengthen; this lengthening must at least be compensated for by shortening the information processing response time by an equal amount.

5. Quotation (Bid) Appearance

The following characteristics have been agreed upon as pertinent to appearance of a quotation or bid (along with their relative importance). In evaluating appearance, a Quotation (Bid) is judged on each characteristic on a scale from 10 (best) to 1 (worst); the points are weighted by relative importance and the total is matched to the description on the overall scale in the Measurement section.

Characteristic	Relative Importance	
Errors	5	There should be no typographical errors such as misspellings or incorrect numbers.
Six copies	5	Six legible copies must be produced.
Reference	4	There should be ready reference to prime fields of reference number, item numbers, quantity, price, and delivery date.
Smudges	3	There should be no carbon or ink smudges or edge impressions.
Linearity	3	Lines of print should be neat and straight.
Symmetry	2	Symmetry between numbers and letters is an important feature of the character set, since description is a mixture of alphabetic and numeric characters.
Impression	2	Print impression should be constant: no hollow letters or varying strength of impression.

Descriptions on the over-all scale in the Measurements section correspond to these point totals:

Outstanding	220 and above
Excellent	200–220
Good	180–200
Fair	160–180
Unsatisfactory	below 160

Two means of producing Quotations (under the present system) were evaluated as follows:

Characteristic	Rubberstamped and Reproduced	Typed
Errors	10(5)–50	4(5)–20
Six copies	10(5)–50	10(5)–50
Reference	6(4)–24	6(4)–24
Smudges	4(3)–12	10(3)–30
Linearity	4(3)–12	10(3)–30
Symmetry	5(2)–10	5(2)–10
Impression	2(2)– 4	10(2)–20
	162 (Fair)	184 (Good)

6. Processable Requests for Quotes/Bids

Two general categories of errors delay processing of quotations and bids. The first category requires inquiry back to the customer or salesman submitting the request, and no processing can be done until an answer is received. The second category requires further investigation, but (while this investigation is going on) the request can be processed.

Processing stops if the request has:

Incomplete product information, such as missing specifications, no power supply, etc.; illogical specifications, such as 110-volt power supply feeding a 220-volt amplifier; unacceptable description of unit or an incorrect identification or item number; illegible information.

Further investigation is required if the request has:

Improper customer designation such as incomplete name or missing address.

7. Standard Products Requested (compared to total requests)

A minor modification is substitution at the subassembly level or higher; below the subassembly level, modification is considered a design function.

Standard products are combinations of catalog and end product items with no substitutions.

Percent of standard products requested may be increased by: broadening the Butodale product line; a higher price differential between standard and nonstandard products; more products of a general purpose nature.

A higher percentage of standard products means that usage of standard parts will increase (with attendant lowering of production unit cost); this permits design flexibility with fewer items in inventory (again affecting production cost) and application of consistent design practices. An important benefit of standardization is the ability to expand or contract the product line without significantly affecting administrative (processing) costs.

No more than 90% standard products plus minor modifications is desired. The remaining 10% represents products requiring engineering design effort; it is the breakpoint for supporting sufficient design capability to create new commercially acceptable products.

8. Dollars of Standard Product Orders (compared to dollars of total orders)

Definitions of minor modifications and standard products are the same.

It is important to note that the Acceptable/Desirable range for minor modifications lies outside the range for standard products. This supports the price differential desired by Butodale: modified products will result in somewhat greater comparable revenue.

QUESTIONS AND PROBLEMS

16-1   What functions are not included in Butodale's **Provide Product Demand** activity?

16-2   What is not included in Butodale's **Provide End Products** activity?

16-3   Describe the scope and boundaries of Butodale's **Provide Product Demand** activity.

16-4   What are the goals and objectives of Butodale's **Provide Product Demand** activity?

16-5   What do *reference* and *symmetry* mean in relation to the appearance of Butodale's quotation bid?

16-6   From the Phase I report one would infer that all the major activities were going to be studied for possible conversion to the computer. In Phase II it appears that the scope of the study has been considerably reduced. Comment.

16-7   In Figure 16-1 we see six listed inputs. Are they all inclusive?

16-8   What freedom do the analysts have in designing the form on which to record the request for quotation or bid?

16-9   In the Phase II report for Butodale, what appears to be the bulk of the work among the required operations? Of what value will be the computer for this work?

16-10 Comment on the four factors that Butodale management desires to use for measuring the effectiveness of the new system.

PART FOUR
DESIGN THE NEW SYSTEM

Part 4 discusses how to conduct Phase III of a system study. Phase III is the design of the new system. Design alternatives are initially formulated around design concepts for one activity. Then, other activities are investigated for possible consolidation. Equipment configurations are analyzed for each alternative and refined into a system solution. Implementation costs are compiled, added to projected operating and maintenance costs, and compared to system benefits to determine the economic impact on the business. Design data are organized into a final report entitled "New System Plan."

New system design is concerned with the development, evaluation, and description of the business information management system that best fulfills requirements established in the Phase II system requirements specification. During Phase III, for each alternative design considered, a broad class of equipment is specified and evaluated against the specified requirements. The most promising solutions are further defined in terms of specific configurations; finally, the best solution is recommended to management.

CHAPTER 17
BASIC SYSTEM DESIGN

17.1 THE DESIGN PROCESS

The requirements report is the critical input to the design process because design alternatives are accepted or rejected on their ability to satisfy specific requirements appearing in the Phase II report. The statement of business goals in that report shows what the new system is expected to accomplish. The activity scope and boundary statement defines for design purposes the size and content of each activity. Input-output, required operations, and resource sheets amplify requirements such as the size and content of input and output records, the rate at which information must move through the system, a summary of processes in each operation and frequency of their execution, and data base characteristics and content. As system designs evolve, measurement factors appearing in the report of requirements can be used to evaluate design alternatives.

In designing a new system, analysts usually center their attention on the dominant activity of the business according to its size, potential savings, or special characteristics. In mechanization or improvement studies, the activity is often selected by management, possibly even before analysts are hired. Various input, output, processing, and file organization possibilities are hypothesized and then merged into alternative system designs. Several options are formulated and evaluated, and a manageable two or three are carried forward to the equipment selection process.

While system implementation itself is outside the scope of this book, it is necessary to show the numbers and types of people required to put the system into operation, when they will be needed, and how long it will take to complete the transition from final design to full system operation. Major preparation costs involved in system implementation and time schedules are prepared. These costs include:

1. Detailed system design
2. Programming and program testing

3. Physical installation
4. Conversion and test
5. Personnel selection and training

As the new system design evolves, the analysts use the measurement factors from the report of requirements to evaluate the performance of alternatives. For the final design, the system is appraised on the basis of its total worth to the business. Business profits, costs (implementation, operation, maintenance, and improvement), return on investment, and cash flow (projected over the estimated life of the new system) are factors typically used in this analysis. These results are then compared to the *base case*—the present system. After these tasks, the new system design is organized and documented in a final report.

17.2 NEW SYSTEM PLAN

The report containing the analysts' recommendations is a concise and complete description of the new system, with an objective judgment of the system's immediate and future value to the business. The report normally contains a preface and five major sections:

1. Management abstract
2. New system in operation
3. Implementation plan
4. Appraisal of system value
5. Appendix

Each section of the report is directed to a particular audience. The management abstract section outlines the study's key recommendations and summarizes the system design for top management. The section on the new system in operation conveys to operating management the special features of the system as it will function after installation. The implementation plan section shows the cost and time required to put the system into operation, and the section on appraisal of system value reveals the cost and profit impact of the system on financial and operating personnel. The appendix contains miscellaneous data which may help those who have to implement and operate the system.

17.3 MAJOR STEPS IN DESIGNING A SYSTEM

System design involves five major steps:

1. *Activity selection* The activity judged to be dominant by management and the study team is selected for initial design.
2. *System element analysis* Major elements (inputs, outputs, processing operations, and files) are identified and evaluated for this activity.
3. *Design alternative formulation* Design alternatives are synthesized and evaluated; the best two or three are accepted for further analysis.
4. *System description* The selected design alternatives are documented with a system description.
5. *Multiactivity integration* Other activities undergo a similar process. Relationships among design alternatives for the activities are analyzed, and appropriate compromises and consolidations are made. A few realistic design alternatives are carried forward.

While system design rewards a high level of creativity, it is more predictable if it is a disciplined effort. A major aid is thinking in terms of design concepts, independent of specific equipment. Imaginative application of design concepts can lead to the major improvements a study team seeks.

The idea of building a design around concepts or ideas can be illustrated by a case study. The National Bank of Commerce, like many other banks, offered its customers a complete range of banking services (checking and savings accounts, Christmas Club, and so on). It processed the information for each service in separate, specialized routines. The analysts considered the design concept of an integrated banking information service which would produce one monthly statement per customer, with each statement covering the entire range of banking services used. Discussion and analysis showed this concept to be feasible. The one-customer-one-statement concept led to important changes in data requirements. The separate file requirements among the several activities of course had led to much similarity across files, and so a central file (data base), to handle all data, was recommended. Similarity of input data requirements for checking and savings accounts led to the use of a checklike document issued by the bank (or written by the customer), rather than conventional deposit and withdrawal slips. Review of proposed legislation modifying the requirement for a savings passbook indicated a good chance that the practice of mailing this document to the customer could be discontinued. This meant that the bank could mail out a monthly or quarterly statement of customer balance and interim transactions. Furthermore, with the central file concept, up-to-the-minute statistics by teller, by branch, or for the entire bank could be made available to direct inquiry from remote locations.

Developing a system design in terms of a concept (in the above case, that of the central file), independently of equipment, can be done for all types of studies. The quality of the design depends on applying sound technical and business judgment, broad knowledge of equipment characteristics and capabilities, awareness of outstanding design concepts from previous studies, thorough training in programming principles, and useful experience in systems analysis. Other technical tools may also be needed in some studies.

17.4 ACTIVITY SELECTION

When multiple activities have been identified, the initial activity to be addressed in designing the new system is selected on the basis of one or more of the following factors:

1. *Dominant performance criteria* A single performance requirement (response time to customer inquiries and orders, for example) makes the activity so important that it overrides other activities.
2. *High affectable dollars* A potentially large savings is involved.
3. *Large size* The activity is large, either in input-output volume or in computing complexity.
4. *Inefficiency* The activity is the most inefficient area of performance in the present system.
5. *Prerequisite* The data base, or functions performed by this activity, is logically required prior to implementing other activities.
6. *Management preference* Management may have its own special reasons for selecting the activity.

17.5 SYSTEM ANALYSIS

After an activity is selected, the analysts must decide on the specifics (for example, inputs, outputs, processing operations, and files) that are to constitute the activity. The operations section of the requirements report is utilized in identifying and evaluating possibilities. Probing, specific questions are asked about each. The volume of input information, the handling of this information, the time it would involve on representative equipment, and accuracy or verification requirements must be examined before deciding which input form is best. Each possibility must be realistic in terms of the available money and implementation time. If the use of optical or magnetic-ink-coded input, for instance, departed from established industry practices, prior acceptance by governmental agencies or industry associations might be required. Many specific possibilities are usually rejected at this point. Known equipment capabilities may not permit economical use of the proposed input or output form or provide the access frequency required for the data or have the computation speed demanded for the proposed method of processing; design is always constrained by presently available technology. Throughout the analysis of design possibilities, the study team must constantly consider the dominant characteristics of the activity; frequently, input-output volumes and specifications indicate such dominance.

Inputs often have to be accepted in the form in which they are received from the outside or from another activity; it frequently happens that input design is really a task of conversion to machine-usable form. Output design frequently involves producing a form acceptable to the environment or to another activity. This may require several intermediate steps, as in an activity using a communications network. In such an activity, inputs may be received originally in oral or handwritten form, converted to machine-readable form such as cards, transmitted over a circuit to a data processing center which again produces cards, and finally edited and processed on a small computer to produce magnetic tape for further large computer operations.

Typical considerations in analyzing input possibilities are:

1. Should inputs received in nonprocessable form be converted, edited, and machine entered, or should they be manually entered?
2. Will each input have to be handled on an as-received (usually a unit) basis, or can inputs be processed in batches?
3. If batched, can inputs be processed randomly as received, or should they be sequenced by designated control fields?
4. What will the significance of input volume variation be on system performance criteria, particularly during peak periods?
5. If optical or magnetic ink character recognition (OCR or MICR)

data are to be directly entered, how will rejected items be handled, online or offline?

Output possibilities are similarly examined:

1. Will reports be printed, or is the output to be in another form, such as voice answerback or direct display blueprints?
2. How much of output content is to be summarized? detailed? listed by exception? Is online access desirable?
3. Which reports must be generated on schedule? on demand? on exception?
4. What will be the general requirements on format, readability, and number of copies?
5. Will there be microfilm or microfiche requirements?
6. Will graphic color or interactive display capability be needed?
7. Will output data be reused? Should it be archived on a mass storage device?
8. Will output go to another activity as a signal, tape record, or other machine-usable form?

After these possibilities have been explored and the inappropriate, unlikely, and unacceptable ones set aside, possible inputs and outputs can be stated as *cards, magnetic tape, machine sensible* for optical scanning or magnetic ink character recognition and the like. This selection of reasonable possibilities takes into account such factors as time restrictions or equipment capabilities, but does not yet specify input-output equipment.

The selection of input-output media is far from simple, and part of the decision depends on what is permitted or available for organizing data. In analyzing files, as in other activity elements, the analyst must isolate and evaluate the dominant characteristics of the activity.

1. To what extent do separate files contain the same data? Can they be consolidated into an integrated data base?
2. Can the file be processed sequentially? Must it be re-sorted for other applications? Should it be organized for direct access?
3. Should part of the data base be distributed for local access? How are local and remote data bases kept in synchronization?
4. Do all files require the same access speeds? Can a mass storage device be used for archival storage?
5. Should a generalized data base management system be used?

After the analysts have postulated answers to questions like these, they will have a better description of file alternatives in terms of file size, average access time, maximum access time, and so on.

When exploring the conceptual aspects of the mechanism to be used for processing data, analysts are primarily concerned with the magnitude and complexity of operations and the impact of these items on the system design. Such points as the following must be analyzed:

1. Should processing be against random or sequential data files?
2. How frequently will operations be executed?
3. What will be the dominant characteristics in operations— arithmetic? logical? relational? edit? lookup?
4. If a host/remote processor configuration is anticipated, how will the workload be split up?
5. How complex will operations logic be, in terms of computing time?
6. Can processing include main-line operations only, or must it include all exceptions? some exceptions?
7. Will operations require significant restart and checkpoint routines? Must remote processors continue operations when the host goes down? How?
8. How automatic is the system to be? Is manual override necessary, or can the system operate automatically without intervention?
9. What kind of auditability should be provided?
10. Must error corrections be made immediately, or can errors be recycled for later processing?

Analysts who have answered questions like these should have arrived at a set of possible processing characteristics that will make it possible to transform data inputs into data outputs. In fact, the information they now possess on input-output, file, and processing characteristics is likely to be sufficient for designing many kinds of systems to handle the information for the activity.

17.6 DESIGN ALTERNATIVE FORMULATION

A design alternative is a specifically stated combination of various input, output, processing, and file element possibilities, built around a design concept. A design concept holds together the separate elements in a design alternative; a design alternative describes how the concept is applied using the elements. In many cases, design alternatives can be built on concepts or approaches that proved successful in earlier installations in the type of business under study. Where pioneering is required, greater design time is usually needed, but possible design alternatives sometimes have to be discarded because of performance imbalances or obvious cost constraints. A solid knowledge of equipment capabilities gives analysts the ability to judge design alternatives intelligently without the time or expense of detailed system design and throughput analysis. The measurement factors in Chapter 13 help evaluate the several design alternatives the study team selects as most promising. The practicality of an appropriate design concept determines to a great extent how the individual possibilities are combined into a system. Four varieties of design concepts are illustrated here.

Regeneration Instead of retaining a large number of answers in memory, it is often possible to store the decision logic necessary to compute or generate each answer as it is needed. When the regeneration, rather than the file reference, principle is used extensively, the smaller files make it possible to eliminate searches and increase access speeds. This approach has been used for product engineering, cost estimating, and tax computations.

Transaction-File Reversal Transaction-file reversal shows how good solutions can evolve through the consideration of extremes or opposites. In a manufacturing business, for example, gross parts and materials requirements are often established by successive explosion of bills of material through several levels of the same structure. In a cumbersome, time-consuming approach, product requirements are thus considered the transactions, and the bills of material are the files. However, by reversing the procedure, considering where-used bills of material records as transactions that are passed against the product requirements (now the file), it should be possible to accomplish the same result in a single pass through the computer at significantly lower cost.

Distributed Processing In multiple-location operations, options exist as to whether to design several independent systems or consolidate data processing operations into a single system or a combination of the two—a distributed processing system. In a company with a widespread network of warehouses, for example, the system can be oriented to the warehouse or to the total network. In a distributed system, the local computers would process certain data unique to the site, perhaps with a local data base, and would periodically communicate with the central (host) computer. Such a decision depends on many different factors: type of products stocked in each warehouse, nature of the market, and uniqueness of the operations at the various locations.

Transaction Driven Entire systems can be built around online processing of each transaction received; the system becomes the sum of the transactions. Transaction driven systems typically involve telecommunications networks and are highly dependent on equipment. For example, airlines reservations systems have thousands of terminals connected to large, duplexed (dual) central processors.

In many industries there are particularly suitable concepts around which such design alternatives can be developed. Online processing, daily cycling, periodic status review, exception reporting, and centralized data processing are a few examples of architectures on which design alternatives can be built. If a standard "for fee" application program pertains directly to an activity, the use of its design approach can certainly be considered one of the principal options.

At the outset of design, the study team deals with pieces and parts (inputs, operations, and so forth). Now, in formulating design alternatives, the team approaches design from an integrated and unified viewpoint; a design is an entity, not an aggregation of parts. Design alternatives are compared with one another, and similar ones are combined until the best two or three remain.

17.7 SYSTEM DESCRIPTION

At this point, sufficient information has been accumulated to prepare a system description, which is essentially a statement of the major inputs, outputs, processing operations, and files needed. No detailed computer program design is formulated, and no attempt is made to state how many input devices, tapes, disks, or printers are desired or what size the main storage should be. The purpose of the system description is to show the basic architecture—the logical flow of information and the logical operations necessary to carry out the particular design alternative. Figure 17–1 is a system description for a multiple warehouse inventory control system. The activity sheet is convenient for this documentation, since it shows a system flow diagram along with information on volumes, time relationships, and specific functions or requirements.

The following narrative, taken from the Atlantic Distributors case, indicates the kind and level of information that should be available at the end of basic system design.

Figure 17–1 A system description for the Inventory Control activity for a wholesale organization.

| Activity Name | INVENTORY CONTROL |

UPDATE STOCK STATUS

Freq: As transactions received

Inputs: 2000, 2010, 2020

Key	Time	Note
1-4	2 HR	
2-4	2 HR	1000
3-4	4 HR	

RESPONSE TO INQUIRY

Freq: As received

Inputs: 2030

Key	Time	Note
5-6	1 MIN	1000

REORDER ANALYSIS

Freq: Daily

Inputs: 4010

Key	Time	Note
7-8	6 HR	1000
8-10	2 HR	1000

REPORTING

Freq: Weekly

Inputs: 4010

Key	Time	Note
11-12	8 HR	1000

INPUTS

Key	Name	Volume
2000	Receipts	500/Day
2010	Withdrawals	10,000/Day
2020	Misc Trans	1,000/Day
2030	Inq's & Ord's	2,000/Day

OUTPUTS

Key	Name	Volume
3000	Stk Status	1,750/Day
3010	Invalid Trans	
3020	Ship Instr	500/Day
3030	Recv'g Cards	500/Day
3040	Purch Ord	100/Day
3050	Exceptions	1,000 Items/Day
3060	Stock Status	20,000 Lines/wk

FILES

Key	Name	Size	Access Rqmts	Note
4000	Recv'g File	20,000 Records	Randm-5 Min	
4010	Master Stock	20,000 Records	Randm- 10 Sec	
4020	Commodity	200 Records	Seq - Daily	1050
4030	Vendor	1,000 Records	Randm-3 Min	1050

Activity Sheet

NOTES

1000 - Maximum allowable per requirements report.

NOTES

1050 - Commodity file is section of vendor file

Figure 17–1 (continued)

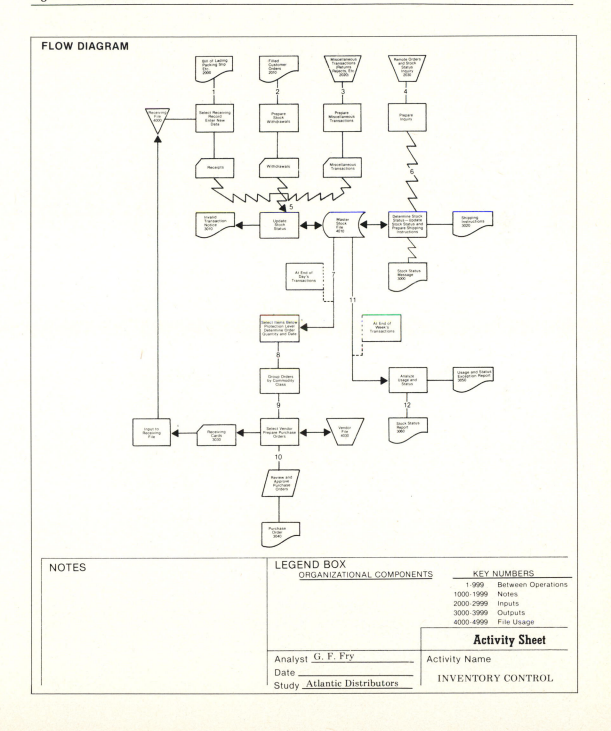

FLOW DIAGRAM

NOTES

LEGEND BOX
ORGANIZATIONAL COMPONENTS

KEY NUMBERS

1-999	Between Operations
1000-1999	Notes
2000-2999	Inputs
3000-3999	Outputs
4000-4999	File Usage

Activity Sheet

Analyst G. F. Fry

Date

Study Atlantic Distributors

Activity Name

INVENTORY CONTROL

Warehouse Inventory Control Activity

This activity is concerned with an inventory control system for a finished goods warehouse. There are many relatively small items stocked in the central warehouse with which the information processing system is associated. Five other auxiliary warehouses, from 100 to 500 miles away, place orders on the central warehouse and may require rapid delivery of critical items. There are four major groups of operations within the system: *updating stock status*, based on actual transactions; *response to inquiries* from auxiliary warehouses and central warehouse; *reorder analysis*, including purchase order preparation; and *weekly analytic reports* to show slow-moving items, major changes in usage rates, behind-schedule reports, and economic lot sizes.

A. Update Stock Status

    1. As material is received, the enclosed paperwork is marked to indicate the quantity received and quality acceptance. The bill of lading or packing slip is then passed against the receiving order file to withdraw the appropriate receiving record (a prepunched card) for each item. Actual quantity received, date received, and quality acceptance code are keypunched, and the card information is then transmitted to the data processing center.

    2. After each customer order is filled, a card is keypunched for each item on the marked-up order, showing actual quantity delivered, customer number, item number, date, and quantity. These withdrawals are transmitted to the data processing center.

    3. A variety of miscellaneous transactions are initiated by the warehouse, the receiving area, and purchasing: returns, rejects of incoming material, recounts, back orders, substitution, and scrap items. A card is prepared for each such transaction with the appropriate code for the transaction: item identification and quantity information are then inserted in the card. These cards are also transmitted to the data processing center.

    4. Transactions are received throughout the day at the data processing center. As each transaction is received, it is processed against the master stock file (on a direct access device) to update the status of each item. Validation checks are made during this operation to ensure that the item number is correct and that the quantity of the transaction is within reasonable limits. Invalid transactions are printed as typewriter output.

B. Remote Orders and Stock Status Inquiry

    5. The order-filling area (in the central warehouse) and the auxiliary warehouses have direct keyboard input to the data processing center by which online inquiries can be made. Availability (or planned availability) for all items can be obtained on an online

basis by keying the item information, quantity desired, and nature of the request.

6. The data processing center interrupts its other processing on receipt of an inquiry to determine stock status and to answer the information request. This is then transmitted back to the proper station. If a reservation or a request to ship is made, appropriate paperwork is prepared and the master stock file modified to show the reservation or withdrawal.

C. Reorder Analysis and Purchase Order Preparation

7. Each night, after all transactions have been posted, the entire master stock file is reviewed. Each item's current balance and planned availability balance are analyzed against expected day-by-day requirements and desired minimum stock levels. Where appropriate, reorder quantity is calculated and reorders are made. The planned due date is set, based on normal delivery cycles. If normal reorder quantity does not give adequate coverage, a specific indication is made.

8. All orders are then sorted by commodity code. Total dollar volume is summarized by commodity.

9. For each commodity code the approved vendor list is reviewed and individual orders are assigned to vendors on the basis of planned participation rates on specific items being ordered, dates required, and current quality-and-date performance by the vendor. Purchase orders are then prepared, and items ordered from the same vendor are grouped together by commodity code. Individual receiving cards are prepared for each item, sent to receiving, and placed in the receiving file. The vendor file is updated to note volume or orders placed and items ordered.

10. The purchase orders are reviewed by the purchasing agent or buyer on the following day, and each is approved and signed. Where changes are required or special decisions needed, the purchasing agent can request detailed information from the master stock file.

D. Stock Status Analysis

11. Weekly, the master stock file is reviewed to determine whether actual usage rates have changed significantly from expected usage rates and to carefully compare current stock status with revised usage. This identifies excessive stocks, overdue orders, and other specific relationships that require management attention. An item-by-item stock status report is issued with an exception report indicating usage and status of each item whose balance or open order is outside planned control limits.

17.8 MULTIACTIVITY INTEGRATION

Where system design encompasses several activities, alternatives are formulated for each activity in the same manner as described above. The resulting best design alternatives for each are then compared with the major activity for resolution of conflicts or incompatibilities. Activities are also reviewed together to determine the potential for compatible consolidation among inputs, outputs, operations, and resources.

It sometimes happens that the characteristics of the dominant activity are so overriding that other considerations are subordinated, and alternatives for the remaining activities tailored to fit this design. Airlines systems are examples of this kind of dominance; the system is designed around the real-time activity of seat reservation, and other activities are accommodated as equipment capacity and available processing time permit.

Developing an efficient solution for activities with diverse profiles can significantly increase equipment requirements. One activity, for example, might call for a very large direct access storage device; another might need a central processing unit with high-speed logical and arithmetic capabilities. However, properly designed, a system using a computer with both tape and direct access files might handle both activities efficiently; conversely, separate smaller computers or even mini-computers with specialized files might prove to be a more economical solution.

Sometimes a balancing activity is added to take advantage of the higher price-performance ratio of larger equipment. An activity requiring extensive computation and limited input-output can be combined with another activity having high input-output volumes and comparatively little computation. Later, when equipment is selected, these two activities together could represent a better total equipment utilization than would be possible for either one alone; hence, the installation is more profitable to the user.

Even the proposed implementation schedule can influence multiple activity decisions. Complexity of installation and lack of trained programmers and analysts often make an extended implementation period necessary. When this occurs, effort has to be first directed to the dominant activity, which is usually scheduled for initial implementation. A compatibility check is then made to ensure that the systems for the later activities will be compatible with the system implemented first.

17.9 **CONSOLIDATION OF FILES: INTEGRATED DATA BASES**

To this point, activities have been treated as independent entities. However, a new design may permit further opportunities for consolidation, especially in regard to common usage of data.

Files having common characteristics, content, and application should be consolidated wherever feasible into a single integrated data base. Consolidation possibilities were shown by several files in the Butodale study. In that company, engineering maintained a large parts file containing data on manufactured and purchased parts, costs, and commodity codes for compiling quotations on requests to bid; three manufacturing sections (standard products, custom-designed products, and spare parts) each supported cost files for preparing product costs; and accounting used another cost file for pricing. This last file was sequenced by part and assembly number, and it showed both part cost and part selling price. A good possibility existed for a common data base to replace these three files, as long as each activity had proper access to the data.

Similar kinds of consolidation possibilities exist among inputs, outputs, and operations. One activity may use the same or similar inputs, or it may produce outputs similar to those of another activity, as demonstrated in the one-customer-one-statement approach of the National Bank of Commerce mentioned earlier in the chapter. Output from one activity is often input to another. Inputs and outputs of the several activities, therefore, are examined for consolidation, or even for combining two sequential activities by eliminating the output-input junction, if care is taken to resolve incompatibilities of form, content, timing, or accuracy of data between activities.

Operations are normally less susceptible to consolidation than inputs, outputs, or files. Nevertheless, they should be checked for possible multiprocessing and multiprogramming when there is a dissimilarity of basic design concepts. Two examples of such dissimilarity are: (1) one activity with low-volume real-time operations, the other a high-volume batch activity, and (2) one activity with high input-output and low computation, the other with high computation. One consolidation often opens up other consolidation possibilities. Taking advantage of the differences in volume and frequency of execution at National Bank of Commerce made possible the combination of several operations through the use of the common transaction document.

When the best two or three integrated design alternatives are put together on activity sheets, both these integrated design alternatives and the earlier individual activity alternatives form the basis for the actual system selection.

SUMMARY

The process of system design leads to the definition of alternative systems. These alternatives become the base from which the selection of a specific system takes place. Experience helps ascertain where basic design should be stopped so that analysts do not become involved in implementation details.

Some analysts find it convenient to go through equipment selection for a single design alternative before developing additional alternatives; others work simultaneously with several alternatives. Both are perfectly reasonable procedures.

QUESTIONS AND PROBLEMS

17–1   For the design phase, how can the data in the present files of a system be related, in tabular form, to the data in the files of the proposed system?

17–2   What problem may arise if a system is designed to merely work with mathematical models, with complete disregard for routine data processing?

17–3   What might be the content of the data files of a mechanized plant maintenance system?

17–4   In most systems which include dynamic files, some of the records become useless for various reasons. As an example, many payroll systems will carry an employee's record for one year after termination of employment and then delete the record from the file. This procedure is known as *purging the file.* As a member of a study team you have been asked to prepare a list of rules for purging the file of a credit bureau. List at least five applicable purging rules the study team might establish during the design phase of a system.

17–5   What are some factors an analyst must consider in the selection of a sequence key format for a customer information file for a commercial bank when designing a new system?

17–6 List five possible formats of a customer name and address in the customer file of a commercial bank data processing application.

17–7 What are the basic questions to be answered in determining the file organization for a data processing system?

17–8 Why is it common to split a manual record into more than one part to form more than one master file?

17–9 Why do management personnel have difficulty in specifying the kind of reports they desire?

17–10 As analysts design a system, how should they think about the following: "As a commodity, information has two characteristics which can give it monetary value—relevance and timeliness. To the extent that it is relevant, it provides useful answers to specific questions, or supplies data to selected individuals; to the extent that it is timely, it is available at the time it is needed or usable. If either of these characteristics is missing, the information is useless and the design of the system is faulty."

17–11 What is the correct amount of data for a company to preserve in its data base?

17–12 What is meant by records retention?

17–13 Why is the government interested in records retention?

17–14 It has been stated that three axioms of business data are:
1. A company cannot afford to collect and process all the data that could be generated by it.
2. A company with an inadequate supply of business data is likely to fail.
3. A company should collect enough data at each stage of its existence to optimize its future earnings and return on investment.

Of what value are these three axioms to the study team during the design phase of a new system?

17–15 Every manufacturing process has maintenance personnel and equipment for performing maintenance on the plant and equipment. Effective management of the maintenance activity is important to a company. What questions might a maintenance management system be expected to answer?

17–16 In an information system for a credit bureau the primary file may be referred to as the *subject file.* This file contains all of the items of information pertaining to individuals' credit history and status. This file, although normally the largest and most important one, is by no means the only one used or maintained at a credit bureau. What might be some of the other files used and maintained by a credit bureau?

17–17 "Effective file maintenance rests upon a set of well-defined and consistent file audit rules." A credit bureau is designing a system for its subject file. What maintenance rules might the analysts set for this file?

17–18 A study of the inventory control system of a company reveals that the company is able to maintain a very small inventory by purchasing frequently and in small lots. Should the system be changed?

CHAPTER 18
SYSTEM SELECTION, IMPLEMENTATION PLANNING, AND EVALUATION

18.1 THE PROCESS OF SELECTION

The development of a system requires the selection of an efficient hardware and software combination for a particular design. Implementation planning for a system involves a thorough analysis and documentation of the expected investment required to install a system. Evaluation of a system involves management's appraisal of the system's value measured by how well it conforms to the cost and performance criteria established for it in Phase II of the system study. These three topics are closely intertwined and will be considered in conjunction with one another in this chapter.[1]

The development of a system is an iterative process. After a design is selected, the evaluation of equipment solutions frequently results in further changes in the configuration, features, or even the design structure itself. Since equipment selection affects and is affected by the design of computer programs, modification of one can directly influence the other and can, in turn, influence alignment of equipment with design alternatives.

The design alternatives, taken with other system requirements, provide the framework that allows the equipment selection to be performed. These requirements can be quite explicit and thus can significantly limit equipment choice. For example, suppose the following three requirements were set for the computing element of a particular system:

1. Must provide magnetic ink character recognition (MICR) for input of transactions

[1]In the remainder of this book it will often be necessary to refer to makes and models of computers for illustrative purposes. The letters XYZ represent any computer make, with model identification indicated by an added capital letter. Thus, XYZ/A is the A model of the XYZ computer.

2. Must create tape output which is compatible with file requirements on an XYZ/R
3. Must provide for immediate inquiry into master file records

Each of these three requirements implies either that certain components must be included in the final system or that certain components may not be included. These facts may simplify equipment selection, but may also build rigidities into the system.

There can also be qualitative boundaries which the system must accommodate. For example, consider the following five constraints:

1. Computer operating time must not exceed two shifts per day, five days per week.
2. Operating cost must be less than the operating cost of the current system.
3. Report ABC must be available to management at noon each day.
4. Cycle, or turnaround, time must be two hours or less; transactions received by 3:00 P.M. must be processed the same day.
5. Availability requirements are such that the system cannot be inoperative for more than two minutes during any hour.

A dollar value is often associated with bringing a factor further inside the boundary limit: For example, decreased cycle time may result in a decrease in open accounts receivable. The choice between equipment configurations meeting all restrictions may be based on the degree to which boundary limits are bettered. The cost-benefits analysis work done in Phase II is helpful in making the trade-offs. Boundary restrictions often limit equipment. Cost may eliminate certain large systems; reliability may require the duplexing of some components.

Initial evaluation of the requirements and the boundaries defines the framework within which equipment can be selected. The requirements are not inviolate; realities may show that some requirements are so expensive that they should be relaxed. A stipulation, for example, that a report be available by 4:00 P.M. one day rather than 8:00 A.M. the next day may be the only factor which forces the selection of a large computer operating one shift per day, rather than a less costly computer operating two shifts per day. Such a requirement must be examined in light of the additional expense directly attributable to it, but since the requirements have by now been reviewed and approved by management, any such change must be cleared before its adoption.

For reasons like this, equipment selection is often a serial, itera-tive process aimed at satisfying design requirements and constraints. These restrictions should be arranged in order of importance of diffi-culty, so that there is a basis for choosing to improve on one of the factors rather than another; that is, so that trade-offs can be properly made.

In summary, the process is as follows:

1. Specify a set of equipment to satisfy a design alternative.
2. Define computer programs using the specified equipment.
3. Estimate the time to execute each program, beginning with the longest running, until a requirement is violated or until all programs have been timed.
4. Iterate, modifying the equipment configuration (or the system design), to remove the violation or to improve its relationship with boundary factors. More components may reduce running time and extra shift; fewer components may increase running time, but decrease overall rental.
5. When the best solution for equipment and programs has been found, document the new equipment solution for that design alternative.
6. After two or three feasible solutions have been timed, go to the next design alternative in the sequence.
7. When all design alternatives have been evaluated, select the best equipment/design combination based on requirements, performance, cost impact upon the business, and implementation and operating costs of the proposed systems.

18.2 ADDITIONAL COMPUTER EQUIPMENT SELECTION CRITERIA

The postulation of equipment alternatives involves the consideration of additional characteristics of the equipment and its support. The most important of these is software support; system control pro-grams, sort/merge programs, programming language compilers and assemblers, data base and data communication (DB/DC) support programs, device access methods, and application programs are the major categories of software. Increasingly, equipment decisions are being made primarily on the availability, reliability, and support of the software itself. Other considerations are hardware and software modularity, compatibility, maintenance; back-up sites where programs could be run in an emergency; and the overall performance of the supplier over the years.

Modularity A feature of computer design that permits the easy addition or removal of component parts of the configuration. Although modularity applies equally to software, the text will normally discuss it in the context of equipment.

If a large activity is to be converted piecemeal to a computer, modularity allows an initial installation of less expensive, slower equipment which will be replaced with faster and/or larger components as volume warrants. Modularity is also significant if volume is expected to grow substantially over time with little or no change in system objectives. The substitution of faster components for slower ones with no change in programming is a most important consideration; examples are the substitution of a faster central processing unit (CPU) for a slower one or the substitution of a disk for a tape unit. Also valuable is the ability to add components, such as more tape units or more main storage, even though taking full advantage of such modularity may require reprogramming if the additional components are to affect performance positively.

Systems Programs Although programming does not take place until the implementation period, an evaluation of the systems software announced or available for the equipment under consideration is vital and often affects the equipment choice.

1. *System Control Programs* These programs are closest to the machine and attempt to make the machine usable by other programs. They schedule the use of such computing facilities as main storage, data channels, and input/output devices; they may provide *multiprogramming* (the ability of many programs to be executed simultaneously) and *multiprocessing* (the ability to engage multiple processors in working on a single program). They provide all of these facilities as a minimum and are often controlled by a job control language.

2. *Language Processors* Compiler and assembler programs take human-understandable programming language programs and convert them to machine-readable form. FORTRAN (Formula Translator), COBOL (Common Business Oriented Language), PL/1 (Programming Language/One), RPG (Report Program Generator), BAL (Basic Assembler Language), APL (A Programming Language) and BASIC (Beginners All-Symbolic

Instruction Code) are widely used computer programming languages. Because the higher level languages such as COBOL and RPG usually permit more rapid coding and debugging (error correction), and despite the fact that Assembler language may produce more efficient running programs, it is almost always preferable to use a higher level language.

3. *Sorts, Utilities* These are generally very efficient programs, written to support specific equipment. They consist of such general functions that they are almost universally usable. Users can often supply parameters to customize particular sorts for their data or can specify how disk-to-printer programs are to perform particular tasks.

4. *Device Access Programs* These programs make it possible for users to reference their data by name, without concern for the physical representation on tapes, disks, etc. Access programs address main storage, telecommunications devices, and other data handling facilities. They greatly reduce the programming effort of the application programmer.

5. *Data Base/Data Communication* (DB/DC) These are programs to assist programmers in managing and manipulating their data bases and/or communication systems. A higher level language is provided such that the user can direct the operations to be performed by the CPU, I/O devices, and remote or local terminals. Each of these normally assumes a particular communication network protocol or expects a particular data file structure.

6. *Application Programs* There are many common applications across a multitude of diverse customers, and others which are usable within a specific industry. Examples of programs in the first category are PERT, simulation, linear programming, text processing, computer assisted instructional systems, a myriad of scientific and statistical calculations, and many standard accounting, sales, and inventory programs. Examples in the latter group would be check processing, life or casualty insurance programs, factory scheduling, capacity planning, and hospital administration. While many of these programs would require modification for particular installations, they can be great time and money savers and may become prime considerations for new, small users. Most application programs and many systems programs are available for a fee, usually lease or purchase.

The programming support for the equipment under consideration is extremely important and complex to evaluate. A careful analysis will pay dividends in both the implementation and operation stages of the life cycle. Another important area of consideration in equipment selection is the assessment of reliability, availability and serviceability, often called RAS. While the words are self-explanatory, this judgment is a complex and important task and can have an important bearing on the equipment selection function.

18.3 PROGRAM DEFINITION

The effectiveness of a specific configuration is determined mainly by analyzing the time and cost of processing data. A first step, therefore, is the organization of the system into programs which break the job down into manageable portions.

Most systems have natural segmentation points for initial performance analysis. In a batch system, for example, segments might be:

1. Input conversion and data validation
2. Sorting
3. Master file updating
4. Output editing and conversion

For an online system, which may be tied directly to company operations, the segments differ somewhat and could be:

1. Inputs
2. Transactions (batch, single)
3. Inquiries
4. Control functions
5. Outputs
6. Reports

After all the programs have been defined, a system chart (or program organization chart) showing the flow of information through the system and the relationship of the programs to files should be prepared. The system chart will show the magnitude and scope of the complete system and aid the analysts in accomplishing the next step, which is the selection by the study team of the number and models of disk drives, tapes, printers, readers, and other components. Equipment features should be identified completely, with a list of the standard and special features needed to fulfill the objectives set for the processing system. If the system is to be handled by equipment already installed, the configuration is fixed; and the programs must be designed to fit the existing equipment.

18.4 TIMING AND COSTING

Each configuration should be evaluated for performance and cost by comparing it to the times and costs of other configurations. This may require a very detailed description of file organization and a review of noncomputer-oriented factors.

The approximate tape-passing time and the number of reels required can be calculated for each file on the basis of volume, tape density, and a tentative record-blocking factor. Tape drives are assigned to achieve a balanced channel condition, and provision is made for error and exception routines.

Utility runs, such as sorts and merges, can be timed from published formulas. For other types of programs, timing is based on tape-passing or disk accessing time and internal processing time. If the system is unbuffered, the time is the sum of input/output time and internal processing time; if the system is buffered (input, output and processing overlapped), the time is the greater of internal processing time or tape-passing time on the channel with the heaviest load.

The time required to locate a record is often critical in analyzing program run times for direct access devices. Various file organization or data management schemes should be studied to determine which will minimize throughput time. Programs are reviewed for improvement in order of their total running times. It may be possible to reduce the number of tape or disk drives, combine short runs, or split long runs for greater efficiency. The best configuration for a design alternative is determined from timing results and from a careful review of other system costs.

System cost is constructed from unit costs for system components, special features, operating supplies, and personnel requirements. A system is made from people, procedures, and equipment. To this point, discussion of system selection has been concentrated on equipment. However, associated procedures also must be examined to take advantage of file organization, better concepts of information storage and retrieval, new transmission equipment, and the like.

There must also be an estimate of the cost of the personnel who operate and maintain the system after it is fully installed. Salaries and clerical support costs are developed from actual payroll data (or industry averages, for new jobs), projected over the useful life of the operating system. Combined with performance and cost data for the equipment, this calculation produces a total operating cost for the new system.

18.5 FINAL SYSTEM SELECTION

Where practical, the process just described for equipment specification, program definition, and timing and cost analysis can be repeated with two or three equipment solutions for a given design alternative. The best configuration for that alternative is then selected. The process is then executed for each design alternative until a final choice can be made among the best solutions for each.

In the final selection process several additional business factors must be reviewed:

1. Growth of the business
2. Cost and ease of implementation
3. Need for system flexibility
4. Other applications and activities
5. Selection and training of personnel
6. Availability of assistance by computer specialists from the equipment manufacturer or independent software firm

One particularly important consideration in system selection is evaluation of implementation and operational cost effects. Analysts must understand the complete system cost to avoid the error of making the final decision solely on the basis of equipment rental and operating costs. When these topics have been examined in conjunction with the special advantages of each system configuration, the final system decision should be the one that is best for the total business, now and in the future.

When a system solution is designated, program description and timing data are reviewed once more to ensure that the best possible design exists prior to final documentation.

Separate activity sheets can be filled out for each program, or they can be combined on a single system flow diagram. Volumes, time relationships, frequency, and other significant data are noted in the tabular area; the system flow diagram can be drawn on the right side of the form, showing inputs, outputs, operations, and files.

Message, file, and operation sheets are used where appropriate. Selective detail is the keynote to documentation; critical areas may require some detailing, but most areas can be treated on a general level.

A summary activity sheet is usually desirable to display the system as an entity, with separate descriptions of equipment and personnel requirements.

18.6 SYSTEM SELECTION EXAMPLE

The process of system selection is illustrated in the following example of a finished stock control and warehousing activity from a multiplant manufacturing concern. Our discussion will center on a decentralized design alternative, a centralized design alternative, and the actual system design selected. The company in our example maintains twenty finished stock warehouses and distribution centers at widely dispersed points throughout the country, each one differing in size and type of items stocked. The study team formulated two basic design alternatives, one for a decentralized, local control system and another for a completely centralized system. During their study of the existing organization, the analysts had found that orders were received at the several warehouses by telephone, in the mail, or on handwritten forms.

Decentralized Concept Under the decentralized design alternative, manual documents would be converted to cards and processed in a computer at least four times a day at each warehouse. A direct access file would be maintained for inventory item balances and pricing data. Output would come in two forms: a printed listing of transactions and updated balances and a card for order picking. Reorder point analysis was scheduled for once-a-day review.

Three general computer configurations were postulated for this alternative, each with direct access storage units:

1. XYZ/A card system with an online printer
2. XYZ/B card system with an online printer
3. XYZ/S system. The acceptance of this configuration would depend largely on the volume of complex calculations.

A fourth possibility was the use of tabulating equipment in conjunction with tub files. Because the study team had to contend with different volumes at different warehouses, there was a chance that any one of these configurations might be appropriate in individual situations.

Starting with the knowledge that the design concept is decentralized and with the fact that several generic systems have been specified, what implications can be made in regard to each system? In the XYZ/A system, for example, the questions involve an alternative:

1. Can sufficient disk files be provided to allow real-time response?
2. Does the inflow have to be considered in batches?

In regard to files:

1. What files are needed?
2. How many transactions occur per day? How are they distributed during the day?
3. How many characters are there in each transaction?
4. Can name and address be coded, or do they come direct?
5. How big is the inventory file?
6. Can the inventory file be combined with the pricing file or name and address file?
7. Are discount data a separate file, or can they be put alongside each item?

The analysts had to answer the following questions on the batching of work:

1. Are inventory reorder point data separate or combined with another file?
2. Are orders separated by geographical location to take advantage of full carloads?
3. Are orders filled by breaking packs or only to full-unit packs?
4. How are modifications handled?
5. What kind of sales records are submitted and maintained?
6. Are accounts receivable part of this activity or separate?
7. Does credit have to be authorized on each order? Should there be a negative file, that is, a list of those who cannot receive credit?

All these questions help to determine the number and size of files. After they defined the files, the analysts decided on batch processing for this activity. Their next step involved an identification of programs, as follows:

1. Sort transactions by item or customer number.
2. Review credit by customer name or number.

3. Sort by geographic location code.
4. Group items into carload lots.
5. Sort carloads by item number.
6. Pass item numbers against the inventory file to produce picking tickets.
7. Sort picking tickets into sequence by location for carload accumulations.
8. Price items from price charts.
9. Re-sort by customer.
10. Perform discount analysis.
11. Produce invoice and accumulate to accounts receivable.

This first pass designation of programs was then reanalyzed to improve its efficiency, and the amount of processing was defined to some extent for each program.

Next, the equipment configuration was expanded in detail by answering these questions:

1. How many disk drives?
2. What speed card reader is needed?
3. What line speed is required for the printer?
4. How many cards are being punched on each run?

Finally, a timing and costing analysis was prepared for each program, which led to further modifications. This entire process was repeated for the other two proposed computers: XYZ/B and XYZ/S. On the basis of the timing and costing results of each configuration, a decision was made on the most feasible one for the decentralized design alternative: one XYZ/A system for each finished stock warehouse and distribution center, and one central XYZ/S system for invoicing.

Centralized Concept The same general approach was applied to the design alternative built around centralized control. Equipment networks were postulated to answer such questions as:

1. What kind of terminals would be needed? What kind of lines?
2. What would line rates be?
3. Would lines be one-way or two-way?
4. Would there be card or tape input terminals or job-oriented terminals? Video or typewriter-like?
5. Centrally, would a computer be used for message exchange, or would some other type of communications equipment be used?

6. Are reliability requirements such that equipment must be duplexed; is there an adequate fallback procedure; or is degraded service acceptable?

As to files, additional questions were:

1. How many logical files are there?
2. How are files organized?
3. How are files addressed?
4. Are files controlled by warehouse or by part number for all warehouses?

These and similar questions were reviewed until a detailed specification of inputs, outputs, and files had been completed.

The programs were quite different from the decentralized alternative, since the system would operate on a real-time basis. Eight or nine major operations were specified for processing transactions and for the associated batch or clean-up programs. A system simulation was considered necessary to evaluate the complexities of interactions and queuing. The analysts used a general purpose simulation program which they found to be effective for this purpose.

Once all these considerations had been weighed, equipment configurations were postulated:

1. Back-to-back XYZ/As
2. Single XYZ/E with an XYZ/B for input-output
3. XYZ/B system for input-output; XYZ/S to handle complex calculations

The configuration was then detailed to show:

1. Features of the equipment
2. Numbers and speeds of tape drives
3. Numbers and sizes of disk files
4. Number of channels between the input-output device and the computer

Performance analysis was considerably more complicated for these alternatives, and again the systems simulator was used. On the basis of time and cost operations, the study team decided on an XYZ/C–XYZ/B combination as the ideal solution, even though this particular configuration had not been specified originally. This solution illustrates how equipment alternatives become modified and blended through successive iterations. This last configuration provided the best compromise since the XYZ/C's high calculating capability, in conjunction with the high input-output capability of the XYZ/B, could also handle the scientific computations of an engineering activity. The remainder of the equipment specification included six tapes, four terminals at each location, and two-way lines.

System Selection The centralized equipment solution was compared with the solution under the decentralized concept. The evaluation of these two included examination of many factors specified in system requirements plus some new, nonequipment oriented elements:

1. Future business growth
2. System flexibility
3. Cost and ease of implementation
4. Training of personnel
5. Programming languages, operating systems, application packages
6. Effect of other applications
7. Cost
8. Impact on organization structure and procedures

When these factors were fully examined and both alternatives reorganized and rearranged, the study team made this final recommendation:

1. Three high-volume warehouses should be assigned separate XYZ/As, although invoicing will be performed centrally.
2. The other seventeen warehouses can be unified under a central XYZ/C–XYZ/B system with a one-hour batch time to eliminate possible queues in the system.

The complete design solution was documented to show detail on the equipment, individual program descriptions, files, inputs, and outputs. The remaining problem was to plan for the implementation of this proposed system.

18.7 PLANNING TO IMPLEMENT THE SYSTEM

An implementation plan thoroughly documents the expected investment in system installation as an important element of total system cost. Estimated time and cost to execute the plan are of primary importance here, rather than the substance and detail of the actual work of implementation.

System implementation planning has a parallel in physical facility planning. Before a commitment is made to proceed with the building of a new plant, management must know what costs are entailed, how long the construction will take, and what the cost of the product will be when produced by the new facility. Only then can a reasonable comparison be made between required investment and benefits to be derived from making this investment.

A substantial investment in time and money is required to transform a drawing board solution into a fully operating system. Investment in implementation is as much a part of the total cost of a new system as the rental or purchase price of equipment. Therefore, it is necessary to prepare an accurate estimate of these costs for management review as part of system recommendations.

In many studies the estimate will reflect the fact that complete systems are rarely installed simultaneously. For instance, an implementation schedule for replacing a tape system with a complex computer network of communications equipment and a disk system may call for a four-step program extending over a period of two to three years:

1. The present application programs are converted to the logic of the new computer and stored in one of the new system's disk files. Transactions are still batched on tape and processed against tape master records.

2. All master records now on magnetic tape are placed in the data base on disk; additional disk units are installed at this point. Transactions enter the system from tape in random sequence and are processed against disk file master records.

3. In-house, or home office, inquiry stations are installed. The data communications management programs must be operational at this point. Application programs are now put into final form. Checkpoint and restart procedures are tested.

4. Terminals are installed in field offices, starting with offices that transmit the greatest diversity of transaction types in order to fully prove system logic.

There is no complete checklist that will apply to every implementation program. However, certain checkpoints are encountered in most schedules, and these are useful when incorporated into a specific preinstallation plan:

1. Establishment of an organization for system implementation
2. Initial education program
3. Physical installation plan

4. Machine room layout and cable order
5. Establishment of conversion procedures
6. Detailed system design, coding, and program testing
7. Selection and training of operating personnel
8. Conversion, system testing, and pilot runs

Two special planning tools or techniques, PERT (Program Evaluation and Review Technique) and CPM (Critical Path Method), are often used in planning preinstallation schedules. If either PERT or CPM is employed, its use at this point should be confined to an overall description of implementation plans; later, when implementation has actually begun, a more detailed network can be developed.

18.8 COST PLANNING

Implementation itself takes place after the new system plan report has been approved. Initial planning for implementation, however, must begin before recommendations are submitted so that analysts can consider the implementation schedule and cost. Implementation cost planning includes five major tasks:

1. Detailed system design
2. Programming and program testing
3. Physical installation
4. Conversion and system testing
5. Personnel selection and training (performed concurrently with other tasks)

An estimate must be prepared showing how long each of these five tasks will take, how many people are needed, how much training each person will require, and how much the plan will cost.

18.9 COST OF DETAILED SYSTEM DESIGN

The new system should be described at a procedural level, during detailed system design, before programming can begin. When developing the implementation plan, however, the analysts' concern is not with the techniques of detailed design, but with the time and cost implications of performing this task: How long will it take? How many trained specialists will it require? How much will it cost in total? These considerations are answered by compiling individual estimates for separate assignments within detailed system design: de-

Figure 18–1 An illustration of how the time and cost plan for implementing the detailed design of a system may be exhibited.

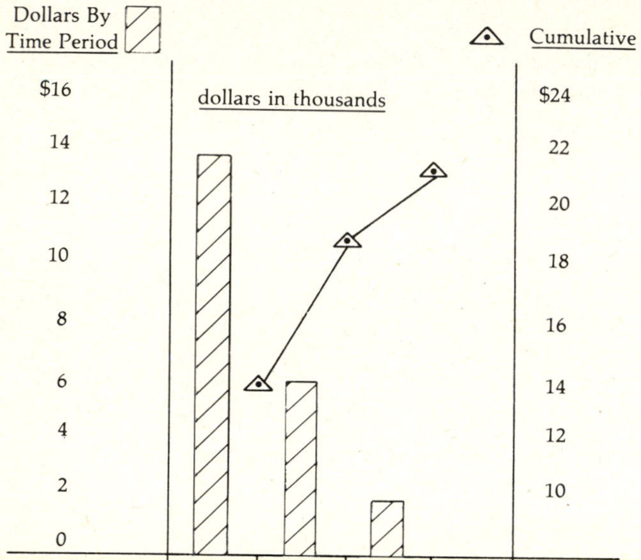
Dollars By Time Period
Cumulative
dollars in thousands
$16
14
12
10
8
6
4
2
0
$24
22
20
18
16
14
12
10

Time Periods	1	2	3	4	
Assignments					Cost
Detailed System Design	10,000				$10,000
Forms Design	2,000	2,000			4,000
File Maintenance Program No. 1	2,000	2,000			4,000
File Maintenance Program No. 2		2,000	2,000		4,000
Totals	$14,000	6,000	2,000		$22,000
Time Periods	1	2	3	4	

veloping program logic and documentation, detailed file design, forms and screen design and layout, report content and layout, and manual procedures.

Estimates are prepared by sampling representative routines, applying experience from comparable prior designs, using appropriate standards, or conducting small-scale desk tests. After individual estimates have been completed for all assignments, they are reviewed and modified, and then an overall plan is prepared.

One method of displaying these data in compact form is illustrated in Figure 18–1. The upper bar graph shows total dollar expenditures in a particular time period; the line graph connecting the triangles shows cumulative total dollars as of that time period using the cumulative value scale on the right. The lower horizontal bar graph shows the period of time over which the assignment is to be performed and the dollars required for the assignment. Totals are accumulated horizontally by task and vertically by time period.

18.10 ESTIMATING THE COST OF PROGRAMMING

As segments of the detailed system design are completed, programming will be initiated. Program flowcharting, coding, creating test data, desk checking, and testing are parts of this process. In developing the implementation cost for the new system, the analysts should estimate the time and money cost of these several programming tasks. The system's software environment, such as control programs, compilers, and DB/DC facilities, will also have an impact on the implementation.

After the basic logic and flow have been defined, a programmer can analyze and rearrange operations to take maximum advantage of computer (and peripheral equipment) characteristics. This reorganization involves evaluation of a number of computer considerations which have an important effect on system performance and efficiency: record blocking, channel balancing, and the use of subroutines, reference tables, multiple printers, and similar technical aspects of data processing. The introduction of these factors will undoubtedly cause some changes in the detailed design. An appropriate cost allowance for this work should be included in the programming estimate.

Time and cost estimates must also be developed for creating test data and for desk checking and code inspections prior to machine testing. In machine testing and debugging, testing packages improve machine utilization and enable more programs to be tested in a given length of time. The analysts should allow for waiting time during debugging, since a computer may not always be immediately available.

After individual modules or subprograms are debugged, they must be linked with other segments. A good time estimate is necessary here. Debugging of individual segments can be predicted with a fair degree of accuracy, but when several programs are integrated into a system, their interaction may be very high. The higher the interaction, the more sharply debugging time increases.

Total programming time can be reduced by using high-level languages, generalized programs, utility programs, and program testing aids. Online programming, structured design and programming, walkthroughs, team programming, and such are often useful in raising programming productivity and decreasing programming errors, and thus reducing the overall program development cost. Often packaged application programs can materially reduce programming time, whether the package is used intact, modified, or as a detail blueprint (system runs, file organization, and record layout).

Actual costs from installed systems and suggested time allowances can be studied for guidance in developing programming estimates. In addition, the analysts obviously should draw upon the experience of programmers. When summarizing the information for management, the analysts may wish to consider a graph with a format similar to that in Figure 18–1.

18.11 PLANNING THE COST OF THE PHYSICAL SITE

The main concern in establishing a physical installation time and cost plan is to provide an adequate time schedule and sufficient construction funds for the work. Of course, if an existing facility is in place, this step can be skipped.

Analysts needing to do this task will find that the various aspects of physical planning such as site selection and construction, air conditioning, equipment and office layout, and electrical and cable requirements have been so thoroughly discussed in other literature that detailed guides are available on both the general subject and individual systems.

The installation estimate can be reported in a form similar to that shown in Figure 18–1, from data supplied by subcontractors or the organization's internal facilities group.

18.12 PLANNING THE COST OF CONVERSION

The size of the conversion task depends on how large a part of the total system is included in the initial change and on how much is consigned to later implementation. A variety of assignments are reflected in the time and cost estimate for conversion:

1. Preparing and editing files for completeness, accuracy, and format
2. Establishing file maintenance procedures
3. Providing training in system operation for using departments and for source-data departments
4. Compiling schedules for the change to the new computer
5. Planning for pilot or parallel operation (In parallel operation, the old and new systems are operated simultaneously for a time on current data; in pilot operation, the new system is checked out extensively, using data from a prior period, before it takes over processing of current operations)
6. Coordinating the conversion

A realistic schedule is based on the amount and type of work to be done and on the availability of personnel to handle it. Appropriate time and costs can be summarized in a form similar to that of Figure 18–1.

18.13 PLANNING THE COST OF PERSONNEL

Each of the foregoing tasks included some personnel cost for doing the work. Since salaries and associated overhead constitute a large part of implementation expense, it is often helpful to show in a separate summary the personnel buildup, by job categories, for all the tasks. Figure 18–2 shows requirements for each position; E represents experienced personnel, and T stands for trainees. The upper numeral in a box indicates the number of persons to be added or released during a stated time period, while the lower numeral reveals the cumulative number in that position at any one time.

Other personnel expenses, beyond the salaries of implementation personnel, are interviewing, testing, rating, and selecting the personnel, and, when they are chosen, training them.

Extensive educational programs are offered on specific data processing systems for those who will do systems analysis, programming, and machine operations jobs, as well as for installation person-

Figure 18–2 A method for showing the number of people needed to implement and operate the computer portion of a new management system.

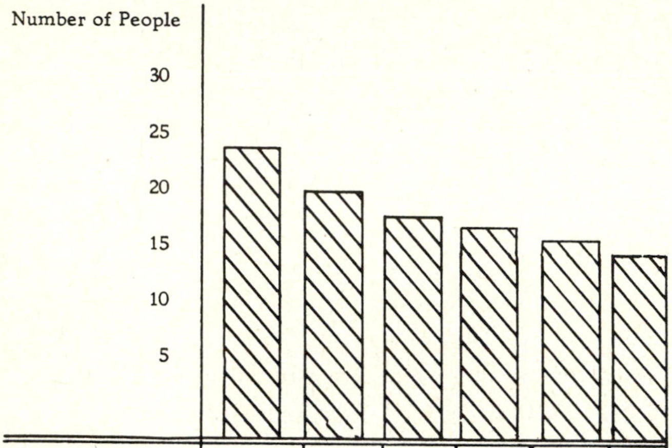

Time Periods	1	2	3	4	5	6
	IMPLEMENTATION				OPERATION	
Manager E	+1 1	0 1	0 1	0 1	0 1	0 1
Systems Analysts E	+4 4	-2 2	-1 1	-1 0	0 0	0 0
Programmers 1/2 E 1/2 T	+12 +12	-4 8	-3 5	-2 3	−1 2	−1 1
Machine Operators 1/2 E 1/2 T	+4 4	+2 6	+2 8	+1 9	0 9	0 9
Maintenance E	+2 2	0 2	0 2	0 2	0 2	0 2
Time Periods	1	2	3	4	5	6

E — Experienced
T — Trainee

Figure 18–3 A method for showing the time and cost relations for training the computer personnel of a new system.

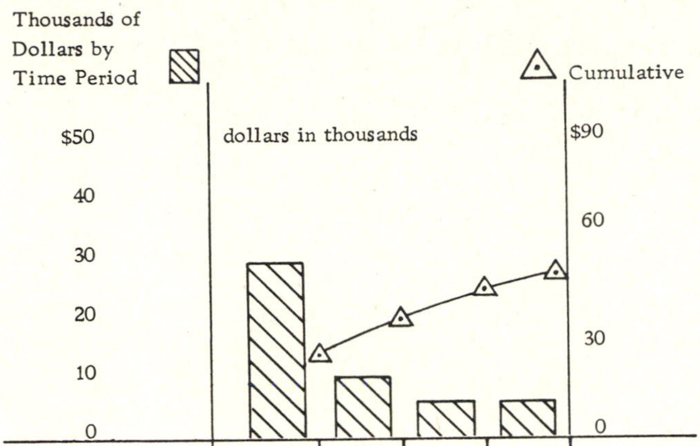

Time Periods	1	2	3	4	Cost
Travel & Living	$ 3,000	$1,000			$ 4,000
Supplies	1,000	500	$ 500	$ 500	2,500
Personnel					
Coordinator	1,000				1,000
Systems Analysts	4,000				4,000
Programmers	16,000	4,000			20,000
Operators	4,000	4,000	4,000	4,000	16,000
Total	$29,000	$9,500	$4,500	$4,500	$47,500
Time Periods	1	2	3	4	

nel and operation supervisors. Job training is also required for data or program librarians, console operators, and auxiliary machine operators. Training is an important factor in a smooth transition to routine system operation. It should allow for this transfer to occur while the business operates at full capacity.

Identifying and scheduling personnel selection, including the hiring or transferring of additional people where appropriate, training, and summarizing time and cost are the final steps in implementation planning. Figure 18–3 illustrates one way of displaying these costs and their time relationships.

18.14 APPRAISAL OF SYSTEM VALUE

Normally the value of a new system to an organization is determined by the management of that organization. Management usually appraises the value of a new system by measuring it against selected decision-making yardsticks. Managers need to consider how the system will affect profits and markets for the next few years; whether there are sufficient funds to support the initial installation; whether money has to be borrowed and if so, for how long; and the economic worth of the system beyond higher operating efficiency and greater flexibility. To address this last issue, a study team should also examine the proposed system in terms other than cost to find out what its ultimate payoff will be.

It is clear that an appraisal of system value must have multiple dimensions to satisfy management. In addition to cost, there must be comparable appraisals for time, flexibility, volume, and accuracy values. It is often difficult to assign values to less tangible measures. Yet they must be evaluated on an economic basis to provide management with information for making sound judgments.

Most of the measurement factors have been outlined in the report on requirements, and they serve individually as guideposts for system design. At this point, the problem is one of establishing the system's total economic impact on the business. This approach can be illustrated by the study of the National Bank of Commerce. The real value of a unified banking system is not just that the depositor is better served and more satisfied. A substantive statement of this value would say:

1. System accuracy, flexibility, and expandability accommodate planned increases (4 percent annually) in the number and amount of deposits. These extra funds will then be available for reinvestment in income-producing endeavors.
2. The system encourages depositors to combine their other banking requirements with this institution. This will lead to increases from profit-generating services.

Because of the new system, these advantages can be further refined with forecasts of change in assets and revenue.

To prepare a comprehensive appraisal of system value, four types of data are needed:

1. New system operating costs, projected over the estimated useful life of the system
2. Present system operating costs, projected over the same period

3. Investment required to bring the new system into full operation (implementation costs)
4. Basic values the new system offers to the organization, expressed in economic terms

When these data are in hand, costs should then be related to values to show the impact of the total system. Comparisons should be made to a consistent base at all times; this base is generally the projection of present system costs. The approach is especially helpful if two or more recommended designs (for example, an online and an offline system) are analyzed in terms of system value. In this situation, the study team evaluates each possible system against the common denominator of the present system instead of less conclusively evaluating one new system against another.

18.15 NEW SYSTEM OPERATING COSTS

One of the outputs from system selection is a description and summary of operating costs for the proposed system. Costs are compiled for the equipment, material, and personnel required to operate and maintain the software. If these figures were not then projected into the future, an estimate of direct operating expense is now developed to cover the useful life of the system, recognizing factors such as anticipated growth and planned expansion.

Estimated equipment, personnel, and other costs are influenced by the potential growth of the business and by the decisions on implementing the system progressively over some period of time. To prepare a cost summary, the analyst must have a sales forecast and the implementation schedule. Marketing forecasts of sales or service levels as developed for other business planning applications can also be useful. If desired, the potential variation in forecast accuracy can be accounted for by stating future expected sales on a probability basis. This method is shown in Figure 18–4. The data represent total revenues for two-year periods. The probabilities, usually set after consultation with management, are used to get a weighted average of estimates. For example, for the two-year period 0 to 1, it was estimated that the probability is 0.1 that revenues will be $12,500,000; that the probability is 0.4 that revenues will be $13,500,000; and that the probability is 0.5 that revenues will be $15,000,000. The weighted average is $14,150,000. This weighted estimate now can be used for forecasting. The other sets of figures are similarly interpreted.

Figure 18–4 Probabilities and estimated revenues for the ten-year period (0 through 9) after implementation begins for a proposed system, in two-year intervals.

0–1		2–3		4–5		6–7		8–9	
Prob.	Am't*	Prob.	Am't*	Prob.	Am't*	Prob.	Am't*	Prob.	Am't*
.1	12.5	.1	16.5	.1	20.0	.1	25.0	.1	30.0
.4	13.5	.4	17.5	.4	21.5	.4	26.5	.4	31.5
.5	15.0	.5	18.0	.5	22.5	.5	28.0	.5	32.5
	14.15**		17.65**		21.85**		27.10**		31.85**

*millions of dollars
**weighted average

The implementation schedule, although emphasizing only the initial installation, also contains plans for implementing other activities. The cost estimate is prepared with due recognition to the equipment and personnel buildup required to support the additional workload.

Equipment costs have to reflect the decision to rent or to purchase. With rental, monthly charges are carried as expense; with purchase, a schedule for monthly depreciation charges and related costs (such as the interest on money borrowed to finance the purchase) is set up. If no decision has yet been reached, parallel descriptions are prepared to show the different cost impacts during a system's life.

Figure 18–5 is an example of a new system operating cost summary. Ordinarily, the data are projected on an annual basis; but where the time span is longer than five years, the figures can be aggregated in two-year sums.

As cost data are compiled, a study team often finds that special analytical techniques are needed to derive valid data. Logical analysis techniques are appropriate for constructing operating costs in some areas of the system—the number of operators required to run communications terminals, for example. Statistical methods are useful for collecting samples of performance. Finally, experimentation and observation techniques can sometimes be applied.

Experimentation involves the manipulation of situations under controlled conditions so that results closely approximate those found in the real world. Experimentation, however, is expensive and should be confined to a limited number of special problems. Simulation, one form of experimentation, may have been employed earlier (especially in design of real-time systems); and if a simulator is already constructed, it can be reused to provide information that will help project costs.

Figure 18–5 Estimated costs for a proposed system in two-year intervals, projected over ten years.

Item	Year	0–1	2–3	4–5	6–7	8–9
Data Processing Equipment		215	240	260	295	295
Personnel		185	185	195	195	205
Materials		120	65	35	35	40
All Other		90	85	90	95	120
Totals (in thousands of dollars)		610	575	580	620	660

Direct observation and the extrapolation of results from known data may also prove useful methods for estimating costs. The former consists of setting up a test situation that evaluates the length of time an operations series takes, while the latter involves determining what the displaceable costs amount to for certain current operations.

18.16 PROJECTING THE COST OF THE EXISTING SYSTEM

A second category of costs necessary for the appraisal of the value of the new system is an estimate of how much the *present* system would cost to operate if maintained over the expected life of the *new* system, with the expected volumes. The cost data to be included are the present personnel, equipment, and other related costs that would be superseded by each new activity. The compilation would cut across conventional departmental boundaries and would reflect the progressive implementation of activities in the business. This makes the costing process complex, but only in this way can costs be compared on a common base.

Balance sheets of financial operations, income and expense statements, and resource usage sheets from the description of the present business are sources for the needed data. Expenses should be projected from current operations to determine how much personnel and equipment costs would be when extended to the higher anticipated volume of future years. Allowances must be made for wage increases, changes in material costs, and trends in cost reduction.

For management review, cost can be summarized and plotted on a graph such as the one in Figure 18–6 to show the difference between projections in present and proposed system operating expense for a ten-year period.

Figure 18–6 A representation of the cumulative cost difference between an existing and a proposed management system, for a ten-year period by two-year intervals.

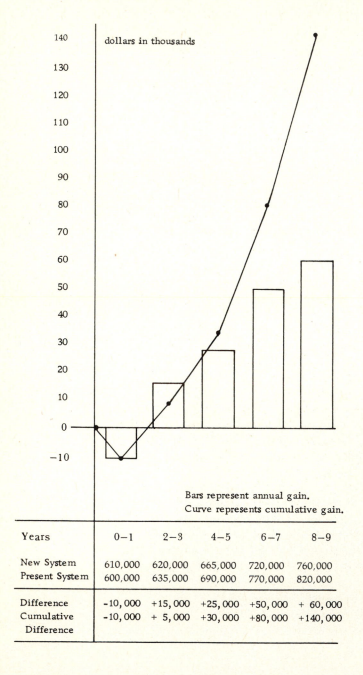

Bars represent annual gain.

Curve represents cumulative gain.

Years	0–1	2–3	4–5	6–7	8–9
New System	610,000	620,000	665,000	720,000	760,000
Present System	600,000	635,000	690,000	770,000	820,000
Difference	–10,000	+15,000	+25,000	+50,000	+ 60,000
Cumulative Difference	–10,000	+ 5,000	+30,000	+80,000	+140,000

18.17 COSTS AS INVESTMENT

After determining the new system operating costs, analysts establish an estimate of implementation costs. Although implementation is a cost in the accounting sense, it also can be viewed as an investment. Management must weigh its value in the same manner as it views new plant construction costs or other projects competing for investment funds. For this reason, implementation costs are customarily regarded as an element of investment during system appraisal.

18.18 ECONOMIC VALUE OF THE NEW SYSTEM

Aside from costs, a study team should consider some of the less tangible ways in which a new system affects the business. What is it worth, for example, to achieve 99 percent accuracy in certain operations rather than 93 percent? A general explanation is not enough; to demonstrate the real value of such an improvement, accuracy must be discussed in economic terms. One approach is to look at business lost because of invoice or statement errors. If a company loses 0.3 percent of its customers annually because of statement errors, and if the new system prevents such errors, this 0.3 percent can be saved. The effect is a 0.3 percent annual gain in customers for the company. The analyst, using additional sales statistics, could then translate this 0.3 percent gain into actual dollars of gross sales.

This type of analysis is applied to each of the factors outlined in the report on requirements and to any other factors added since that report was presented. The results demonstrate how the new system will perform in regard to each factor and what economic value is assigned to this performance. Some factors to consider are:

1. Decrease in the length of a product or service processing cycle
2. Improvement in product or service quality
3. Shortened response time to inquiries from prospective customers
4. Effect on other classes of investment and resources (for example, accounts receivable, utilized floor space, and inventories)
5. Increased employment stability
6. Better maintenance of delivery promises to customers
7. Greater stock availability to service a variable demand
8. Effect of cost reduction from elimination of spoilage, waste, and obsolete materials

18.19 RELATING COSTS TO VALUE

In a final step, the several analyses of cost and value are drawn together to present a complete and integrated appraisal for the new system. This is best accomplished through displays meaningful to management: profit and loss, return on investment, and cash flow statements.

Profit and Loss Statement The cost-value relationship can be portrayed in financial report style with a summary-of-operations statement for the entire business or for some selected part of it. Figure 18–7 illustrates this method of presentation. The method requires the projection of data to develop additional information.

Estimates of future conditions and events must be conservative, reasonable, and believable. The sales forecast is a case in point. If, for example, one benefit from the proposed system is reduced cycle time or faster response to customer inquiries, management will want to know what direct effect this will have on future markets, on material costs, and on selling price. Unless the impact of the benefit can be predicted with assurance by the marketing department, the conservative approach is to use the same sales forecast for both present and proposed systems.

Projection of cost data can be simplified by separating from the computations those costs that are not affected by the change in the system. Within the other cost areas, the analysts establish dollar figures for factors such as personnel changes, cost reduction improvements, waste and spoilage reductions, quality improvements, and differences in fixed and variable costs. One study team conducted a broad analysis of this type by interviewing each department head. Supervisors were asked to pinpoint how their costs would change with the new system, down to individual job classifications and related expense areas. Nonaffected costs were set aside, and the supervisors' estimates were adjusted for the greater volumes anticipated over the next few years. Results were then organized in an operations statement similar to Figure 18–7.

Return on Investment Another form of value appraisal is the computation of the return on investment in the new system. This form of analysis is designed to demonstrate the value of a proposed investment in terms of earnings by measuring present system cost, new system cost, and investment differences.

Figure 18–7 An illustration of a financial statement portraying the cost-value relationship between an existing and a proposed information management system.

(4-year average—$ in 000)

	Present	Proposed	Difference
Net Sales Billed	$8710	$8830	+$120
Costs of Sales	7560	6950	− 610
Direct Material	3280	3040	− 240
Data Processing Equipment	30	110	+ 80
Other Indirect Costs	430	350	− 80
Nonaffected Costs	1930	1930	−
Gross Income	1150	1880	+ 730
Total Income Tax	600	980	+ 380
Net Income	550	900	+ 350
Percent to Sales	6.3	10.2	+ 3.9

Figure 18–8 shows the result of such an analysis. Year by year system operating costs were projected over four time periods, along with the level of inventory required to support the forecasted sales. (Inventory can be projected by simulations—for example, by applying significant ratios such as turnover by inventory class and number of weeks of inventory on hand—or by calculating balances remaining from estimated shipment schedules.) Comparable data were developed for the proposed system; the differences are shown in Lines 5 and 6.

The dollar value of the inventory reduction was determined on the basis of estimated savings from reduced obsolescence and deterioration, space savings, and opportunity costs. In this case it amounted to 25 percent, as is shown on Line 7. The net operational improvement (Line 8) was developed by adding the operating cost difference (Line 5) to the dollar value of the inventory reduction (Line 7) for each forecast period. Implementation costs and equipment purchase costs were totaled to show investment (Line 9). Return on this investment (Line 10) was found by dividing average yearly improvement by the implementation and equipment costs (Line 9). The Line 8 total, $1,200,000, was divided by number of time periods, four, to produce $300,000 average yearly improvement.

Cash Flow The display of the expected impact of the proposed system on the cash position of the business enables management to have sufficient funds available to meet commitments as they arise. A

Figure 18-8 An illustration of how return on investment estimates for an existing and a proposed system can be prepared for management review.

	Time Periods	1	2	3	4	Total
Present System	(1) Operating Costs	$ 300,000	$ 330,000	$ 370,000	$ 450,000	$1,450,000
	(2) Inventory Level	2,000,000	2,200,000	2,400,000	2,800,000	9,400,000
New System	(3) Operating Costs	350,000	300,000	300,000	350,000	1,300,000
	(4) Inventory Level	1,200,000	1,200,000	1,300,000	1,500,000	5,200,000
	(5) Operating Costs Difference (1) - (3)	-50,000	+30,000	+70,000	+100,000	150,000
	(6) Inventory Level Difference (2) - (4)	800,000	1,000,000	1,100,000	1,300,000	4,200,000
	(7) Value of Inventory Reduction 25% of (6)	200,000	250,000	275,000	325,000	1,050,000
	(8) Net Operational Improvement (5) + (7)	150,000	280,000	345,000	425,000	1,200,000
	(9) Implementation plus Equipment Costs	1,200,000				
	(10) Return on Investment	25% per year				

cash flow analysis is useful in showing, over time, the monetary requirements of the business, and it helps the financial officers develop plans in support of the new system needs.

A cash flow analysis is illustrated in Figure 18-9. Total implementation investment was calculated for the period prior to operation, and net operational improvements (same as Line 8, Figure 18-8) were inserted for each following time period. An incremental inventory level difference was computed by subtracting each period's inventory level difference from that of the prior period (Line 6, Figure 18-8). Equipment purchase costs were included on Line 4 to reflect three equal annual payments; this capital charge was depreciated for a five-year life beginning in the second period. Net cash flow is net operational improvement added to inventory level incremental difference and equipment depreciation, with implementation investment and equipment purchase price then subtracted. Cumulative cash flow is the total of the previous year's cumulative cash flow and the current year's net cash flow.

Figure 18–9 An illustration of a method for analyzing the cash flow for an organization installing a new system. The data are from Figure 18–8.

Time Periods	0	1	2	3	4
1. Total Implementation Investment	$600,000				
2. Net Operational Improvement		$150,000	$280,000	$345,000	$425,000
3. Inventory Level Incremental Difference		800,000	200,000	100,000	200,000
4. Purchase of Equipment	200,000	200,000	200,000		
5. Depreciation of Equipment		80,000	120,000	120,000	120,000
6. Net Cash Flow (2)+(3)+(5)−(1)−(4)	−800,000	+830,000	+400,000	+565,000	+745,000
7. Cumulative Cash Flow	−800,000	+30,000	+430,000	+995,000	+1,740,000

Cash flow can also be shown as in Figure 18–10. The main line in the graph shows the projected total cash outflow and inflow annually for a four-year period. An examination of the graph reveals that $800,000 additional cash is required to place the system in operation, but that funds will be generated fast enough to permit repayment toward the end of the first period of operation.

While these are several of the ways of relating projected costs and values of a proposed system to an existing system, much of the information contained in a review of value depends on the projection of future events. It is therefore advisable for the analysts to explain in their report how the key cost-value comparisons were developed. Also, they should describe the impact of these comparisons on the operations of the organization. Major results of the appraisal should be emphasized, particularly with regard to two points: the time it will take for the system to pay back the initial investment and the magnitude of future profits once the system is in operation for a given time period.

Figure 18–10 An illustration of a method for portraying the net annual cash flow projected for a proposed system for a five-year period (0 through 4).

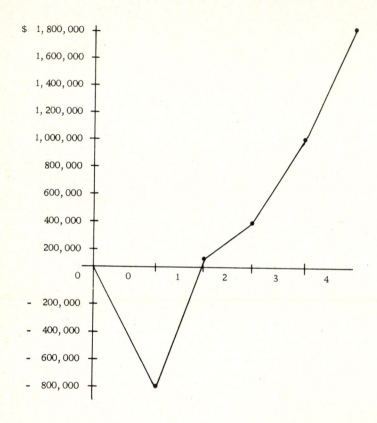

SUMMARY

The development of a system is an iterative process. The equipment must meet the system requirements and conform to qualitative constraints. Considerations in equipment alternatives include modularity, system programs, and application programs. The effectiveness of a particular configuration is determined mainly by analyzing the time and cost of processing the data. A system flow diagram illustrates the flow of information through the system and the relationship of programs and files. An implementation plan thoroughly documents the expected investment in system installation. Implementation planning consists of determining the cost of detailed system design, programming, program testing, physical planning, conversion, and personnel selection and training. Graphs and tables may be useful for illustrating these costs to management. Management usually appraises the value of a new system by how well it compares to selected decision-making yardsticks, such as those developed in Phase II. A comprehensive appraisal of system value includes new system operating costs, present system operating costs, investment required for the new system, and basic values the new system offers to the organization. A complete and integrated appraisal of the new system views its impact on profit and loss, on return on investment, and on cash flow.

QUESTIONS AND PROBLEMS

18-1 The credit manager for a department store makes frequent use of information from a credit bureau. The bureau, considering installing a data processing system, asks the manager's opinion as to whether the department store should install a terminal to have direct communication with the computer. As a system analyst for the store, how would you advise the credit manager?

18-2 Visit a company that has a computer and prepare a report on the programming languages used.

18-3 Distinguish between *hardware* and *software* with respect to a computer system.

18-4 What costs might a company reduce if it implements a system which will provide inventory control so that a smaller, but sufficient, inventory is maintained?

18-5 During a study you are assigned the task of gathering the costs associated with the purchasing activity of the company. What departments of the company should you consider as contributing to the total purchasing activity cost?

18-6 "A good system on a poor computer is better than a poor system on a good computer." Comment.

18-7 What is a queue or a waiting line?

18-8 Why does the computer play such an important role in simulation?

18-9 What is the relationship between the *Monte Carlo* method and simulation?

18-10 What is a deterministic model? a probabilistic model?

18-11 What are some major differences between COBOL, ALGOL, FORTRAN, and PL/1?

18–12 When establishing reorder points for items in an inventory control system, what factors should the analysts take into consideration?

18–13 It has been recommended that before a study of a distributor's salable products inventory system is begun, the following information about the inventory should be prepared:
1. Distribution by value of items in sequence by annual dollar sales.
2. Distribution by value of vendors in sequence by annual dollar sales.
3. Distribution of items within vendor in sequence by annual dollar sales.

Of what value would this information be to the study team and to management?

18–14 Describe three factors for measuring the effectiveness of a newly designed system for the purchasing activity of a company.

18–15 List the fields of information, other than customer name and address, which may be included in an account record in a file of personal checking accounts in a commercial bank for which a new system is being designed.

18–16 What are some of the tangible advantages, other than cost, of an online data processing system for credit authorization in a department store?

CHAPTER 19
DESCRIBING A NEW SYSTEM

19.1 THE DESIGN PROCESS

Automated techniques have not been developed for the design of a new business system to fulfill the requirements defined during the Phase II study. The reason is that design is a creative process, one which requires an unpredictable number of variables.

In approaching the design of a new system, the most valuable information available to the analyst is a description of the system as it is and an analysis of what the new system must accomplish. The analysis should contain the operations and processes required. The analyst who receives this input must translate the information and judgments into a new system design.

An overall system profile based on information flow, such as is shown abstractly in Figure 19-1, is also useful as a preliminary guide. Of course, to serve a particular situation, this abstraction would have to be converted to the specific terminology of the activity.

As a first attack on the problem of developing a new system, the analyst normally produces several alternative designs that possibly can fulfill the requirements. Through consultation with management, the analyst can narrow the choice to two or three potential solutions. These have to be investigated in more detail until one is selected as a practical optimum.

When an acceptable design evolves, it must be described; and for this purpose the descriptive forms from Phase I are used. In describing the projected system, analysts usually support the forms by more exhaustive documentation, and the level of detail is typically greater. The analyst is aware that the forms in the third phase will be used to set up a new system; hence complete and precise information is generally required.

The new system as designed is present initially only in the mind of the designer; the design must still be communicated to others. A description of the mechanism of the system is important to management, to other systems engineers who may help implement the system, and to analysts themselves.

The use of the basic forms described in Chapters 8 and 14 assures

Figure 19–1 An illustration of an overall system profile based on the processing of data. The I represents input. D represents daily. W represents weekly. R represents output.

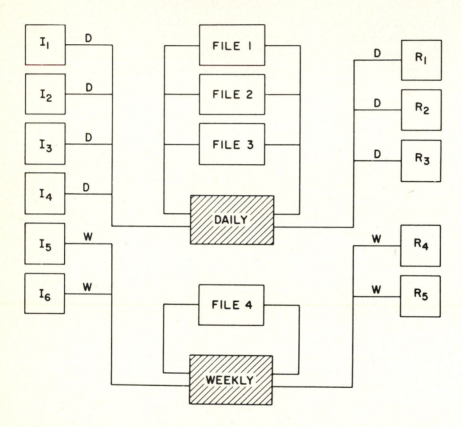

the designer that he or she has probably not overlooked anything significant. If there has been an omission, the lack should show up on the activity or operation sheets.

The principal difference between the use of the forms in a Phase I study and a Phase III description is the level of detail and the amount of supporting documentation. The aim of the Phase III description remains the same as in the earlier survey: to show what the system will do, working from given inputs to produce desirable outputs through the use of what resources and facilities.

19.2 DESCRIBING A NEW SYSTEM

The description of a planned system normally starts with the activity sheet (or sheets) and ends with the resource usage sheet. The first step is to prepare the flow diagram on the activity sheet. If only one activity has been considered in the study, the procedure is straightforward. If the system as designed covers an unwieldy number of operations—say, more than twenty-five—it may be necessary to break the activity into parts and consider each part as a separate activity for documentation purposes.

The flow diagram is the key to the validity of the subsequent documentation. The analyst should see to it that it fully represents the activity; that all inputs, outputs, and files are referenced; that no essential operation is omitted. Required operations sheets from the requirements report are valuable guides in preparing the flow diagram.

The tabular section of the activity sheet can then be filled in. Frequency of inputs to and outputs from operational sequences, and average- and peak-volume data for operations within the sequences can be obtained from input-output and required operations sheets. Notes and supporting documents are prepared and attached. The process of supporting the basic documentation continues throughout Phase III; as additional supporting data are produced, they are entered on or attached to activity and operation sheets.

The operation sheets exploding the individual boxes on the activity sheet are next prepared. All three summary documents from the Phase II analysis are valuable in guiding the preparation of operation sheets. Equipment designations are noted on the sheet, and specifications are attached as support. Narrative descriptions in detail are frequently valuable for unusual procedures which the operation sheet may not completely explain.

Message and file sheets are next prepared for all inputs, outputs, and information resources. Copies of document specifications, file equipment specifications, and distribution lists are appended.

The resource usage sheet is prepared last. The references to departments which appear on the activity sheet are primary inputs to the construction of the new resource usage sheet. These are the departments concerned with the activity, the ones which form the framework of the business segment within which the activity takes place.

The procedure is again straightforward. Selecting a common lower level if possible, the analyst should distribute the operating departments in related groups across the bottom of the upper sections of the resource usage sheet. A few short interviews will then permit the construction of levels above the common lower level. The organizational lines should be traced back until they come together in one management box. The procedure is not unlike drawing a family tree.

The personnel quantities and costs are next gathered and entered. As in Phase I, employees in any lower-level components not shown on the chart are put into the lower boxes for totaling, while upper-level boxes show only their own immediate employee totals.

A new cost tabulation is then prepared. For the purpose of describing a projected system, cost estimates are perfectly valid. Costs of personnel, machines and equipment, materials, and so forth are summarized for each of the organizational components in the bottom level and for higher-level components directly concerned in the activity. These costs are summed horizontally in the column for totals.

Costs included in the activity being described are then tabulated below the inclusive tabulation for the section of the business. These, too, are summed horizontally in the column for totals. Data such as the average amount of money invested in inventories or accounts receivable are tabulated and identified in the two unmarked columns at the far right of the resource usage sheet.

Refinement and correction of each form to bring all of them into agreement with each other, and addition of notes or appendixes to support and explain peculiarities of the system are final steps in the procedure. The end product should be a clear description of the system as it will be installed.

The basic operations of the new system are traced on the activity sheet, while the framework within which the activity takes place is displayed on the resource usage sheet. Details of processing steps and of the equipment that will perform them are described on the operation sheets. The message and file sheets provide details of the information inputs, outputs, and resources.

The descriptive forms, working with the detailed supporting documentation, should communicate all the information needed to describe the new system in operation. The five descriptive forms, coupled with the three summary forms used in Phase II, thus provide a related approach by which an analyst can derive the facts needed to study a system, determine what the system should be doing, and then design and describe a system to do the required job.

19.3 STRUCTURE OF THE REPORT

The report describing the design of a new system proposes a course of action for management. It has two major objectives:

1. Provide management with an understanding of the new system, stressing economic value to the business.

2. Furnish supporting data for objective evaluation by technical and functional specialists within the business.

The report must put across its message succinctly, with awareness of reader interest and point of view.

Analysts should liberally use charts, graphs, and pictures to illustrate complex points difficult to describe in the text, statistical data, equipment layout, work flow, and personnel organization. In addition, the five basic documentation forms should be used as necessary, since they permit descriptions from a general level down to the detail desired. Normally, these basic documents are included in the appendix, although the resource usage sheet and activity sheets often appear in the main body of the report.

As far as the physical report is concerned, six sections are suggested and illustrated in Figure 19–2. The sections are:

1. Preface. Contains (1) a letter of transmittal from the study team to management, with recognition of study participants and contributors, (2) a general introduction, and (3) a table of contents.
2. Management abstract. A concise, executive-level summary of key system recommendations and study results.
3. New system in operation. Describes how the job will be done, directed toward operating management. Should highlight the mechanisms built in to insure maintainability so that the system will be usable over the planned period of operation.
4. Implementation plan. Shows time and cost of system implementation. Directed toward managers responsible for financial operations, planning, and implementation.
5. Appraisal of system value. Portrays economic impact and value of the new system, aimed at financial and operating management.
6. Appendix. Displays selected background data on detailed procedures for methods and programming personnel.

The following sections of this chapter cover each of the six sections of the report.

19.4 PREFACE

The transmittal letter to management notes the formal conclusion of the analysts' work in designing a new system. The original scope and objectives of the study are reviewed, along with any major changes

Figure 19-2 Structure of the report presenting management with the design of the new system.

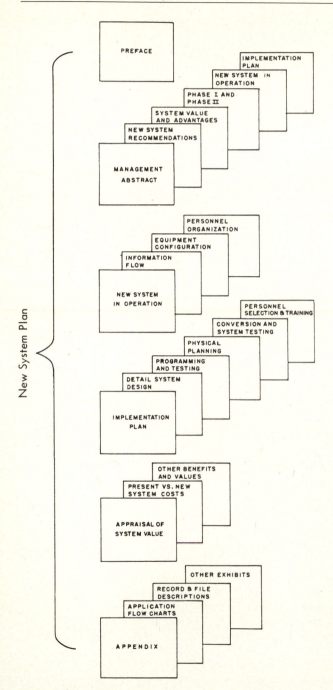

in either. The study team is described, and mention is made of special assistance supplied by other persons or groups.

An introduction to the report and a table of contents form the rest of the preface.

19.5 MANAGEMENT ABSTRACT

The nucleus of the new system plan is the management abstract. It should be written so that an executive can gain insight and understanding into the proposed new system quickly, without burden of excessive detail. It describes the system at an overview level and serves as an extended table of contents for the balance of the report.

In this critical section, management expects to see precise and accurate statements about the investment potential of the new system. The abstract, then, must include a basic appraisal of the new system's essential values and advantages to the business. The subject matter must be thorough but selective, and the abstract must cover only significant facts, stated in an orderly and logical manner.

However brief, an abstract should cover:

1. Recommended course of action with regard to the new system
2. Appraisal of system advantages, benefits, and savings
3. Review of results from the present system analysis and future system requirements
4. New system operating costs
5. Review of investment required for implementation

New System Recommendations The system solution proposed to management is the concluding recommendation of the study team. The new system is defined and described in broad outline; general advantages are cited for its introduction and acceptance into the business. This kind of recommendation is illustrated by an excerpt from the report of a case study.

Following a thorough examination of the present business at Collins and McCabe, and specification of system requirements, we recommend the installation of a computer-based communications system. This data processing system will provide complete brokerage service for Collins and McCabe through integration of communications and accounting operations.

The communications network will bring remotely located data to a central processing area, forward them for action, and return processed data to originating locations for prompt satisfaction of customer requirements and efficient recording and reporting of information.

A complete range of brokerage operations will be handled electronically, with minimum manual intervention. The real-time nature of the system is made possible by computer control of transmission facilities. Online data will permit the system to accept many different types of entries for processing against customer and securities files.

System Value and Advantages Since information and conclusions are presented in order of their interest to management, the economic value of the proposed system is discussed next. Management generally looks first for direct dollar savings, then for intangible improvements. Value must be demonstrated by how the new system will produce added profits and how the capital structure of the business is affected over the estimated useful life of the system.

To portray value objectively, selected exhibits described in Chapter 18 are used along with a narrative explanation. Figure 19-3 shows how expected savings were graphically illustrated in the Collins and McCabe report.

Exhibits can be further supported with statements of savings and benefits in specialized areas. Each factor must be described in terms of direct economic value to the business. Faster, more accurate reports are an advantage, to be sure; but an attempt should be made to translate such intangible benefits into economic value. In the Collins and McCabe report, values were shown for:

1. Improved customer service through specific reductions in elapsed time
2. Greater computational accuracy through error-checking procedures
3. Capacity for growth in transaction volume—without significant increases in clerical cost
4. Reductions in after-hours operation for transaction and record posting

The actual value of these and other benefits was shown to demonstrate advantages beyond savings in operating costs.

Present Business Description and System Requirements Specification One or two paragraphs are inserted in the report to review distinctive features from the present business description. Brief facts on products or services, markets, present sales volumes, rate of growth, organization structure, and the like might be combined into a comprehensive statement.

Figure 19–3 A graph taken from the Collins and McCabe case study showing estimated initial costs (negative values) and the savings by month over the first four years of a new system, beginning with implementation.

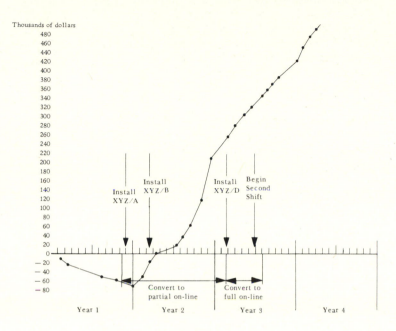

Activity requirements for the future system are also outlined here in one or two pages. Goals and scope for each activity are specified in narrative form, as in the following example for an insurance company:

This activity handles details of new business for Custodian Life Insurance Company from receipt of an application at the home office to completion of the policy and related records for transmission to the customer. In the last three years, applications processed have increased from 8,565 to 9,811. Volume is expected to increase gradually over the next few years (no sudden increase is expected).

New business applications are vital to the prosperity of Custodian. Quick and efficient processing of applications will assist greatly in stimulating even more new business and in keeping costs down.

Or, the goals and scope can be specified in a two-part list:

The new activity performs these functions:

Review application and related forms
Request medical and policyholder history
Underwrite applications

Assemble application data
Calculate premiums

The new activity does not perform these functions:

Determine outside underwriting services
Determine underwriting standards
Set limits on policy size
Determine medical standards
Determine premium rate schedule

Cost limitations, policy constraints, or any other considerations affecting the activity are noted at this point.

New System in Operation This part of the management abstract describes how the new system will appear in full operation. Managerial uses of data are emphasized, rather than the mechanics of processing data. Discussion of operating highlights and characteristics should employ terminology used by the management audience.

The content may be organized around a summary system flowchart or around a modified flow diagram as in Figure 19–4 from Collins and McCabe. Description is focused on major inputs, operations, and outputs, the mainline events, and salient features. Thus, management can acquire an understanding of the system in operation without becoming involved in detailed procedures.

Conciseness applies equally well to the equipment description. Frequently, the explanation can be blended with the system operations discussion, as in the following excerpt from a case study:

The data processing center is the heart of the system. Communication lines form the main arteries over which vital reservations data is transferred between agents and the center.

The design of the data processing center is based on two major subsystems: the XYZ/F data processing system and a bank of disk storage units.

The central processing unit performs all logical and decision-making functions required in the reservation process.

The data channel is similar to a subsidiary computer and uses a semi-independent stored program to control the flow of data between the computer memory and a group of input and output devices. Several data channels may operate concurrently in the XYZ/F system.

Data from communication lines enters the processing center through the transmission control unit. Among other functions, this device assembles message characters arriving on the communication lines into groups, checks these groups for errors, and moves them into the main computer storage unit.

Figure 19—4 Real-time traffic flow as a modified flow diagram taken from the Collins and McCabe case study.

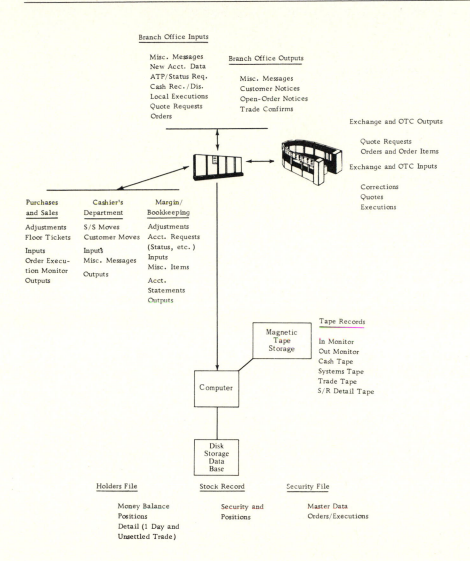

Large-capacity disks store the reservation records. These disks contain records of seat inventory, availability, current passenger reservations, current flight information, fares, and infrequently used computer programs. Reading and recording mechanisms, operating automatically under control of the central processing unit, locate records to be read or recorded at high speed.

The profile of new system operation is completed with a short summary of new positions and specialized job skills required. Personnel requirements can be illustrated graphically by means of an organization chart that shows how the new system differs from the present in positions and in alignment of duties.

Implementation Plan The timetable and the costs associated with implementation form the final section of the abstract. A composite exhibit is prepared from the separate task schedules and is shown in Figure 19–5. Beginning with an estimated start date, costs and time are projected for each implementation task, detailed system design, programming, testing, installation, conversion, and personnel selection and training. A one-paragraph description of each task is included with the exhibit, similar to the following explanation of personnel selection and training:

This task involves the selection and education of personnel capable of effectively performing functions such as systems analysis, programming, documentation, and console operation. The selection procedures will include aptitude tests, educational qualifications, and past experience reviews. Training will involve both classroom and on-the-job training.

19.6 NEW SYSTEM IN OPERATION

The new system operation as described in the management abstract is expanded to provide further information for operating managers and other personnel of the business. Data may be condensed and summarized under three headings:

1. Information flow
2. Equipment and software requirements
3. Personnel organization

Information Flow The broad system description and pictorial diagram in the management abstract is reoriented to convey more detail

Figure 19–5 An illustration of a composite summary of implementation costs prepared for the management abstract of a new system plan.

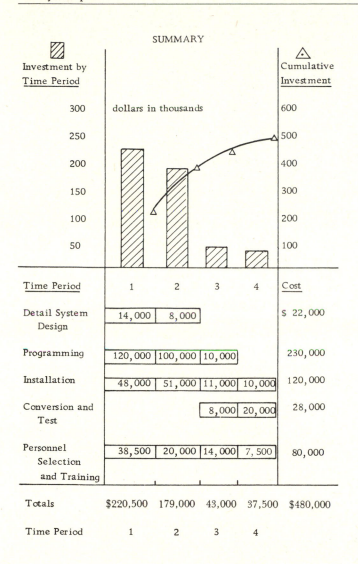

Time Period	1	2	3	4	Cost
Detail System Design	14,000	8,000			$ 22,000
Programming	120,000	100,000	10,000		230,000
Installation	48,000	51,000	11,000	10,000	120,000
Conversion and Test			8,000	20,000	28,000
Personnel Selection and Training	38,500	20,000	14,000	7,500	80,000
Totals	$220,500	179,000	43,000	37,500	$480,000
Time Period	1	2	3	4	

on information flow for operating personnel. General terms are replaced by specialized nomenclature associated with equipment descriptions and flowcharting techniques.

Explanation, as before, is highly visual. Description may be maintained at a single level of detail; or it may work down progressively from a total system flow diagram through activity diagrams to operation flowcharts, as illustrated in Figure 19–6 for a state tax agency study. Data for this part of the report is extracted from the activity sheets prepared earlier for designing the new system.

Narrative explanations can be attached to the flowcharts or can be integrated into a running system description. In the Typical State case study, the diagram shown in Figure 19–6 was prepared to document the system design. A statement for the operation **Correction of Edit-Found Errors** illustrates how narrative can supplement and support the presentation in the flow diagram.

Input to the taxpayer error correction routine consists of error cards. Cards are given to clerks, who interpret them and write corrections directly on the cards (those cards that cannot be corrected are destroyed, and corrections are made at the computing center). Cards that can be corrected are of two kinds: those that can be handled locally and those that require information from the master file located at the computing center. In either case, after referring to the source document file or to the appropriate master file at the computer center, the clerks write correct data on the cards. The cards are keypunched, verified, and sorted by document number. They are now ready to be used in correcting the taxpayer error tapes, which are then sent to the computing center.

Equipment Configuration Each unit of proposed equipment is identified by name and number and related to the other equipment on a single display. Physical characteristics and functions of significant units are discussed in a paragraph. The programming needed to support the installation is specified along with the source—manufacturer, independent software firm, and so on. Software requirements may include any or all of the following: operating system, language compilers, utility programs, data base or data communication managers, special application programs.

Personnel Organization A proposed personnel organization chart has already been included in the management abstract; the specific duties of each new position are outlined. Delegations of responsibility and authority are also specified, since they apply to the data process-

Figure 19–6 An example of a system diagram prepared for a new system in the operation section of a new system plan.

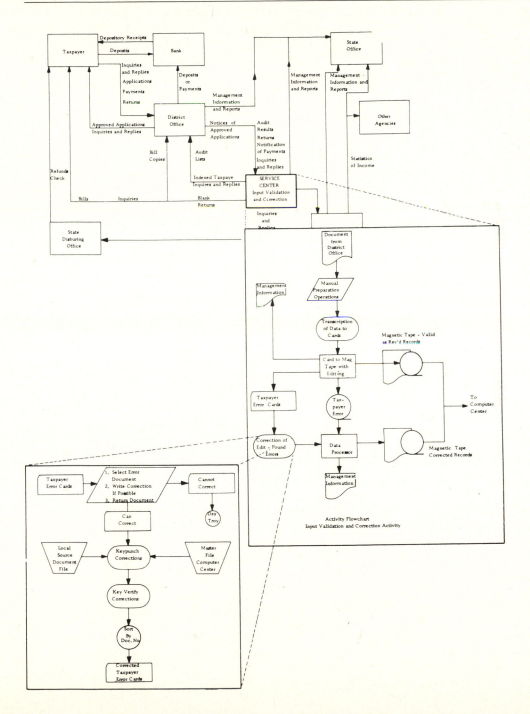

ing group and that group's relationship with external organization components.

There are generally four categories of full-time information processing personnel:

1. *Systems analysts* Responsible primarily for the design of the system, they act as advisors to the programmers in systems problems; they may also serve as programmers.

2. *Application programmers* Translate the flowcharts to machine-acceptable language. This work includes the preparation of detail flowcharts and HIPOs and the writing and testing of programs.

3. *Systems programmers* Responsible for installing and maintaining the system software required to keep the facility operational.

4. *Operators*
   a. Console operators In charge of operations in the machine room during actual running of the equipment.
   b. Librarians Responsible for the receipt, storage, and issuance of removable storage mediums, such as tapes and disks.
   c. Data control clerks Log and establish controls on all incoming and outgoing jobs. Also set up and maintain job schedules.

19.7 IMPLEMENTATION PLAN

Various implementation task schedules discussed in Chapter 18 are placed in this report section to expand the implementation summary of the management abstract. These exhibits, along with backup narrative, provide a sufficient amount of implementation detail, although some study teams have used PERT diagrams to further illustrate time and cost relationships. The Collins and McCabe report, for example, contained brief narrative accounts on each of the five tasks; major cost and service events were then itemized, showing when equipment and procedures would be installed, and the cost associated with each event.

Figure 19–7 from the Collins and McCabe case study uses a somewhat different technique of displaying personnel buildup during implementation as compared with the bar graphs in Chapter 18.

Figure 19–7 An example of a method for presenting the projected change in programming and systems personnel for a new system. The graph was taken from the Collins and McCabe case study.

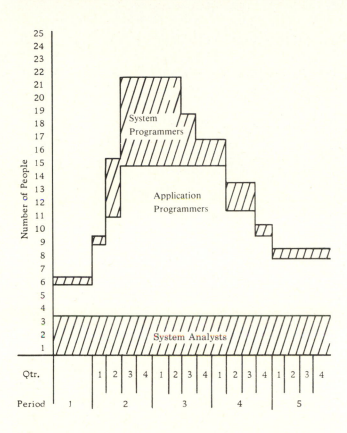

19.8 APPRAISAL OF SYSTEM VALUE

The management abstract emphasized economic values of the system in terms of profits, cash flow, and return on investment. In this section, system advantages are examined as they pertain to other operating personnel in accounting, facilities, and property departments. Two kinds of information are generally included:

1. Cost comparisons between the present system projected into the future and the proposed new system over its useful life
2. Detailed descriptions of other system benefits and values

Personnel, materials, data processing rental or depreciation, and related expenses are drawn from the cost summaries illustrated in

Chapter 18. These are supplemented with narrative to indicate breakeven points, trends, and other important features.

Specific reasons for rejecting alternate proposals can also be noted here. At Collins and McCabe, alternate solutions for pure message switching, for message switching and order matching, and for common-carrier service were evaluated and reasons listed for the rejection of each one.

A discussion of this nature leads to an evaluation of other system advantages and benefits, including such intangible values as flexibility, efficiency, improved service, reliability, and so on. Where assumptions are made in estimating the cost of these factors, the basis for arriving at values should be carefully explained. Any values developed as described in Chapter 18 and not covered in the management abstract should be discussed here.

19.9 APPENDIX

The appendix is a technical validation and detailing section that contains information of primary use to methods and programming personnel. It is not a catchall for study detail that does not fit elsewhere. Emphasis is directed in particular to critical and advanced elements of the study.

The appendix includes such subjects as:

1. Simulation data on message flow, volumes, equipment utilization, networks, and so forth
2. Data base and message descriptions
3. Sample (and demonstration) programs
4. Application flowcharts and/or HIPOs
5. Physical planning detail
6. Detailed equipment characteristics
7. Disk and tape requirement calculation
8. Detailed software characteristics—purchased/licensed
9. Derivation of formulas and calculations
10. Training course descriptions
11. Documentation forms

The five basic documentation forms (resource usage, activity, operation, message, and file sheets) are included, since they permit description in the necessary depth. But certain types of data require other media for description (program flowcharts, manual procedures, and network diagrams).

SUMMARY

The new system plan is both a description of the study team's solution to a major business problem and a formal presentation to management for decision and action. It is the culmination of a system study, providing management with sufficiently penetrating, thorough, and validated information to make sound decisions about future systems that will promote the short- and long-term growth of the business. The next step is management's directive to proceed with system implementation and operation.

QUESTIONS AND PROBLEMS

19-1 What automated techniques could be developed for designing a new system?

19-2 What are two kinds of information which are generally included in the appraisal of system value?

19-3 In the report describing the new system, what is included in:
a) management abstract,
b) implementation plan?

19-4 Describe one similarity between the system design process and the determination of system requirements.

19-5 A system has been designed to select from a skills inventory file those individuals who have certain characteristics of education, product knowledge, specific field skill, and experience with product components. Prepare a Venn diagram to show the effect of such a combinatorial search. Would the diagram be of any value in the management abstract of the report for the proposed system?

19-6 What subjects are usually included in the appendix of the report describing the new system?

19-7 When an analyst begins the design phase for a new system, what two main kinds of information are important for his or her use? Where can the information be found?

19-8 Why is a management abstract needed in the "New System Plan" if all the information is in the rest of the report?

19-9 In Figure 19-3 we notice that the plan for the new system implies that more than two years will be needed for implementation. Why does it take so long to get a system into operation?

19–10 What would be the most significant aspect to management of the diagram in Figure 19–6?

CHAPTER 20
A NEW SYSTEM PLAN
FOR BUTODALE

20.1 GUIDE TO BUTODALE'S NEW SYSTEM PLAN

This chapter displays the new system plan developed for the composite case study, Butodale. Although derived basically from an actual report, the plan is modified to conceal the company's identity, to adapt it to book form and yet illustrate concepts and principles. The study is not designed to be analyzed for the adequacy or accuracy of its equipment recommendations. The appendix is omitted for reasons of length.

The new system plan for Butodale proposes a basic batch-oriented approach to the problem, an approach that is appropriate for an organization with limited experience with computers. In time, the system would probably evolve into an online system for immediate response.

The reader will recall that the six main parts of the new system plan are preface, management abstract, new system in operation, implementation plan, appraisal of system value, and appendix. Within each of these, except for the implementation plan, the subdivisions of Butodale's new system plan closely follow the suggestions set forth in Chapter 19. The implementation plan intermixes topics. Analysts may find the outline in Figure 19–2 convenient for management presentations or as a check list during a study. Similarly, management and operating personnel studying the report should find the outline helpful as a reading guide.

After an initial review, readers might find it useful to imagine themselves chief decision makers on Butodale's computer-evaluation committee. On the basis of this report, would you install the computerized system, retain the existing system, or take some alternative course of action? Does the letter of transmittal convey the information that permits you to grasp the study team's point of view and main conclusions? Does the general introduction adequately recap the Phase I and Phase II reports? Does it provide an adequate frame of reference for the Phase III report?

Your main interest will probably be centered on the management

abstract where you find the team's recommendations. The first recommendation asks for your positive decision to proceed to implement the new system plan. Next, under the summary of system
values and advantages you will find the payoff and the cost. An economic advantage of $240,000 per year for the new system is pro-
jected—an important factor if the report convinces you that this potential is attainable. The remainder of the abstract should provide
you with an overview of how the new system will operate and how
the study team proposes to implement it.

The next few sections of the report will be of special significance to
your financial and technical staff. The information flow and recommended equipment is of prime concern to your technical people to
evaluate whether it will do the work necessary to accomplish the goals
and objectives for the **Provide Product Demand** activity. Financial
management must evaluate the rental or purchase costs of the equipment and the personnel costs of staffing the new department.

The graphic representation of the implementation plan shows at a
glance the steps needed to change from the existing system to the
new system. A figure in the division of the report appraising the value of the new system gives you the net financial picture. A column
carries forward the figures from the resource usage sheet of the Phase
I report, and, when compared with another column shows the before
and after cost of the **Provide Product Demand** activity. A later
column isolates cost increases and decreases by department for this
activity, with a net $240,000 reduction.

The nonfinancial benefits and values of the new system are presented in the final pages of the report. The potential benefits outlined
here for your evaluation must be considered carefully, as they may be
of even more importance than any cost savings. After looking at the
report through the eyes of the chairman of the computer evaluation
committee, the reader can also review the report as the chief financial
executive in Butodale. In the same manner, the reader might profitably consider the report from other viewpoints, such as that of the
manager of product engineering or engineering services. Once out of
the top level of decision making, the reader will begin to explore the
technical detail more carefully.

20.2 A NEW SYSTEM PLAN FOR THE BUTODALE ELECTRONICS COMPANY

Mr. Ansel T. Benson
Butodale Electronics Company
Danvers, Massachusetts

Dear Mr. Benson:

Last October, a study was undertaken to determine the
extent to which computers could be used for automating
Company activities. Since the presentation of our two
earlier reports, our scope has centered on the activity of
providing the demand information for Butodale's products.
This activity involves engineering design in response to
customer orders and preparing bids and quotations for
potential customers. The study was completed in late April.
Briefly, our findings are as follows:

1. The provide product demand activity can be
   automated.
2. Utilization of a computer for this activity will
   result in economic savings and other tangible
   advantages to Butodale.
3. Special design calculations, now done manually,
   also can be effectively accomplished by data
   processing equipment.

The attached report includes a summary of the study
objectives, an analysis of the present system and a
description of the proposed new system. Further, we include
a proposed implementation schedule.
This report will assist you in appraising the potential
value of data processing equipment in handling this part
of Butodale's operations. We believe the recommendations
are sound and substantiated by the information available
and the various analyses that have been made.
We appreciate the excellent cooperation you and the other
members of management have given us during this study.
In particular, we want to commend the work of Messrs.
L. K. White, T. R. Fellows, P. K. Ragonese, and K. R.
Sherman for their special contributions to and cooperation
with the members of the study team. Finally, we wish to
acknowledge the help received from the sales representative
and systems engineers of the XYZ Computer Company.

Yours very truly,

R. L. Casey
Project Coordinator

CONTENTS

I PREFACE—GENERAL INFORMATION

Objectives
Project Scope
Organization of the Study

II MANAGEMENT ABSTRACT

New System Recommendations
System Value and Advantages
Phase I and Phase II
New System in Operation
Implementation

III THE NEW SYSTEM IN OPERATION

Information Flow
Detailed System Flow
Equipment
Organization

IV IMPLEMENTATION PLAN

V APPRAISAL OF SYSTEM VALUE

Present vs New System Costs

Other Benefits and Values

VI APPENDIX (NOT INCLUDED)

I PREFACE—GENERAL INFORMATION

Six months ago a study was begun to examine the existing information processing system at Butodale, to establish requirements for a new system, and to design and propose a new system, employing automated procedures as much as possible. After the completion of Phase II, it was decided to concentrate our efforts on the provide product demand activity.

Objectives

The five objectives set for the provide product demand activity are:

1. Satisfy customer information requests.
2. Perform engineering design.
3. Supply information for cost accounting and management control.

4. Inform customers of order disposition and schedules.
5. Provide information to manufacturing.

Project Scope

Essentially, the complete activity of providing product demand involves accounting, sales and service, administration and advertising, product engineering, and engineering services functions of the company. Those operations within this activity that are directly involved in the automated aspects of the system are concerned with the engineering design for customer orders and preparing bids and quotations for potential customers. Both the requests and the orders may be for standard or nonstandard analog computers or modifications to installed computers.

Requests for standard analog computers are processed routinely and the customer is furnished information which includes price quotations, descriptions, layouts, diagrams, and other data necessary for the potential customer to make the purchase decision.

Requests for nonstandard analog computers are handled specially and involve engineering reviews, engineering design and layout, and the compilation of special cost data. The customer is furnished the same kind of data for nonstandard computers as for standard computers.

When a formal order is received from a customer, it must be edited and clarified and then detail-designed for communication to manufacturing.

In brief, this report concerns those operations involved with the receipt of customer orders, customer requests for bids and quotations, producing quotations and specifications in response to requests, and providing detailed engineering design documents in response to formal orders.

Organization of the Study

The project was organized into three phases: Phase I, which comprised the study of the existing manual system in relation to its environment; Phase II, the analysis of the product line and its specifications to determine system requirements; and Phase III, the design and evaluation of the new system.

In *Phase I,* the project team reviewed pertinent Company and industry literature in order to describe Butodale's present operations, the industry background, the major policies and practices, and the Company's principal objectives. The conclusions were verified by interviews with Company executives. Following this first step, the basic structure of the Company was outlined in the following areas:

products and markets

materials and suppliers

finances

personnel

facilities

Finally, interviews were conducted in the sales and order processing department, the engineering department, and the manufacturing department to determine time and volume data. Historical data and actual samples of present orders were reviewed in order to arrive at accurate analyses of cost. Descriptions of all procedures, supporting documents, resources, and costs related to activities were prepared and included in the Present Business Description report, which was submitted to Butodale management.

In order to determine the requirements for the projected system, *Phase II* was organized to include (1) an analysis of customer specifications, (2) a structural description of the general-purpose analog computer, (3) a parts analysis, and (4) the definition of the design logic for selected standard and nonstandard models. An analysis of customer specifications was performed which identified each unique specification and indicated a value or range of values for each.

By reviewing Company product manuals, interviewing appropriate personnel, and perusing many blueprints, the major assemblies, subassemblies, and parts were identified and their relationships defined. This information was synthesized in a generic model list demonstrating the relationships among parts and assemblies at different structure levels.

Next, a detailed parts analysis was performed in which product and parts characteristics were identified and documented, and a value or range of values assigned to each one. Characteristics were separated into fixed and variable. The greatest effort was spent on the variable characteristics since these express the real parameters of the product line and its potential expandability.

The final step was the determination of the design logic which connects the customer specifications to the product characteristics. One approach was to group, structure and tie parts characteristics back to individual customer specifications through the medium of the design logic. Alternately, the design logic was brought out by working first with customer specifications and progressing down to the product and parts characteristics.

Throughout the design-logic determination, it was necessary to record this information so as to be readily communicated to all concerned, including engineers, analysts, and programmers. For this purpose, flowcharts and decision tables were utilized because of their ability to display complex interrelationships among data in simplified form and at several different levels of descriptive language. We summarized our findings in the System Requirements Specifications report, which was accepted by Butodale management in February.

In *Phase III*, the final phase, the specifications of the new system were agreed upon during several conferences with management, and the system was then designed in detail. One part of this development was to restructure the existing design logic found in Phase II so that a general approach was made to each design problem. In this manner, great flexibility and breadth of coverage was included.

An evaluation of the proposed new system as compared to the present system was conducted to determine: (1) Does the new system meet the criteria set for it? (2) Is technical feasibility demonstrated? (3) What are the actual dollar savings plus intangible advantages?

In order to provide concrete proof of the feasibility of the automated design concepts and to show particular solutions to the types of problems encountered in the design of an analog computer, a demonstration for selected portions of the product was developed. This demonstration covered enough of the product line and the product to indicate that complete coverage is feasible.

Finally, the newly designed ADE/BUT (Automated Design Engineering for Butodale) System and the demonstration were fully documented.

II MANAGEMENT ABSTRACT

New System Recommendations

For Butodale to gain the benefits of an automated system, the following steps should be taken:

1. Approve and begin implementation of the system described in this report.
2. Assign four engineers familiar with the engineering functions of the general-purpose analog computer line to participate in the implementation of the system.
3. Order the necessary XYZ equipment for installation in late September.

Each of these recommendations is documented and substantiated in this report. A detailed description of the present system and other information on the computer programming techniques to be used is contained in the Appendix to this report.

System Value and Advantages

The proposed system offers the following advantages to Butodale:

1. Estimated direct cost savings of $240,000 per year.
2. A decrease in the elapsed time for quotation preparation from one week to one day.
3. In product engineering, the actual elapsed time in the new system will be less than three days. Under the present system, one to two months are required for new orders.
4. Clerical, computational, and design errors will be substantially reduced

because of the inherent accuracy and reliability of the data processing equipment.
5. Standardization of parts and models without loss of flexibility will enable increased order quantities of identical parts for manufacturing.
6. Provide experience to Butodale so that like systems can be developed for other product lines, such as data plotters.

Phase I and Phase II

There are two main results that stand out from the present business description at Butodale.

1. The total market for general purpose analog computers is growing and Butodale is capturing a large share of the market.
2. The Provide Product Demand and Provide End Products activities are of such a character as to be likely candidates for automation.

After this report was presented, the study team was authorized to proceed with the Phase II study to determine the requirements for automating these two activities.

During the Phase II study, the requirements were specified for both the Provide Product Demand and Provide End Products activities. The report was presented to management in February. After this presentation, management decided to consider the Provide Product Demand activity first. Thus, the main outcome of the Phase II study was management's authorization to proceed with the design of the ADE/BUT System for the Provide Product Demand activity.

New System in Operation

The automated design engineering system for Butodale will consist of a man-machine complex designed to most effectively utilize the education, experience, and creativity of the engineer while relieving him of the necessity for completing tedious and routine tasks. The product lines processed will include standard and nonstandard general-purpose analog computers.

Requests for quotations and bids will be processed by entering customer requirements and pre-engineering results. These will be processed by XYZ/C computer in order to produce the required equipment list with prices and necessary information for preparation of drawings. Results developed during this phase are retained for later use if the order is received.

The receipt of an order initiates a similar input process in which any customer changes and pre-engineering are incorporated. The results are the engineering specifications, drawing backups, information for drafting of required drawings, and a machine-readable product record describing the complete product.

This product record enables the system to handle future modifications as they are received. For analog computers for which there is no existing machine-readable product record, one will be prepared from the job file when the first modification order for that particular computer is received.

The cost of operating the system is $238,960 per year, which is balanced against a present cost of $479,245 per year, resulting in potential savings of $240,285 per year when the system is in full operation.

Implementation Plan

It is recommended that the new system be implemented over a nineteen-month period. During this time the team will reach several "milestones."

1. Order the necessary equipment for delivery in September.
2. Establish the proper organization to implement and install the new system.
3. Prepare the physical site.
4. Provide for training the project group by XYZ personnel in the necessary programming technology.
5. Complete the analysis of the general-purpose analog computer product line and prepare the detailed logic design.
6. Begin programming.
7. Install the computer and related equipment.
8. Test and debug the programs.
9. Begin parallel operations.
10. Begin full operations of the new system.

III THE NEW SYSTEM IN OPERATION

Information Flow

1. **System Design Approach** The system proposed is the result of the comprehensive study of the existing system conducted by the study team. The new system represents a unified systems approach in that the total problem was surveyed and the system then designed to fulfill a goal-directed activity of Butodale Electronics. The goal which the system will fulfill is:

   Prepare for use by the manufacturing department all information necessary for the production of general-purpose analog computers in response to customer orders; prepare responses to customer requests for quotations and bids.

2. **Description of the System** The broad aspects of the operating system are pictorially presented in two figures. Figure 20–1 is an activity model of the ADE/BUT System. Both the present system and the ADE/BUT System must accept as inputs customer requests for quotations, customer requests for bids, and customer orders. The new system will

Figure 20–1 Schematic model of Butodale's automated design engineering system for the Provide Product Demand activity.

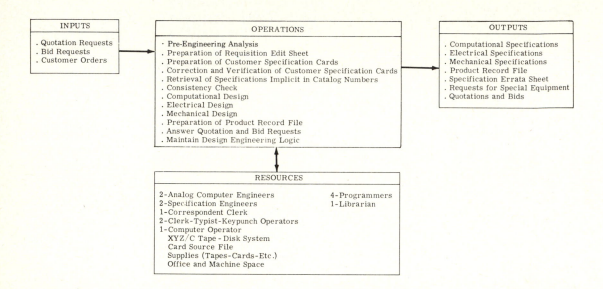

INPUTS	OPERATIONS	OUTPUTS
. Quotation Requests . Bid Requests . Customer Orders	· Pre-Engineering Analysis . Preparation of Requisition Edit Sheet . Preparation of Customer Specification Cards . Correction and Verification of Customer Specification Cards . Retrieval of Specifications Implicit in Catalog Numbers . Consistency Check . Computational Design . Electrical Design . Mechanical Design . Preparation of Product Record File . Answer Quotation and Bid Requests . Maintain Design Engineering Logic	. Computational Specifications . Electrical Specifications . Mechanical Specifications . Product Record File . Specification Errata Sheet . Requests for Special Equipment . Quotations and Bids

RESOURCES

2-Analog Computer Engineers   4-Programmers
2-Specification Engineers   1-Librarian
1-Correspondent Clerk
2-Clerk-Typist-Keypunch Operators
1-Computer Operator
  XYZ/C Tape-Disk System
  Card Source File
  Supplies (Tapes-Cards-Etc.)
  Office and Machine Space

also accept inquiries from engineers. The system produces engineering specifications divided into computational, electronic, and mechanical sections, requests for special purchases, and a bill of materials. In the ADE/BUT System, the product-record file may be thought of as a bill of material. The answers to requests for quotes or bids are in a form which can be sent to the customer. In addition to these outputs, the ADE/BUT System provides a specification errata sheet on which are listed any customer specification errors or inconsistencies which the computer program detects and cannot resolve. This sheet can also be used for communication with the customer.

Connecting the inputs and the outputs are the operations necessary to accomplish the goals of the system with the resources which are to be used in these operations. The operations are listed in Figure 20–1 and detailed in the following sections. The resources consist primarily of the personnel and equipment which make up the man-machine complex that is the ADE/BUT System. In addition, there are supplies, office equipment, and physical space.

Figure 20–2 is a general flow diagram of the operations listed in the previous figure. Manual operations are shown as ovals and machine functions as a rectangle. The first step is the translation of the customer orders, or bid and quotation requests, into a form which can be efficiently handled by the computer. This is accomplished by filling in a requisition edit sheet, an example of which is shown in the Appendix. In the next operation, the requisition edit sheet is used for preparation of

Figure 20–2 The general flow of operations shown in Figure 20–1 for Butodale's Provide Product Demand activity.

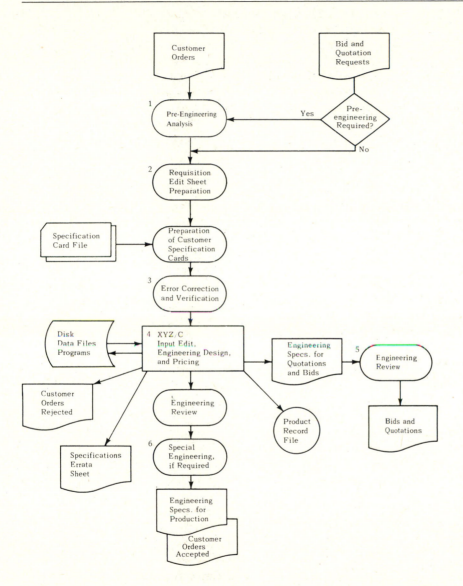

customer specification cards to serve as input to the computer program. This is accomplished by keypunching information from the specification edit sheet and, where possible, using prepunched cards covering standard information. After the cards are completed, they are checked and verified both manually and mechanically.

The cards thus prepared are read into the XYZ/C computer and form the input data for the computer programs. One of the first functions performed by the program is to make an extensive logic and accuracy check on the customer specifications. At this point any errors or inconsistencies are printed out on a specifications errata sheet. The actual design will continue if the magnitude and nature of the errors detected permit; otherwise the design is abandoned and a customer-order rejection notice prepared.

The design proceeds serially, designing first the computational elements, then the electrical portions, and finally the mechanical components. Throughout the design, the engineering specifications are printed out, and the parts and subassemblies as generated or selected are written on the product-record file.

If any manual design is called for, the order is listed for special engineering. Engineering specifications are produced for answering quotation and bid requests; these are sent to customers after an engineering review. An engineering specification for production undergoes an engineering review and is sent to manufacturing for scheduling and advance ordering, and customer acceptance is forwarded for formal orders. The product-record file would form a logical input to an automated inventory planning and control system.

Detailed System Flow

The following sections provide additional detail concerning the individual operations shown in Figure 20–2 and discussed in general above.

1. **Pre-Engineering Analysis** The first operation is pre-engineering analysis, which is required for about 10 percent of the orders to identify them for general-purpose analog computers and to provide key technical data.

2. **Requisition Edit and Preparation of Customer Specification Cards** The next operation is the preparation of a requisition edit sheet from the request for quotation, request for bid, and customer order. The preparation of the requisition edit sheet serves the function of converting the customer's terminology into standard specification terminology. This is accomplished principally by checking appropriate boxes on the edit sheet to indicate the alternatives selected by the customer. In addition,

it will be necessary to write in certain variables which can take on continuous or nearly continuous values, that is, ranges and catalog numbers.

From this completed requisition edit sheet, prepunched cards are pulled from the specifications card file for the standard specifications indicated on the requisition edit sheet and printed on the cards. The other values that have been shown are now keypunched into additional specification cards.

3. **Verification and Error Correction** The cards are first listed to provide an easy visual check. The listing is compared with both the original customer order and the requisition edit sheet to check for editing errors and pulling or keypunch errors. Detected errors are corrected and the checking procedure is repeated.

4. **Computer Operations** The operations included in the computer programs are the heart of the ADE/BUT System. The size and complexity of these programs preclude any but a general description of their operations in this summary. The Appendix contains an example showing the design process in more detail. The checked and verified cards whose preparation is described above form the input to the computer. The first computer operation is to retrieve the customer specifications which are implied by the catalog numbers, values, and ranges. The individual customer specifications are next allowed to supplement and modify retrieved specifications in order to represent the total customer requirements.

An extensive internal check is now performed to insure consistency of the final specifications. If consistency errors are found, or if it is necessary to assume missing values, messages are printed to this effect on the specifications errata sheet. If design can proceed with reasonable assumptions, the order continues in the main line; if not, an order rejection notice is printed, the design process is terminated, and the next order is begun.

If no errors are encountered, the design now proceeds serially designing the computational, electrical, and mechanical components. Three design techniques are used for the design programs. The first is a selection of existing parts or subassemblies and their implicit assembly according to the specific detail drawing on the basis of the customer specifications and internally generated specifications. The second technique is to use the computer for calculations of values and conditions which can be expressed mathematically. Circuit parameter calculations are an example of this. The calculated values for components such as resistors are referred to a standard circuit drawing. The third technique is to utilize the high speed of the computer to iterate using the design logic many times, and using different assumptions to develop balanced solutions. At the end of each iteration, the result is compared against acceptance criteria. If the criteria are not met, the basic assumptions are modified to improve the results and the next iteration commences.

As the design proceeds, the engineering specifications are listed on the printer and required parts and subassemblies are written on the product record file. If any special engineering is required, special cards are punched for later printing.

5. **Special Engineering Operations** Operations 5 and 6 in Figure 20–2 describe special engineering procedures. The engineering specifications produced in the computer phase are either sent to manufacturing (after special engineering, if required) or are used in the preparation of answers to quotation requests and bids. The product-record file could provide an input to an automated inventory planning and control system. An automated inventory system would include the ability to summarize parts and assembly requirements. This would be used for reducing inventories, checking for reorder points, forecasting, and ordering special purchased parts.

6. **Description of Design Philosophy** One of the prime considerations in the automation of design engineering is that the design logic is never static; rather it is in a continuing, dynamic state of change as in any other management system. Thus, the computer programs which represent this logic must reflect these changes. The ADE/BUT System is designed with this in mind. One technique for insuring this flexibility is to provide detailed documentation of the logic in a modular form. This is accomplished through the use of master flowcharts for an effective overview and detailed decision tables, which are easily understood by all interested personnel (engineers, programmers, and analysts) and are inherently modular. This procedure allows changes to be prepared and confirmed by those most knowledgeable—the engineers themselves.

Equipment Configuration

In order to implement the ADE/BUT System at Butodale, we recommend that an XYZ/C computer system be installed. This equipment will give the capacity and flexibility needed to carry out the automated program for the Provide Product Demand activity for the general-purpose analog computer and allow compatible growth for future expansion into other product lines and activities. Our recommendation is based on the following considerations:

1. The present unit record system in Finance is being used approximately one full shift, amounting to almost 176 hours of usage a month. Additional applications in the area of cost and inventory control are

**Figure 20–3 Recommended equipment for ADE/BUT in the
Provide Product Demand activity.**

Qty.	Type	Model	Description	Monthly Rental	Purchase Price
1	XYZ	C	Processing Unit	$3,280	$176,000
1	XYZ	3	Inquiry Station	180	9,000
1	XYZ	500	Card Read Punch	500	25,000
1	XYZ	1000	Printer	795	39,750
2	XYZ	10	Disk Storage	1,200	46,000
4	XYZ	9	Magnetic Tape Units	1,160	54,000
			Total	$7,115	$349,750

already planned for this equipment. For both technical and workload reasons, it is not feasible to plan on using this punched-card system for a project of such large scope and complexity as ADE/BUT. As a future project, this equipment should be replaced with a computer compatible with the XYZ/C or on a shared basis with a larger XYZ computer.

2. We estimate that the ADE/BUT System will utilize the XYZ/C tape-disk system an average of 4 hours per day to process the current volume of requests and orders for general-purpose analog computers. On peak days, processing of current requests for quotations and orders may fill an entire 8-hour day. In addition, the time not utilized on the machine by processing current orders will be used for modifying, expanding, and testing the ADE/BUT System for the general-purpose analog computer line.

3. One of the most important considerations is the need to recommend a system which will have the capacity to expand this computer-application concept to other product lines and other applications. The knowledge gained in implementing the ADE/BUT System for the general-purpose analog computer line will provide the capability to expand into other important areas, such as forecasting and cost-estimating. Figure 20–3 is a summary of equipment costs.

Organization

The automated design engineering system will occupy a position of considerable importance in Butodale operations. For this reason, it is recommended that a separate organizational group be created to implement and operate the system.

The most important justification for such an organization is that the people operating and implementing the system must be familiar with its procedures, capabilities, and limitations. By organizing these people into one group, the communication of necessary information is facilitated.

Figure 20–4 Personnel needed during the implementation and full operation of the ADE/BUT System.

Personnel Needed	During the 19 months of implementation	Annually for full operation after implementation
Analog Computer Engineers	4	1
Programmers	4	2
XYZ/C Operator	1	1
Correspondent Clerk	1	1
Keypunch Operators	2	2
Librarian	1	1
XYZ Systems Engineers	2	
Number		
Butodale Personnel	13	8
XYZ Personnel	2	
Cost		
Butodale Personnel	$182,000	$75,500

Also, these personnel can and essentially will be interchangeable in that they will be involved in both implementation and operation. This interchangeability increases the flexibility of the system and enables it to more effectively meet peak demands.

Personnel requirements will vary throughout the stages of implementation and operation. In the initial implementation stage, four engineers familiar with the general-purpose analog computer line will be required. Only one engineer will be required for operations.

After about six months, the program will be partially implemented. By then a portion of the system will be operational and the remainder will be in the process of completion. During this time, the personnel will be split into two groups. The plans for personnel are summarized in Figure 20–4.

Column 1 of Figure 20–4 lists the personnel needed for implementation and operation of the new system. These are principally Butodale personnel with some participation by XYZ personnel. Column 2 gives the full-time equivalents of personnel during the 19 months of implementation.

Column 3 contains the full-time equivalents for personnel after the system is in full operation.

IV IMPLEMENTATION PLAN

The transition period during which a new system is being installed can be difficult and expensive. For this reason, it is necessary to plan thoroughly the tasks to be accomplished. This section details a recommended plan for the implementation of the Butodale ADE system.

Figure 20–5 A graphic representation of the major tasks, estimated times, and milestones during the implementation phase of the ADE/BUT System.

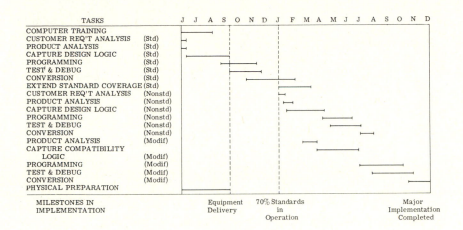

The plan covers a period of 19 months. At the end of this time it is anticipated that the major implementation effort will have been completed. Due to the dynamic nature of the system, however, there will be continued implementation, modification, and maintenance of the system throughout its life.

Figure 20–5 presents a pictorial representation of the plan, detailing major tasks with estimated times, and indicating "milestones" in the implementation of the system. The duration and calendar times allotted for the tasks are indicative of the expected requirements.

The plan is organized to provide an orderly transition from the existing manual system. Throughout this period, portions of the product line will be in the process of conversion to the automated system. Thus, the transition will be gradual and will produce minimum disorder in both the new and the old system.

One of the major objectives of this implementation plan is to endeavor to place a substantial portion of the product line into operational status as rapidly as possible. This is desirable from two standpoints.

a. First and primarily, it is anticipated that this portion will help cover the cost of the continued implementation of the system, thus insuring Butodale a maximum and rapid return on the out-of-pocket investment.

b. It will provide maximum training to Butodale personnel, as they will have been exposed to the full spectrum of the tasks involved in implementation.

In order to insure the above advantages it is recommended that Butodale provide a total of four engineers familiar with the engineering functions within the general-purpose analog computer line. In addition, it is recommended that a keypunch operator-clerk and a programmer be added as soon as implementation begins. These personnel will form the nucleus for the continued implementation and operation of the ADE/BUT System.

For its part, XYZ personnel will provide continued support and will also provide additional technical support as needed during implementation.

The first "milestone" is the installation of the XYZ equipment necessary for this application. The next is the completion of the implementation of the first portion of the standard-product line. The operation of this portion will provide savings to help offset its own costs and the continued implementation costs. The final "milestone" shown is the point at which the major implementation efforts will have been completed. The proposed system will then be in operation.

Key steps in the implementation plan are:

1. *Schools* It is desirable to have the Butodale implementation and operating personnel thoroughly familiar with all aspects of programming and operating the system. For this reason, it is planned for all personnel to attend classes during June and July at the XYZ Education Center in Boston. These 2- to 8-week schools will provide a knowledge of the equipment and the PL/1 programming language.

2. *Analysis and Design Logic* During this step the design-logic and system approach used for the preliminary demonstration will be reviewed and modified as necessary to fit the operating system. In addition, those areas not covered by the example in the Appendix will be thoroughly analyzed and recorded in the form of flowcharts and decision tables.

3. *Programming* In parallel with the analysis, as sections of the design logic are completed, conversion of flowcharts and decision tables into programs will commence. In the latter stages of the programming step, it will be necessary to add another key entry operator to the group. In addition to his or her data input duties, this operator will perform many clerical duties which will arise in the analysis and conversion.

4. *Test and Debug* The magnitude and complexity of the programs involved in the ADE/BUT System will dictate extensive testing and debugging. It is XYZ policy to provide a number of hours of free test time prior to installation of a system. The XYZ/C test system is located in Boston. In the 90 days prior to the delivery of the computer, a number of trips to the data center will be necessary to test the programs. As each new section of the system is described in modular form and coded in PL/1 it can be independently checked out with sample data. In this way the analysis, flowcharts, decision tables, coding, and design logic can be tested as a unit, thus minimizing total test time.

An additional recommendation is that a limited parallel operation be started immediately and continue through installation. Once or twice a month a number of current customer orders should be put through the sample system as it is expanded to include the newest proven additions. This will aid in further testing the selected computational, electrical, and mechanical assemblies as they are programmed. This will also aid in pointing out the more common inconsistencies and errors so that these may be added to the specification-consistency check program. In this way an even more powerful checking feature can be built into the system prior to installation, and the system when installed will be that much more error free and efficient.

In addition to the initial test of the programs, the arrival of the computer system will initiate a period of intensive testing and debugging. At this time, a machine operator should be added to the team to free the engineers and programmers from these operations. This operator will continue with the system during full operation.

5. *Conversion* As the programs begin to approach a debugged state, parallel running of the ADE/BUT System with the present system should commence. This will be concurrent with continued testing and debugging. Parallel runs of one to one and a half months should bring the system to the point where productive output can be expected. At that state, it is anticipated that 70% of the standard general-purpose analog computers will be designed completely. Other portions of the line will be designed to various stages by the ADE/BUT System with manual intervention to complete the designs. At this time, the return will begin to equal the operating cost.

Continued addition of the logic for the portions of the remaining line will bring the system coverage to the estimated 95% in an additional period of two months. As more and more of the line is added to the system, the advantages and savings to Butodale will reach their full potential.

6. *Physical Planning* Prior to the actual arrival of the computer system, facilities for it must be prepared. These facilities take the form of an air-conditioned room, preferably with a raised floor to accommodate cables. It has been estimated, based on experience of other users and advice from the XYZ Company, that such a room will cost approximately $15,000, this low cost being due to the extensive facilities available.

V APPRAISAL OF SYSTEM VALUE

Present vs New System Cost

The analysis of the present system conducted during the first phase of the study by the study team provides the background against which the new system can be evaluated. In most systems comparisons, it is unusual to have the wealth of material which has been made available by Phase I of this study. In the evaluation, full use of these figures and examples has been made. The results represent the best estimates of the existing conditions and projections of the future system in operations that can be made by the team members.

1. **Product Line Coverage** It is anticipated that the proposed system will be capable of processing approximately 95% of the engineering effort involved in the general-purpose analog computer line. The remaining 5% consists of such types as export orders and other complex or unique installations.

   Also significant to Butodale is the inclusion of modifications to existing configurations. As the market in analog-computer equipment is growing, the ability to process these jobs automatically will become of increasing importance to help customers grow with their existing equipment.

2. **Cost Comparison of Present and New System** The prime justification for the proposed system is the direct-cost savings made available by allowing the computer to assume the many routine, repetitive tasks involved in this area. The Appendix contains the detailed analysis of the costs associated with the present system. Figure 20–6 summarizes the overall costs associated with the activity of providing product demand. The seven columns in the figure are explained below, column by column.

   1. Under the new system, in addition to the six departments involved in providing product demand, it will be necessary to set up a new department, the ADE computer department.
   2. The cost of providing product demand was presented in the report from Phase I. These are the same cost figures as in the resource usage sheet of Phase I.
   3. The costs in this column represent all of the old system costs that will be eliminated by the installation of the new system.
   4. The cost figures in this column represent the remaining functional costs within Butodale which are not affected by the installation of ADE/BUT.
   5. Each cost figure in this column represents the added costs after the computer system is installed. Of special interest here is the cost of machine rental, personnel, and other costs that arise with the new computer department such as program maintenance. This $196,000 increase represents a new cost item.
   6. This column shows the total costs of providing product demand among the six old departments and the new computer department under the ADE/BUT System.
   7. The figures in this column represent the cost savings of ADE/BUT, department by department. We show the new costs associated with the system as a negative savings (−$196,000). The main factor in this

Figure 20–6 Summary cost and savings analysis for the Provide Product Demand activity under the present system and under ADE/BUT. All figures are in thousands of dollars.

Department	Present Provide Product Demand Annual Cost	Eliminated Costs from Present System	Remaining Functional Costs	Added Costs under New System	New Provide Product Demand Annual Cost	Annual Savings of ADE/BUT
Management	24	8	16		16	8
Accounting	32	7	25		25	7
Sales and service	1,052	282	770	108	878	174
Administration	265	104	161	10	171	94
Product engineering	126	106	20	41	61	65
Engineering services	152	120	32	32	64	88
ADE computer department				196	196	−196
Total	1,651	627	1,024	387	1,411	240

column, and indeed in the entire table, is the overall cost saving of $240,000 per year to Butodale if ADE/BUT is implemented.

3. **Implementation Costs** There are three main aspects to the costs of implementation. First to be considered are the personnel, then the equipment, and finally, supply and other costs. During this period there will be some overlap between the operations under the present system and those under the new one.

We summarize the implementation costs for 19 months as follows:

Butodale personnel	$182,000
Equipment rental	106,725
Other conversion costs	78,370
Total cost	$367,095
Estimated net operational savings during implementation	143,756
Net implementation cost:	$223,339

From these figures, we see that Butodale must expect to spend a net of $223,339 during the 19 months of implementation. Thus, at the rate of $20,000 monthly savings under ADE/BUT, it will require 11 months after implementation to recover the capital invested, not including interest on the investment. There is a total of 30 months therefore until Butodale begins to realize a net savings from ADE/BUT for the Provide Product Demand activity. After that, the cost savings will be approximately $240,000 per year. A fuller breakdown of these cost and savings figures may be found in the Appendix. They were developed by the study team and represent estimates using the best available data and conservative projection methods.

Other Benefits and Values

1. **Faster Response Time** An area of great potential value to Butodale is the reduced elapsed time associated with orders processed in the automated system.

   One particular advantage is that the reduced proposal time will encourage the transmission of increased numbers of field requirements for proposals to the plant. This will serve to allow the sales engineer in the field to spend more time with customers and potential customers. In addition, reduced engineering time for orders will result in decreased lead time and an improved competitive position for Butodale.

   The ADE/BUT System has provided sufficient personnel in order to respond to proposals and orders on an average of one day each. However, it is recognized that there must be sufficient lead time prior to manufacturing to enable proper shop loading. This time is considered to be approximately one week.

2. **Accuracy and Consistency** "To err is human" and, because of this, every manual system endeavors, with varying degrees of success, to cope with the human element. The larger and more complex the operation, the more human error will tend to compound itself. In the present system, it is difficult to assign a dollar value to the errors existing. It is, however, recognized that they are substantial.

   Errors may arise from such sources as transposition of digits, incorrect transcription, calculation, and many other sources. In the proposed system such errors are virtually eliminated due to the inherent reliability and accuracy of electronic data processing equipment.

   Typically, for a product as sophisticated as a general-purpose analog computer a number of engineering solutions exist for a given set of customer requirements. Thus, there is no guarantee that two engineers doing the same job would come up with the same result. However, a best approach does exist. It is this best-design solution for which the logic will be incorporated in the ADE/BUT System. The result is that the best engineering solution is consistently produced without sacrificing the flexibility of the system.

   It has been estimated by the Butodale operating personnel that, under the existing manual system, 75% of all orders reaching manufacturing contain some form of error. These errors take on many forms but most can be traced to the human element. One prime source of error is in the material being selected for manufacturing.

a. Engineering errors—either through the specification engineers or through the bill of material clerks.
b. Incorrect updating of bill of material or drawings.
c. Typing or selection errors in the factory-order preparation.
d. Storeroom material selection errors.

All of these errors except (d) can be greatly reduced by the ADE/BUT System with its elimination of much of the human element and its extensive programmed and manual checks.

These problems are easily solved by a man-machine complex such as the ADE/BUT System. Calculations are completed rapidly and accurately by the computer. In the design and updating of the programs, the best criteria are selected for each case from all of the approaches presently being used. Thus, under the ADE/BUT System, the design produced for a given set of specifications would be consistently the same unless altered by later engineering changes. It would represent the best design philosophy available, produce mathematically and logically accurate results, and would be done at computer speed.

If it were necessary to present justification for the ADE/BUT System on the basis of only one area, the increased accuracy, reliability, and consistency of the system would have been selected as the one with the most potential value to Butodale.

3. **Flexibility** One of the prime objectives of the design of a system is to insure flexibility. Engineering applications are by their very nature dynamic; new technologies are constantly being developed, new engineering procedures and standards are evolved. Also, for a semicustom-engineered product such as analog computers, the system must be capable of responding to a large percentage of the wide range of nonstandard requirements that the customer may specify.

These criteria have been considered in the design of the ADE/BUT System. In order to insure the necessary flexibility, a number of procedures and techniques have been employed. In computer programs, ease of modification is achieved by modularity, by use of higher level programming languages, and by thorough documentation of the programs. The ADE/BUT System programs will be written primarily in PL/1. PL/1 is a largely machine-independent computer language which provides very powerful mathematical and logical facilities. The English-like statements are particularly easy to understand and to modify, even in engineering applications.

The goals of modularity and documentation are advanced through the use of a logic-recording technique referred to as decision tables. This is a method of describing and recording complex logical situations which contains better structured information than the more conventional narrative or flowchart means of documenting logic. Furthermore, decision tables are easily understood by programmers and engineers alike. Not only are they ideal for capturing and recording logic for programming, but they serve as their own documentation.

The structure of decision tables is such that related logic tends to group naturally into modules. This inherent modularity will be preserved in the programs. Engineering changes dealing with a particular portion of the design logic can be made by changing only those tables involved.

By the use of these techniques, and by keeping the need for modularity and documentation firmly in mind during the implementation period, the flexibility so necessary for an automated system will be achieved.

4. **Future Expansion** The ADE/BUT System as proposed will be a continually expanding system. As it progresses through its various stages of implementation, the system will grow to encompass essentially the total scope of the general-purpose analog computer line.

An area for which there is great potential for future expansion is that of digital plotter systems. At the present stage of development, plotter engineering is primarily of a prototype nature. That is, design criteria and procedures are in the process of being established. Each system at this time is relatively unique. In the future, as plotter systems begin to replace the electromechanical systems, they will move from a prototype status into an engineering procedure similar to the analog computer.

The initial introduction of a new product is a particularly advantageous stage for utilization of automated design engineering. The design logic is fresh and easily captured. It can in fact be developed with a computerized system in mind. There is no background of historical results with which the new system must cope. In particular, the system can be designed to handle automatically future additions to engineered products.

The experience gained by Butodale in implementing and operating the automated system will be of great value in future expansions to other product lines.

The second area for expansion is to extend the boundaries of the system to include many of the functions now performed in manufacturing, engineering, order control, and scheduling.

In addition to the above, there are other types of applications which, while not a part of an ADE/BUT System, are its logical outgrowths. One such is an inventory system that could be used with the ADE/BUT System. Other possibilities exist in the financial and accounting control areas.

It is likely that there are other areas of management in which the computer sophistication and system analysis ability gained by Butodale personnel will be profitably used in the future.

QUESTIONS AND PROBLEMS

20-1 Prepare a flowchart in the format of the chart in Figure 20-2, to show the input data and output reports of the registration activity of a university. Assume that a student data master file, a student academic master file, and a course timetable master file are available for use.

20-2 A study team has determined that the primary purpose of a system to record and control customer information in a charge account file in a department store is to bill the customer and collect the monies due. When proposing such a system a study team could also include advantages which the system would have for
a) credit promotion,
b) sales promotion,
c) bad debt analysis,
d) account solicitation analysis,
e) attorney effectiveness.
What might the team include in its proposal as advantages for each of these areas?

20-3 A university may use a computer to process its data for a wide range of purposes. Prepare an overall flow diagram indicating the system that might be considered for student services, once the student is accepted.

20-4 Discuss some factors which indicate that an engineering design system should be automated.

20-5 Into what three major segments may a production control system be divided?

20-6 What type of information would be desirable from the material control phase of a production management system?

20-7 What type of information would be desirable from the manufacturing control phase of a production management system?

20-8 Prepare a flowchart to show the logic of the input edit and engineering design shown as Operation 4 in Figure 20-2.

20-9 Prepare a flowchart to show the processes necessary to accomplish the verification and correction of input cards indicated as Operation 3 in Figure 20-2.

20-10 Prepare a flowchart showing in more detail the processes in Operations 1 and 2 in Figure 20-2.

20-11 Why is a letter of transmittal included in the Phase III report for Butodale and not in the previous two Butodale reports?

20-12 How does the model in Figure 20-1 help management understand the new system?

20-13 In Figure 20-2 how many computer runs are indicated? Will this be true in the actual system?

20-14 In Figure 20-3 we see a large difference between the purchase price and monthly rental of the proposed computer equipment. Should Butodale rent or purchase the equipment?

20-15 How will the actual implementation differ from the plan in Figure 20-5?

20-16 The large changes in the cost figures among the departments in Figure 20-6 mean major personnel changes. How can this be done without demoralizing personnel?

CHAPTER 21
STAGES 2 AND 3: IMPLEMENTATION AND OPERATION

21.1 RELATIONSHIP OF THE THREE STAGES

The three stages in the life cycle of a system—study and design, implementation, and operation—are shown in Figure 21–1. Having covered Stage 1 in detail, this final chapter will provide an overview of Stages 2 and 3. Although each has its own characteristics and methods, no one stage is independent of the others. They are interdependent and require coordination of the study team, the implementation team, and the operating personnel if they are to accomplish the goals set for the system.

After reviewing and approving the new system proposal, management may want the plan implemented immediately. However, a hastily installed system may well encounter difficulties and fail to accomplish its objectives as defined in the study and design stage. Careful planning and control are required for proper system installation and operation, and this chapter provides an overview and discusses some of the more critical points of installing and operating a system.

21.2 RESPONSIBILITY FOR INSTALLATION AND OPERATION

Signing a lease or purchase agreement with a computer manufacturer for equipment puts the responsibility for its installation and operation not with the manufacturer, but with the user. The system belongs to the company. The company must live with the system, and the employees of the company must install, operate, and maintain it. Management therefore must designate those personnel who will be responsible for the installation and operation stages.

The physical site for the computer installation must also be designated by management. Power requirements, floor loads, air conditioning, and space for programming and operating personnel are factors in determining the physical site.

Figure 21-1 The development of a system.

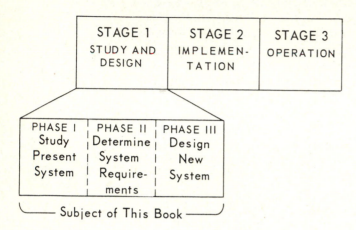

The equipment manufacturer can assist the company in personnel selection criteria and physical site requirements. But the manufacturer should only be looked to for advice, guidance, and teaching.

21.3 PERSONNEL REQUIREMENTS

The most important personnel decision made by management is the selection of the individual who will be responsible for the installation and operation of the new system. This person may also direct the computer department in converting additional applications to the equipment. (In this section we have assumed for completeness that this is the initial computer installation for a company. Where this is not the case, many of these people will already be in place.)

Requirements for this position usually include a degree in business administration, engineering, or one of the sciences. In addition to the educational requirements, the person selected must have creative ability and drive. He or she must also be able to deal with management and supervisory personnel because this is the person who will provide the primary liaison between the computer department and the other departments of the company. As additional applications are converted to the computer, this position of system manager becomes increasingly important, and in many companies this becomes one of the key management positions.

The system manager may be either the leader of the study team or one of its members, a present employee of the company, or someone hired from outside. There are advantages and disadvantages to both the internal and the external source. A present employee has knowledge of the company's operations and policies, but often must be trained in computer techniques. A new employee has training and experience in the use of computers, but will have to be indoctrinated in the operations and policies of the company. Whichever source is used, management must realize that the position requires the full efforts of the individual, who must receive the complete support of company management.

The source of programming and operating personnel may also pose a problem to management. If present company employees can be made available for these positions, the equipment manufacturer may advise tests to evaluate their ability to perform programming and operating duties. If present employees are not available or not capable, then new employees must be hired. Assistance in locating qualified applicants can usually best be obtained through the company's personnel office or through personnel agencies. Many agencies now specialize in computer personnel and can generally supply lists of qualified applicants.

If company personnel are to be trained in programming, system software and operating the equipment, the manufacturer may provide classroom teaching and home study courses or possibly online computer assisted training. Sufficient time and money must be allotted for such education since programming personnel may spend several months in training before writing any programs for the new system.

Other personnel, such as department managers and supervisors whose work will be affected by the new system, should also be educated in the concepts of computers and data processing. Seminars for this purpose can usually be provided by the equipment manufacturer, by management associations, by consultants, or by universities. Proper indoctrination of this group of company personnel is important for the successful installation and operation of the system. These are the people who will supervise the preparation of the input for the system and will receive and use its output. The installation of the computer sometimes causes this group concern about the future of their jobs or worry that the new system will disrupt their ability to carry out their work successfully. These concerns can be eliminated, or at least reduced, through proper education and communication.

21.4 STAGE 2: IMPLEMENT AND INSTALL

The second stage—implement and install—in the life cycle of a business system includes detailed system design, test planning, coding and unit testing, documentation, system testing, parallel operation, and conversion to the new system. The time and effort required for each of these steps will vary from one system to another. Each step is important and all are interrelated.

Figure 21–1 shows the sequence of steps and the feedback paths from one step to one or more other steps. These feedback paths are an important part of implementation and are discussed in the following sections in conjunction with steps that generate the feedback.

21.5 DETAILED SYSTEM DESIGN

Detailed system design includes the development of the precisely defined logic required to control the data flow through the system and the detail design of the files themselves. System flow diagrams, program flowcharts or HIPOs, and record and screen layouts are the outputs. The logic and sequence of processing the data are defined by the flowcharts. The position-by-position contents of every record are specified by the record layouts. The flowcharts (or HIPOs) for each program, together with the data base layouts which describe the inputs to and outputs from the program, are used by the programmer during the coding, testing, and documentation steps.

A complete review or walk-through of the total flow of data through the system is desirable before the coding step begins, as a change in the data or processing in one program may affect one or more other programs. Thus, there is considerable feedback within the detailed design implementation step. If, as one program is designed—input, process, output—it is passed on for coding before all programs are defined, the changes which affect the upstream programs already in coding must be made.

File design is less difficult if a system is being converted from one machine-readable medium to another and if the file structure and content are to remain similar. Thus, if the present system is basically a card-processing implementation, the record contents are well defined from past experience. If the same basic system is to be converted to tape, the tape record layout can be simply an aggregation of known card images. The combining of the records into files will change because of the change in medium. Available space should be left in the records wherever possible for future additions to the system.

21.6 TEST PLANNING

Testing the system consists of: (1) testing each program independently (unit test) and (2) testing all the programs of the system by processing sets of data through all the programs (system test). Another level of testing, integration testing, which takes place between unit testing and system testing, is sometimes recognized. The distinction between integration and system testing disappears when a top-down approach to building the system is used: As modules (programs) succeed in properly executing the unit test cases, they are promoted to the library which constitutes the lastest version of the system. Thus, all the testing of the system includes the testing of the new modules.

Developing criteria and data which will test every combination of operations in the system under all possible conditions is usually an impossible task. Even when the system serves only one activity of the company, the integration of operations is typically complex, and a set of inputs that will trigger all possible combinations of operations will be difficult to establish. As the number of activities that the system is to serve increases, the possible combinations of operations increase geometrically, and the difficulty of developing comprehensive test criteria and data increases accordingly.

Test data may be created so that they will test all reasonable combinations of operations. Rather than creating artificial test data, it may be better to obtain real data in a machine-readable medium from previous application history. It is more difficult to plan the testing of online, interactive systems. Test drivers often have to be written to simulate the environment and data impacts on the system as it will exist when operational. It may be necessary to develop scripts for test personnel at terminals interacting directly with the system to use in insuring that the functions described in the new system documentation perform properly. As in developing test scenarios for all types of programs, a great deal of effort must be spent devising tests for improper input data recognition; the system must be made as foolproof as possible.

As shown in Figure 21–2, the test planning step can generate feed-

Figure 21–2 Sequence and feedback of steps in Stage 2.

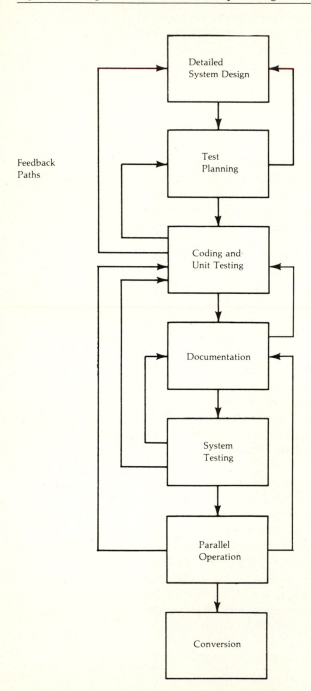

Feedback
Paths

back to the detailed system design step. Although functional specifications (what the system must do) are the prime input to the test planning step, it often develops that deficiencies in the design are identified by simply walking through the paper system one more time.

21.7 CODING AND UNIT TESTING

The detailed program specifications developed in the design step are followed explicitly in writing the program code. The flowcharts or HIPO diagrams portray the sequence and logic of the process steps, and the data base description provides a precise definition of the input, intermediate, or output data. The highest level programming language available should be used (*e.g.*, COBOL, PL/1, BASIC, FORTRAN), except in very unusual cases when an Assembler language is necessary or other installation standards require its use.

The maintenance and modification of the programs over their useful life may well cost more than their initial writing. Therefore, it is prudent to utilize as many of the existing facilities of the operating system as is possible rather than new code requiring maintenance. Additional software available with the equipment being used, such as data base managers, data communications managers, sort/merge programs, industry-specific application programs, and utilities programs may also be indicated. Techniques such as structured programming have shown over time that programs built in this fashion tend to be much more error free, and, more importantly, also facilitate modification as the requirements of the system change over time.

Unit testing is the process of running test cases against the program and observing the results to be sure that they are consistent with those projected in the test planning step. The code is continuously corrected until the expected results are obtained. Both the unit testing and the coding are greatly enhanced in terms of increased productivity when an online application development environment exists. Programmers are able to compose, modify, and test their programs from their keyboards without having to wait for keypunching, job execution, and other interruptions which make the programming task discontinuous.

21.8 DOCUMENTATION

It is extremely important that each program be properly documented. It must be remembered that the documentation must be such that another person, not now familiar with the programs, must be able to use and understand the material. The computer itself may be employed in developing the program documentation. Information about each program should be recorded in a standardized format and collected into a file folder, a loose-leaf binder, or some other device for keeping the material together. Items which should be included in the documentation are:

1. A narrative description of each program, briefly describing its inputs, outputs, and function
2. Equipment operating instructions for setting up and executing the program
3. Samples of all printouts produced
4. Flowcharts or HIPOs of the logic of the program
5. Program listings
6. Record layouts of all input to or output from the module
7. A list of all constants in the program which require periodic updating (for example, the FICA rate) and the procedure for changing them
8. A description of any tables used by the program and the method by which they can be updated

Much of the documentation can be incorporated into the program through the use of *comments*. Almost all assemblers/compilers provide for the entering of notations in the source program. These notes, or comments, are not steps in the program, but are useful in providing required documentation. As an example, a comments line at the beginning of a program could state that the program contains the FICA rate which should be checked every January 1 for possible change. The line in the program which contains the FICA rate as a constant can be preceded or followed by comments describing the constant and how it can be changed.

Comments lines in the source program are among the most valuable and most practical methods of program documentation. The comments remain with the source program and are printed in all source program listings. Thus, each time the program is assembled or compiled, a new listing, including comments, is automatically prepared. The comments must of course be updated as changes are made to the program, or they will lose their value. The self-documenting program is the goal one should strive for.

The use of *documentation standards* within the organization facilitates the preparation, communication, interpretation, and maintenance of the documentation. These standards include record layouts, printer layouts, flowchart symbols, operating instructions format, and the use of comments within the programs.

Since a complete system will include at least some manual operations, the procedures for them must be prepared and documented. These procedures for people are the equivalent of the program for the computer. Narrative, flowchart, and decision-table formats may be used for documenting these procedures. Samples of completed forms and computer input and output should be included in the procedures to give them clear meaning for operating personnel reference.

21.9 SYSTEM TESTING

System testing is performed according to the script developed in Step 2. It is done when all of the programs have demonstrated that they can execute the unit tests faultlessly. As mentioned earlier, if the development was not accomplished using a top-down structured approach, an intermediate level of integration test may need to be conducted—a process which continuously adds programs and subsystems to the nucleus programs until the entire system is together in one piece. The purpose of system testing is to insure that all of the programs can operate in concert and produce the end results described in the new system description.

The entire configuration may not be installed when system testing is initiated. For example, only a portion of the processors and their associated terminals may be installed in a distributed system, the plan being to add sites upon completion of the pilot system. In cases like this, test drivers are often used to provide simulated data as though the remote sites were providing it. Simulation programs are often used to estimate the performance of the system as it will operate when fully installed.

As shown in Figure 21–2, the system test step can generate feedback to the documentation and coding steps, which may in turn affect the system specifications developed in detail design. If the testing process indicates many changes in the code, file design, or system design, then a careful review of the entire implementation effort is called for.

21.10 **PARALLEL OPERATION**

The parallel operation step is a continuation of the testing process but it uses real data generated currently by the system. The full system may be operated in parallel, or it may be desirable to execute all of the operations on only a portion of the system. As an example, one product at a time of the full product line may be processed in parallel. When parallel operation on the one product is proven correct, additional products can be added to the parallel test. As another example, if a company installs a system to perform route accounting, it may test in parallel, using only eight or ten routes of the total number of routes. If the sample group of routes is handled correctly by the system, additional routes may be added to the test, or all the routes may then be converted to the new system. When only a portion of a system is to be operated in parallel, the selected portion should be as representative of the full system as possible.

During parallel operation the performance and outputs of the new system are compared with the performance and outputs of the existing system. These comparisons may indicate errors in the new system and cause feedback to previous steps as shown in Figure 21−2. If errors are detected, programming, file design or system design must be changed to correct the condition. It is not unusual to detect some errors during parallel operation, but the cause of the error should be easily corrected. If the previous steps are well done and coordinated, serious errors or omissions will not be found during parallel operation.

Although parallel operation is highly desirable for final testing of any system, several factors must be considered. Some of these are:

1. The new system usually produces outputs that the existing system does not—or could not—produce, making direct comparison of content difficult.
2. The inputs to the new system may be radically different from those of the existing system, requiring additional care in making comparisons. Because of the different inputs to the old and new systems, separate controls may have to be maintained and reconciled.
3. The cost of the parallel operation may be high, since it is a duplicate effort.

4. Parallel operation should be continued for only a limited time. During parallel operation, the operating personnel continue to depend on the existing system. The availability of the existing system may discourage rapid conversion to the new system. Therefore, parallel operation should be continued only until some preset level of performance is attained.

21.11 CONVERSION TO THE NEW SYSTEM

The final step in the implementation stage is full conversion to the new system. This step may take days, weeks, or months. The required time depends on:

1. The volume and medium of the existing records. Converting card records to tape or disk is normally not too difficult, since the conversion can be performed by machines. However, converting from manual records to a computer medium can be an extensive task.
2. The people and equipment available to perform the conversion. Recording manual records in machine readable form may require additional personnel and equipment.
3. The need to convert the existing records. Management may decide that it is important only to place new records in the new system and convert the existing records slowly, or not at all. This approach minimizes or eliminates much of the conversion step.
4. The number of terminal workstations to come online. Installing additional local and remote equipment and the training of personnel are often the pacing factors.

The primary difficulty in converting is that business must continue while the conversion takes place. The records being converted must customarily be available to operating personnel. The most practical approach to conversion is to convert existing records in controllable units or groups which can be temporarily frozen while conversion takes place. Accounting controls on the conversion groups should be established to insure that they are correctly recorded in the new system. Special programs are usually required for validating the converted records before entering them into the files of the new system.

Personnel, customers, vendors, stockholders, and others who may be affected by the conversion of the existing records should be advised of the change. If the payroll application is being converted, employees should be notified of the change; if billing or accounts receivable records are being converted, customers should be notified; if purchasing or accounts payable are being converted, vendors should be notified. Notification to affected parties may not always be necessary, but the value of such notification should be examined for each conversion.

The conversion schedule and procedures should be defined and agreed to early in the installation stage. If the volume of records to be converted is large, a special conversion team is desirable. The team can test existing files for completeness, and if the same data is available from one or more existing files, the team can recommend which data should be secured from which file.

If the existing files do not contain all the data desired for the new system (because the data for all new records entering the system have been expanded), a decision must be made as to the value of obtaining such data for the existing records. If the existing files are highly volatile, so that the life of a given record is short, then it may not be necessary to convert them at all.

Some companies have taken the approach of not converting any existing records until the new system is completely satisfactory, using only new records as input. This approach is good if there is no relationship between new records and existing records, and if space and personnel permit two systems to be operating at the same time.

Regardless of the method used, conversion is usually a difficult task and often is not given enough consideration by analysts or by management. Frequently, poor conversion techniques are the cause of dissatisfaction by employees, customers, and others who are affected by the new system.

21.12 STAGE 3: OPERATE, EVALUATE, MODIFY, AND MAINTAIN

The third stage — operate, evaluate, modify, maintain — in the life cycle of a business system is concerned with the day-to-day use of the system. Effective use of the system requires coordination among the many departments that participate in the system completely or partially.

Figure 21–3 shows the relationship of management, the computer department, and three operating departments labelled A, B, and C. The solid lines represent authority and control, and the dotted lines

Figure 21–3 Relationship of the computer department to management and the operating departments.

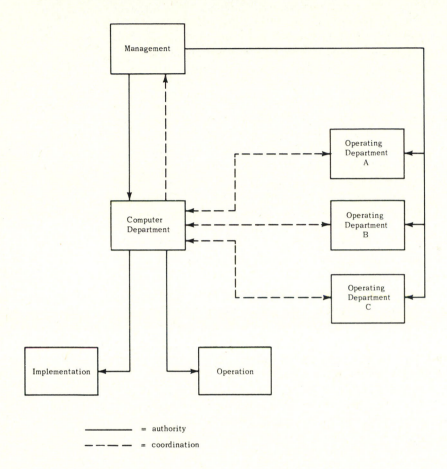

represent coordination. The need for this coordination and the means by which it can be achieved is discussed in the following sections in conjunction with the more important details of each step in Stage 3.

Many of the larger computers have very sophisticated system control programs that automatically handle many of the functions described in the following sections. The procedures described here are for a basic system environment—a batch, nonmultiprogrammed operation.

21.13 SYSTEM OPERATION: SCHEDULING

The operation of a computer-based system consists of the computer department functions plus the computer-related functions of the departments supplying input to the computer and using the output from the computer. The operation of the system should be considered as a production function. As in any production function, scheduling is of prime importance. Complete system scheduling consists of:(1) scheduling the computer and its related equipment and (2) coordinating the computer room schedule with the work flow to and from the operating departments.

Scheduling within the computer room should begin with a monthly or weekly schedule showing the time of each unit of equipment necessary to achieve the processing required. When the system is first installed, this schedule can be developed from time estimates based on testing and parallel operation. The schedule can be refined as experience is gained in daily operation. It will usually require some day-by-day adjustment, but a specified weekly or monthly schedule does establish a basic framework of equipment needs.

The schedule should include known periodic jobs which are performed only quarterly, semiannually, or annually. As an example, if the computer is being used for a payroll application, additional time will be needed each quarter and at year-end to prepare federal and state reports. If the computer is used for a sales analysis application, there may be several quarterly reports to be prepared, and the required time for preparing these reports should be recognized in the schedule.

The second factor in sound scheduling is coordination with the operating departments. When several departments supply data to the computer (and this is often the case), the scheduling of the receipt of data from the departments must be established and adhered to. The computer department cannot meet its own internal schedule if the data input schedule is not met.

Thus, if payroll checks are to be prepared by the computer on, say, Wednesday morning, all data for check preparation must be ready by that time. Input data, such as hours worked by each employee, rate changes, new hires, changes in deductions, and so on, must be proved and available at check-preparation time. If the system is such that this input data must be processed through one or more programs for proof and validation, then that processing should be scheduled sufficiently in advance to permit the results to be reviewed and corrected by the payroll department. Since the input data cannot be processed through the proof and validation programs until they are in machine-readable form, conversion to machine medium must be completed according to schedule.

The sequence of work flow that will most facilitate meeting desired schedules can be established by the use of critical path techniques. Even an unsophisticated schedule network may reveal points of delay in the work flow and assist in making necessary changes. Whenever possible, the overall schedule should allow some slack time for potential difficulties.

One method of encouraging proper coordination in scheduling between the computer department and the operating departments is to have the manager or supervisor of computer operations meet with the managers or supervisors of the operating departments to review the schedule for the coming week. Any anticipated delays can be discussed and adjustments in the schedule agreed to by all concerned. Management itself may be responsible for anticipated delays because it may choose not to close the period until certain transactions are recorded. Depending on the structure of the system, considerable processing may be delayed until these transactions are completed.

The proper scheduling of the operations of the system can be complex and can involve many departments. The dotted lines between the computer department and the operating departments, and between the computer department and management shown in Figure 21-3 represent the coordination needed to develop and attain desired schedules.

21.14 SYSTEM 'OPERATION: PERSONNEL AND PROCEDURES

The basic personnel complement for computer room operations is one or more equipment operators. The total number of personnel needed depends on the type and amount of equipment and the number of effective processing hours required. A system using a computer having only card input and card and printer output will usually require card sorters and collators. Operators are needed for the sorting and collating equipment, as well as for the computer. A similar system using tape or disk to accomplish the sorting and merging functions will require fewer operators. A one-shift operation will, of course, require less personnel than a two- or three-shift operation.

Standardized operating procedures should be defined for the equipment operators. The data-handling procedures for each program should be prepared in a format easily followed by the operators. A manual of instructions for data handling for each program is initially developed during the programming and documentation steps of Stage 2. These instructions can be modified and amplified, if need be, by the manager or supervisor of computer operations. The equipment manufacturer can often assist in the preparation of operating procedures by supplying forms designed for ease in recording such procedures.

An important part of the procedures for computer operations is the control system, which is established for checking computer output. In smaller installations, the computer-room supervisor may maintain such controls. In larger installations, one or more control clerks may be designated to perform this duty. In either case, the primary controls should be established by the operating department for whom the processing is performed. Thus, if the computer is used in an accounts receivable application, the total accounts receivable balance with which the statements prepared by the computer should agree can best be determined by the accounts receivable department.

The coordination needed to facilitate balancing to established controls is expressed in Figure 21–3 by the dotted lines between the computer department and the operating departments.

21.15 EVALUATING AND MODIFYING THE SYSTEM

The evaluation of the system is performed by management, by supervisory personnel who have day-to-day contact with the system, or by technical specialists who are effective system auditors. Minor changes that will significantly improve the efficiency of the system can be proposed after it is in operation. Desired changes are made by the implementation or system maintenance personnel. Designers must take extreme care to be sure that changes which improve one portion of the system do not harm other portions. The efficiency analysis should continue over the life of the system.

Factors included in the evaluation of the system include cost, throughput, usefulness of output, and ability of the operating departments to work with the system. Minor changes in data flow or equipment may have a significant effect in reducing cost and in improving throughput. Changes in report format may easily improve the usefulness of the output. Additional education and indoctrination of operating department personnel can improve their ability to work with the system.

21.16 MAINTAINING THE SYSTEM

Maintenance contributes significantly to the continued usefulness of the system. Both *fixes* to the programs to correct defects (sometimes called negative maintenance) and *improvements* to the programs (positive maintenance) are implied by the word maintenance. A system may be judged as operating poorly if it simply has not been properly maintained. Frequently the machine may be thought defective when it is in fact lacking correct system maintenance. For example, incorrect invoices may be prepared by the computer, not because of any machine malfunction, but because the program was not changed to reflect a change in a sales tax rate. The change may have required only changing one constant in the program; but if it is not changed, or if it is changed improperly, all computations using this factor will be incorrect.

System maintenance is usually performed by assigned implementation or maintenance personnel who are thoroughly familiar with the system. Major system maintenance may require the assistance of additional programmers and complete testing to be sure that the changes are made accurately without disturbing the successful operation of the system.

Flexibility incorporated into the initial system design can greatly facilitate system maintenance. As an example, consider an application which includes the preparation of a sales analysis with a description of each product sold. The input to the program which produces the sales analysis report may contain only the code of each product and not the description. The description for each product can be obtained during the program processing from descriptions included in the program as constant information. Each time a new product is added, a change in the program must be made. If a table of product codes and descriptions is used in place of various constants, the table can be updated independently and the new product handled without any changes in the program itself.

Another important factor in facilitating system maintenance is proper program documentation. It is never known when a program may have to be changed to effect system maintenance. The time allotted for the change may be brief, and even the programmer who originally wrote the program may have difficulty in locating the instructions or module which should be changed. Good documentation will assist greatly in locating the area to be changed. If at the time of writing the original program it is known that changes will be required from time to time, then comments can be included in the program explaining how a change can be made.

System maintenance may also include the writing of new programs to prepare additional reports. A change in company policy, federal or state law, or in management personnel may make additional reports necessary. Thus, a new member of the sales or marketing staff may be well satisfied with existing reports, but may also have definite and specific requirements for additional information from the system. The raw data could be available in the system with only one or two program modules required to prepare the desired additional report.

21.17 RETURN TO STAGE 1

A system that operates for any long period of time may become technologically obsolete, at which time it no longer supports the goals of the business. Then Stage 1—Study and Design—in the life cycle of a business system should again be undertaken. The existing system must, of course, continue to operate during the new study and design stage. Fortunately, the experience gained during the life of the existing system will be of great value in determining the requirements of the next generation system. The life of a system can seldom be accurately predicted, and the cycle of study and design; implement and install; operate, evaluate and maintain; study and design; and so on continues indefinitely. Even if the organization is absorbed by another organization, the life cycle of the system will continue, if only as a subsystem of a larger system in the new organization.

SUMMARY

After the new system plan is approved, the normal course of events is to execute the implementation plan as developed by the analysts who designed the new system. The initial positive act on the part of the company is often to sign a contract for the computer and related equipment. However, the responsibility for implementing, operating, and maintaining the system remains with the company. In the typical situation, it is company personnel who study the existing organization, design the new system, implement the system, operate the system, and maintain it.

The manufacturer of the equipment usually is able to provide test facilities, education in programming and computer operations, and general guidance. However, it takes a significant amount of time, effort, money, and ability in a company to install, operate, and maintain a computerized system for management or information-system processing.

During the implementation stage, documentation standards should be established, the system designed in detail, the files organized and laid out. There must be programming and documentation of the system; test data must be developed; and the system must be tested. This is followed by parallel operation and, finally, conversion to the new system.

To put the new system in operation, new relationships have to be established between the affected operating departments and the computer department. Schedules have to be established for data inputs received from the operating departments and for the data outputs and reports to be sent to them. Cooperation and coordination are important ingredients in a successful system.

Eventually, the passage of time will have brought about so many internal or external changes that it will again be necessary to study the existing system and to design another one. Business systems imitate natural ones in being born, growing while they serve a useful purpose, and then dying.

QUESTIONS AND PROBLEMS

21–1   If systems require study, design, and implementation on a
continuing basis, how have many companies managed to
survive as long as they have without constantly improving
their systems?

21–2   What is the relationship between the implementation
personnel and the operating personnel of the data
processing department?

21–3   Visit a company with a computer and report on the number
and titles of the employees in the programming and
operating sections of the data processing department.

21-4   Suggest why a plan that calls for simultaneous conversion of all areas of a new system at one time is likely to encounter severe difficulties.

21-5   Why are standards necessary in programming and operating departments?

21-6   Why are accounting control totals important for conversion to the new system?

21-7   What is the difference between the people who install a system and the people who keep it going once it has been put into operation?

21-8   If a company signs a contract for a computer, should the computer manufacturer be responsible for getting the system to work?

21-9   Why is the selection of the senior person to install and operate the system so important?

21-10 Why do systems change during implementation? If the design had been done correctly the first time, should it not be suitable for implementation?

GLOSSARY

The technical vocabulary in the field of computers and data processing systems draws heavily on words that already exist in the English language, but often uses them with different meanings. English meanings are always subject to change. A particular word has one meaning in a certain place and at a certain time, but quite a different meaning at another place or another time. Even a group of people with similar interests may not be able to agree on the meaning of a word or term or on a method for defining the word or term.

Perhaps the most difficult problem for a noncomputer person reading a computer-related book is that some of the words and terms are defined by using expressions and concepts that are also not familiar. For this reason, some readers may want to return to certain parts of the book several times to fully understand the technical usages. To aid them, we present the following glossary; the reader should also refer to sources noted in the bibliography. This glossary emphasizes words used in this book and defines them accordingly.[1]

Activity. A logically related set of operations, usually self-contained, with few ties to the surrounding environment; directed toward satisfying one or more fundamental business goals.

Activity Requirements Model. A pictorial means of showing the relationship of required and imposed inputs, outputs, operations, and resources.

Activity Sheet. A diagram showing the flow of operations within a single activity and system characteristics such as volumes and times recorded in tabular form.

Affectable Costs. The costs of a business which can be changed by a new system, for example, reduced personnel, waste reduction.

Algorithm. A set of rules or steps pertaining to a constructive calculating process designed to lead to the solution of a problem in a finite number of steps.

---

[1]Permission to reprint those words identified by an asterisk has been obtained from the American National Standards Institute, Inc., 1430 Broadway, New York, N.Y. 10018, with accreditation to "American National Dictionary for Information Processing, X3/TR-1-77." ISO refers to the International Standards Organization.

Alphameric. A generic term for alphabetic letters, numeric digits, and special characters which are machine-processable. Synonymous with alphanumeric.

Analog Computer. A computer which represents variables by physical analogies. Thus, any computer which solves problems by translating physical conditions such as flow, temperature, pressure, angular position, or voltage into related mechanical or electrical quantities and uses mechanical or electrical equivalent circuits as an analog for the physical phenomenon being investigated. In general, it is a computer which uses an analog for each variable and produces analogs as output. An analog computer measures continuously, whereas a digital computer counts discretely.

Analog Data. Data represented in a continuous form, as contrasted with digital data represented in a discrete (discontinuous) form. Analog data are usually represented by means of physical variables such as voltage, resistance, and rotation.

Analysis. The breaking up of study subjects into manageable elements for individual evaluation.

Analyst. A person skilled in the definition of problems and the development of logical procedures and data structures for their solution, especially methods which may be implemented on a computer.

Application. The system or problem to which a computer is applied.

Assembler. A computer program which operates on symbolic input data to produce, from such data, machine instructions by carrying out such functions as translation of symbolic operation codes into computer operating instructions; assigning locations in storage for successive instructions; or computation of absolute addresses from symbolic addresses. An assembler generally translates input symbolic codes into machine instructions item for item, and produces as output the same number of instructions or constants as were defined in the input symbolic codes.

*Associative Storage. (1) (ISO) A storage device whose storage locations are identified by their contents, or by part of their contents, rather than by their names or positions. Synonymous with content-addressed storage. (2) Contrast with parallel search storage.

Audit Trail. A system of providing a means for tracing items of data from one processing step to the next, particularly from a machine produced report or other machine output back to the original source data.

Automation. (1) The implementation of processes by automatic means; (2) the theory, art or technique of making a process more automatic; (3) the investigation, design, development, and application of methods of rendering processes automatic, self-moving, or self-controlling.

Batch Processing. A systems approach to processing where a number of similar input items are grouped for processing during the same machine run.

*Baud. A unit of signaling speed equal to the number of discrete conditions or signal events per second. For example, one baud equals one-half dot cycle per second in Morse code, one bit per second in a train of binary signals, and one 3-bit value per second in a train of signals each of which can assume one of eight different states.

*Binary. (1) (ISO) Pertaining to a selection, choice, or condition that has two possible values or states. (2) (ISO) Pertaining to a fixed radix numeration system having a radix of two.

Bit. Contraction of "binary digit," the smallest unit of information, which is dual-state (one or zero, on or off, mark or space).

Boolean Algebra. A process of reasoning, or a deductive system of theorems using a symbolic logic and dealing with classes, propositions, or on-off circuit elements. It employs symbols to represent operators such as *and*, *or*, *not*, *except*, *if*, *then*, etc., to permit mathematical calculation.

Business Goals. In addition to making a profit and providing employment, business goals are the special contributions a business makes to its environment. For example, the primary goal of an appliance company is to manufacture and distribute appliances.

Byte. A group of bits handled as a unit; may be a character, a part of a word, or a word.

Cathode Ray Tube (CRT). An electronic vacuum tube, such as a television picture tube, that can be used to display graphic images.

Central Processing Unit (CPU). (1) The unit of a computer system which contains the main storage, arithmetic unit, logical unit, and special registers. (2) All that portion of a computer exclusive of the input, output, peripheral, and in most instances, storage units.

Centralized Data Processing. Data processing performed at a single, central location on data obtained from several geographical locations or managerial levels. Distributed data processing involves processing at various managerial levels or geographical points throughout the organization.

Character. One symbol of a set of elementary symbols such as those corresponding to the keys on a typewriter. The symbols usually include the decimal digits 0 through 9, the letters A through Z, punctuation marks, operation symbols, and any other single symbols which a computer may read, store, or write.

Checkpoint Restart. A point in a program at which sufficient information can be stored to permit restarting the computation from that point.

COBOL. CO-mmon B-usiness O-riented L-anguage. (1) A data processing language that makes use of English-like statements. (2) Pertaining to a computer program which translates a COBOL language source program into a machine language object program.

Communication Network. A complex of data communication equipment, data links, and channels that connects one or more data processing systems.

*Compile. (1) (ISO) To translate a computer program expressed in a problem-oriented language into a computer-oriented language. (2) To prepare a machine language program from a computer program written in another programming language by making use of the overall logic structure of the program, or generating more than one computer instruction for each symbolic statement, or both, as well as performing the function of an assembler.

*Computer Language. (ISO) A computer-oriented language whose instructions consist only of computer instructions. Synonymous with machine language.

*Computer Network. A complex consisting of two or more interconnected computing units.

Conversion. (1) The process of changing information from one form of representation to another; such as, from the language of one type of machine to that of another or from magnetic tape to the printed page. Synonymous with data conversion. (2) The process of changing from one data processing method to another or from one type of equipment to another; e.g., conversion from punch card equipment to magnetic tape equipment.

CPM (Critical Path Method). Similar to, but differs technically from PERT. CPM is concerned primarily with time and cost and does not consider the problem of uncertainty of time for each activity. The terminology of CPM differs from PERT, as an event in PERT is a node in CPM, and an activity in PERT is a job in CPM. A critical path is the longest path through a network.

Cybernetics. The field of technology involved in the comparative study of the control and intracommunication of information handling machines and nervous systems of animals and man in order to understand and improve communication.

Data. A general term used to denote any or all facts, numbers, letters, and symbols that refer to or describe an object, idea, condition, situation, or other factors. It connotes basic elements of information which can be processed or produced by a computer.

*Data Base. (1) (ISO) A set of data, part of the whole of another set of data, and consisting of at least one file that is sufficient for a given purpose or for a given data processing system. (2) A collection of data fundamental to a system. (3) A collection of data fundamental to an enterprise.

Data Base Administrator. An individual responsible for designing and controlling the data bases of an organization.

Data Base Management System. The programs required to build, maintain, and utilize a data base.

Data Communication. Data transferred between various locations via communications facilities.

Data Dictionary. A catalogue of an organization's data bases including names and structures.

Data File. A collection of related data records organized in a specific manner. For example, a payroll file (one record for each employee, showing his rate of pay, deductions, etc.) or an inventory file (one record for each inventory item, showing the cost, selling price, number in stock, etc.). See also data set.

*Data Hierarchy. A data structure consisting of sets and subsets such that every subset of a set is of lower rank than the data of the set.

*Data Management. (1) The function of controlling the acquisition, analysis, storage, retrieval, and distribution of data. (2) In an operating system, the computer programs that provide access to data, perform or monitor storage of data, and control input/output devices.

Data Processing. (1) The preparation of source media which contain data or basic elements of information, and the handling of such data according to precise rules of procedure to accomplish such operations as classifying, sorting, calculating, summarizing, and recording. (2) The production of records and reports.

Data Security. See security.

Data Set. The major unit of data storage and retrieval in the operating system, consisting of a collection of data in one of several prescribed arrangements and described by control information to which the system has access.

DB/DC. Data base/data communication.

Debug. To detect, locate, and remove mistakes from a program or malfunctions from a computer.

Decision Table. A visual method for displaying the cause-and-effect relationship in systems logic. A means of relating conditions and actions through decision rules.

Digital Computer. A computer which processes information represented by combinations of discrete or discontinuous data in contrast to an analog computer for continuous data. More specifically, it is a device for performing sequences of arithmetic and logical operations, not only on data but on its own program. Still more specifically, it is a stored program computer capable of performing sequences of internally stored instructions, as opposed to calculators, on which the sequence is impressed manually.

*Display Tube. A tube, usually a cathode ray tube, used to display data.

Distributed Function. In data communication, the use of programmable terminals, controllers, and other devices to perform operations that were previously done by the processing unit, such as managing data links, controlling devices, and formatting data.

Documentation. The group of techniques necessary for the orderly presentation, organization, and communication of recorded specialized knowledge, in order to maintain a complete record of reasons for changes in variables. Documentation is necessary not so much to give maximum utility as to give an unquestionable historical reference record. Documentation records decision logic, program reference information, and data structure.

Environment. Those factors outside a business (and hence outside the scope of the study) which influence the business. Included in the environment are items such as competitors, geographical considerations, market status, and customer attitudes.

External Storage. A storage device outside the computer which can store information in a form acceptable to the computer, e.g., cards, tapes, disks.

Feedback. The part of a closed loop system which automatically brings back information about the condition of the variable being controlled.

Field. An assigned area in a record to be filled with information.

File. A collection of related records treated as a unit. In inventory control, one line of an invoice forms an item, a complete invoice forms a record, and a set of records forms a file. In general, an organized collection of information directed toward some purpose. The records may or may not be in sequence.

File Maintenance. The processing or periodic modification of a file to effect changes in the file which occurred during a given period; for example, updating a master file.

File Sheet. A form used to support the operation sheet which describes a collection of messages or an information file.

Flowchart. A series of symbols connected by lines to demonstrate a sequence of events and decisions.

Gantt Chart. A method of showing scheduling requirements in chart form. The method was developed by Henry L. Gantt prior to World War I. In a typical Gantt chart the time required for completion of each step of a process is expressed as a bar across a sheet with the length of the bar denoting the total time required for the step. This method quickly shows overlapping steps.

General Section. This section of the Phase I report describes the environment in which the business operates, and the position of the business in that environment.

Generic System Description. The logical flow of information and the logical operations necessary to carry out a particular design without regard to equipment required to perform the task.

Goals. Those contributions (usually products or services) an organization wishes to make to its environment. Goals define the purpose and objectives of the organization.

Hardware. The physical equipment or devices forming a computer and peripheral units.

*Heuristic Method. (ISO) Any exploratory method of solving problems in which an evaluation is made of the progress toward an acceptable final result using a series of approximate results.

Hierarchical File. A data file organized in a tree structure with some records subordinate to others.

HIPO (Hierarchy Input Process Output). A documentation technique for describing systems. An alternative to flowcharts and decision tables.

Host Computer. (1) The primary or controlling computer in a multiple computer operation. (2) A computer used to prepare programs for use on another computer or on another data processing system; for example, a computer used to compile, link edit, or test programs to be used on another system. (3) The primary or controlling computer in a data communication system.

Implementation. The process of constructing a system to perform the tasks specified in the design while meeting the measurement criteria.

Implementation Plan. A description of the steps to install a new system, with cost and time schedules involved.

*Information. (ISO) (1) The meaning that a human assigns to data by means of the known conventions used in their representation. (2) The collection of facts or other data especially as derived from the processing of numbers or words; often used in a broader sense than data.

Information Processing. A less restrictive term than data processing, encompassing the totality of scientific, business, and word processing operations performed by a computer and people.

Information Retrieval. The recovery of desired information or data from a collection of documents, or other records.

Input. Information or data transferred from an external storage medium into the internal storage of the computer.

Input-Output. A term for the equipment used to provide information for, and accept it from, the computer and the actual data flowing into and out of a system.

Input-Output Sheet. A summary form used in Phase II to record the required input and output characteristics. Message sheets can be used for supporting material if more detail is required.

Inquiry. (1) A request for information from storage, e.g., a request for the number of available airline seats; (2) a machine statement to initiate a search of library documents.

Interactive. Pertaining to an application in which each entry calls forth a response from a system or program, as in an inquiry system or an airline reservation system. An interactive system may also be conversational, implying a continuous dialog between the user and the system. See also inquiry.

Interface. A common boundary or physical connection between automatic data processing systems or parts of a single system. May also be used for program interrelationships.

Key. (1) A group of characters which identifies or is part of a record or item; thus any entry in a record or item can be used as a key for collating or sorting purposes. (2) A marked lever manually operated for entering a character; e.g., a typewriter, paper tape perforator, card punch, manual keyboard, digitizer, or manual word generator. (3) A lever or switch on a computer console for the purpose of manually altering computer action.

Keypunch. (1) A special device to record information in cards or paper tape by punching holes in the cards or tape to represent letters, digits, and special characters. (2) To operate a device for punching holes in cards or tape.

Language. A system for representing and communicating information or data between people or between people and machines. Such a system consists of a carefully defined set of characters and rules for combining them into larger units, such as words or expressions, and rules for word arrangement or usage to achieve specific meanings.

Linear Programming. A technique of mathematics used in operations research for solving certain kinds of problems involving many variables where a best value or set of best values is to be found.

Logic. (1) The science dealing with the criteria or formal principles of reasoning and thought. (2) The systematic scheme which defines the interactions of signals in the design of an automatic data processing system. (3) The basic principles and application of truth tables and interconnection between logical elements required for arithmetic computation in an automatic data processing system.

Management Abstract. A synopsis of the Stage 1 study for management evaluation, describing the proposal concisely but completely with background material on the current system and requirements for the new system.

Mark-Sense. To mark a position on a punched card or other specially designed form with special pencil, for later sensing by machines.

Mass Storage. (1) (ISO) Storage having a very large storage capacity. (2) The storage of a large amount of data which is also readily accessible to the processing unit of a computer.

Mathematical Model. A mathematical representation of a process, device, or concept.

Measurement. Various criteria for evaluating system performance, such as time, reliability, accuracy, cost, efficiency, etc., comprise a means of system measurement. The way in which a future system is to be measured is established in Phase II before it is designed.

Message. (1) A group of words, variable in length, transported as a unit; (2) a transported item of information; (3) any communication of information, formal document, informal letter, or oral statement.

Message Sheet. A form used to support the operation sheet which provides information about system inputs and outputs.

Model. A representation of something to be made or already existing. A model may be physical, schematic, or mathematical. A mathematical model is a formula selected as a representation of a social or natural law. For business purposes, mathematical models are used to explain or predict changes in a system. Mathematical models are the foundation for simulating a system on a computer. Physical models include prototype machines and factory mock-ups. Schematic models include flow diagrams, PERT networks, system flowcharts, and so on.

Module. (1) An interchangeable plug-in item containing components. (2) An incremental block of storage or other building block for expanding the computer capacity. (3) The input to, or output from, a single execution of an assembler, compiler, or linkage editor; a source, object, or load module; hence, a program unit that is discrete and identifiable with respect to compiling, combining with other units, and loading.

Multiplex. The process of transferring data from several storage devices operating at relatively low transfer rates to one storage device operating at a high transfer rate in such a manner that the high-speed device is not obliged to wait for the low-speed devices.

Multiprocessor. A system or machine complex with multiple arithmetic and logic units for simultaneous use.

Multiprogramming. Multiple object programs, residing in a single system internal memory, that are alternately executed by a processor to gain greater throughput through simultaneous input, output, and processor operations.

Network. A system of connected points—for example, terminals connected by communications channels and some form of exchange. Also used in CPM and PERT to describe the arrangements of tasks.

Offline. Descriptive of a system and of the peripheral equipment or devices in a system in which the operation of peripheral equipment is not under the control of the central processing unit.

Online. Descriptive of a system and of the peripheral equipment or devices in a system in which the operation of such equipment is under control of the central processing unit; online operation is required if information reflecting current activity is to be introduced into the data processing system as it occurs. Thus, online processing requires online peripheral equipment.

*Operating System. (ISO) Software that controls the execution of computer programs and that may provide scheduling, debugging, input/output control, accounting, compilation, storage assignment, data management, and related services.

Operation. A related set of processes which, when initiated by a trigger, converts inputs to outputs utilizing resources. An activity contains multiple operations which in turn contain multiple processes.

Operation Sheet. Describes the processing steps which make up an operation and shows the inputs, resources, and outputs in relation to the processes.

Operational Section. This section of the Phase I report defines activities and relates them to the established framework of the business.

Operations Logic. The means of transforming inputs to outputs; a definition of the cause and effect relationship between inputs and outputs.

Operations Research. The use of analytic methods adapted from mathematics for solving operational or planning problems. The objective is to provide management with a logical, mathematical basis for making sound predictions and decisions. Among the common scientific techniques used in operations research are the following: linear programming, probability theory, information theory, game theory, Monte Carlo method, and queuing theory.

Optical Scanning. A technique for machine recognition of characters by their visual images.

Output. The information transferred from the internal storage of a computer to secondary or external storage, or to any device outside of the computer.

Overview. A broad-gauge, general description of a business.

Password. A unique string of characters that a program, computer operator, or user must supply to meet security requirements before gaining access to data.

Peripheral Equipment. The auxiliary machines which may be placed under the control of the central computer. Examples are card readers, card punches, magnetic tape units, and high speed printers. Peripheral equipment may be used online or offline depending upon computer design, job requirements, and economics.

PERT (Program Evaluation and Review Technique). A management information and control system used in the planning, control, and evaluation of progress of a project. It is time-oriented and uses a network usually expressed in diagram form. The network consists of events connected by activities.

Plotter. A visual display or board in which one or more variables are graphed automatically.

Process. One of the actions taking place within an operation. Usually describable by a single statement; e.g., "Locate information in file," or "Compile report on scrap losses."

Process Control. Pertaining to systems whose purpose is to provide automation of complex physical operations. Usually relates to continuous processes like refining and paper manufacture. Sometimes called control systems.

Program. (1) The complete plan for the solution of a problem, more specifically the complete sequence of machine instructions and routines necessary to solve a problem. (2) To plan the procedures for solving a problem. This may involve, among other things, the analysis of the problem; preparation of a flow diagram; preparing detailed code; testing; allocation of storage locations; specification of input and output formats; and incorporating a particular computer run into a larger data processing system.

Programmer. A person who prepares problem-solving procedures and flowcharts and who may also write and debug routines.

Queuing. A study of the patterns involved and the time required for discrete units to move through channels; e.g., the elapsed time for auto traffic at a toll booth or employees in a cafeteria line.

Random Access. Pertaining to the process of obtaining data from or placing data into storage when there is no sequential relation governing the requests. Normally this is done on devices (like disks) where the access time to storage locations is relatively independent of location (not the case for magnetic tape). Also called direct access.

Rating Scales. A means of establishing targets for measurement factors. Unacceptable, acceptable, and desirable ranges of performance may be placed on some linear or other scale for later evaluation of planned or actual performance.

Real-Time Operation. The use of the computer as an element of a processing system in which the times of occurrence of data transmission are controlled by other portions of the system, or by physical events outside the system, and cannot be modified for convenience in computer programming. Such an operation either proceeds at the same speed as the events being monitored or at a sufficient speed to analyze or control external events happening concurrently. This is online processing with immediate response. Data can be handled in a sufficiently rapid manner so that the results of the processing are usefully available at the data sources. Airlines reservations, information inquiry, and bank teller operations are examples of real-time systems.

Record. (1) A group of related facts or fields of information treated as a unit, thus a listing of information, often in printed or printable form. (2) To put data into a storage device.

Regeneration. The concept of computing answers on demand from decision logic rather than storing massive amounts of precomputed data.

Required Operations Sheet. A summary form used in Phase II to record inputs, outputs, processes, and frequency information for required operations.

Resource. The means of performing operations; e.g., personnel, equipment and facilities, inventories and information.

Resource Sheet. A summary form used in Phase II to record the logically necessary material and informational resources.

Resource Usage Sheet. A form which, when completed, shows the organization and cost by organizational component and by activity. A summary form developed in Phase I.

Routine. A sequence of machine instructions which carry out a well defined function.

Satellite Computer. (1) A computer that is under the control of another computer and performs subsidiary operations. (2) An offline auxiliary computer.

Scope and Boundary. A description of the operations performed by an activity and a description of what is not performed.

Security. Prevention of access to or use of data or programs without authorization.

Simulation. Simulation in its general meaning is the act of assuming the mere appearance of something without the reality of the thing being studied. This can be done in many ways. (1) One can construct replicas of the thing to be studied. (2) Another method is mathematical. In this method, the variables of the system are related by mathematical equations, and the system is then analyzed by manipulating these mathematical symbols. (3) A third method is heuristic or logical. In this method, the analyst draws upon background and experience and then uses his or her best judgment and intuition in preparing a descriptive model that can predict the behavior of the system with the passage of time. (4) A fourth method is to use a computer to play a dominant role. In this method, the mathematical and logical relations are expressed in computer programs, and the random variables are introduced on a probabilistic basis. Numeric data are entered, and then the computer goes through simulation runs to predict expected system behavior.

Software. The totality of programs and routines used to extend the capabilities of computers, such as operating systems, compilers, assemblers, application programs, and subroutines.

Source Program. A computer program written in a language designed for ease of use by people to express certain problems or procedures.

Storage. (1) (ISO) The action of placing data into a storage device. (2) (ISO) The retention of data in a storage device. (3) * A storage device.

Structural Section. This section of the Phase I report amplifies the description of the business in terms of inputs, outputs, and resources.

Structured Programming. A technique for organizing and coding programs that reduces complexity, improves clarity, and makes them easier to debug and modify. Typically, a structured program is a hierarchy of modules that each has a single entry point and a single exit point; control is passed downward through the structure without unconditional branches to higher levels of the structure.

Subsystem. A secondary or subordinate system, usually capable of operating independently of, or asynchronously with, a controlling system.

Synthesis. The combining of parts or elements into an entity, requiring logical reasoning in advancing from principles and propositions to conclusions.

System. A set of methods and procedures utilizing a combination of personnel, equipment, and facilities working to produce outputs.

System Requirements Specification. A series of information packets, each of which describes requirements for one activity within the business which will satisfy a business goal.

System Analysis. The examination of an activity, procedure, method, technique, or business to determine what must be accomplished and how the necessary operations may best be accomplished.

System Planner. A person responsible for creating, designing, and implementing systems within a business. A planner must have insight, understanding, imagination, determination, and effective analysis and synthesis tools to successfully complete his or her tasks.

Teleprocessing. Communication and processing of information which is received from or sent to remote locations.

Terminal. (1) A point in a system or communication network at which data can either enter or leave. (2) A device, usually equipped with a keyboard and some kind of display, capable of sending and receiving information over a communication channel.

Time Sharing. The use of a device for two or more purposes during the same overall time interval, accomplished by interspersing component actions in very short time periods. Normally implies that the computer skips from job to job without regard to whether the first job has yet been completed.

Top-Down Programming. The design and coding of computer programs using a hierarchical structure in which related functions are performed at each level of the structure.

Trigger. Any phenomenon, physical or otherwise, that sets an operation in motion. Triggers may fall in any of four categories: receipt of an input, a time or frequency per unit of time, receipt of multiple inputs, or a combination of inputs and times.

Turn-Around Time. The total time from job request to job delivery.

Unified Systems Approach. The business is treated as an entity, business goals are defined and refined, and an operating system is created to satisfy and further these goals. Oriented toward goals and activities which attain goals, and not toward personnel, equipment, or organization structure.

Unit Record Equipment. The machines and equipment using punch cards. The group of equipment is often called tabulating equipment because the main function of installations of punch card machines for some years before the first automatic digital computer was to produce tabulations of information resulting from sorting, listing, selecting, and totaling data on punch cards.

Virtual Storage. (ISO) The storage space that may be regarded as addressable main storage by the user of a computer system in which virtual addresses are mapped into real addresses. The size of virtual storage is limited by the addressing scheme of the computing system and by the amount of auxiliary storage available, and not by the actual number of main storage locations.

BIBLIOGRAPHY

The amount of published material on the application of computers to management, business, and scientific problems has become quite extensive and is growing as rapidly as the industry. Following is an annotated guide to:

1. Basic books
2. Bibliographies
3. Journals and magazines
4. Glossaries
5. Selected overview papers

The interested reader will want to check regularly a selected few of the reviews, digests, and journals cited to keep abreast of current developments in the field of management systems and computer applications.

American National Dictionary for Information Processing. Computer and Business Equipment Manufacturers Association, 1977.

   This glossary, considered by many people to be the most authoritative of its kind, was developed by Committee X3 of the American Standards Association and sponsored by CBEMA. The American Standards Association has published recommended standards on several other areas of computers and data processing including a code for information interchange, flowchart symbols, FORTRAN, bank magnetic ink characters, and so on.

Anthony, R. N. *Planning and Control Systems—A Framework for Analysis.* Boston, Mass.: Harvard Graduate School of Business Administration, 1965.

   This book is of value to those who study and use planning and control systems and to management personnel in general. The book establishes a framework intended to be useful in planning control and operational systems. It describes the distinguishing characteristics of the main elements of the framework and shows how failure to make these distinctions has led to mistakes in designing and using systems.

Archibald, R. D., and Villoria, R. L. *Network Based Management Systems (PERT/CPM)*. New York: Wiley, 1967.

This book is a guide to the use of PERT and CPM. It is of use to the reader who merely seeks orientation in the subject or one who wishes to apply these techniques. Case studies, some quite detailed, illustrate PERT and CPM applied to projects ranging from the introduction of a new product to the construction of an apartment house.

Aron, Joel D. *The Program Development Process*. Reading, Mass.: Addison-Wesley, 1974.

The field of systems programming grew out of the efforts of many programmers and managers whose creative energy went into producing practical, utilitarian systems programs needed by the rapidly growing computer industry. Programming was practiced as an art in which each programmer invented his or her own solutions to problems with little guidance beyond that provided by immediate associates. In 1968, the late Ascher Opler, then at IBM, recognized that it was necessary to bring programming knowledge together in a form accessible to all systems programmers. Surveying the state of the art, he decided that enough useful material existed to justify a significant codification effort. On his recommendation, IBM decided to sponsor The Systems Programming Series as a long-term project to collect, organize, and publish those principles and techniques that would have lasting value throughout the industry. This is the first book in the series.

Atlas of Applications, Volumes I, II, and III. (Forms GC20-1764, GC20-1768, GC20-1783.) International Business Machines Corporation, 1133 Westchester Avenue, White Plains, New York.

An alphabetical bibliography of quantitative methods applied to business, industry, science, and engineering. Volumes I and II cite 11,300 references covering the years 1961–1974; Volume III is a collection of 2,500 references to journal articles and papers given at conferences, primarily covering 1975.

Bibliography of Data Processing Techniques. (Form F20-8172.) International Business Machines Corporation, 1133 Westchester Avenue, White Plains, New York.

This bibliography and associated classification system provide a means to identify selected IBM publications which, either wholly or in part, document data processing techniques information. Part I of the bibliography lists publications alphabetically within major subject classification. Part II contains abstracts of the publications in form number sequence only.

Bibliography on Simulation. (Form C20-1741.) International Business Machines Corporation, 1133 Westchester Avenue, White Plains, New York.

This bibliography provides the user with an extensive list of publications in the field of simulation. Anyone desiring a quick review of the literature concerning simulation would do well to search through this bibliography.

Boole, George. *The Laws of Thought.* New York: Dover Publications, 1961.

This is the first American printing of the 1854 edition of Boole's *An Interpretation of the Laws of Thought,* on which are founded the mathematical theories and probabilities. For the reader interested in Boolean algebra, this book is basic. To anyone interested in analysis, this book represents a foundation of logical reasoning.

Brooks, Frederick P., Jr. *The Mythical Man-Month.* Reading, Mass.: Addison-Wesley, 1975.

Brooks's conclusions are intended for professional programmers, professional managers, and especially professional managers of programmers. Although written as separate essays, the book has a central argument, in Chapters 2 to 7. Brooks believes that large programming projects suffer management problems different in kind from small ones, because of division of labor. He believes the critical need to be the preservation of the conceptual integrity of the product itself. These chapters explore both the difficulties of achieving this unity and methods for doing so. The later chapters explore other aspects of software engineering management.

Bross, Irwin J. *Design for Decision.* New York: Macmillan, 1953.

Some years ago, Bross prepared this book so that the nonmathematician could understand the meaning of statistical decision making. The book has now become the classic in its field and is possibly the most widely referenced work of its kind. All management and systems people will benefit from reading this book, whatever their work. It explains in everyday language the same procedures for decision making that are being applied to the study, design, implementation, and operation of data processing systems. The topics covered include the history and nature of decision, prediction, probability, values, rules for action, operating as a decision maker, sequential decisions, data models, sampling, measurement, statistical inference, statistical techniques, and design for decision.

Cases in Data Processing: Intercollegiate Bibliography. Intercollegiate Case Clearing House, Boston, Mass.: Harvard Graduate School of Business Administration, 1965.

This bibliography contains a listing of about ninety case studies in data processing grouped into the following divisions:

1. Preliminary study. Choice of equipment. Purchase or lease.
2. Systems. Flow of information. Data needed.
3. Introduction of data processing equipment. Conversion of its use.
4. Data processing center or company.
5. Mathematical programming.
6. Simulation.
7. Other techniques. Procedures.
8. Miscellaneous applications.

For each case there is an abstract, a listing of the course and subjects covered by the case, the setting of the case, the management positions involved by the case, and a method of identification of the case. These cases are available for a fee by writing to the address given above. Upon request, the bibliography will be supplied from the same address.

Churchill, C. W., Ackoff, Russell, and Arnoff, E. Leonard. *Introduction to Operations Research.* New York: Wiley, 1957.

The methods of statistics, operations research, and management science have been mentioned as useful techniques. The book generally considered the classic in this field is the one cited here. Even though it was published many years ago, it is still basic. Furthermore, the reader should have no difficulty obtaining a copy as it has had a wide acceptance, and most libraries will have it. The book provides a general introduction to linear programming, queuing theory, replacement theory, and similar areas that affect management. The authors cite case histories to illustrate many of the concepts.

Collins, J. H., "Systems Analysis before Systems Design." *Proceedings of Guide 45*, Volume 1. Chicago: Guide International, October– November 1977, pp. 391–397.

The contention of this paper is that without good computer and teleprocessing systems analysis, we may fail to get the very real benefits which rapidly developing technology could bring us.

Methodology is a way of going about a project, an intellectual basis for doing the job properly. The importance of a good methodology for engineering complex systems may not be discussed often enough. Thus, for example, the methodology for carrying out a project in a conventional engineering discipline is often taken for granted, although there have been recent developments in these disciplines. Improvements in approach are therefore being sought and found. The application of a systems approach provides one of these improvements. In this paper the deficiencies in current system analysis methodologies are identified, and examples are given of how a systems approach can overcome these deficiencies.

Communications, Computing Reviews, Computing Surveys and *Journal of the Association for Computing Machinery*, 1133 Avenue of the Americas, New York 10036.

The *Journal* (published quarterly) is the pioneer scholarly publication in the computer sciences and is the primary publication in theoretical computer science, including automata theory, programming theory, numerical analysis, programming languages, logical design, switching theory, and all tributary domains in computing. *Communications* is a monthly broad-based publication which covers topics of technical interest. Consisting mainly of by-lined reports on advances in computer science, *Communications* also includes news of the profession and industry, ACM activities, official notices, and committee reports. Its departments represent programming languages, techniques, scientific applications, business applications, information retrieval, medical applications, and others. *Computing Reviews* (monthly) covers the literature on computing and its pertinent applications. More than a thousand volunteer specialists, from the United States and abroad, serve as reviewers who provide critical evaluation of books, papers, articles, films, and video presentations. More than 200 serial publications are scanned for pertinent material so that advances and developments can be reviewed. *Computing Surveys* is a quarterly journal, aimed at the broader interests of the computing community and oriented to readers with a minimal background in the areas covered. It presents reports of the state of the art in the most vital areas of current practice. These four—*Journal, Communications, Reviews,* and *Surveys*—play a significant role in the fields relating to computers.

Couger, J. Daniel. "Evolution of Business Systems Analysis Techniques." *ACM Computing Surveys*, Volume 3, No. 3, September 1973.

The paper presents the results of a comprehensive literature search covering approaches for analysis of business systems. The author focuses attention on the fact that whereas hardware technically was advancing at a very rapid rate, the technology of defining requirements and integrating systems into the fabric of an organization lagged behind the technology development.

Couger, J. Daniel, and Knapp, Robert W. *Systems Analysis Techniques.* New York: Wiley, 1974.

This book consists of a series of articles describing techniques covering Phases I and II of the System Development Cycle, similar in concept to Phases I and II of *Management Systems.* It covers general systems theory, techniques for determining whether a system should be automated, and finally, both manual and automated techniques to aid in the process.

Data Management. Data Processing Management Association, 505 Busse Highway, Park Ridge, Illinois.

This journal is the official publication of the Data Processing Management Association, which is regarded by many people as the major organization representing the business and management use of computers. The association sponsors the Certificate in Data Processing. A study of the journal will provide the reader with a good idea of the data processing functions of computers.

Datamation. Technical Publishing Company, 1301 South Grove Avenue, Barrington, Illinois.

Datamation is published monthly and is aimed at management people in the area of computers, data processing, systems information and related subjects. It usually contains about ten articles on timely subjects such as conversion problems or experiences, advances and trends in hardware and software, computing developments a decade hence, real-time computing, peripheral and package program characteristics, and many other subjects relating to computers. Most of the articles are not very technical. In addition to the articles, there are several features including things such as looking ahead, news items, new products, new literature, worldwide report, Washington report, books, people, and advertisements. *Datamation* is probably the most widely read single publication in the computer planning and programming field.

Data Processing Digest. Canning, Sisson, and Associates, 1140 South Robertson Boulevard, Los Angeles, California.

The *Digest,* published monthly, contains an analytical summary of the current major articles and books concerning computers and data processing. Any organization with a significant interest in management systems should make sure its computer department sees the *Digest*. Its summaries of the current books, articles, and happenings in computer related fields provide a wealth of material that can be of considerable benefit.

Data Processing Glossary. (Form GC20-1699.) International Business Machines Corporation, 1133 Westchester Avenue, White Plains, New York.

This glossary contains definitions of over 5,000 words, terms, concepts, and abbreviations.

Data Security Controls and Procedures—A Philosophy for DP Installations. (Form G320-5649-01.) International Business Machines Corporation, 1133 Westchester Avenue, White Plains, New York.

This publication is addressed to installation systems management, and it presents measures for limiting risk in data processing activities. It attempts to answer questions such as how security requirements are reconciled with production needs, how control can be exercised over system programming activities, operations, and systems development, and who should be made responsible for security. Emphasis is on controls and procedures as they relate to data security; their use in the accomplishment of other objectives is treated in passing. Physical security measures and backup and recovery measures are only dealt with as they relate to planning.

Davis, R. "Systems of the 1980's—The U.S. Perspective." *Proceedings of the 35th Conference on a Preview of the 1980s and Distributed Processing*, Amsterdam, Holland, November 18–20, 1975. National Bureau of Standards, Washington, D.C.: Document No. EC35, Session C, 1976, pp. 27–43.

Computer systems of the 1980s will be used in applications such as data acquisition and validation, record keeping, management information systems, real-time control, real-time monitoring, modeling, simulation, individualized services, scheduling, allocation, dispatching, and scientific and research investigations. These systems will serve primarily two sets of customers. One set is composed of large single organizations using computer systems to manage diversified activities and economic communities using computer systems to link members together. The second set will be individual users needing autonomous dedicated computer systems which can be interconnected to larger computer service networks or other individuals. The 1980s will see computer networks containing computers and computer modules of all sizes, independent memories, and a large variety of access terminal and automated input devices. However, the present lack of information controls, privacy safeguards, audit procedures, performance measures for real-time control systems, interface standards, software validation, and documentation standards will have to be overcome to assure acceptability of the envisioned systems.

Drucker, Peter. *Management — Tasks. Practices. Responsibilities.* New York: Harper & Row, 1974.

This book is a study of management as an organized body of knowledge. It deals with the techniques of effective management, looks at management externally, and studies its tasks and requirements as well. The emphasis is on needed accomplishments and results, including all areas of managerial concern.

Ferber, Robert. *The Handbook of Marketing Research.* New York: McGraw-Hill, 1974.

This handbook brings together in one volume much information on the many areas of marketing research. Of particular interest is Part B of Section II, which covers the topic of surveys. Each of the ten chapters in Part B covers a separate key technique. Among the topics included are survey design, a variety of data collection methods, analysis of results, and interviewing techniques.

Flowcharting Techniques. (Form C20-8152.) International Business Machines Corporation, 1133 Westchester Avenue, White Plains, New York.

For the reader who has little or no knowledge of flowcharting methods, this manual serves as a good introduction. It describes in detail the preparation of system and program flowcharts. It stresses the fact that adherence to standard techniques for the preparation of flowcharts of data processing systems and procedures greatly increases effectiveness of communication between the programmers, analysts, and the many groups with whom they deal.

Fry, James P., and Sibley, Edgar, II. "Evolution of Data Base Management Systems." Published in Association for Computing Machinery, *Computing Surveys*, Volume 8, No. 1, March, 1976, pp. 7–42.

This paper deals with the history and definitions common to data base technology. It delimits the objectives of data base management systems, discusses important concepts, defines terminology for use by other papers in this issue, traces the development of data base systems methodology, gives a uniform example, and presents some trends and issues. Prepared in cooperation with the University of Michigan, Ann Arbor, Graduate School of Business Administration.

Grooms, David W. "Data Base Management."(Citations from the NTIS Data Base.) *National Technical Information Service*, Springfield, Va., April 1976.

The advent of online systems and the increasing problems of file organization, file maintenance, and file structures of data bases have required that data base management systems be studied and developed. This bibliography of federally funded research cites the development of these software packages and implementation of data base management systems into various information systems. Guidelines are also included for managers to use in optimizing and modeling data bases. (Contains eighty-six abstracts.)

Hall, A. D. *A Methodology for Systems Engineering.* New York: Van Nostrand, 1962.

This book is still widely referenced as an excellent introduction to the concepts and philosophy of systems design and analysis.

Installation Management Bibliography. (Form GF20-8172-12.) April 1977. International Business Machines Corporation, 1133 Westchester Avenue, White Plains, New York.

This bibliography describes selected IBM publications on the management of data processing, data security, and generally useful application development techniques. Publications intended for a specific data processing system are normally excluded. The publications included are texts, manuals, briefs, articles, certain forms and templates, reference indexes, and catalogs. The bibliography provides the titles, order numbers, and abstracts. Items are clustered by topic and sorted by title; a second list is in order-number sequence showing the current items.

Journal of the Operations Research Society of America. Mount Royal and Guilford Avenues, Baltimore, Maryland.

This journal, published bimonthly, would be of interest primarily to people with a good mathematical background. It, like *Management Science,* is aimed at the quantitative solution of management problems. It also has book reviews. Some of the topic areas include information systems, Bayesian decision theory, linear programming, marketing models, critical path methods, economic order quantities, Markov chains, simulation, queuing, and life testing. In brief, the *Journal* would keep an organization up to date on developments in this field.

Kepner, Charles H., and Tregoe, Benjamin B. *The Rational Manager.* New York: McGraw-Hill, 1965.

Managers solve problems and make decisions by experience, but they often do so inefficiently, wasting time, money and energy. Yet managers themselves rarely realize this. There are rational processes behind these two essential management functions, but they have long been unrecognized or misunderstood. This book shows managers how to improve their problem solving and decision making by using information efficiently. The thesis of the book is that, because information is the raw material with which managers work, the most effective way to improve managerial performance is to improve the use of information.

Lazzaro, Victor, ed. *Systems and Procedures.* Englewood Cliffs, N.J.: Prentice-Hall, 1968.

The objective of this handbook is to bring together information on the various systems and procedures techniques—such as work measurement, EDP, PERT, forms control, and systems analysis—into a single comprehensive volume that can be used as a ready reference guide for readers interested in acquiring a general knowledge of the subject. The book is particularly useful for students of systems and procedures and for personnel responsible for making management and operating studies and related improvements. Each chapter was written specifically for this book by a recognized authority in the field, thereby making it possible to produce a comprehensive work on systems and procedures.

McCracken, D. D. *Structured COBOL Programming.* New York: Wiley, 1976.

This book is written for the person who wants to get a rapid grasp of the application of computers to the problems of business. COBOL has been the most widely used language for such work and is an excellent vehicle for the study of computer applications. All of the essential COBOL functions are explained fully within the framework of realistic applications in a case study format. The book is therefore considerably more than a simple text on COBOL.

McFarlan, F. Warren, and Nolan, Richard L. *The Information Systems Handbook.* Homewood, Ill.: Dow Jones–Irwin, 1975.

This book provides thorough guidance to executives in planning and utilizing the data processing system most useful to their company. The past two decades have seen a truly remarkable growth in the importance of data processing systems in the management of corporations. The increase in the complexity of equipment and programs together with the concomitant increase in the complexity of the organizations they serve confronts data processing executives with a bewildering array of responsibilities. This handbook is designed to help these executives meet these new responsibilities effectively.

McMillan, Claude, and Gonzalez, Richard F. *Systems Analysis — A Computer Approach to Decision Models.* Homewood, Ill.: Irwin, 1965.

This book considers the use of the computer for simulation and includes discussion of inventory systems, Monte Carlo simulation, queuing concepts, management planning models, and a study in total systems simulation.

McNurlin, Barbara C. "Using Some New Programming Techniques." *EDP Analyzer*, Volume 15, November 1977.

This report describes some uses of IPTs (Improved Programming Technologies) as examples of how users might improve the software development process. The use of IPTs is categorized into three groups: (1) For designing software, including top-down design, HIPO (Hierarchy plus Input Process Output) and pseudocode. (2) For building software, including development support library, structured programming, top-down programming, and chief programmer teams. (3) For testing software, including structured walk-throughs and interactive debugging and testing.

Management Science. The Journal of The Institute of Management Sciences, Mount Royal and Guilford Avenues, Baltimore, Maryland.

TIMS is a professional association whose aim is to identify, extend, and unify scientific knowledge pertaining to management. The journal is prepared in three sections. Section A is aimed at the scientific community. Section B is aimed primarily at management. Section C is a bulletin for news and announcements. There are some excellent book reviews. Although the tone of the journal is quantitative, and would appeal mostly to people with a mathematical background, there are many articles that could be profitably read by systems people in general.

Mayer, H. C., Ball, F. W., and Low, D. W. *Selected Bibliography of Application Development.* November 1975. International Business Machines Corporation, 1133 Westchester Avenue, White Plains, New York.

This document has been compiled over several years to provide background material on the variety of programming techniques, productivity technologies, and the development process that relate to an application development project. The topics covered in this bibliography include applications using decision tables, conversion of decision tables to computer programs, programming by questionnaire, structured programming, modular programming, chief programmer team concepts, top-down design and development, customizing of applications, automatic software design, and application development process.

Mills, Harlan D. "Software Development." *Transactions on Software Engineering*, Volume 2, No. 4. IEEE, December 1976.

Software development has emerged as a critical bottleneck in the human use of automatic data processing. Beginning with ad hoc heuristic methods of design and implementation of software systems, problems of software maintenance and changes have become unexpectedly large. This paper contends that improvement is possible only with the use of mathematical rigor in software design and development methodology. Software development should be done incrementally with continuous user participation and replanning. This paper serves as a history of the data processing area; it is well structured to show how the pieces fit together in creating a software system.

Moehrke, D. P., and Dunham, M. D. "Top-Down Design Using Information Modeling." *Proceedings of Guide* 41, Volume 1. Chicago: Guide International, November 1975, pp. 278–286.

In recent years much of the data processing industry has come to recognize the importance of the design portion of software system development. Consequently, a variety of procedures and tools has been used in the evolution of a project from feasibility study through system design, detail design, and implementation. This paper describes a single consistent methodology to conduct an effective business system design from a top-down functional decomposition at a very high level. It begins with the definition of high level business objectives and results in a detailed definition of implementation specifications.

Montalbano, Michael. *Decision Tables*. Chicago: Science Research Associates, 1974.

This book provides a good general review of the subject of decision tables and then backs it up with a fairly detailed technical explanation as to the structure and logic of tables. The book then reviews rules on completeness and consistency, compares decision tables with flowcharts, and discusses decision table translators. This is one of a number of texts which explain the use of decision tables and provide guidance to people who have found them to be a convenient alternative to the usual flowchart or narrative forms.

Morrison, Philip, and Morrison, Emily, eds. *Charles Babbage and His Calculating Engines*. New York: Dover Publications, 1961.

This book contains selected writings by Charles Babbage and others. It explains the reasons for the development of and the mechanics and logic of Babbage's machine, including his idea for a large-scale computer. Not only is the book interesting for its coverage of the problems of computation in the early 1800s; it is also excellent for its discussion of management problems in developing advanced systems in backward surroundings.

Myers, Glenford J. *Reliable Software through Composite Design*. New York: Petrocelli/Charter, 1975.

The purpose of this book is solving problems by defining a set of design measures, strategies, and techniques collectively known as composite design. This technology is used in the design of highly modular programs. Reducing a program's complexity has a positive effect on its quality and cost.

Orr, K. T. "Introducing Structured Systems Design." *Proceedings of Guide* 43, Volume 2. Chicago: Guide International, November 1976, pp. 718–726.

Structured systems design is a new concept. It is not simply just a warmed-over version of traditional systems design approaches. Structured systems design, like structured programming, is hierarchical, modular, and logically organized. In addition, structured systems design is also output oriented and data structured.

Pooch, U. W. *Computer Graphics, Interactive Techniques, and Image Processing 1970–1975—A Bibliography*. College Station: Texas A&M University, 1976.

Computer graphics, interactive techniques and image processing are among the developments in the constantly evolving computer science field. This bibliography attempts to compile all articles, books, conference papers, and technical reports about computer graphics and man-machine interaction that have been published in English from 1970 to 1975. The bibliography contains 683 entries cross-referenced by the following subject headings: computer graphics, computer graphics languages, computer graphics algorithms, computer graphics software, books, computer graphics in color, theoretical foundations, collective bibliographies, and computer graphics applications.

Schmidt, Richard N., and Meyers, William E. *Electronic Business Data Processing*. New York: Holt, Rinehart and Winston, 1963.

This is primarily a text to be used in teaching the principles of data processing from the management point of view. A review of the book will give the reader a good insight into the kind of work that is involved during the implementation stage of computer-based systems.

Schmidt, Richard N., and Meyers, William E. *Introduction to Computer Science and Data Processing.* New York: Holt, Rinehart and Winston, 1965.

This book is designed as a nonmathematical introduction to computers and their use. It would be of value to management or systems personnel who wish to obtain a basic understanding of the concept and operation of a stored-program computer.

Schoderbek, Peter P., ed. *Management Systems.* New York: Wiley, 1967.

This book contains a set of fifty-one readings related to management and systems. The readings begin with an article by Kenneth E. Boulding, "General Systems Theory: The Skeleton of Science," which provides the theme for the book. The other articles cover the many and diverse fields with which this subject is concerned. The section on models and simulation opens with an article called "Models," by Irwin D. J. Bross, and concludes with an article, "Management Control Systems," by Joel M. Kibbee. The final section of the book covers information retrieval. This book attempts to link the basic concepts employed in management systems to reveal their interrelationships.

Systems and Procedures Journal. Systems and Procedures Association, 7890 Brookside Drive, Cleveland, Ohio.

A person who desires to find out more about the kind of work done by systems and procedures people should examine this journal and the official book, *Business Systems,* published by the Association. Other publications of the Association include *Total Systems, Joint Man/Machine Decisions, Profile of a Systems Man, Systems Film Catalog, An Annotated Bibliography for the Systems Professional, Ideas for Management*, and many others of interest to systems analysts.

Taggart, William M., Jr., and Tharp, Marvin O. "A Survey of Information Requirements Analysis Techniques." *ACM Computing Surveys*, Volume 9, No. 4, December 1977.

This paper is a comprehensive survey of the literature specifically concentrating on information requirements analysis. In general, it covers an area in which organizations should spend considerable effort, the part of the systems effort prior to system design.

Teichroew, Daniel. "A Survey of Languages for Stating Requirements for Computer-Based Information Systems." *Proceedings: AFIPS, 1972*, Fall Joint Computer Conference.

Teichroew focuses attention in this methods review paper on ways in which the information needs of the user can be uncovered and documented effectively from the perspective of the systems designer.

Teichroew, Daniel, and Winters, Edgar. "Recent Developments in System Analysis and Design." *Atlanta Economic Review*, Volume 26, No. 6, November/December 1976, pp. 39–46.

Major improvements are necessary in the methods analysts use to develop system requirements. These improvements should address the problems of communication, consistency, and completeness. In order to make a significant improvement in these areas, the authors recommend the use of a problem statement language and a problem statement analyzer. The use of these methods in an operating environment is outlined. Participants in systems development who have used these computer-aided techniques agree that a significant improvement is evident.

Wiener, Norbert. *Cybernetics, or Control and Communication in the Animal and the Machine.* 2d ed. Cambridge, Mass.: Massachusetts Institute of Technology Press, 1961.

This book is the all-time classic on the theory of systems. It deals with a study of human control functions and the mechanical and electrical systems designed to replace human beings. It requires a certain level of mathematical maturity to benefit from this study. For those without a mathematical background, Wiener's *Human Use of Human Beings* covers the same topics from a nonmathematical point of view.

INDEX

THE DRYDEN PRESS
SERIES IN MANAGEMENT

William F. Glueck, Consulting Editor